NEW SOCIOLOGY LIBRARY
No. 1

General Editor: Professor NORBERT ELIAS
Department of Sociology, University of Leicester

The Sociology of Sport

The Sociology of Sport

A Selection of Readings

Edited by
Eric Dunning
Lecturer in Sociology at the University of Leicester

With a foreword by
Professor Norbert Elias

FRANK CASS : LONDON

First published in 1971 by
FRANK CASS AND COMPANY LIMITED
Gainsborough House, Gainsborough Road
London E11 1RS

Second impression 1976

ISBN 0 7146 2293 1

Printed in Great Britain by offset lithography by
Billing & Sons Ltd, Guildford, London and Worcester

For Judy

Contents

PART III

Acknowledgements

I should like to take this opportunity to record my thanks to the contributors to this volume for permission to publish or reprint their essays here. Special thanks are due to those who have permitted me to publish papers which have not so far appeared elsewhere. I should also like to express my gratitude to those of my friends and colleagues with whom I discussed various parts of the Reader. I have benefited considerably from their critical comments. In this connection, I should like particularly to thank Ilya Neustadt for his patient reading of the original draft of the General Introduction and Norbert Elias both for including *Readings in The Sociology of Sport* in his New Sociology Library series and for the many lively and enjoyable sessions we have spent working on the joint essays which are published here. Thanks are also due to Clive Ashworth, Mike Attalides, Nicos Mouzelis and Sami Zubaida for commenting on various parts of the interstitial material. Last but not least, I should like to thank my brother, Roy Dunning, for his help in translating one of the articles from German. The several hours of patient labour he put in went far beyond what could normally be asked of a brother, especially in consideration of the fact that the sociological jargon in both the English and the German versions clearly represented a source of continual offence to his literary sensitivity.

Foreword

by Norbert Elias

This collection of essays on the sociology of sport, edited and anno-
tated by Eric Dunning, apart from giving information about specific
issues, should help towards a better understanding of the functions
of sport in our society. A reviewer surveying some recent books on
the philosophy of sport under the heading "Locker Room Metaphysics",* referred to the difficulty of identifying the place of sport
on the general map of human interests and activities. One may find
that a sociological approach is of help in one's search for such an
orientation.

In some respects no doubt, the place of sport is changing though
perhaps not quite in the manner which seems to attract most attention. It is sometimes assumed that sport, in the good old days, was
exclusively an occupation for gentlemen and amateurs and also that
it used to be less violent. In actual fact, some sports always had the
twofold character as amateur and spectator sport, including cricket,
even though the spectators were largely country gentlemen and noblemen who paid retainers rather than an entrance fee and who added
spice to their entertainment by betting. In the past, moreover, sport
activities, including boxing and football, were far more violent than
they are today. Some widespread assumptions about the changes in
sport, on closer view, turn out to be legends.

At the same time, certain changes which are not legendary are
perhaps less in the public eye. The twin phenomena of the institu-
tionalisation and bureaucratisation of sport are on the increase.
Public authorities on the local, the regional and the national level are
tending to regard education for sport and sport itself as their concern.
From being exclusively people's private affair, sport activities are
becoming over a wider area directly or indirectly dependent on public
financial help. They are coming, therefore, directly or indirectly
under public control. In some countries, sport is already totally

* Anthony Quinton, Locker Room Metaphysics, *The New York Review
of Books*, Vol. XIII, No. 3, 21 August, 1969, p. 21 ff.

controlled by the state authorities. More research is needed in order to asses the effects of this change.

Perhaps one may be allowed to point to another of the current legends about the place of sport in contemporary societies which studies in the sociology of sport can help to dispel. Sport education has found its accepted place within the educational framework of our time under the slightly misleading name of "physical education". This expression reflects an old tradition of thinking which persists even in educational institutions although it has long since lost its scientific basis. It implies that one type of education is exclusively concerned with the "mind" and another exclusively with the "body". Both types, according to this tradition, are defined in terms of different but equally rational and utilitarian purposes. "Physical education", for instance, may find its overt justification in the contribution it can make to people's health and, less overtly, in its contribution to people's soldierly virtues and capacities. Perhaps, if public money is to be spent on "physical education", this type of justification is both useful and convincing enough.

Sociological enquiries, however—and no doubt psychological enquiries too—cannot help taking note of the fact that sport involves a person as a whole and not only his "physique". They strongly suggest that the place of sport in our society cannot be understood if one divides men conceptually and institutionally into "mind" and "body", and men's education, therefore, into "mental" and "physical" education. The function of sport as an inducement to mental exercise and well-being is not less significant than its function as an inducement to physical exercise and well-being; it is hardly possible to separate the one from the other. By considering sport education one-sidedly as "physical education" only, one narrows its task unduly. One excludes from its aims and tasks the function it has for a person's social and emotional development and concentrates only on the function it has for that of his muscles. It might be preferable to call it clearly and simply "sport education" and consider it as an integral part of the general education of men—with sufficient safeguards for the protection of those young people who do not take to sport.*

In educational as well as in sociological discussions about sport, one tends to argue as if "sport" were still the relatively unified phenomenon which it is believed to have been at previous stages of its development. One distinguishes between amateur and professional sport—often enough with tongue in cheek—and tends to idealise the

* Dislike of sport, like that of mathematics, may well be produced or increased by inadequate methods of teaching, especially by the disregard for individual differences of social and emotional dispositions and aptitudes.

former at the expense of the latter. But the distinction itself is no longer wholly appropriate to what one actually observes. A better conceptual approximation to the social development of our time would be a "sport continuum" spread between two poles: high achievement sport, such as that practised at the Olympic games and performed by professionals as well as by amateurs (though the latter seem to be losing out) and leisure sport with its two subdivisions, spectator sport and active leisure sport. Spectator sport is a form of leisure sport so far as the spectators are concerned, and high performance sport, though of course in varying degrees, so far as the performers are concerned. Active leisure sport, which in any education for leisure is likely to find increasing attention, is a classifying name for the wide range of sport activities undertaken actively by people for their own enjoyment, from the game of soccer played by young workers in their lunch hour on a meadow near their factory to the game of golf or tennis played by people who can use the amenities of a club, and the half-hour weekly swim or the mountain walk of old people who no longer compete. There are many intermediary forms. But sociologically as well as educationally the distinction may be found useful. High achievement sport is more spectacular and draws a good deal of attention to itself. It can easily overshadow in our reflections the very great part played in contemporary societies by the leisure-sport activities of ordinary people. In the context of a high achievement sport, even amateurs—perhaps for the sake of their country—undergo a long, hard and highly specialised training, elements of which may spill over into ordinary sport education. One should bear in mind therefore that the sociological as well as the educational aspects of the types of sport near the two poles of the continuum are different. As time for leisure activities is expanding, one may be able to take more note of the fact that sport, like other leisure activities, can be a recurrent source of social and emotional refreshment without having to fear that people may grumble because they feel public money should not be spent on education for pursuits which provide excitement and pleasure, but only on activities which have a truly "rational" purpose such as physical strength or health. In actual fact, it is a highly "rational" aim to enlarge people's capacity for leisure enjoyment, among others, through the mastery of a sport. One may find that some of the studies selected by Mr. Dunning for inclusion in this volume point in that direction.

Amsterdam, 1970.   NORBERT ELIAS

Preface

The sociology of sport is a new but rapidly expanding field of sociological research. It seeks to understand the part played by sports in society and to unravel the complex social forces which have helped to shape and which are currently leading to transformations in their character. This book of readings is designed as an introduction to the subject. It is aimed not only at students of sociology but also at teachers and students of physical education, sports writers and other non-sociologists who wish to increase their understanding of the many and varied relations between sport and society. Hopefully, it may also stimulate more sociologists to undertake work in the field than have done so in the past.

A few words about the organisation of the book may help the reader to understand the underlying rationale. It is divided into three main parts: *Some Concepts and Theories; The Development of Sports and Games*; and *Aspects of Sports in Modern Society*. Part III, the longest of the three sections, is subdivided under the following headings: *Sports and Socialization*; *Class and Race in Sport; Sport as an Occupation*; and *Problems of Conflict and Social Control in Sport*. These titles indicate central problem areas in the field. Their selection has partly been determined by the nature and scope of the literature available. There are some significant gaps due to the fact that the sociology of sport is a recently established specialism in the discipline. Thus, it has proved impossible to include anything specifically on sport and the economy or on what is probably one of the most critical current issues, namely the tendency in many countries towards increasing control of sport by the state, a trend which appears to be occurring largely as a result of the growing significance of sport in international relations. Each of these important issues, however, is touched on more or less briefly at various points throughout the volume.

At the beginning of each section, there is a short introduction which attempts to indicate relationships between particular articles and to place the themes they deal with in a wider sociological context. These introductions also specify some of the central sociological questions raised by the various problem areas. They are all of a fairly elementary kind. By aiming them at this level, it seemed that they were more likely to be understandable to newcomers and be- ginners in sociology than if they were directed simply at a readership of trained specialists in the discipline.

Coverage in the Reader is fairly comprehensive. A number of sociological issues are discussed in relation to a wide variety of sports and games including soccer, rugby, American football, athle- tics, boxing, wrestling, baseball, and bullfighting. As is indicated by this list, the sports of several countries are dealt with but the focus is not simply on sports in the modern era. Those of ancient Greece, medieval and early modern Britain are also discussed as well as the processes of development involved in the formation of modern Association, Rugby and American football. In short, the Reader is based on a comparative and developmental orientation to the soci- ology of sport. Such an approach seeks to clarify the nature of modern sports by viewing them in terms of a wide social and histori- cal perspective. Thus, comparison between the sports of different countries and of societies at different stages of social development makes it easier to clarify the central structural and functional charac- teristics of modern sports. Viewing them developmentally focuses at- tention on the processes at work within them, in the past as well as in the present. Sports are not fixed, unchanging entities that have always existed in their modern forms and will always continue to do so. Their modern character emerged gradually over time and they are continuing currently to change. In order to understand them fully, it is crucial to study both their past and present patterns of develop- ment. That is why this Reader is organised in terms of a develop- mental as well as a comparative perspective. Such an orientation to the sociology of sport would appear to hold out the greatest hope for securing further advance in what has been up to now one of the most neglected areas in sociology.

General Introduction

Sport as a Field of Sociological Enquiry

Sport is something people tend to take for granted. They may like it or dislike it but they do not usually question it or see it as posing problems which require an explanation. In particular, they rarely ask questions concerning its development or its role in society as a whole. It is just this type of question, however, which forms the central subject matter of the sociology of sport. A few words about why they are sociologically interesting and important may help the reader to gain a clearer perspective on the type of issues that are dealt with in this volume.

Playing and watching sports and games is one of the most popular leisure activities in the world today. One or two figures on the numbers engaged in Association Football ("soccer") must suffice in this context as a rough measure of the magnitude of "sports involvement". In Great Britain alone, somewhere in the region of half a million boys and men regularly play organised "club" soccer. Around a million, women as well as men, pay every Saturday to watch the drama and the spectacle offered in matches organised by the Football League.[1] This number would be multiplied several times if one could reliably estimate the countless others who regularly watch the live and recorded matches offered on television in the comfort of their own homes or who follow the game in the national and the local press. It would be multiplied even more if one had data on the numbers of people who play and watch soccer in countries all over the world. Some idea of the numbers involved can be gained from the fact that a television-satellite link-up made it possible for the 1966 World Cup Final played at Wembley between England and West Germany to be watched "live" by 400,000,000 people.[2] Few peacetime events apart from the first moon-landing can have evoked such widespread interest. Few can have been watched simultaneously by such large numbers of people. There is clearly some truth in the statement recently made by the sports and drama critic Laurence Kitchin that, apart from science, soccer is the only "global idiom" but it is an oversimplification.[3] Soccer is by no means the only sport which is nowadays played and watched all over the world. Others such as athletics, tennis, boxing and golf also have a world-wide following. Others still, such as rugby, cricket and hockey are limited to a smaller number of countries but are also widely watched and played. And, of course, sports are not restricted simply to matches between teams and individuals within particular countries. They are played internationally, too, and have come to represent today one of the most frequent sources of regular contact between people from different countries.

Data such as these—ideally of course, one would want them to be far more detailed and precise—suggest that sports are a leisure pursuit which is not only popular, but of some social importance. Exactly how important they are is a matter for sociological investigation but there can be little doubt that the "sports movement" is one of the most far-flung social movements of our time. It appears to be very deeply rooted. In some sense or another, it cuts right across the boundaries of class, race, religion, ethnic group and nation. That is why it poses questions for the sociologist. The questions raised in this connection can be divided into two basic categories: problems of development and change in sports and games and problems of their functions.[4] Perhaps it will help the general reader if just a few of the questions which arise in relation to each of these two categories are listed at this juncture:

PROBLEMS OF DEVELOPMENT AND CHANGE IN SPORTS AND GAMES

How and why has sport come to play such a prominent part in so many different countries nowadays? Has it always been important? Is it a universal "leisure institution" found in societies all over the world and in every era whatever the type and level of social development? Or is it something new, a specifically modern social phenomenon the development of which is perhaps connected with the rise of industrial nation-states and with the changing balance between work and leisure that occurs in connection with a process of industrialisation? What patterns of change can be detected currently in sports and games? How are they connected with patterns of change in society at large? Are sports, for example, tending to become more highly regulated and organised more along bureaucratic lines? Are they becoming more competitive? Is it true that they are becoming more violent than has ever been the case before? Do such changes, if they are occurring, represent a threat to the enjoyable and playful character of sports? In short, are they threatening to diminish their central function as leisure activities?

PROBLEMS OF THE FUNCTIONS OF SPORT AND GAMES

What contributions are made by sports and games to the life of the individual and to the society of which he is a member? What, for example, is the nature of the satisfactions derived by amateurs from playing sports? Are they primarily of a physical kind such as benefit to health, or do they also contain important psychological and social components such as the experience of pleasurable excitement gained in playful competition or pleasure derived from friendships formed on the sportsfield? Why do not only professionals for whom sport is their work but also amateurs for whom it is a leisure pursuit take the games they play so seriously? What is the nature of the satisfactions derived from watching as opposed to playing sports? Does identification with a sports team represent a means whereby people can identify with the wider social units—city, county, country—which their team represents? In this sense, do sports act as a unifying agency which to some extent counteracts the divisive force of class, race, religion and other, similar types of social unit which simultaneously unite certain groups of men and divide them from others? Do sports serve to give the individual in the "lonely crowd" of our impersonal modern "mass society" a sense of belonging to some wider social grouping and help to bring order, meaning and a sense of continuity into his life? Why is riotous and openly violent behaviour so frequent an accompaniment of spectatorship at sports events? Is such behaviour a result of the sometimes near-fanatical level of identification and involvement of sports fans with the teams that they support, or does it come about due to factors which are essentially extraneous to the game as such? What are the effects of sport on international relations? Do sporting competitions help to promote peace and international understanding as has sometimes been maintained, are they "neutral" with respect to international relations, or do they exert an influence which is positively harmful?

The questions outlined above are primarily concerned with sports as a type of leisure pursuit. But sport, of course, is nowadays more than just a leisure occupation. It has come to form an important part of the "entertainments industry" in countries such as Britain. It regularly attracts countless thousands of paying spectators for whom it is a leisure pursuit. The money they pay, however, enables substantial numbers of people to be employed as players, managers, coaches, trainers, groundsmen and administrators. Many more are engaged in the manufacture, sale and maintenance of sports facilities and equipment to say nothing of the writers, reporters, broadcasters and television commentators who earn their livings wholly or partly by writing and commentating on the field of sports. Numerous sociological questions are raised by sport as part of the entertainments industry and by the various types of careers that have grown up in connection with it. Here are just a few of them:

PROBLEMS OF SPORT AS PART OF THE ENTERTAINMENTS INDUSTRY

How and why has the development of modern society given rise to the emergence of a sports "industry"? How and in what ways is this development connected with the changing patterns of work and leisure, production and consumption which are typically associated with a process of industrialisation? What are the effects of the "sports industry" on the economics of production and consumption? Does it represent a drain on time, energy, money and resources which might otherwise be spent more profitably or does its "product" help to refresh people who are tired from their work or represent an essential outlet for the release of repressed tensions thus serving as a means for enabling them to work and produce more effectively? Does sport, in this connection, represent a social enclave where people can behave in a more openly emotional manner than is usually permitted to them, in this way acting as a counter to the routines, restraints and controls which tend to be all-pervasive in a society such as ours? What is the nature of organisations in the sports industry? Are they, and can they be, oriented simply towards making a profit as is the case with business enterprises of other kinds? Or does a profit-orientation pose a threat to the sports themselves, turning them into commercial spectacles which cease to be sports in any meaningful sense of that term? Is there a tendency for professional sports organisations to become highly formalised and bureaucratic? If so, does this typically lead to conflicts between the "line" (officials, managers etc.) and the "staff" (players) of a type similar to those which often occur in other bureaucratic organisations? What are the nature and the consequences of the career in sport? Does it, like education, represent an avenue whereby boys from the working classes can climb permanently to higher levels of wealth and social standing than might otherwise be possible for them? Or does it lead simply to a temporary elevation with the consequence that they become highly dissatisfied once their short playing careers are over—perhaps because they are not qualified for occupations which would provide them with the financial means for obtaining a standard and a style of living commensurate with that to which they have become accustomed as players? And what about professional sportsmen who never make it to the top? What happens to them when their playing days are over?

These are the sorts of issues to which the essays in this volume are addressed. They are focused above all on problems of development, structure, function and change in the sphere of sports. As such, they are rather different from the type of issues that are usually dealt with in books, newspapers and magazine articles on the subject. These, most frequently, are concerned with reporting particular matches or with discussing the careers and performances of particular teams and individual players. They tend to contain lists of results, descriptions of "epic" struggles to win the League or Cup and anecdotes relating incidents in the private lives of players. In the main, their authors concentrate on the top levels of professional sport. Only rarely do they discuss the lower reaches of the "profession" or say anything about its amateur counterparts. Often, they "glamorise" the subject and inject false elements of drama and excitement into it, instead of reporting it soberly and in a factual manner. In so far as they do discuss issues rather than single matches or single individuals, they rarely take the wider or the long-term view. They tend to focus on the "here and now", on sports as if they existed in a social and historical vacuum. They do not stand back from their subject in order to gain a clearer perspective or try to view the sport they are discussing in relation to patterns of social structure and social development in society as a whole. Nor do they usually ask questions about the functions of sports whether for individuals or for units in society at large. They tend to take it for granted, as something which is simply "there" and inherently enjoyable. They do not usually see it as posing questions which require an explanation. When, on rare occasions, they do ask questions of this sort, the answers that they give often consist of plausible but unexamined ideas such as the notion that sports serve in some way or another as a character-forming agency, that they act as a channel for the relatively harmless expression of aggressive impulses, or that they represent an agency which is helpful in promoting peace and international understanding. A principal task of the sociologist is to subject ideas of this kind to empirical test, to carry out research which brings evidence to bear concerning their validity. This is one of the central objects of this Reader. Many of the articles which follow are concerned with critically examining "ideologies" which have grown up in the sphere of sports. As one will see, on close inspection many of them turn out to be myths.

NOTES

1 "The Football Industry—I", *Planning* (P.E.P. Report), Vol. XVII, No. 324, 26 February, 1951, p. 157.

2 Richard L. Strout, "The National Game: Soccer?", *Christian Science Monitor*, 26 March, 1967.

3 Laurence Kitchin, "The Contenders", *The Listener*, 27 October, 1966.

4 Strictly speaking, of course, it is impossible to separate problems of development and change from problems of function. They are treated separately here solely for purposes of convenience and clarity of exposition.

PART I

SOME CONCEPTS AND THEORIES

Introduction

The term "sociology" has come increasingly into vogue in Britain over the past few years. Almost every newspaper, radio or television commentator on social affairs is nowadays referred to as a sociologist. During the same period, sociology has become one of the most rapidly expanding subjects in higher education. Departments of Sociology have been established in most of our universities yet, despite the speed with which the subject is expanding, there is widespread misunderstanding concerning its nature and its objects. It is widely believed, for example, that the main task of the sociologist is to collect factual information which can serve as a guide in formulating policies and implementing decisions of a practical kind but few sociologists would agree with this definition of their role. As is implicit in the General Introduction, sociology is the scientific study of societies. Like any other science, it is concerned in the first instance with analysis and understanding *as such* and not with the *immediate* solution of practical problems. Understanding is a prerequisite for intelligent action and experience has shown that the scientific method is the best available to man as a means of furthering understanding.

Scientific method, whether in physics, biology, economics or sociology consists in a combination of empirical observation and theory building, of the factual and the analytic. Concepts—general terms which specify distinguishable classes of objects, events and processes—serve as media for precise communication among scientists. Theories serve in the analysis and interpretation of known facts. They give them broader meaning by indicating ways in which they are related to different classes of facts, thus placing them within a wider framework of knowledge. They also serve as guides to future research by helping one to formulate questions and by suggesting—in the form of hypotheses—trends and relationships which seem probable, but which, at any given time, cannot be supported by reference to observable facts. In this manner, theories help to direct research into systematically related channels.

At present, concept formation and theory construction in the sociology of sport are not particularly advanced. It has only proved possible, therefore, to include articles of a largely preliminary kind in this introductory section. They illustrate the type of questions which sociologists ask in relation to sport and suggest a series of concepts and hypotheses likely to prove useful in sociological research in this area. They attempt, for example to identify and explain observable trends in the development of sports and some of the consequences which follow from these trends. They propose hypotheses concerning the functions of sports, that is, concerning their intended and unintended contributions to individual and social life which explain why people take part in and encourage them. In addition, they point to some of the respects in which the sociology of sport can help in the solution of wider problems of sociological research and sociological theory.

The section opens with an extract from Jan Huizinga's *Homo Ludens*—"man the player"—entitled "The Play Element in Contemporary Civilization". The principal thesis advanced in *Homo Ludens* is that play is behaviour which involves freedom from restraint. According to Huizinga, it has played a central part in the development of civilisation. Freedom from restraint, he argues, is essential for innovation and, on that account, for the creation of culture generally. However, Huizinga defines play in a broad sense to cover creative lack of restraint in general. He does not restrict use of the term to its common meaning. Thus, for him, play is involved in the creative work of the scientist, the painter, the poet and the novelist. It is not located simply in the field of sports and games.

Huizinga believes that modern civilisation lacks potential for the further development of culture. This is because much of the "play-element" characteristic of earlier ages was lost in the nineteenth century as a result of industrialisation. Industrial societies are tending to become more and more rigid and bureaucratic in character. Innovation is stifled because people are increasingly expected to conform to strict rules and regulations. The extract from *Homo Ludens* included here, tackles the apparent paradox posed for this argument by the fact that the nineteenth century witnessed not only the consolidation and spread of industrial forms of civilisation but was also the principal starting point for the development of modern sports. On the face of it, this development would seem to indicate that the nineteenth century was a period in which at least a certain type of play forms flourished. According to Huizinga, however, the development of sports in no way contradicts his overall thesis. Modern sports themselves, he argues, along with science, industry and the arts, are tending to become increasingly subjected to restraint with the result that they no longer represent forms of play.

Huizinga, of course, is correct in detecting a trend towards increasing systematisation and rationalisation in modern sports but he sees only one side of the coin. There is reason to doubt whether this trend has led to a destruction of sports as forms of play. It seems unlikely, for example, that sports such as football could have come to attract large numbers of players and spectators if the "play-element" in them had been destroyed entirely. Organisation and systematisation are essential if large numbers of people are to play and watch a single game played according to unified rules. They are prerequisites for the "democratisation" of a sport. They make the enjoyment of playing and watching available to people from different classes, different regions and different countries. Rules, furthermore, which limit and control the types and amounts of violent physical contact in sports are necessary in the more civilised climate of opinion which prevails in industrial nation-states. Organisation, rationalisation and civilisation between them do pose a threat to spontaneous enjoyment but it is clearly possible to effect a balance. How this balance between organisation, civilising restraints and spontaneity has been achieved in sports such as football, in such a manner that they continue to attract large numbers of players and spectators who derive enjoyment from them, is by no means entirely clear. It represents an important problem for research in the sociology of sport.

Huizinga's essay is followed by "The Classification of Games" by Roger Caillois. This is a chapter from his *Man, Play and Games*, a book which was strongly influenced by *Homo Ludens*. Caillois, however, is concerned with games as such and not with the "play-element" in civilisation as a whole. As a result, he is able in his approach to encompass more of the detail and complexities of sports and games than was possible for Huizinga. In the chapter included here, he proposes a typology of games based on four main categories of recurrent dimensions which he detects in them: what he calls *agon, alea, mimicry* and *ilinx*. He assigns games to these categories in accordance with the degree to which competition, chance, simulation or the experience of vertigo is their dominant element. In addition, he subdivides the games in each of these categories in terms of the dimensions of *paidia* and *ludus*, namely the degree to which they are spontaneous or highly regulated. The four main categories are "ideal types", rarely to be found in their pure form in reality. Most games, in fact, as Caillois sees them, contain more than one element though in any given game a particular element may be dominant. Thus, *agon* is the dominant element in football and cricket but elements of chance or *alea* are also involved in the sense that choice of ends or who shall bat first is determined by the toss of a coin. Both *agon* and *alea*, moreover, are present in card games, such as bridge and poker, in almost equal proportions. That is, they are contest games in which the outcome is decided both by the chance distribution of the cards and by the strategies employed by the contending parties.

Caillois' typology is very useful. Apart from the fact that it specifies the major dimensions of games of different types, it provides a comprehensive framework for classifying them in a meaningful and orderly manner. In this way, it helps to make sense of a vast array of seemingly diverse phenomena. It also enables one to make some headway in coming to grips with the complex problem of defining precisely what is meant by "sport". Sports, according to Caillois, are principally a type of "agonistic" or competitive games which involve a component of physical movement and more or less physical strength and skill. However, chance, simulation and even vertigo can also be present in them in varying degrees. Thus, uncertainty with respect to the outcome is a key element in all sports which is why they tend to become associated with gambling; a form of simulation is often involved in being a spectator, in the sense that spectators sometimes identify with the players they are watching, and vicariously experience their actions and emotions—triumph when they win, dejection when they lose; and sports such as skiing, high-jumping and pole-vaulting allow the participants to experience a type of vertigo.

Caillois' classification thus represents a brilliant attempt to come to grips with a very complex issue. He did not, however, address himself at any length to the question of the functions performed by sports and games. An interesting hypothesis in this respect is developed by C. E. Ashworth in his paper "Sport as Symbolic Dialogue" which is the third essay in this section. Ashworth's article is an essay in social psychology, written in terms of a "symbolic interaction" frame of reference. In contrast to the currently dominant type of social psychology which explains human behaviour in terms of postulated universal "needs", "drives" or "motives" such as the need to obtain pleasure and to avoid pain or the need for approval, this perspective focuses on the concept of "identity". Ashworth begins by illustrating the difference between this perspective and the currently dominant one by comparing how these two positions would analyse sports and games. In terms of the dominant view, he argues, the complexity of modern society is seen as persistently generating frustrations for the members of its constituent groups. Hostilities accumulate which have to be controlled in some way or another. Sports represent an institutionalised means for controlling them. They provide opportunities for people to release accumulated aggression against each other in a manner and a setting that is not disruptive to the society's overall co-operative system. Seen in these terms the F.A. Cup is "civilised civil war"; the Olympic Games "civilised world war".

According to Ashworth, the perspective of symbolic interaction enables one to understand many aspects of sports and games which cannot be accounted for in terms of the dominant type of theory. To know what he is, he argues a man must compare himself with others. The values of Western society state that all men are equal, but the built-in inequalities of this type of society create conditions which render fair comparison almost impossible in the normal run of everyday life. On the sports field, however, modern man insists on equality, i.e. on strict formal rules which make factors, other than ability, equal for all participants. Sports thus provide a kind of egalitarian utopia in which the rich and the poor, the handsome and the ugly, the white and the black can subject themselves to a symbolic test unhampered by accidents of wealth or poverty, looks or skin colour. In this sense, Ashworth hypothesises, sports represent a kind of simulated scientific experiment, an experiment in living which enables men to see what they are in relation to each other under conditions which satisfy the demands of the comparative experimental method as closely as is possible in real life. This hypothesis, he suggests, enables one to explain why teams and individuals are never interested in playing against opponents who are weaker than they are. Under such conditions, they would know in advance that they would win and no test would be involved. If sports were simply a question of releasing aggression, people would seek out opponents over whom victory would be certain. But under such circumstances, games would be impossible; no one would be able to find a certain loser. Violence would again become uncivilised. Among other things, this hypothesis provides a convincing explanation of why sports are taken so seriously in modern society. If Ashworth is correct, this seriousness does not represent a corruption of the "pure-play" element in sports of the kind hypothesised by Huizinga. It is a necessary component of them.

Ashworth's essay is followed by "American Sports: Play and Display" by Gregory P. Stone. This is also written from the standpoint of symbolic interaction. Unlike Ashworth, however, who is implicitly critical of the thesis propounded by Huizinga, Stone for the most part explicitly supports it. His essay is concerned with an analysis of the way in which sport is caught up in the tensions and anomalies of American society such as those between work and play, production and consumption and the battle of the sexes. His principal contribution is the distinction which he draws between the antagonistic principles of "play" and "display". Wherever they are present, he argues, spectators destroy the play-content of a sport. "The sport becomes a spectacle," as he puts, "*dis*-play". It is played for the spectators rather than for the players. The enjoyment of the former becomes of paramount importance. The sport loses its character of spontaneity and playful innovation and begins to become a type of ritual, predictable and even predetermined in its outcome.

The attendance of spectators in large numbers is certainly a characteristic development in many fields of modern sport. It probably does represent a threat to the play-element in such sports from the players' point of view. It seems reasonable, however, to suggest that Stone's analysis does not reach quite to the heart of the matter. What appears to be important is not the mere presence or absence of spectators, but whether or not the players are dependent on attracting spectators for their livelihood; in short, whether they are professionals dependent on money taken at the gate. Under such conditions, the wishes of spectators must be taken into account. The sport must be made attractive from their point of view but this is not the case with amateur games which draw large crowds such as rugby union. The development of this game shows very clearly that it is possible for a game to be run for the sake of the players and yet to be attractive for spectators. By their mere presence, spectators do not necessarily destroy the playful character of a sport: they do not necessarily lead it to become spectacular display though the pressures in this direction are probably greater in a highly commercialised society such as the United States than they are in a society such as England which, up to the present at least, has remained somewhat less commercialised and where the traditions of the "gentleman amateur" are much more firmly entrenched. To point this out, however, is by no means to detract from the usefulness of the conceptual distinction drawn by Stone. This is a very complex issue and his analysis directs attention forcefully to a form of tension which is critical in modern sport. It thus prepares the way for a deeper sociological understanding of many contemporary issues such as the controversy over amateurism and professionalism.

The final essay in this section is "Dynamics of Sport Groups with Special Reference to Football" by Norbert Elias and Eric Dunning. It is different from the others in that the authors are not simply concerned with issues related to the sociology of sport; instead they attempt to clarify certain basic sociological concepts such as that of "configuration". They also try to lay the foundations for a sociological theory of sports which concentrates on their dynamics, on the processes at work within them which tend to make them change. In addition, their essay shows how the sociology of sport can play a part in the further development of the discipline as a whole. Thus they use their analysis of football as a springboard, first, to develop a critique of small groups research in sociology, and second, in order to propose a way of overcoming an inadequacy characteristic of much modern sociological theory: the failure to develop a single theory which can account not only for the co-operative but also for the conflictful nature of human social relations. A brief discussion of these wider issues may help to make this essay clearer for the non-sociologist.

The dominant type of small groups research in modern sociology is highly "positivistic" and principally concerned with conducting experiments on group behaviour under controlled laboratory conditions. This, it is felt, can help sociological research to approximate the precision achieved in the physical sciences. According to Elias and Dunning, however, such experiments can only be marginally useful since it is impossible to simulate "real life" social structures and social situations in the laboratory. The groups assembled there are *ad hoc* and artificial; they have no permanence, no meaning in the lives of their members, no connections and no functions in the wider society. Theories constructed about them are likely to be highly formal and of little relevance to the understanding of behaviour and social structures in society at large. "Natural" small groups such as groups of football players are far more useful as subjects for sociological research. However, it is important to study them as social "configurations". One cannot understand what takes place on the football field without focusing on the interdependence of the two teams as part of a single configuration. What their members do cannot be understood by considering them in isolation. A combination of moves by one side produces a combination of counter-moves by the other, each side acting in more or less perfect unison in accordance with their skill. Where they are present, spectators also influence events on the field of play. They, too, form part of an overall social configuration which, in its turn, is implicated in a variety of configurations of relationships in the wider society. Thus, the social class of the players, their ethnic or religious group memberships, the relations between these various groupings, the type and effectiveness of the apparatus for social control employed by the state, all have to be taken into account in order to provide a complete picture. Journalists, writers, psychologists and even some sociologists often try to explain the behaviour of individuals or groups as if they existed in isolation. They do not take sufficient account of the complex configurations of social relations in which they are implicated. As a result, they often fail to provide an adequate explanation.

Any configuration of human relationships, moreover, whether between two individuals such as in a marriage or between two groups such as employers and employees, always has a dual nature: it is both co-operative and conflictful. A man and his wife, for example, need each other for love, companionship and sexual satisfaction. They co-operate in building a home and bringing up their children, but each also needs a degree of autonomy in relation to the other in order to retain a sense of individuality. Furthermore, their relationship involves several points of tension, for example, in relation to members of their wider families, perhaps particularly their "in-laws", or in relation to other men and women whom they may find sexually attractive. In similar fashion, employers need employees to work for them and the latter have to work in order to obtain a living. But disposal of the money earned from selling what they produce and the employer's power which limits the autonomy of the employees in the work-place represent points of conflict. The employer issues orders which the employees are compelled to obey. Their freedom is strictly limited unless they form a trade-union and fight for it.

This complexity, this "Janus-headed" character of social configurations, has not been adequately captured in modern sociological analysis. On the one hand, theories have been propounded which stress co-operation and harmony: on the other, theories which stress conflict and antagonism. Elias and Dunning suggest that the study of sport-games such as football might represent a way of solving the dilemma since they cannot be understood except as a form of controlled tension, one which clearly involves both co-operation and conflict at the same time. In this manner, research into football and other, similar sports might make a contribution to our understanding of wider, more important sociological issues such as problems of union-management, class and international relations.

CHAPTER 1

The Play Element in Contemporary Sport*

Johann Huizinga

Let us not waste time arguing about what is meant by "contemporary". It goes without saying that any time we speak of has already become an historical past, a past that seems to crumble away at the hinder end the further we recede from it. Phenomena which a younger generation is constantly relegating to "former days" are, for their elders, part of "our own day", not merely because their elders have a personal recollection of them but because their culture still participates in them. This different time-sense is not so much dependent on the generation to which one happens to belong as on the knowledge one has of things old and new. A mind historically focused will embody in its idea of what is "modern" and "contemporary" a far larger section of the past than a mind living in the myopia of the moment. "Contemporary civilisation" in our sense, therefore, goes deep into the nineteenth century.

The question to which we address ourselves is this: To what extent does the civilisation we live in still develop in play-forms? How far does the play-spirit dominate the lives of those who share that civilisation? The nineteenth century, we observed, had lost many of the play-elements so characteristic of former ages. Has this leeway been made up or has it increased?

It might seem at first sight that certain phenomena in modern social life have more than compensated for the loss of play-forms. Sport and athletics, as social functions, have steadily increased in scope and conquered ever fresh fields both nationally and internationally.

Contests in skill, strength and perseverance have, as we have shown, always occupied an important place in every culture either in connection with ritual or simply for fun and festivity. Feudal society was only really interested in the tournament; the rest was just popular recreation and nothing more. Now the tournament,

---

* Chapter 12 of *Homo Ludens: A Study of the Play Elements in Culture,* by Johann Huizinga, translated by R. F. C. Hull (after Huizinga's own translation). Routledge and Kegan Paul, 1949.

with its highly dramatic staging and aristocratic embellishments, can hardly be called a sport. It fulfilled one of the functions of the theatre. Only a numerically small upper class took active part in it. This one-sidedness of medieval sporting life was due in large measure to the influence of the Church. The Christian ideal left but little room for the organised practise of sport and the cultivation of bodily exercise, except in so far as the latter contributed to gentle education. Similarly, the Renaissance affords fairly numerous examples of body-training cultivated for the sake of perfection, but only on the part of individuals, never groups or classes. If anything, the emphasis laid by the Humanists on learning and erudition tended to perpetuate the older under-estimation of the body, likewise the moral zeal and severe intellectuality of the Reformation and Counter-Reformation. The recognition of games and bodily exercises as important cultural values was withheld right up to the end of the eighteenth century.

The basic forms of sportive competition are, of course, constant through the ages. In some the trial of strength and speed is the whole essence of the contest, as in running and skating matches, chariot and horse races, weight-lifting, swimming, diving, marksmanship, etc.[1] Though human beings have indulged in such activities since the dawn of time, these only take on the character of organised games to a very slight degree. Yet nobody, bearing in mind the agonistic principle which animates them, would hesitate to call them games in the sense of play—which, as we have seen, can be very serious indeed. There are, however, other forms of contest which develop of their own accord into "sports". These are the ball-games.

What we are concerned with here is the transition from occasional amusement to the system of organised clubs and matches. Dutch pictures of the seventeenth century show us burghers and peasants intent upon their game of kolf; but, so far as I know, nothing is heard of games being organised in clubs or played as matches. It is obvious that a fixed organisation of this kind will most readily occur when two groups play against one another. The great ball-games in particular require the existence of permanent teams, and herein lies the starting-point of modern sport. The process arises quite spontaneously in the meeting of village against village, school against school, one part of a town against the rest, etc. That the process started in nineteenth-century England is understandable up to a point, though how far the specifically Anglo-Saxon bent of mind can be deemed an efficient cause is less certain. But it cannot be doubted that the structure of English social life had much to do with it. Local self-government encouraged the spirit of association and solidarity. The absence of obligatory military training favoured the occasion for, and the need of, physical exercise. The peculiar form of education tended to work in the same direction, and finally the geography of the country and the nature of the terrain, on the whole flat and, in the ubiquitous commons, offering the most perfect playing-fields that could be desired, were of the greatest importance. Thus England became the cradle and focus of modern sporting life.

Ever since the last quarter of the nineteenth century games, in the guise of sport,[2] have have been taken more and more seriously. The rules have become increasingly strict and elaborate. Records are established at a higher, or faster, or longer level than was ever conceivable before. Everybody knows the delightful prints from the first half of the nineteenth century, showing the cricketers in top-hats. This speaks for itself.

Now, with the increasing systematisation and regimentation of sport, something of the pure play-quality is inevitably lost. We see this very clearly in the official distinction between amateurs and professionals (or "gentlemen and players" as used pointedly to be said). It means that the play-group marks out those for whom playing is no longer play, ranking them inferior to the true players in standing but superior in capacity. The spirit of the professional is no longer the true play-spirit; it is lacking in spontaneity and carelessness.[3] This affects the amateur too, who begins to suffer from an inferiority complex. Between them they push sport further and further away from the play-sphere proper until it becomes a thing *sui generis*: neither play nor earnest. In modern social life sport occupies a place alongside and apart from the cultural process. The great competitions in archaic cultures had always formed part of the sacred festivals and were indispensable as health and happiness-bringing activities. This ritual tie has now been completely severed; sport has become profane, "unholy" in every way and has no organic connection whatever with the structure of society, least of all when prescribed by the government. The ability of modern social techniques to stage mass demonstrations with the maximum of outward show in the field of athletics does not alter the fact that neither the Olympiads nor the organised sports of American Universites nor the loudly trumpeted international contests have, in the smallest degree, raised sport to the level of a culture-creating activity. However important it may be for the players or spectators, it remains sterile. The old play-factor has undergone almost complete atrophy.

This view will probably run counter to the popular feeling of today, according to which sport is the apotheosis of the play-element in our civilisation. Nevertheless popular feeling is wrong. By way of emphasising the fatal shift towards over-seriousness we would point out that it has also infected the non-athletic games where calculation is everything, such as chess and some card-games.

A great many board-games have been known since the earliest times, some even in primitive society, which attached great importance to them largely on account of their chanceful character. Whether they are games of chance or skill they all contain an element of seriousness. The merry play-mood has little scope here, particularly where chance is at a minimum as in chess, draughts, backgammon, halma, etc. Even so all these games remain within the definition of play as given in our first chapter. Only recently has publicity seized on them and annexed them to athletics by means of public championships, world tournaments, registered records and press reportage in a literary style of its own, highly ridiculous to the innocent outsider.

Card-games differ from board-games in that they never succeed in eliminating chance completely. To the extent that chance predominates they fall into the category of gambling and, as such, are little suited to club life and public competition. The more intellectual card-games, on the other hand, leave plenty of room for associative tendencies. It is in this field that the shift towards seriousness and over-seriousness is so striking. From the day of ombre and quadrille to whist and bridge, card-games have undergone a process of increasing refinement, but only with bridge have the modern social techniques made themselves master of the game. The paraphernalia of handbooks and systems and professional training has made bridge a deadly earnest business. A recent newpaper article estimated the yearly winnings of the Culbertson couple at more than two hundred thousand dollars. An enormous amount of mental energy is expended in this universal craze for bridge with no more tangible result than the exchange of relatively unimportant sums of money. Society as a whole is neither benefited nor damaged by this futile activity. It seems difficult to speak of it as an elevating recreation in the sense of Aristotle's diagoge. Proficiency at bridge is a sterile excellence, sharpening the mental faculties very one-sidedly without enriching the soul in any way, fixing and consuming a quantity of intellectual energy that might have been better applied. The most we can say, I think, is that it might have been applied worse. The status of bridge in modern society would indicate, to all appearances, an immense increase in the play-element today. But appearances are deceptive. Really to play, a man must play like a child. Can we assert that this is so in the case of such an ingenious game as bridge? If not, the virtue has gone out of the game.

The attempt to assess the play-content in the confusion of modern life is bound to lead us to contradictory conclusions. In the case of sport we have an activity nominally known as play but raised to such a pitch of technical organisation and scientific thoroughness that the real play-spirit is threatened with extinction. Over against this tendency to over-seriousness, however, there are other phenomena pointing in the opposite direction. Certain activities whose whole *raison d'être* lies in the field of material interest, and which had nothing of play about them in their initial stages, develop what we can only call play-forms as a secondary characteristic. Sport and athletics showed us play stiffening into seriousness but still being felt as play; now we come to serious business degenerating into play but still being called serious. The two phenomena are linked by the strong agonistic habit which still holds universal sway, though in other forms than before.

The impetus given to this agonistic principle which seems to be carrying the world back in the direction of play derives, in the main, from external factors independent of culture proper—in a word, communications, which have made intercourse of every sort so extraordinarily easy for mankind as a whole. Technology, publicity and propaganda everywhere promote the competitive spirit and afford means of satisfying it on an unprecedented scale. Commercial competition does not, of course, belong to the immemorial sacred play-forms. It only appears when trade begins to create fields of activity within which each must try to surpass and outwit his neighbour. Commercial rivalry soon makes limiting rules imperative, namely the trading customs. It remained primitive in essence until quite late, only becoming really intensive with the advent of modern communications, propaganda and statistics. Naturally a certain play-element had entered into business competition at an early stage. Statistics stimulated it with an idea that had originally arisen in sporting life, the idea, namely, of trading records. A record, as the word shows, was once simply a memorandum, a note which the inn-keeper scrawled on the walls of his inn to say that such and such a rider or traveller had been the first to arrive after covering so and so many miles. The statistics of trade and production could not fail to introduce a sporting element into economic life. In consequence, there is now a sporting side to almost every triumph of commerce or technology: the highest turnover, the biggest tonnage, the fastest crossing, the greatest altitude, etc. Here a purely ludic element has, for once, got the better of utilitarian considerations, since the experts inform us that smaller units—less monstrous steamers and aircraft, etc.—are more efficient in the long run. Business becomes play. This process goes so far that some of the great business concerns deliberately instil the play-spirit into their workers so as to step up production. The trend is now reversed: play becomes business. A captain of industry, on whom the Rotterdam Academy of Commerce had conferred an honorary degree, spoke as follows:

Ever since I first entered the business it has been a race between the technicians and the sales department. One tried to produce so much that the sales department would never be able to sell it, while the other tried to sell so much that the technicians would never be able to keep pace. This race has always continued: sometimes one is ahead, sometimes the other. Neither my brother nor myself has regarded the business as a task, but always as a game, the spirit of which it has been our constant endeavour to implant into the younger staff.

These words must, of course, be taken with a grain of salt. Nevertheless there are numerous instances of big concerns forming their own Sports Societies and even engaging workers with a view not so much to their professional capacities as to their fitness for the football eleven. Once more the wheel turns.

NOTES

1 A happy variation of the natatorial contest is found in Beowulf, where the aim is to hold your opponent under water until he is drowned.

2 It is probably significant that we no longer speak of "games" but of "sport". Our author may not have been sufficiently familiar with the development of "sport" in the last ten or twenty years, here and in America, to stress the all-important point that sport has become a business, or, to put it bluntly, a commercial racket. Trans.

3 Note G. K. Chesterton's dictum: If a thing is worth doing at all it is worth doing badly! Trans.

CHAPTER 2

The Classification of Games*

Roger Caillois

The multitude and infinite variety of games at first causes one to despair of discovering a principle of classification capable of sub-suming them under a small number of well-defined categories. Games also possess so many different characteristics that many approaches are possible. Current usage sufficiently demonstrates the degree of hesitance and uncertainty: indeed, several classifications are em-ployed concurrently. To oppose card games to games of skill, or to oppose parlour games to those played in a stadium is meaningless. In effect, the implement used in the game is chosen as a classificatory instrument in the one case; in the other, the qualifications required; in a third the number of players and the atmosphere of the game, and lastly the place in which the contest is waged. An additional over-all complication is that the same game can be played alone or with others. A particular game may require several skills simultane-ously, or none.

Very different games can be played in the same place. Merry-go-rounds and the diabolo are both open-air amusements. But the child who passively enjoys the pleasure of riding by means of the move-ment of the carousel is not in the same state of mind as the one who tries as best he can to correctly whirl his diabolo. On the other hand, many games are played without implements or accessories. Also, the same implement can fulfil different functions, depending on the game played. Marbles are generally the equipment for a game of skill, but one of the players can try to guess whether the marbles held in his opponent's hand are an odd or even number. They thus become part of a game of chance.

This last expression must be clarified. For one thing, it alludes to the fundamental characteristic of a very special kind of game. Whether it be a bet, lottery, roulette, or baccara, it is clear that the player's attitude is the same. He does nothing, he merely awaits the outcome. The boxer, the runner, and the player of chess or hop-

* Chapter 3 from *Man, Play & Games*, by Roger Caillois, London, 1962, translated by Meyer Barash.

scotch, on the contrary, work as hard as they can to win. It matters little that some games are athletic and others intellectual. The player's attitude is the same: he tries to vanquish a rival operating under the same conditions as himself. It would thus appear justified to contrast games of chance with competitive games. Above all, it becomes tempting to investigate the possibility of discovering other attitudes, no less fundamental, so that the categories for a systematic classification of games can eventually be provided.

After examining different possibilities, I am proposing a division into four main rubrics, depending upon whether, in the games under consideration, the role of competition, chance, simulation, or vertigo is dominant. I call these *agon, alea, mimicry,* and *ilinx,* respectively. All four indeed belong to the domain of play. One *plays* football, billiards, or chess (*agon*); roulette or a lottery (*alea*); pirate, Nero, or Hamlet (*mimicry*); or one produces in oneself, by a rapid whirling or falling movement, a state of dizziness and disorder (*ilinx*). Even these designations do not cover the entire universe of play. It is divided into quadrants, each governed by an original principle. Each section contains games of the same kind. But inside each section, the different games are arranged in a rank order of progression. They can also be placed on a continuum between two opposite poles. At one extreme an almost indivisible principle, common to diversion, turbulence, free improvisation, and carefree gaiety is dominant. It manifests a kind of uncontrolled fantasy that can be designated by the term *paidia.* At the opposite extreme, this frolicsome and impulsive exuberance is almost entirely absorbed or disciplined by a complementary, and in some respects inverse, tendency to its anarchic and capricious nature: there is a growing tendency to bind it with arbitrary, imperative, and purposely tedious conventions, to oppose it still more by ceaselessly practising the most embarrassing chicanery upon it, in order to make it more uncertain of attaining its desired effect. This latter principle is completely impractical, even though it requires an ever greater amount of effort, patience, skill, or ingenuity. I call this second component *ludus.*

I do not intend, in resorting to these strange concepts, to set up some kind of pedantic, totally meaningless mythology. However, obligated as I am to classify diverse games under the same general category, it seemed to me that the most economical means of doing so was to borrow, from one language or another, the most meaningful and comprehensive term possible, so that each category examined should avoid the possibility of lacking the particular quality on the basis of which the unifying concept was chosen. Also, to the degree that I will try to establish the classification to which I am committed, each concept chosen will not relate too directly to concrete experience, which in turn is to be divided according to an as yet untested principle.

In the same spirit, I am compelled to subsume the games most varied in appearance under the same rubric, in order to better demonstrate their fundamental kinship. I have mixed physical and mental games, those dependent upon force with those requiring skill or reasoning. Within each class, I have not distinguished between children's and adults' games, and wherever possible I have sought instances of homologous behaviour in the animal world. The point in doing this was to stress the very principle of the proposed classification. It would be less burdensome if it were perceived that the divisions set up correspond to essential and irreducible impulses.

FUNDAMENTAL CATEGORIES

Agon. A whole group of games would seem to be competitive, that is to say, like a combat in which equality of chances is artificially created, in order that the adversaries should confront each other under ideal conditions, susceptible of giving precise and incontestable value to the winner's triumph. It is therefore always a question of a rivalry which hinges on a single quality (speed, endurance, strength, memory, skill, ingenuity, etc.), exercised, within defined limits and without outside assistance, in such a way that the winner appears to be better than the loser in a certain category of exploits. Such is the case with sports contests and the reason for their very many subdivisions. Two individuals or two teams are in opposition (polo, tennis, football, boxing, fencing, etc.), or there may be a varying number of contestants (courses of every kind, shooting matches, golf, athletics, etc.). In the same class belong the games in which, at the outset, the adversaries divide the elements into equal parts and value. The games of checkers, chess, and billiards are perfect examples. The search for equality is so obviously essential to the rivalry that it is re-established by a handicap for players of different classes; that is, within the equality of chances originally established, a secondary inequality, proportionate to the relative powers of the participants, is dealt with. It is significant that such a usage exists in the *agon* of a physical character (sports) just as in the more cerebral type (chess games for example, in which the weaker player is given the advantage of a pawn, knight, castle, etc.).

As carefully as one tries to bring it about, absolute equality does not seem to be realisable. Sometimes, as in checkers or chess, the fact of moving first is an advantage, for this priority permits the favoured player to occupy key positions or to impose a special strategy. Conversely, in bidding games, such as bridge, the last bid-der profits from the clues afforded by the bids of his opponents. Again, at croquet, to be last multiplies the player's resources. In sports contests, the exposure, the fact of having the sun in front or in back; the wind which aids or hinders one or the other side; the fact, in disputing for positions on a circular track, of finding oneself in the inside or outside lane constitutes a crucial test, a trump or disadvantage whose influence may be considerable. These inevitable imbalances are negated or modified by drawing lots at the beginning, then by strict alternation of favoured positions.

The point of the game is for each player to have his superiority in a given area recognised. That is why the practise of *agon* pre-supposes sustained attention, appropriate training, assiduous appli-cation, and the desire to win. It implies discipline and perseverance. It leaves the champion to his own devices, to evoke the best possible game of which he is capable, and it obliges him to play the game within the fixed limits, and according to the rules applied equally to all, so that in return the victor's superiority will be beyond dispute.

In addition to games, the spirit of *agon* is found in other cultural phenomena conforming to the game code: in the duel, in the tourna-ment, and in certain constant and noteworthy aspects of so-called courtly war.

In principle, it would seem that *agon* is unknown among animals, which have no conception of limits or rules, only seeking a brutal victory in merciless combat. It is clear that horse races and cock fights are an exception, for these are conflicts in which men make animals compete in terms of norms that the former alone have set up. Yet, in considering certain facts, it seems that animals already have the competitive urge during encounters where limits are at least implicitly accepted and spontaneously respected, even if rules are lacking. This is notably the case in kittens, puppies, and bear cubs, which take pleasure in knocking each other down yet not hurting each other.

Still more convincing are the habits of bovines, which, standing face to face with heads lowered, try to force each other back. Horses engage in the same kind of friendly duelling: to test their strength, they rear up on their hind legs and press down upon each other with all their vigour and weight, in order to throw their adversaries off balance. In addition, observers have noted numerous games of pur-suit that result from a challenge or invitation. The animal that is overtaken has nothing to fear from the victor. The most impressive example is without doubt that of the little ferocious "fighting" willow wrens. "A moist elevation covered with short grass and about two meters in diameter is chosen for the arena," says Karl Groos. The males gather there daily. The first to arrive waits for an adversary, and then the fight begins. The contenders tremble and bow their heads several times. Their feathers bristle. They hurl themselves at each other, beaks advanced, and striking at one another. Never is there any pursuit or conflict outside the space delimited for the tourney. This is why it seems legitimate for me to use the term *agon* for these cases, for the goal of the encounters is not for the antagonist to cause serious injury to his rival, but rather to demonstrate his own superiority. Man merely adds refinement and precision by devising rules.

In children, as soon as the personality begins to assert itself, and before the emergence of regulated competition, unusual challenges are frequent, in which the adversaries try to prove their greater endurance. They are observed competing to see which can stare at the sun, endure tickling, stop breathing, not wink his eye, etc., the longest. Sometimes the stakes are more serious, where it is a question of enduring hunger or else pain in the form of whipping, pinching, stinging, or burning. Then these ascetic games, as they have been called, involve severe ordeals. They anticipate the cruelty and hazing which adolescents must undergo during their initiation. This is a departure from *agon*, which soon finds its perfect form, be it in legitimately competitive games and sports, or in those involving feats of prowess (hunting, mountain climbing, crossword puzzles, chess problems, etc.) in which champions, without directly confronting each other, are involved in ceaseless and diffuse competition.

Alea. This is the Latin name for the game of dice. I have borrowed it to designate, in contrast to *agon*, all games that are based on a decision independent of the player, an outcome over which he has no control, and in which winning is the result of fate rather than triumphing over an adversary. More properly, destiny is the sole artisan of victory, and where there is rivalry, what is meant is that the winner has been more favoured by fortune than the loser. Perfect examples of this type are provided by the games of dice, roulette, heads or tails, baccara, lotteries, etc. Here, not only does one refrain from trying to eliminate the injustice of chance, but rather it is the very capriciousness of chance that constitutes the unique appeal of the game.

Alea signifies and reveals the favour of destiny. The player is entirely passive; he does not deploy his resources, skill, muscles, or intelligence. All he need do is await, in hope and trembling, the cast of the die. He risks his stake. Fair play, also sought but now taking place under ideal conditions, lies in being compensated exactly in proportion to the risk involved. Every device intended to equalise the competitors' chances is here employed to scrupulously equate risk and profit.

In contrast to *agon*, *alea* negates work, patience, experience, and qualifications. Professionalisation, application, and training are eliminated. In one instant, winnings may be wiped out. *Alea* is total disgrace or absolute favour. It grants the lucky player infinitely more than he could procure by a lifetime of labour, discipline, and fatigue. It seems an insolent and sovereign insult to merit. It supposes on the player's part an attitude exactly opposite to that reflected in *agon*. In the latter, his only reliance is upon himself; in the former, he counts on everything, even the vaguest sign, the slightest outside occurrence, which he immediately takes to be an omen or token— in short, he depends on everything except himself.

Agon is in vindication of personal responsibility; *alea* is a negation of the will, a surrender to destiny. Some games, such as dominoes, backgammon, and most card games, combine the two. Chance determines the distribution of the hands dealt to each player, and the players then play the hands that blind luck has assigned to them as best they can. In a game like bridge, it is knowledge and reasoning that constitute the player's defence, permitting him to play a better game with the cards that he has been given. In games such as poker, it is the qualities of psychological acumen and character that count.

The role of money is also generally more impressive than the role of chance, and therefore is the recourse of the weaker player. The reason for this is clear: *Alea* does not have the function of causing the more intelligent to win money, but tends rather to abolish natural or acquired individual differences, so that all can be placed on an absolutely equal footing to await the blind verdict of chance.

Since the result of *agon* is necessarily uncertain and paradoxically must approximate the effect of pure chance, assuming that the chances of the competitors are as equal as possible, it follows that every encounter with competitive characteristics and ideal rules can become the object of betting, or *alea*, e.g. horse or greyhound races, football, basketball, and cock fights. It even happens that table stakes vary unceasingly during the game, according to the vicissitudes of *agon*.[3]

Games of chance would seem to be peculiarly human. Animals play games involving competition, stimulation, and excess. K. Groos, especially, offers striking examples of these. In sum, animals, which are very much involved in the immediate and enslaved by their impulses, cannot conceive of an abstract and inanimate power, to whose verdict they would passively submit in advance of the game. To await the decision of destiny passively and deliberately, to risk upon it wealth proportionate to the risk of losing, is an attitude that requires the possibility of foresight, vision, and speculation, for which objective and calculating reflection is needed. Perhaps it is in the degree to which a child approximates an animal that games of chance are not as important to children as to adults. For the child, play is active. In addition, the child is immune to the main attraction of games of chance, deprived as he is of economic independence, since he has no money of his own. Games of chance have no power to thrill him. To be sure, marbles are money to him. However, he counts on his skill rather than on chance to win them.

Agon and *alea* imply opposite and somewhat complementary attitudes, but they both obey the same law—the creation for the players of conditions of pure equality denied them in real life. For nothing in life is clear, since everything is confused from the very beginning, luck and merit too. Play, whether *agon* or *alea*, is thus an attempt to substitute perfect situations for the normal confusion of contemporary life. In games, the role of merit or chance is clear and indisputable. It is also implied that all must play with exactly the same possibility of proving their superiority or, on another scale, exactly the same chances of winning. In one way or another, one escapes the real world and creates another. One can also escape himself and become another. This is *mimicry*.

Mimicry. All play presupposes the temporary acceptance, if not of an illusion (indeed this last word means nothing less than beginning a game: *in-lusio*), then at least of a closed, conventional, and, in certain respects, imaginary universe. Play can consist not only of deploying actions or submitting to one's fate in an imaginary milieu, but of becoming an illusory character oneself, and of so behaving. One is thus confronted with a diverse series of manifestations, the common element of which is that the subject makes believe or makes others believe that he is someone other than himself. He forgets, disguises, or temporarily sheds his personality in order to feign another. I prefer to designate these phenomena by the term *mimicry*, the English word for mimetism, notably of insects, so that the fundamental, elementary, and quasi-organic nature of the impulse that stimulates it can be stressed.

The insect world, compared to the human world, seems like the most divergent of solutions provided by nature. This world is in contrast in all respects to that of man, but it is no less elaborate, complex, and surprising. Also, it seems legitimate to me at this point to take account of mimetic phenomena of which insects provide most perplexing examples. In fact, corresponding to the free, versatile, arbitrary, imperfect, and extremely diversified behaviour of man, there is in animals, especially in insects, the organic, fixed, and absolute adaptation which characterises the species and is infinitely and exactly reproduced from generation to generation in billions of individuals: e.g. the caste system of ants and termites as against class conflict, and the designs on butterflies' wings as compared to the history of painting. Reluctant as one may be to accept this hypothesis, the temerity of which I recognise, the inexplicable mimetism of insects immediately affords an extraordinary parallel to man's penchant for disguising himself, wearing a mask, or playing a part— except that in the insect's case the mask or guise becomes part of the body instead of a contrived accessory. But it serves the same purposes in both cases, viz. to change the wearer's appearance and to inspire fear in others.[4]

Among vertebrates, the tendency to imitate first appears as an entirely physical, quasi-irresistible contagion, analogous to the contagion of yawning, running, limping, smiling, or almost any movement. Hudson seems to have proved that a young animal "follows any object that is going away, and flees any approaching object". Just as a lamb is startled and runs if its mother turns around and moves towards the lamb without warning, the lamb trails the man, dog, or horse that it sees moving away. Contagion and imitation are not the same as simulation, but they make possible and give rise to the idea or the taste for mimicry. In birds, this tendency leads to nuptial parades, ceremonies, and exhibitions of vanity in which males or females, as the case may be, indulge with rare application and evident pleasure. As for the oxyrhinous crabs, which plant upon their carapaces any alga or polyp that they can catch, their aptitude for disguise leaves no room for doubt, whatever explanation for the phenomenon may be advanced.

Mimicry and travesty are therefore complementary acts in this kind of play. For children, the aim is to imitate adults. This explains the success of the toy weapons and miniatures which copy the tools, engines, arms, and machines used by adults. The little girl plays her mother's role as cook, laundress, and ironer. The boy makes believe he is a soldier, musketeer, policeman, pirate, cowboy, Martian,[5] etc. An aeroplane is made by waving his arms and making the noise of a motor. However, acts of mimicry tend to cross the border between childhood and adulthood. They cover to the same degree any distraction, mask, or travesty, in which one participates, and which stresses the very fact that the play is masked or otherwise disguised, and such consequences as ensue. Lastly, it is clear that theatrical presentations and dramatic interpretations rightly belong in this category.

The pleasure lies in being or passing for another. But in games the basic intention is not that of deceiving the spectators. The child who is playing train may well refuse to kiss his father while saying to him that one does not embrace locomotives, but he is not trying to persuade his father that he is a real locomotive. At a carnival, the masquerader does not try to make one believe that he is really a marquis, toreador, or Indian, but rather tries to inspire fear and take advantage of the surrounding licence, a result of the fact that the mask disguises the conventional self and liberates the true personality. The actor does not try to make believe that he is "really" King Lear or Charles V. It is only the spy and the fugitive who disguise themselves to really deceive because they are not playing.

Activity, imagination, interpretation, and *mimicry* have hardly any relationship to *alea*, which requires immobility and the thrill of expectation from the player, but *agon* is not excluded. I am not thinking of the masqueraders' competition, in which the relationship is obvious. A much more subtle complicity is revealed. For nonparticipants, every *agon* is a spectacle. Only it is a spectacle which, to be valid, excludes simulation. Great sports events are nevertheless special occasions for *mimicry*, but it must be recalled that the simulation is now transferred from the participants to the audience. It is not the athletes who mimic, but the spectators. Identification with the champion in itself constitutes *mimicry* related to that of the reader with the hero of the novel and that of the movie-goer with the film star. To be convinced of this, it is merely necessary to consider the perfectly symmetrical functions of the champion and the stage or screen star. Champions, winners at *agon*, are the stars of sports contests. Conversely, stars are winners in a more diffuse competition in which the stakes are popular favour. Both receive a large fanmail, give interviews to an avid press, and sign autographs.

In fact, bicycle races, boxing or wrestling matches, football, tennis, or polo games are intrinsic spectacles, with costumes, solemn overture, appropriate liturgy, and regulated procedures. In a word, these are dramas whose vicissitudes keep the public breathless, and lead to denouements which exalt some and depress others. The nature of these spectacles remains that of an *agon*, but their outward aspect is that of an exhibition. The audience are not content to encourage the efforts of the athletes or horses of their choice merely by voice and gesture. A physical contagion leads them to assume the position of the men or animals in order to help them, just as the bowler is known to unconsciously incline his body in the direction that he would like the bowling ball to take at the end of its course. Under these conditions, paralleling the spectacle, a competitive *mimicry* is born in the public, which doubles the true *agon* of the field or track.

With one exception, *mimicry* exhibits all the characteristics of play: liberty, convention, suspension of reality, and delimitation of space and time. However, the continuous submission to imperative and precise rules cannot be observed—rules for the dissimulation of reality and the substitution of a second reality. *Mimicry* is incessant invention. The rule of the game is unique: it consists in the actor's fascinating the spectator, while avoiding an error that might lead the spectator to break the spell. The spectator must lend himself to the illusion without first challenging the decor, mask, or artifice which for a given time he is asked to believe in as more real than reality itself.

Ilinx. The last kind of game includes those which are based on the pursuit of vertigo and which consist of an attempt to momentarily destroy the stability of perception and inflict a kind of voluptuous panic upon an otherwise lucid mind. In all cases, it is a question of surrendering to a kind of spasm, seizure, or shock which destroys reality with sovereign brusqueness.

The disturbance that provokes vertigo is commonly sought for its own sake. I need only cite as examples the actions of whirling dervishes and the Mexican *voladores*. I choose these purposely, for the former, in technique employed, can be related to certain children's games, while the latter rather recall the elaborate manoeuvres of highwire acrobatics. They thus touch the two poles of games of vertigo. Dervishes seek ecstasy by whirling about with movements accelerating as the drumbeats become ever more precipitate. Panic and hypnosis are attained by the paroxysm of frenetic, contagious, and shared rotation.[6] In Mexico, the *voladores*—Huastec or Totonac—climb to the top of a mast sixty-five to one hundred feet high. They are disguised as eagles with false wings hanging from their wrists. The end of a rope is attached to their waists. The rope then passes between their toes in such a way that they can manage their entire descent with head down and arms outstretched. Before reaching the ground, they make many complete turns, thirty according to Torquemada, describing an ever-widening spiral in their downward flight. The ceremony, comprising several flights and beginning at noon, is readily interpreted as a dance of the setting sun, associated with birds, the deified dead. The frequency of accidents has led the Mexican authorities to ban this dangerous exercise.[7]

It is scarcely necessary to invoke these rare and fascinating examples. Every child very well knows that by whirling rapidly he reaches a centrifugal state of flight from which he regains bodily stability and clarity of perception only with difficulty. The child engages in this activity playfully and finds pleasure thereby. An example is the game of teetotum[8] in which the player pivots on one foot as quickly as he is able. Analogously, in the Haitian game of *mais d'or* two children hold hands, face to face, their arms extended. With their bodies stiffened and bent backward, and with their feet joined, they turn until they are breathless, so that they will have the pleasure of staggering about after they stop. Comparable sensations are provided by screaming as loud as one can, racing downhill, and tobogganing; in horsemanship, provided that one turns quickly; and in swinging.

Various physical activities also provoke these sensations, such as the tightrope, falling or being projected into space, rapid rotation, sliding, speeding, and acceleration of vertilinear movement, separately or in combination with gyrating movement. In parallel fashion, there is a vertigo of a moral order, a transport that suddenly seizes the individual. This vertigo is readily linked to the desire for disorder and destruction, a drive which is normally repressed. It is reflected in crude and brutal forms of personality expression. In children, it is especially observed in the games of hot cockles, "winner-take-all", and leapfrog in which they rush and spin pell-mell. In adults, nothing is more revealing of vertigo than the strange excitement that is felt in cutting down the tall prairie flowers with a switch, or in creating an avalanche of the snow on a rooftop, or, better, the intoxication that is experienced in military barracks—for example, in noisily banging garbage cans.

To cover the many varieties of such transport, for a disorder that may take organic or psychological form, I propose using the term *ilinx*, the Greek term for whirlpool, from which is also derived the Greek word for vertigo (*ilingos*).

This pleasure is not unique to man. To begin with, it is appropriate to recall the gyrations of certain mammals, sheep in particular. Even if these are pathological manifestations, they are too significant to be passed over in silence. In addition, examples in which the play element is certain are not lacking. In order to catch their tails dogs will spin around until they fall down. At other times they are seized by a fever for running until they are exhausted. Antelopes, gazelles, and wild horses are often panic-stricken when there is no real danger in the slightest degree to account for it; the impression is of an overbearing contagion to which they surrender in instant compliance.[9]

Water rats divert themselves by spinning as if they were being drawn by an eddy in a stream. The case of the chamois is even more remarkable. According to Karl Groos, they ascend the glaciers, and with a leap, each in turn slides down a steep slope, while the other chamois watch.

The gibbon chooses a flexible branch and weighs it down until it unbends, thus projecting him into the air. He lands catch as catch can, and he endlessly repeats this useless exercise, inexplicable except in terms of its seductive quality. Birds especially love games of vertigo. They let themselves fall like stones from a great height, then open their wings when they are only a few feet from the ground, thus giving the impression that they are going to be crushed. In the mating season they utilise this heroic flight in order to attract the female. The American nighthawk, described by Audubon, is a virtuoso at these impressive acrobatics.[10]

Following the teetotum, *mais d'or*, sliding, horsemanship, and swinging of their childhood, men surrender to the intoxication of many kinds of dance, from the common but insidious giddiness of the waltz to the many mad, tremendous, and convulsive movements of other dances. They derive the same kind of pleasure from the intoxication stimulated by high speed on skis, motor-cycles, or in driving sports cars. In order to give this kind of sensation the intensity and brutality capable of shocking adults, powerful machines have had to be invented. Thus it is not surprising that the Industrial Revolution had to take place before vertigo could really become a kind of game. It is now provided for the avid masses by thousands of stimulating contraptions installed at fairs and amusement parks.

These machines would obviously surpass their goal if it were only a question of assaulting the organs of the inner ear, upon which the sense of equilibrium is dependent. But it is the whole body which must submit to such treatment as anyone would fear undergoing, were it not that everybody else was seen struggling to do the same. In fact, it is worth watching people leaving these vertigo-inducing machines. The contraptions turn people pale and dizzy to the point of nausea. They shriek with fright, gasp for breath, and have the terrifying impression of visceral fear and shrinking as if to escape a horrible attack. Moreover the majority of them, before even recovering, are already hastening to the ticket booth in order to buy the right to again experience the same pleasurable torture.

It is necessary to use the word "pleasure", because one hesitates to call such a transport a mere distraction, corresponding as it does more to spasm than to an entertainment. In addition, it is important to note that the violence of the shock felt is such that the concessionaries try, in extreme cases, to lure the naive by offering free rides. They deceitfully announce that "this time only" the ride is free, when this is the usual practice. To compensate, the spectators are made to pay for the privilege of calmly observing from a high balcony the terrors of the co-operating or surprised victims, exposed to fearful forces or strange caprices.

It would be rash to draw very precise conclusions on the subject of this curious and cruel assignment of roles. This last is not characteristic of a kind of game, such as is found in boxing, wrestling, and in gladiatorial combat. Essential is the pursuit of this special disorder or sudden panic, which defines the term vertigo, and in the true characteristics of the games associated with it: viz. the freedom to accept or refuse the experience, strict and fixed limits, and separation from the rest of reality. What the experience adds to the spectacle does not diminish but reinforces its character as play.

FROM TURBULENCE TO RULES

Rules are inseparable from play as soon as the latter becomes institutionalised. From this moment on they become part of its nature. They transform it into an instrument of fecund and decisive culture. But a basic freedom is central to play in order to stimulate distraction and fantasy. This liberty is its indispensable motive power and is basic to the most complex and carefully organised forms of play. Such a primary power of improvisation and joy, which I call *paidia*, is allied to the taste for gratuitous difficulty that I propose to call *ludus*, in order to encompass the various games to which, without exaggeration, a civilising quality can be attributed. In fact, they reflect the moral and intellectual values of a culture, as well as contribute to their refinement and development.

I have chosen the term *paidia* because its root is the word for child, and also because of a desire not to needlessly disconcert the reader by resorting to a term borrowed from an antipodal language. However, the Sanskrit *kredati* and the Chinese *wan* seem both richer and more expressive through the variety and nature of their connotations. It is true that they also present the disadvantages of overabundance—a certain danger of confusion, for one. *Kredati* designates the play of adults, children, and animals. It applies more specifically to gamboling, i.e. to the sudden and capricious movements provoked by a superabundance of gaiety and vitality. It applies equally to illicit sex relationships, the rise and fall of waves, and anything that undulates with the wind. The word *wan* is even more explicit, as much for what it defines as for what it avoids defining, i.e. specifying games of skill, competition, simulation, and chance. It manifests many refinements of meaning to which I will have occasion to return.

In view of these relationships and semantic qualifications, what can be the connotations and denotations of the term *paidia*? I shall define it, for my purposes, as a word covering the spontaneous manifestations of the play instinct: a cat entangled in a ball of wool, a dog sniffing, and an infant laughing at his rattle represent the first identifiable examples of this type of activity. It intervenes in every happy exuberance which effects an immediate and disordered agitation, an impulsive and easy recreation, but readily carried to excess, whose impromptu and unruly character remains its essential if not unique reason for being. From somersaults to scribbling, from squab-ble to uproar, perfectly clear illustrations are not lacking of the comparable symptoms of movements, colours, or noises.

This elementary need for disturbance and tumult first appears as an impulse to touch, grasp, taste, smell, and then drop any accessible object. It readily can become a taste for destruction and breaking things. It explains the pleasure in endlessly cutting up paper with a pair of scissors, pulling cloth into thread, breaking up a gathering, holding up a queue, disturbing the play or work of others, etc. Soon comes the desire to mystify or to defy by sticking out the tongue or grimacing while seeming to touch or throw the forbidden object. For the child it is a question of expressing himself, of feeling he is the cause, of forcing others to pay attention to him. In this manner, K. Groos recalls the case of a monkey which took pleasure in pulling the tail of a dog that lived with it, each time that the dog seemed to be going to sleep. The primitive joy in destruction and upset has been notably observed by the sister of G. J. Romanes in precise and most meaningful detail.[11]

The child does not stop at that. He loves to play with his own pain, for example by probing a toothache with his tongue. He also likes to be frightened. He thus looks for a physical illness, limited and controlled, of which he is the cause, or sometimes he seeks an anxiety that he, being the cause, can stop at will. At various points, the fundamental aspects of play are already recognisable, i.e. volun-tary, agreed upon, isolated, and regulated activity.

Soon there is born the desire to invent rules, and to abide by them whatever the cost. The child then makes all kinds of bets—which, as has been seen, are the elementary forms of *agon*—with himself or his friends. He hops, walks backwards with his eyes closed, plays at who can look longest at the sun, and will suffer pain or stand in a painful position.

In general, the first manifestations of *paidia* have no name and could not have any, precisely because they are not part of any order, distinctive symbolism, or clearly differentiated life that would permit a vocabulary to consecrate their autonomy with a specific term. But as soon as conventions, techniques, and utensils emerge, the first games as such arise with them: e.g. leapfrog, hide and seek, kite-flying, teetotum, sliding, blindman's buff, and doll-play. At this point the contradictory roads of *agon, alea, mimicry,* and *ilinx* begin to bifurcate. At the same time, the pleasure experienced in solving a problem arbitrarily designed for this purpose also intervenes, so that reaching a solution has no other goal than personal satisfaction for its own sake.

This condition, which is *ludus* proper, is also reflected in different kinds of games, except for those which wholly depend upon the cast of a die. It is complementary to and a refinement of *paidia*, which it disciplines and enriches. It provides an occasion for training and normally leads to the acquisition of a special skill, a particular mastery of the operation of one or another contraption or the discovery of a satisfactory solution to problems of a more conventional type.

The difference from *agon* is that in *ludus* the tension and skill of the player are not related to any explicit feeling of emulation or rivalry: the conflict is with the obstacle, not with one or several competitors. On the level of manual dexterity there can be cited games such as cup-and-ball, diabolo, and yo-yo. These simple instruments merely utilise basic natural laws, e.g. gravity and rotation in the case of the yo-yo, where the point is to transform a rectilinear alternating motion into a continuous circular movement. Kite-flying, on the contrary, relies on the exploitation of a specific atmospheric condition. Thanks to this, the player accomplishes a kind of auscultation upon the sky from afar. He projects his presence beyond the limits of his body. Again, the game of blindman's bluff offers an opportunity to experience the quality of perception in the absence of sight.[12] It is readily seen that the possibilities of *ludus* are almost infinite.

Games such as solitaire or the ring puzzle, although part of the same species, already belong to another group of games, since they constantly appeal to a spirit of calculation and contrivance. And lastly, crossword puzzles, mathematical recreations, anagrams, olorhymes[12] and obscure poetry, addiction to detective stories (trying to identify the culprit), and chess or bridge problems constitute, even in the absence of gadgets, many varieties of the most prevalent and pure forms of *ludus*.

It is common knowledge that what to begin with seems to be a situation susceptible to indefinite repetition turns out to be capable of producing ever new combinations. Thus the player is stimulated to emulate himself, permitting him to take pride in his accomplishment, as against those who share his taste. There is a manifest relationship between *ludus* and *agon*. In addition, it can happen that the same game may possess both, e.g. chess or bridge.

The combination of *ludus* and *alea* is no less frequent: it is especially recognisable in games of patience, in which ingenious manoeuvres have little influence upon the result, and in playing slot machines in which the player can very crudely calculate the impulsion given to the ball at various points in directing its course. In both these examples, chance is still the deciding factor. Moreover, the fact that the player is not completely helpless and that he can at least minimally count on his skill or talent is sufficient reason to link *ludus* with *alea*.[14]

Ludus is also readily compatible with *mimicry*. In the simplest cases, it lends aspects of illusion to construction games such as the animal made out of millet stalks by Dogon children, the cranes or automobiles constructed by fitting together perforated steel parts and pulleys from an Erector set, or the scale-model planes or ships that even adults do not disdain meticulously constructing. However, it is the theatre which provides the basic connection between the two, by disciplining mimicry until it becomes an art rich in a thousand diverse routines, refined techniques, and subtly complex resources. By means of this fortunate development, the cultural fecundity of play is amply demonstrated.

In contrast, just as there could be no relationship between *paidia*, which is tumultuous and exuberant, and *alea*, which is passive anticipation of and mute immobility pending the outcome of the game, there also can be no connection between *ludus*, which is calculation and contrivance, and *ilinx*, which is a pure state of transport. The desire to overcome an obstacle can only emerge to combat vertigo and prevent it from becoming transformed into disorder or panic. It is, therefore, training in self-control, an arduous effort to preserve calm and equilibium. Far from being compatible with *ilinx*, it provides the discipline needed to neutralise the dangerous effects of *ilinx*, as in mountain climbing or tightrope walking.

Ludus, in itself, seems incomplete, a kind of makeshift device intended to allay boredom. One becomes resigned to it while awaiting something preferable, such as the arrival of partners that makes possible the substitution of a contest for this solitary pleasure. Moreover, even in games of skill or contrivance (e.g. patience, crossword and other puzzles) which exclude or regard as undesirable the intervention of another person, *ludus* no less inspires in the player the hope of succeeding the next time when he may obtain a higher score. In this way, the influence of *agon* is again manifested. Indeed, it enriches the pleasure derived from overcoming an arbitrarily chosen obstacle. In fact, even if each of these games is played alone and is not replaced by an openly competitive one, it can easily and quickly be converted into a contest, with or without prizes, such as newspapers organise on occasion.

There is also an aspect of *ludus* that, in my opinion, is explained by the presence of *agon* within it: that is, that it is strongly affected by fashion. The yo-yo, cup-and-ball, diabolo, and ring puzzle appear and disappear as if by magic and soon are replaced by other games. In parallel fashion, the vogues for amusements of a more intellectual nature are no less limited in time; e.g. the rebus, the anagram, the acrostic, and the charade have had their hours. It is probable that crossword puzzles and detective stories will run the same course. Such a phenomenon would be enigmatic if *ludus* were an individual amusement, as seems superficially to be the case. In reality, it is permeated with an atmosphere of competition. It only persists to the degree that the fervour of addicts transforms it into virtual *agon*. When the latter is missing, *ludus* cannot persist independently. In fact, it is not sufficiently supported by the spirit of organised competition, which is not essential to it, and does not provide the substance for a spectacle capable of attracting crowds. It remains transient and diffuse, or else it risks turning into an obsession for the isolated fanatic who would dedicate himself to it absolutely and in his addiction would increasingly withdraw from society.

Industrial civilisation has given birth to a special form of *ludus*, the hobby, a secondary and gratuitous activity, undertaken and pursued for pleasure, e.g. collecting, unique accomplishments, the pleasure in billiards or inventing gadgets, in a word any occupation that is primarily a compensation for the injury to personality caused by bondage to work of an automatic and picayune character. It has been observed that the hobby of the worker-turned-artisan readily takes the form of constructing complete scale models of the machines in the fabrication of which he is fated to co-operate by always repeating the same movement, an operation demanding no skill or intelligence on his part. He not only avenges himself upon reality, but in a positive and creative way. The hobby is a response to one of the highest functions of the play instinct. It is not surprising that a technical civilisation contributes to its development, even to providing compensations for its more brutal aspects. Hobbies reflect the rare qualities that make their development possible.

In a general way, *ludus* relates to the primitive desire to find diversion and amusement in arbitrary, perpetually recurrent obstacles. Thousands of occasions and devices are invented to satisfy simultaneously the desire for relaxation and the need, of which man cannot be rid, to utilise purposefully the knowledge, experience, and intelligence at his disposal, while disregarding self-control and his capacity for resistance to suffering, fatigue, panic, or intoxication.

What I call *ludus* stands for the specific element in play the impact and cultural creativity of which seems most impressive. It does not connote a psychological attitude as precise as that of *agon*, *alea*, *mimicry* or *ilinx*, but in disciplining the *paidia*, its general contribution is to give the fundamental categories of play their purity and excellence.

Besides, *ludus* is not the only conceivable metamorphosis of *paidia*. A civilisation like that of classical China worked out a different destiny for itself. Wisely and circumspectly, Chinese culture is less directed towards purposive innovation. The need for progress and the spirit of enterprise generally seem to them a kind of compulsion that is not particularly creative. Under these conditions the turbulence and surplus of energy characteristic of *paidia* is channellised in a direction better suited to its supreme values. This is the place to return to the term *wan*. According to some, it would etymologically designate the act of indefinitely caressing a piece of jade while polishing it, in order to savour its smoothness or as an accompaniment to reverie. Perhaps this origin clarifies another purpose of *paidia*. The reservoir of free movement that is part of its original definition seems in this case to be oriented not towards process, calculation, or triumph over difficulties but towards calm, patience, and idle speculation. The term *wan* basically designates all kinds of semi-automatic activities which leave the mind detached and idle, certain complex games which are part of *ludus*, and at the same time, nonchalant meditation and lazy contemplation.

Tumult and din are covered by the expression *jeou-nao*, which means literally "passion-disorder". When joined to the term *nao*, the term *wan* connotes any exuberant or joyous behaviour. But this term *wan* must be present. With the character *tchouang* (to pretend), it means "to find pleasure in simulating." Thus *wan* coincides fairly exactly with the various possible manifestations of *paidia*, although when used alone it may designate a particular kind of game. It is not used for competition, dice, or dramatic interpretation. That is to say, it excludes the various kinds of games that I have referred to as institutional.

The latter are designated by more specialised terms. The character *hsi* corresponds to games of disguise or simulation, covering the domain of the theatre and the spectacle. The character *choua* refers to games involving skill and ability; however, it is also used for contests involving jokes or puns, for fencing, and for perfection in practising a difficult art. The character *teou* refers to conflict as such, cock fighting or duelling. It is also used for card games. Lastly, the character *tou*, not to be applied to children's games, covers games of chance, feats of daring, bets, and ordeals. It also is the name for blasphemy, for to tempt chance is considered a sacrilegious wager against destiny.[15]

The vast semantic area of the term *wan* makes it even more deserving of interest. To begin with, it includes child's play and all kinds of carefree and frivolous diversion such as are suggested by the verbs to frolic, to romp, to trifle, etc. It is used to describe casual, abnormal, or strange sex practices. At the same time, it is used for games demanding reflection and forbidding haste, such as chess, checkers, puzzles (*tai Kiao*), and the game of nine rings. It also comprises the pleasure of appreciating the savour of good food or the bouquet of a wine, the taste for collecting works of art or even appreciating them, voluptuously handling and even fashioning delicate curios, comparable to the Occidental category of the hobby, collecting or pottering. Lastly, the transitory and relaxing sweetness of moonlight is suggested, the pleasure of a boat ride on a limpid lake or the prolonged contemplation of a waterfall.

The example of the word *wan* shows that the destinies of cultures can be read in their games. The preference for *agon, alea, mimicry,* or *ilinx* helps decide the future of a civilisation. Also, the channelling of the free energy in *paidia* towards invention or contemplation manifests an implicit but fundamental and most significant choice.

TABLE 1
Classification of Games

	Agon (Competition)		*Alea* (Chance)	*Mimicry* (Simulation)	*Ilinx* (Vertigo)
Paidia Tumult Agitation Immoderate laughter	Racing Wrestling Etc. Athletics	not regu- lated	Counting-out rhymes Heads or tails	Children's initiations Games of illusion Tag, Arms Masks Disguises	Children "whirling" Horseback riding Swinging Waltzing
Kite- flying Solitaire Patience Crossword puzzles	Boxing, Billiards Fencing Checkers Football Chess		Betting Roulette		Volador Travelling carnivals Skiing Mountain climbing Tightrope walking
Ludus	Contests Sports in general		Simple complex, and continuing lotteries*	Theatre Spectacles in general	

N.B.—In each vertical column games are classified in such an order that the *paidia* element is constantly decreasing while the *ludus* element is ever increasing.

* A simple lottery consists of the one basic drawing. In a complex lottery there are many possible combinations. A continuing lottery (e.g. Irish Sweepstakes) is one consisting of two or more stages, the winner of the first stage being granted the opportunity to participate in a second lottery.

NOTES

1 Karl Groos, *The Play of Animals* (English translation; New York: D. Appleton & Co., 1898, p. 151).

2 For example, in the Balearic Islands for *jai-alai*, and cockfights in the Antilles. It is obvious that it is not necessary to take into account the cash prizes that may motivate jockeys, owners, runners, boxers, football players, or other athletes. These prizes, however substantial, are not relevant to *alea*. They are a reward for a well-fought victory. This recompense for merit has nothing to do with luck or the result of chance, which remain the uncertain monopoly of gamblers; in fact it is the direct opposite.

3 As has been aptly remarked, girls' playthings are designed to imitate practical, realistic, and domestic activities, while those of boys suggest distant, romantic, inaccessible, or even obviously unreal actions.

4 O. Depont and X. Coppolani, *Les confréries religieuses musulmanes* (Algiers, 1887), pp. 156–9, 329–39.

5 Description and photographs in Helga Larsen, "Notes on the Volador and Its Associated Ceremonies and Superstitions", *Ethnos*, 2, No. 4 (July, 1937), 179–92, and in Guy Stresser-Péan, "Les origines du volador et du comelagatoazte", *Actes du XXVIII Congres International des Américanistes* (Paris, 1947), 327–34. I quote part of the description of the ceremony from this article (translated by M.B. from French text):

"The chief of the dance or K'ohal, clad in a red and blue tunic, ascends in his turn and sits on the terminal platform. Facing east, he first invokes the benevolent deities, while extending his wings in their direction and using a whistle which imitates the puling of eagles. Then he climbs to the top of the mast. Facing the four points of the compass in succession, he offers them a chalice of calabash wrapped in white linen just like a bottle of brandy, from which he sips and spits some more or less vaporised mouthfuls. Once this symbolic offering has been made, he puts on his headdress of red feathers and dances, facing all four directions while beating his wings.

"These ceremonies executed at the summit of the mast mark what the Indians consider the most moving phase of the ritual, because it involves mortal risk. But the next stage of the 'flight' is even more spectacular. The four dancers, attached by the waist, pass underneath the structure, then let themselves go from behind. Thus suspended, they slowly descend to the ground, describing a grand spiral in proportion to the unrolling of the ropes. The difficult thing for these dancers is to seize this rope between their toes in such a way as to keep their heads down and arms outspread just like descending birds which soar in great circles in the sky. As for the chief, first he waits for some moments, then he lets himself glide along one of the four dancers' ropes."

6 (Toton in the French text. M.B.)

7 Groos, *op. cit.*, p. 208.

8 *Ibid.*, p. 259.

9 Observation cited by Groos, *ibid.*, pp. 92–3:

"I notice that the love of mischief is very strong in him. Today he got hold of a wineglass and an egg cup. The glass he dashed on the floor with all his might and of course broke it. Finding, however, that the egg cup would not break when thrown down, he looked round for some hard substance against which to dash it. The post of the brass bedstead appearing to be suitable for the purpose, he raised the egg cup high above his head and gave it several hard blows. When it was completely smashed he was quite satisfied. He breaks a stick by passing it down between a heavy object and the wall and then hanging on to the end, thus breaking it across the heavy object. He frequently destroys an article of dress by carefully pulling out the threads (thus unravelling it) before he begins to tear it with his teeth in a violent manner.

"In accordance with his desire for mischief he is, of course, very fond of upsetting things but he always takes great care that they do not fall on himself. Thus he will pull a chair towards him till it is almost over-balanced, then he intently fixes his eyes on the top bar of the back, and when he sees it coming over his way, darts from underneath and watches the fall with great delight; and similarly with heavier things. There is a washstand, for example, with a heavy marble top, which he has with great labour upset several times, but always without hurting himself." (G. J. Romanes, *Animal Intelligence*, New York, D. Appleton & Co., 1897, p. 484.)

10 This had already been observed by Kant. Cf. Y. Hirn, *Les jeux d'enfants* (French translation; Paris, 1926), p. 63.

11 (Olorimes (in French) are two lines of poetry in which each syllable of the first line rhymes with the corresponding syllable of the second line. Caillois suggested the following couplet from Victor Hugo as an example:

Gal, amant de la reine, alle, tour magnanime
Galamment de l'arène a la Tour Magne, a Nimes

From correspondence with Callois. M.B.)

12 The development of slot machines in the modern world and the fascina-tion or obsessive behaviour that they cause is indeed astonishing. The vogue for playing slot machines is often of unsuspected proportions. It causes true obsessions and sometimes is a contributing factor to youth's entire way of life. The following account appeared in the press on 25 March, 1957, occasioned by the investigation conducted by the United States Senate that same month:

"Three hundred thousand slot machines manufactured by 15,000 em-ployees in 50 factories, most of which are located in the environs of Chicago, were sold in 1956. These machines are popular not only in Chicago, Kansas City, or Detroit—not to speak of Las Vegas, the capital of gambling—but also in New York. All day and all night in Times Square, the heart of New York, Americans of all ages, from schoolboy to old man, spend their pocket money or weekly pension in an hour, in the vain hope of winning a free game. At 1485 Broadway, 'Playland' in gigantic neon letters eclipses the sign of a Chinese restaurant. In an immense room without a door dozens of multicoloured slot machines are aligned in perfect order. In front of each machine a comfortable leather stool, reminiscent of the stools in the most elegant bars on the Champs-Elysées, allows the player with enough money to sit for hours. He even has an ash tray and a special place for his hot dog and Coca Cola, the national repast of the poor in the United States, which he can order with-out budging from his place. With a dime or quarter, he tries to add up enough points to win a carton of cigarettes. In New York State it is illegal to pay off in cash. An infernal din muffles the recorded voice of Louis Armstrong or Elvis Presley which accompanies the efforts of the small-time gamblers. Youths in blue jeans and leather jackets rub shoulders with old ladies in flowered hats. The boys choose the atomic bomber or guided-missile machines and the women put their hand on the 'love meter' that reveals whether they are still capable of having a love affair, while little children for a nickel are shaken, almost to the point of heart failure, on a donkey that resembles a zebu. There are also the marines or aviators who listlessly fire revolvers." (D. Morgaine, translated by M.B.)

The four categories of play are represented: *agôn* and *alea* involved in most of the machines, *mimicry* and illusion in the imaginary manoeuvering of the atomic bomber or guided missile, *ilinx* on the shaking donkey.

It is estimated that Americans spend 400 million dollars a year for the sole purpose of projecting nickel-plated balls against luminous blocks through various obstacles. In Japan, after the war, the mania was worse. It is estimated that about 12% of the national budget was swallowed up annually by slot machines. There were some installed even in doctors' waiting rooms. Even today, in the shadow of the viaducts, in Tokyo, between the trains "is heard the piercing noise of the pachencos, the contraptions in which the player strikes a steel ball which gropingly traverses various obstacles and then is lost forever. An absurd game, in which one can only lose, but which seduces those in whom the fury rages. That is why there are no less than 600,000 pachencos in Japan. I gaze at these rows of dark heads fascinated by a ball that gambols against some nails. The player holds the apparatus in both hands, no doubt so that his will to win shall pass into the machine. The most compulsive do not even wait for one ball to run its course before hitting another. It is a painful spectacle." (James de Coquet, *Le Figaro*, 18 February, 1957, translated by M.B.) This seduction is so strong that it contributes to the rise of juvenile delinquency. Thus, in April of 1957, the American newspapers reported the arrest in Brooklyn of a gang of juveniles led by a boy of ten and a girl of twelve. They burglarised neighbourhood stores of about one thousand dollars. They were only interested in dimes and nickels, which could be used in slot machines. Bills were used merely for wrapping their loot, and were later thrown away as refuse.

Julius Siegal, in a recent article entitled "The Lure of Pinball" (*Harper's*, 215, No. 1289 (October, 1957), 44–7), has tried to explain the incredible fascination of the game. His study emerges as both confession and analysis. After the inevitable allusions to sexual symbolism, the author especially stresses a feeling of victory over modern technology in the pleasure derived from slot machines. The appearance of calculation that the player reflects before projecting the ball has no significance, but to him it seems sublime. "It seems to me that when a pinballer invests his nickel he pits himself—his own skill—against the combined skills of American industry" (p. 45). The game is therefore a kind of competition between individual skill and an immense anonymous mechanism. For one (real) coin, he hopes to win (fictive) million, for scores are always expressed in numbers with multiple zeros.

Finally, the possibility must exist of cheating the apparatus. "Tilt" indicates only an outer limit. This is a delicious menace, an added risk, a kind of secondary game grafted on to the first. Curiously, Siegal admits that when depressed, he takes a half-hour's detour in order to find his favourite machine. Then he plays, confident that the game "... assumes positively therapeutic proportions—if I win" (p. 46). He leaves reassured as to his skill and chances of success. His despair is gone, and his aggression has been sublimated.

He deems a player's behaviour at a slot machine to be as revealing of his personality as is the Rorschach test. Each player is generally trying to prove that he can beat the machine on its own ground. He masters the mechanism and amasses an enormous fortune shown in the luminous figures inscribed on the screen. He alone has succeeded, and can renew his exploit at will. "... He has freely expressed his irritation with reality, and made the world behave. All for only a nickel" (p. 47). The responsibility for such an ambitious conclusion is the author's. What is left is that the inordinate success of slot machines (in which nothing is won but the possibility of playing again) appears to be one of the most disconcerting enigmas posed by contemporary amusements.

13 The Chinese also use the word *yeou* to designate idling and games in space, especially kite-flying, and also great flights of fancy, mystic journeys of shamans, and the wanderings of ghosts and the damned.

14 Game analogous to ring puzzles: nine links form a chain and are traversed by a rod attached to a base. The point of the game is to unlink them. With experience, one succeeds at it, careful not to call attention to a quite delicate, lengthy, and complicated manipulation where the least error makes it necessary to start again from the beginning.

15 From data provided by Duyvendak in Huizinga (*op. cit.*, p. 32), a study by Chou Ling, the valuable observations of Andre d'Hormon, and Herbert A. Giles' *Chinese-English Dictionary*, 2nd ed. (London, 1912), pp. 510–11 (*hsi*), 1250 (*choua*), 1413 (*teou*), 1452 (*wan*), 1487–1488 (*tou*), 1662–1663 (*yeou*).

Sport as Symbolic Dialogue*

C. E. Ashworth

The individual classifies not only the object world around him, i.e. the world of things, processes and relations, but also himself. He defines himself as some-thing or another. In other words, he is an object to himself. This process of self-objectification is fundamentally no different from his objectification of the "external" world. Such self concepts as "boy", "man", "businessman", "Englishman", "fool", etc., define how one relates to the world in the same way as one's objectifications of the "external" world define how the respective objects in it relate to each other. Thus, "I *cannot* wear that skirt because I am a man" can conceivably be said with the same certainty with which one says "water *cannot* flow uphill". Societies differ in the extent to which self identity is as unambiguous as the laws of gravitation. So, too, do they differ in the extent to which respective identities are mutually confirmed and agreed upon. In the event of ambiguous identities or mutually incompatible ones, societies differ in their conception of what *rules* of thought will ultimately resolve ambiguity and incompatibility. If social life can be conceived of as a game by which identities are established, tested, and possibly abandoned, then games can be conceived of as idealised forms of social life which establish identity with a consensual certainty that in social life itself, is not always possible. They do so by their *rules*, rules which create just those conditions which allow human thought to be certain of itself, given its own rules about how "reality" and "appearance", the "general" and the "particular", "essence" and "existence", are to be respectively known and separated.

Let us illustrate our conception of social life as a game and then pass on to our conception of games as social life.

A factor common to all human identities is that they develop, maintain themselves, and change in conjunction with *others* making a series of similar objectifications, i.e. in symbolic interaction. For example, if "I *am* intelligent" and "you *are* intelligent", this means that I have classified both myself and you in terms of the concept or

* This essay is published here for the first time.

symbol "intelligence". If, however, my definition of intelligence assumes that "intelligence recognises intelligence" and if I perceive you, by your actions, as *not* recognising *my* intelligence, then I am presented with a problem of knowledge. In such a "situation"—a totality of thoughts and actions-being-thought-about—either I or you must *become* "stupid", or some such other concept denoting the absence of intelligence. "Self as stupid" preserves *your* "intelligence", both to me and to you. If, however, I remain "intelligent", to myself at least, in the face of your disconfirming attitude, then you must become "stupid", a fact which you may or may not recognise. The point about this example is that it shows that each of us systematically brings the other into being, although our respective beings, or selves, may not be mutual. There is a simultaneous process whereby our respective symbolic systems, those systems of concepts and definitions by which we recognise *what* an object or event is, resolve themselves into an "equilibrium", or inner consistency, in the very process of their mutual assimilation of, and accommodation towards, the actions of the other. The rules in this system of interaction are the rules of cognition which enable either me or you "to win", that is to assimilate the negating attitude of the other into our already existing system of definitions. To "lose" to to be forced, by virtue of one's *own* rules, to accommodate to the *other's* definition. Life is thus a game whether rules are *agreed* upon or not because cognition is unavoidably governed by rules—those rules which establish identity in a continual state of becoming and ambiguity—but it is not an *idealised* game because the mutuality of rules is not necessarily guaranteed so that *outcomes* can be mutual and not individual.

Human action can be understood if one considers the totality of objectifications that individuals make, both of themselves and of the object world. This totality I shall call "self-being-in-the-world". To illustrate: if, in my view, "society progresses", then I am literally *brought into being* as "an object of progress". I come into focus to myself in a manner which fits the "form" of the world in the same way that to a Marxist the world "calls him" to rebel against it. However, if a "slave" defines himself as "free", two mutually preclusive self concepts within his *own* rules of thinking, then he is *anxious* about his not-being-in-the-world, i.e. not being in "the world of slavery" *or* "the world of freedom". He hovers, as in a perceptual figure/ground reversal, between two incompatible worlds within which he cannot be *one-self*. Ultimately, it is his *conviction* that will decide what he "wants" to be. If he is "free" then he will "want" to rid himself of the objectification "self as slave", an identity he does not accept as "real" or "necessary", but as illegitimately imposed by others, an identity that need-not-be in the same way that water does not *have* to be hot *or* cold. Alternatively, the establishment of himself as "slave" in "a world of slavery" will lead him to regard "freedom" as either illusion or evil or as both. It is both unnecessary and misleading to appeal to abstract "needs", "wants", or "motives" in order to explain his action. There is no universal desire for freedom, sex, money, power, security, survival etc. Man enters into a symbolic dialogue with the universe *as to what he is*, his own inner *conviction* or otherwise being sufficient to account for his actions, and the anxiety of his not-being, being sufficient to account for his "wants", or his "movement towards or away from". If a man defines slavery as both "natural" and "necessary", and his own being-a-slave as "God's will", then he will "enjoy" slavery in the same way that all of us "enjoy" *any* mode of being that is unambiguous, apparently immutable, and in which we participate fully.

"Common sense", however, and much of the current psychological and sociological literature would object to the notion of social life as symbolic dialogue on the grounds that it ignores human motivation. It seems almost self-evident to explain the behaviour of both the business man and the bank robber in terms of their common "desire for money". What more needs to be said? Why clutter up and complicate our explanations with such lavish and esoteric phrases as "symbolic dialogues", when concepts like "need", "drive", "want", "motive", "desire", etc. are available for such purposes? Such an argument seems to offer us a temptingly simple conception of man in society. If man can be endowed with certain universal characteristics like the old nineteenth-century "pleasure/pain principle", or the modern "need for approval" then all the empirical similarities and differences between men in different societies, in different parts of the world, and in different periods of history, can be explained in terms of the satisfaction of these universals under varying environmental conditions. Thus, while modern man achieves *his* security by accumulating money, the primitive achieves his by subordinating himself to strong all-embracing family ties. In this way, both the behaviour of the primitive and of modern man are parsimoniously explained by appeal to an *identical* principle, namely the operation of the "need for security" under diverse environmental conditions. Science often defines itself as aiming at simplicity of this type.

Let us illustrate the dialogue between conceptions of man as motivational, as having certain universal primary needs and certain culturally idiosyncratic, derived needs, and the notion of man as engaged in a symbolic dialogue with the universe, as a being that simply *is* what is "true", and let us do this by comparing how these respective imageries would deal with games and sport.

A popular explanation of why people are interested in, and participate in, games run as follows. In modern society, people belong to innumerable groupings; generational, sexual, religious, occupational, regional and national. The complexity of modern life requires that these groupings co-operate with each other in a manner that is precise, regulated and highly "civilised". Such groupings, however, besides mutually co-operating with each other also mutually frustrate each other. Now to perpetuate the co-operation that we have mentioned as being necessary means that the accumulated hostilities which develop as a result of the frustrations must be "controlled". Games, competitive games, thus provide opportunities for people to release accumulated aggression against each other in a manner and setting that is not disruptive to the co-operative system. Meanwhile, the extent to which the rules of sport equalise conditions for the respective participants, or the extent to which they are "biased" towards one or other of the contestants, is a reflection of the relative power position of the various groupings in the larger social framework.

Games are thus motivated by "the need to release aggression", aggression that is accumulated as a result of the day to day interaction and mutual frustration that various groups impose upon each other. In other words, games satisfy our wants in a specific way, in a way that is simultaneously "functional" for both "us" and "society". Games can be called a form of civilised violence that parallels the controlled, but nevertheless universally generated. violence of real life. The F.A. Cup is thus "civilised civil war". while the Olympic Games are "civilised world war". Such an explanation applies to both players and spectators, the latter "vicariously participating in violence" or "identifying with the violence of the team". By comparing man to some kind of hydraulically self-regulating steam valve, this approach has the glamour of modern science about it, namely it is simple, factual and presumably testable. But where is the "symbolic dialogue with the universe"?

To know *what* he is, a man compares himself with others. As we said earlier, identities bring each other into being: Thus. self knowledge derives from knowledge of the other and *vice versa*. For example, "he *is* rich" because he has more money than others, but the others *must* be there with their "lack" of money for his "richness" to come into being. Conversely, their "poverty" derives from his "wealth". However, Western culture is relatively unique in that it does not accept such comparisons as *definitive* of being, as adequate in themselves for the establishment of certainty, and yet comparisons of this kind must be made in order that definitions can be arrived at in the first place. Let us illustrate.

Even though a Russian might admit that economic wealth is evidence of "superiority", he will not necessarily admit that America has a superior socio-economic system to Russia simply because it is richer. Nor would such unwillingness on his part be an example of "unconscious self deception" or "rationalisation", as many Freudian psychologists would have us believe. The Russian will claim that, although wealth *is* a test of "being superior", it is so only under comparable conditions. He will claim that his country was hampered by a feudal past and by devastating wars, conditions which did not operate in America. To abstract oneself out of, for purposes of "genuine" comparison, the unique historical configurations that have constituted one's being is a peculiarly Western habit of cognition.

Likewise a Negro or a working man may well admit, particularly today, that the ability to acquire money is evidence of "intelligence" but neither is likely to admit that he is therefore "less intelligent" than men who are richer. In a manner "formally" similar to the Russian in the previous example, each will claim that he never had the "chances" that the rich men did. If this is the case, then how do people compare themselves and thus know themselves at all? Western thinking puts modern man in a terrible dilemma of identity. Western society requires the individual to make comparisons, indeed it is only via comparisons that identity is acquired and sustained at all, but it creates *conditions* which render comparison well nigh impossible.

Scientists resolve this dilemma by *experimentation*, that is they compare objects, persons and processes under identical and controlled conditions, conditions, they believe, that enable them to know what things "are really like", in and for themselves. Could we not compare a game to a simulated experiment, an experiment in living that enables men to see *what they are* under conditions that satisfy the comparative, experimental method? Perhaps it is the "unconscious rules of cognition" that form the structure which will enable us to understand the diversity and changes of sport in human history.

This "structuralist" hypothesis might, perhaps, enable us to understand many aspects of games and sport which are not accounted for in the earlier "common sense" or "scientific" theory. Although games were common in the pre-industrial west, and still are in non-western societies, they differ from modern western games in that they are not experiments in the scientific, positivistic sense. In feudal Europe, two villages would play "football" against each other even though the terrain over which they played consistently "favoured" one side against the other. For example, one village might have been uphill *vis à vis* the other, or have had more horses for its players to ride upon. Nor would the contestants have "minded" this fact. Only modern Western man abstracts himself from his social setting and from the conditions that have made up his life in order to see "what he is really like". To themselves, feudal villagers *were what they were*; they could not conceive of themselves *apart from* the village that was "uphill" or "downhill". Modern Western man can and, indeed, insists on doing so before he is *convinced* that a legitimate comparison of himself with others has been made. The recent uproar and concern over the oxygen level in the Mexico Olympics reflects this. Doubt was cast on whether "the winners" of certain races "really" had won. Similarly, feudal games would seem "unfair" to the modern man. However, to the people of the times, who had different rules of cognition by which identity could legitimately be established, a tournament between knights would be judged quite "fair"; even though one had a horse and armour while the other one did not.

Modern man insists on "equality" in sport, i.e. on strict formal rules that make "extra-ability" factors equal for every one. This is because he *defines* himself as equal; therefore any test of difference must reconstruct the "essence of the world", namely a utopian equality that allows "natural" differences to be observed in such a way that they cannot be "confused" with the accidentality of social life that neither starts from nor approximates to this ideal state. On a cricket field, as on any field of modern sport, the rich and the poor, the handsome and the ugly, the white and the black, are comparing themselves with each other in an egalitarian "communistic" utopia that subjects their respective beings to a test, a symbolic test, that is unhampered by their wealth or poverty, their looks or their colour. In "real life", such factors "interfere"; therefore "real life" does not establish adequately the nature of being or identity. Social life is still a game itself, but its outcomes, its victors and losers, are all profane, deceptive illusions, while on the field of sport outcomes are "sacred", that is they reconcile "essence" and "existence", they make that which appears-to-be, *real*.

Thus, sport *is* a "symbolic dialogue" and in modern Western society it symbolises the strict requirements of *how* a dialogue should be conducted. Only this view of sport can explain the otherwise mysterious fact that specific individuals or teams are never interested in playing against those individuals or teams against whom they *know in advance*, that they will win. To win at sport consistently makes participation uninteresting for the simple reason that no "test" is involved. Knowing beforehand makes it unnecessary to gain knowledge. "Being-uncertain" makes a "test" essential, to use the language of science. If games were a mere question of releasing aggression, then opponents would be looked for against whom victory, and thus self aggrandisement, would be certain; meanwhile potential opponents would refuse to play but would themselves look for yet weaker opponents, and so on. Thus no one would ever play through mutual inability to find a "certain loser" and violence would once more become "uncivilised".

CHAPTER 4

American Sports: Play and Display*

Gregory P. Stone

Society has often been likened by its students to a game, but, like other more frequently encountered social science metaphors such as the machine or the organism, the game itself is usually unquestioned. Its significance is only to be found in that which it represents. Thus the well known "game theory" of von Neumann and Morgenstern, for example, has contributed to our knowledge of economic behaviour, political behaviour, and conflict. More recently, fantastic insights have been accomplished in psychiatry by construing the relation between the psychiatrist and his patient as a game.[1] Yet, little, if anything, has been said about what our economic or political life can tell us of games or play. Concurrent with its representational value, the game is interpreted as a "childish thing". George Herbert Mead has shown how play and games may be viewed symbolically as phases in the emergence of selfhood, and Jean Piaget has studied with admirable care the relation between the child's orientation to the rules of the game and his larger moral development. These efforts are mentioned not to detract in any way from their value but rather to indicate something of the circumlocution that has seemingly attended our studies of play and games. The substantive investigation of play has been largely eschewed by social scientists. Consequently, there is little to *report* here about American sport, but much to *suggest*.[2]

Jan Huizinga in his remarkable little study of man, the player,[3] notes that play is certainly prior to culture, for all young animals may be observed to gambol and frisk about. But puppies and kittens may at times be envied. Animal play is not interpreted. Ernst Cassirer would have said their play is responsive, not responsible. Man, on the other hand, imbues his play with meanings and affect,

---

* The original version of this paper was published in the *Chicago Review*, IX (Fall, 1955), pp. 83–100 and reprinted in Eric Larrabee and Rolf Meyersohn (eds.), *Mass Leisure* (Glencoe, Illinois: The Free Press, 1958), pp. 253–64. For this collection, the original article has been considerably revised and updated.

arranges it, stylises it. And in America, at least among the "middle mass" of the large cities and suburbs, the old styles of play seem somehow to apply no longer, while the new emergent styles are not yet widely apprehended and nowhere clearly understood. Play is often conceived in archaic restraint and carried on in frenzies of un-restraint. Americans are uneasy with play, sometimes inept. Even in their discussions of leisure, as David Riesman has observed,[4] many of our people seem uncomfortable. Nor are sociologists immune to such discomfort. Nelson Foote, in a plea for a "social science of play", apparently felt constrained to protest his "deadly serious-ness".[5] The uneasiness that accompanies our view of play may well afford the simplest and most efficient explanation for the lack of social science inquiries into the nature of play.[6] At the same time and in the light of the ambivalence and anomalies it suggests, it may afford a fruitful point of departure for our own discussion of Ameri-can sport.

Huizinga rested his case for the thesis that civilisation develops *in* and *as* play largely upon his detection of an agonistic component—a competition or contest—in various phases of life among diverse civilisations. Yet what is relevant here is not only that play is a contest or that it manifests tension and uncertainty, but that it is also *contested*. Play both embraces the contest and is caught up in the larger contests, tensions, ambivalences, and anomalies of society. A brief glance at the history of sport and play in Western civilisation demonstrates this. As our social organisation has shifted from a system of estates, through a system of production and classes, to an arrangement of consumption and masses, play and sport have always been affected by the cleavages and processes built into such organisa-tional patterns. The significance of archery for the early maintenance of aristocratic power lay behind most of the medieval bans against such sports as football, golf, and bowling. In a sense the pre-eminent place assigned to production in the nineteenth century had the effect of insulating sport and play or restricting most sports to the play-grounds of the leisure classes and placing sports in the hands of amateurs who would perform conspicuously and graciously to gain the esteem and deference of exclusive status-linked audiences. Nor has the massification of sport, implying its commercialisation and professionalisation, emerged uncontested on the contemporary scene. Professional sport experienced many early setbacks in its struggle to break out of the dignified amateurism and exclusiveness of the nine-teenth century.

The point is this: because of their intrinsic agonistic character and the fact of their involvement in the "agony" of the larger society, sport and play are fraught with anomalies. A consideration of some of these anomalies should reveal something of the significance that sport and play have for Americans.

THE PRODUCTION AND CONSUMPTION OF SPORT

The anomalous quality of sport may be grasped at once when its production or industrial character is placed over and against its appeal as a product to be consumed. From 1910 to 1960 the proportion of persons employed in amusement, recreation, and related services has almost doubled, but it is still less than 1% of the total labour force. As a matter of fact, although the number of workers employed in these services increased slightly between 1950 and 1960 (from 493,433 to 502,879), the proportion in the labour force declined somewhat from 0.9% to 0.8%. Within this small segment of the labour force, the most notable change in occupations has occurred in the professional and semi-professional occupations which contributed more than one-half of all workers in the industry in 1910, declined to about one-fourth in 1950, and by 1960, comprised just over one-fifth. Although it is difficult to interpret these census data accurately because of the heterogeneity of some of the categories, they may well attest to the proliferation of related occupations that seems to have characterised the growth of sport in America. With the players themselves—the producers of games—the picture is strikingly different. In 1950 professional athletes comprised a microscopic proportion of all workers (0.02%). Even so, that proportion represented a sharp increase in numbers over 1940. In that decade professional athletes increased their numbers 61%, a greater increase than for the other professional occupations considered as a whole (37.4%) and greater than the increases of the entire labour force (25.2%). This growth in the number of professional athletes, however, has been extremely short-lived. With the death of minor league ball clubs and other small sports enterprises, like local boxing clubs, the number of workers employed as athletes declined almost unbelievably in the fifties. In 1950 there were 11,597 employed athletes. By 1960 that number had shrunk to 4,224—a 63.6% decrease. At the last available count, then, the proportion of working athletes had shrunk to 0.01% of all employed workers, and, more impressive, less than 1% (0.8%) of all workers employed in amusement, recreation, and related services.

As a matter of fact, sport would seem to present a unique occupational morphology among American industries. Although 0.8% of all workers employed in amusement, recreation, and related services were professional athletes in 1960, the proportion for *all* paid employees in baseball, football, and other sport promotions in 1963 was 2.9% and that proportion has remained constant since 1954.[8] Those engaged first hand in the production of the commodity—the game or the match—constitute a minority within the industrial complex, while those engaged in the administration, promotion, and servicing of the production constitute a sizable majority. The occupational structure of the industry has the character of an inverted pyramid.

We may note in passing an additional peculiarity of the occupational character of sport. It would seem to be readily apparent that the occupation is one in which the work cycle differs from that of most occupations. Specifically, the worker has a relatively short productive work life,[9] and generally his occupational experience does not qualify him for any other skill.[10] Currently the aversion to "subject matter men" (specialists) in some educational circles may merely reflect larger trends in social mobility. As Riesman suggests, it would seem that there is "a new pattern in American business life: if one is successful in one's craft, one is forced to leave it"[11]—the "subject matter" may, in fact, be losing its significance for mobility in professional and business occupations. The athlete, however, is involved in different mobility patterns. As opposed to the "skills of gregariousness and amiability", it has been proposed that "skill democracy . . . based on respect for ability to do something tends to survive only in athletics".[12] Not only are the athlete's opportunities for mobility considerably constricted by the intrinsic brevity of his career, but, once that brief career has ended, he leaves it whether he is successful or not. Perhaps the career of the boxer may dramatise, if not precisely speak for, the case of the professional athlete in America:

> Boxers find further that, despite their success in the sport, their careers terminate at a relatively early age . . . Since boxing has been the vocational medium of status attainment and since they have no other skills to retain that status, many boxers experience a sharp decline in status in their postboxing careers. As an illustration, of ninety-five leading former boxers (i.e., champions and leading contenders), each of whom earned more than $100,000 during his ring career, eighteen were found to have remained in the sport as trainers or trainer-managers; two became wrestlers; twenty-six worked in, "fronted for", or owned taverns; two were liquor salesmen; eighteen had unskilled jobs, most commonly in the steelmills; six worked in the movies; five were entertainers; two owned or worked in gas stations; three were cab-drivers; three had newsstands; two were janitors; three were bookies; three were associated with the race tracks (two in collecting bets and one as a starter); and two were in business, one of them as a custom tailor.[13]

When these findings are regarded in light of the fact that the chances of success in boxing are, indeed, relatively slim, the negligible opportunity for larger social success to be found in boxing circles is sharply underscored. Specifically, of a sample of 127 fighters whose careers were traced from 1938 to 1952, 84.2% remained in the local preliminary or semi-windup category; 8.7% became local headliners; and 7.1% achieved national recognition.[14] It does not seem unreasonable to surmise that similar barriers confront other professional athletes in their quest for ultimate success.

Moreover, inferences about the impact of sport on the national economy certainly do not provide impressive figures. Between 1959 and 1963, the relative contribution of *all* amusement, recreation, and related services, except motion pictures, to the national income did not reach one-half of one per cent (0.39% in 1959 and 0.41% in 1963). Of all services, the contribution of amusement, recreation, and related services, except motion pictures, to the national income has remained at about three and one-half per cent since 1937 (1937—3.7%; 1950—3.5%; 1953—3.3%; 1959—3.4%; and 1963—3.3%).[15] Given the way in which the above data have been reported, the contribution of spectator sports can only be surmised from other figures. Baseball, football, and other sports clubs and promotional establishments made up only 1.8% of all amusement, recreation, and related establishments, except motion pictures, in 1948; and, by 1963, that proportion had shrunk to 0.6%. Receipts, pay roll, and paid employees witnessed a similar decline in the same period—12.4% to 4.0%, 13.9 to 6.4%, and 5.7 to 2.9%, respectively.[16]

If we consider the sheer dollar outlay for spectator sports to estimate the place they assume in American consumption, the figures remain unimpressive. In 1963 Americans devoted 6.0% of their personal consumption expenditures to recreation services,[17] while admissions to spectator sports consumed only 0.12% of such expenditures. Even so, the small proportion expended on admissions represented an increase since 1959 (0.08%) proportionally greater than the increase in expenditures for all recreation services (5.8% in 1959). However, *consumption must be writ large*, and, then, the place that sport occupies in American consumption is awesome. We read, hear, and view sport in America. The pervasiveness of our interest may be readily illustrated, if not documented. In 1955, my morning paper at the time, the Detroit *Free Press*, devoted five pages to sporting news (roughly four hundred column inches excluding advertising) and two and one-half pages to news of business and industry (roughly two hundred and forty column inches). Available back issues acknowledged that that issue was not at all unrepresentative. Twelve years later, in a different place, I found four pages devoted to sporting news and four pages to news of business and industry in the Minneapolis *Tribune*. Column inches, excluding advertising, were about equal (355 and 346 respectively). However, that was Thursday, 11 May, 1967. The Minnesota Twins had not played on the preceding day, nor was there much else, except for the routine, to report in the world of sport.[18] Again, back issues showed little deviation from the pattern observed twelve years earlier in Detroit. In addition to the disproportionate space given sports in the press, we ought to note the time given sportscasts on radio and TV, and particularly the "battle of the networks": the purchase of the New York Yankees by CBS and the further "triumph" of that network in gaining exclusive rights to the telecasting of NFL football, left NBC with the AFL, and ABC with a long, cold, empty season in 1966.

In this paper, it is possible to provide only a modest beginning for interpreting the function of sport for the American consumer; and, as yet, no thoroughgoing studies have been made. Let us anticipate. We suspect, for example, that the sports pages in the daily newspaper are important for many consumers primarily because they provide some confirmation that there is a continuity in the events and affairs of the larger society. A certain reassurance may be gained from following sporting news that is not possible from following current events, the continuity of which is not readily discernible for many readers. Indeed, the discontinuity of world affairs has been ironically conceptualised as a "credibility gap". A newspaper cartoon, the source of which I have forgotten, serves as an example. President Johnson is depicted standing on the brink of the Grand Canyon and surveying its magnificence—"Incredible! " he mutters to himself. In addition to imposing order upon the vicissitudes of the larger uncertain social scene, the consumption of sports may have the latent function of bringing continuity into the personal lives of may Americans. Team loyalties formed in adolescence and maintained through adulthood may serve to remind one, in a nostalgic way, that there are areas of comfortable stability in life—that some things have permanence amid the harassing interruptions and discontinuous transitions of daily experience.[19]

Certainly the personal identities of those who have followed the successes and failures of the Boston (and Milwaukee) Braves, Brooklyn Dodgers, New York Giants, Philadelphia Athletics (members of the original National Associational of Baseball Players), and the St. Louis Browns have not been unaffected by the deprivation of identification incurred by the moves of those teams.[20] But these are speculations. Research is needed to explore the various ramifications. In this regard, may not the boxing fan "suffer" somewhat more than the baseball fan? The New York Yankees or the Cleveland Indians can always come back, but Joe Louis or "Sugar Ray" Robinson never can.

WORK AND PLAY

Disparities revealed by our overview of the character of American sport may be both reflections of and contributions to the tension between work and play in American life. Work has been for a century or more the means *par excellence* of acquiring the treasured symbols of our society. There has been no ethical alternative. Furthermore, Max Weber has demonstrated that the ethic of work in America was fortified early by the sanctions of Protestantism. The consequences are clear. We know that athletics were at their lowest ebb in England during the Puritan rule and that of Charles II. Such tendencies have survived in the contrasting views American Protestant and Catholic churches have maintained towards lotteries, gambling, or *gaming*. Only in the 1920's did the American Protestant churches relax their rules towards such games, and then it was with the stipulation that they be played for amusement only. Risk and gain were cemented in the context of work, never in the context of play. The work-place and the playground were sharply set apart. During the nineteenth century and on into this century, perhaps (as Riesman has somewhere suggested) up to the death of Henry Ford, work and play stood at a distance. The distances between the child and the man, the sexes, the home and the factory or the office, the gentleman and the worker, the Protestant and the Catholic, night and day, Saturday and Sunday—all recorded the gap between work and play.

Now the distances diminish. Long pants no longer signify the adult male, and, as the symbols of adulthood are captured by children, youth creeps into middle age—men of forty-five are "boys". Women are now engaged in all occupations, and boys and girls enter the schools hand in hand through the same doors.[21] The factory becomes a ranch house; the home, a tool shop. The *leisure class* that inspired the irony of Veblen has become a *leisure mass*. Religion embraces science and psychoanalysis, and diverse churches unite in national committees. Increments of pay lure the working man out of the day into the night. Saturday no longer mobilises the household.[22] All these mitigations of distance are ramified in the world of sports and play. For with the loss of the social frame that once insured their separation, work and play have spilled over their former bounds and mingle together in American life. However, the amalgam is new, untested, strange. Traces of the old distance remain and are expressed in vital anomalies.

Consider how Americans speak of sport. Baseball, basketball, football, golf, hockey, and tennis—these sports are "played". The participants are "players". Huizinga speaks of the superfluous character of play, its disinterestedness, its extraordinary and unreal character. "It is never a task."[23] Certainly the sports mentioned here are unreal—a sort of "voluntary hallucination", as Nelson Foote has put it.[24] Yet precisely those sports that are "played" have become work in America. Here is the matrix of professional athletics.

However, the "players of sport" are not, literally, "sportsmen"! Sportsmen are hunters and fishermen, archers, skiers, yachtsmen, sports-car drivers, leisure-time fliers of airplanes, parachute jumpers, or campers. Note that these sports are never literally "played", nor may they assume the character of work. They are peopled almost entirely by amateurs. When they do become work, they become occupations that bear no reference to leisure. Fishing is a primary *industry*. Another alternative permits such sports to become tutorial in character. "Working sportsmen" can be guides, tutors, or counsellors.

There are, of course, exceptions. Boxing, bowling, and wrestling, for example, are not "played"; but note the extraordinarily difficult path each has had to follow to gain public acceptance as a professional sport. Every state in the union has at one time outlawed "prize fights", and it was not until 1917, when boxing became an integral part of the U.S. Army's physical training programme, that legal bans were significantly relaxed. The American Bowling Congress is in no small measure the outcome of a social movement designed to secure public respect for the sport. And the movement may have succeeded. Of all amusement, recreation, and related services, except motion pictures, bowling led in the proportion of establishments (11.1%), per cent of business receipts (22.5), and per cent of all payrolls in those services (21.6) as of 1963.[25] Wrestling can scarcely be considered a professional sport. We shall see that it is best considered drama. As play becomes increasingly transformed into work, however, we may well be witnessing an end to the distinction between amateur and professional *sport*. The democratisation of games has the consequence of confining amateur *play* to smaller and smaller circles in the status order. Specifically, as golf has been made available to the leisure mass, amateurs and professionals participate together boldly and in an undisguised manner—the "pro-am tournament" is commonplace.[26] This was not always the case. The commingling of professional and amateur golfers was cloaked, not too long ago, in the guise of a teacher-student relationship. The "pro" was usually attached to some country club, though he seldom "worked" at that club. The unattached "pro" is now no longer a rarity. Young golfers, aspiring to participation in pro tournaments, frequently go to a school, conducted under the auspices of the PGA, to qualify for invitations to such matches. *In the United States, sports that were once work are never played, but these engage the "players" —the amateurs. Sports that were never work are always played, and these engage the "workers"—the professionals.*[27] In the latter transformation, amateurism is being forced out, and this is all the more the case, as universities and colleges become "feeder farms" for professional teams, and amateur sports, such as tennis and golf, feed players into professional circles.

The intertwining of work and play is carried over into daily life. More and more we work at our play and play at our work. Reuel Denney, Everett Hughes, and David Riesman have observed again and again that our play is disguised by work and *vice versa.* Consequently, we begin to evaluate our leisure time in terms of the potential it has for work—for us to "do it ourselves", and we evaluate our work in terms of the potential it has for play. I have noted in another discussion[28] my son's remark, made when he was seven years old, that he wanted to be a sociologist so he could hunt, fish, and play golf. Among other things, this betrays a process of stylisation—a process that becomes exacerbated in periods of transition from one pattern of social organisation to another. Huizinga asks, "Is not the birth of a style itself a playing of the mind in its search for new forms?" He notes in the same passage that "a style lives from the same thing as does play, from rhythm, harmony, regular change and repetition, stress and cadence".[29] Perhaps in our archaic groping for new forms of work to replace the old in an age where production is being replaced by consumption as a central organising phase, the play style, being the most fundamental style, is most readily available and the one with which we have been most intimate for the greater part of our lives. Thus, we endow our work with qualities of play. Yet the old limitations upon play are not easily forgotten, and often we may stylise our work, for example, with the idiom and phraseology of sport, omitting to carry over and apply the ethic. Crucial moral problems are posed, then, for a significant number of Americans. We can play at our work for the enjoyment of it, thereby enriching it; or we can play at work to conceal it from ourselves, thereby shrugging off responsibility for it.[30] Similarly, our stylisation of play with the work form may ennoble or debase it. Certainly the ultimate ethical outcome is not at all clear.

THE BATTLE BETWEEN THE SEXES

Sports would appear to be caught up in the contest of the sexes in American life as well as in the contest between work and play. In viewing American sport the observer may be suddenly impressed with the "masculine bias" of his observations. When I asked one of my colleagues what he thought about the general function of sport in American life, he thought first of hunting and fishing, and described the function of sport as providing a vehicle of "escape" from civilisation—a way for the *boys* to go out, drink, and avoid shaving. His wife maintained that he was "like a little boy" when he went on his fishing trips. I would prefer to discern a more positive quality in his "irresponsible fishing". Women, above all, are taboo on hunting and fishing trips.[31] The masculine symbolism of hunting and fishing is clear (even though women are now capturing some of the symbols—they have their hunting fashions and styles), and, of course, the possibility must be considered that the hunter or fisherman may not be trying to "escape" anything. Perhaps men go on such trips to accentuate their masculinity and independence (responsibility)—to be more male than they are—rather than to "escape" responsible sexuality. But, paradoxically, man owes his maleness to women, i.e. a man is only a man because he differs from women. The sexes are intrinsically dependent upon one another for their identity. It is in a striving for autonomy and independence that Thurber's "battle between the sexes" is conceived; and it is a battle that can never, by definition, be won, although at different times and in different places one of the contestants may win a temporary advantage. The hunting or fishing trip may be viewed merely as a tactic in the battle, and I suggest that the hunter or fisherman is striving to achieve an autonomous masculinity with his hunting or fishing companions. This is often reinforced by the decorum of the trip which prohibits going into the town tavern "on the make", although getting drunk is quite within bounds. Even erotic revery may be censored at the camp fire. Preferably the revery is autonomously masculine and often consists solely of heroic legends and myths where *men only* play the role of heroes.

In discussing the function of American sport my colleague distinctly confined his remarks to the purpose it served himself and other men. We have little knowledge of the feminine player or sporting enthusiast (in 1950, 706 of the 11,597 professional athletes were women; by 1960, that number had dwindled to 336), except that some "feminine players" are "masculine females". We have even less knowledge of the female spectator, and least knowledge of the spectator of female players.

Let us consider the female fan. Her plight is effectively dramatised by an uncertain, confused, and querulous letter addressed by a female fan to a sports columnist:

> I'm a woman who has loved baseball all of her life. When I was nine or ten, I remember keeping box scores of all the games. My father's friends were always amused and gladly would explain the game to me.
>
> But now that I'm older, what happens? Did you ever notice men when women talk baseball to them? They put on a frozen smile and try to change the subject or get away from you.
>
> I still like baseball. But what fun is it for women to take an interest in it when they can't discuss it with men who know more about it?
>
> If baseball is slipping, it's the men who are making it slip . . by not including women fans in their baseball conversations.[32]

Age and sex are the fundamental anchorages of personal identity. That both are problematical *vis-à-vis* their validation in sport and play is underscored in the letter quoted above. Perhaps the female fan, even more than the male hunter or the fisherman, is engaged in a quest for sexuality.[33] At least a suggestion of this possibility may be found in the contest between players and spectators that is waged in the wrestling arena.

In the case of wrestling it was my impression some years ago that I saw more females in the background of my TV set when I viewed wrestling matches than when I viewed other games and contests. I was able to get some confirmation for this early impression from David Riesman, who found evidence for this in interviews carried on in the Kansas City study of ageing. Unfortunately, the interviews were not directly concerned with sport. Now, the matter is clear. Vance Packard has reported that "a Nielsen check of TV fans watching wrestling matches revealed that ladies outnumbered men two to one."[34] My own study of wrestling shows the greatest concentration of wrestling spectators and fans among older, lower status women.[35]

That study, however, failed to cast much light on the precise attraction wrestling has for the female spectator. Some who are psychoanalytically oriented might suggest the sadomasochistic qualities of wrestling and consider the vicarious gratification derived from viewing the match. This seems not at all convincing to me. It merely attaches a different name to what is going on, for one thing; but, for another, boxing is certainly a bloodier sport, although the boxer's code requires that overt manifestations of pain be suppressed by the contestants while the wrestler's code demands that pain, fear, viciousness, and unsportsmanlike conduct be overtly expressed. Yet

these expressions are intentionally farcical, and I can not permit myself to believe that our women spectators are enchanted by the farce.
This, as we shall see, does not mean that the farce is inconsequential.

Other observers have noted the sexual representations inherent in
various wrestling holds. Guessing that women spectators are middle-
aged and, therefore, were introduced to sex in a period before, as
Nelson Foote has put it, sex became play,[36] these observers have
speculated that the woman spectator of wrestling experiences vicarious gratification from the pain inflicted by one (male) wrestler upon
the other (male) in the sexually suggestive position. This kind of
analysis makes somewhat more sense to me than the first, since we
now know that most women spectators are older.

Let me return to the conception of wrestling as a deliberate and
contrived farce. Wrestling is a mockery of the spectator; and, when
many spectators are women, it is women who are mocked. This may
partially explain the once popular "feminisation" of wrestling. Although wrestlers appear in many parts on the arena stage—Indians,
Arabian sheikhs, atavistic monstrosities, and futuristic supermen—
the role of the feminised wrestler is most relevant here. His mere
presence in the sports arena was another manifestation of sexual tension along Thurberian lines. Moreover, in his mockery of the demon-
strative vociferous female spectator, the wrestler, in fact, became a
woman. The female wrestler completed the cycle of the farcical
feminisation of the sport. Today it seems that the earlier mockery of
the female has reintroduced the male to the wrestling arena, for there
are few "Gorgeous Georges" on the wrestling stage, at least in the
Midwest at this time. Yet, in pre-match TV ballyhoo, wrestlers
harshly impugn one another's masculinity. For example, the
"Crusher" contemptuously refers to the "championship" tag team
of Larry Hannig and Harley Race as the "Dolly Sisters". Sure
enough, their hair seems to have gradually lengthened and become
more blond during their stay in the Minneapolis area, probably
signalling the incipience of a new feminine cycle.

Such remarks suggest a final matter that must be considered before
we close our general overview of sport and play, namely, the problem
posed by the spectacular elements of American sport.

GAMES AND SPECTACLES

To this point we have largely treated various ways in which larger
social tensions modify the character of American sport. Now we
must turn to possible modifications of sport that are intrinsically
generated. We would contend that all sport is affected by the antinomial principles of play and dis-play. These principles, in turn,

summarise the contrasting character of games and spectacles, and historically have come to represent basic differences between whole societies. In a sense the glory of ancient Greece is expressed by play and the games, the vain-glory of Rome by the spectacles and dis-play of the Caesars. Thucydides observed that the brilliant Spartan commander, Brasidas, was received by the multitudes at Scione with honour befitting an athlete. Moreover, competition for the Olympic crown never threatened the status of the most highborn competitor. In contrast, any Roman patrician appearing in public as a charioteer was stigmatised, and Roman names were conspicuous by their absence from the gladiatorial lists. The difference was, of course, never so dramatically clear-cut. Tendencies towards dis-play are to be found in the late history of ancient Greece, and tendencies towards play in the early history of Rome. Obviously, too, the internal differentiations of any society along sex, age, and status axes preclude wholesale characterisations of societies. The illustrations, however, do lay bare the noble character of the game as opposed to the ignoble character of the spectacle.

Play and dis-play are precariously balanced in sport, and, once that balance is upset, the whole character of sport in society may be affected. Furthermore, the spectacular element of sport may, as in the case of American professional wrestling, destroy the game. The rules cease to apply, and the "cheat" and the "spoil-sport" replace the players. Yet even here counterforces are set in motion. If we may, discontinuously, resume our analysis of wrestling, we would note that there is always the "hero" who attempts to defeat the "villain" within the moral framework of the rules of the game. It is a case of law *versus* outlaw, cops and robbers, the "good guys" *versus* the "bad guys". Symbolically the destruction of the game by the spectacle has called into existence forces of revival which seek to re-establish the rules, but these forces are precisely symbolic— representative. They are seldom able to destroy the spectacular components of the dis-play. They are part of the spectacle itself.

The point may be made in another way. The spectacle is predictable and certain; the game, unpredictable and uncertain. Thus spectacular dis-play may be reckoned from the outset of the performance. It is announced by the appearance of the performers— their physiques, costumes, and gestures. On the other hand, the spectacular play is solely a function of the uncertainty of the game. The spectacular player makes the "impossible catch"—"outdoes himself". He is *out of character*. The "villains" and "heroes" of the wrestling stage are *in character*. They are the *dramatis personae* of a pageant—an expressive drama. Consequently their roles have been predetermined. The denouement of the contest has been decided at its inception, and the "hero" is unlikely to affect the course of events.

These things would seem to lie at the base of the American humanist's aversion to many aspects of contemporary sport and play. The game, inherently moral and ennobling of its players, seems to be giving way to the spectacle, inherently immoral and debasing. With the massification of sport, spectators begin to outnumber participants in overwhelming proportions, and the spectator, as the name implies, encourages the spectacular—the dis-play.[37] In this regard the spectator may be viewed as an agent of destruction as far as the dignity of sport is concerned. There is a tension between the morality of the game and the amorality of the spectator (immoral in its consequences). There are many examples of this, but perhaps the most striking is the case of Maurice "The Rocket" Richard, *spectacular* offensive player for the Montreal Canadians. Fines were of dubious value for bringing "The Rocket" into line following his frequent infractions of the rules ("immorality"), for his fans would inevitably raise funds sufficient to overcompensate for his losses. This action alone tends to break down the morality of the game. However, the ultimate disparity between the immoral demands of the spectator and moral demands of the game was achieved, when, as we know, Montreal experienced its worst riot in recent years in public response to the suspension of "The Rocket" for the remainder of the hockey season.[38]

But massification and the consumption of American sport will be with us yet a while. Perhaps one of the most pressing problems facing the social science analyst of sport in America is the problem of how the spectator becomes caught up in the dignity of the game he witnesses to the extent that his consumership of sport is ennobling rather than debasing. Only when that problem is solved and the solution is applied, will play become a legitimate ethical alternative to work in America.

IN CONCLUSION

I have attempted here to demonstrate how certain tensions in American society—between production and consumption, work and play, and between the sexes—how the tension between play and display contained within sport, itself, cast sport in a uniquely American mould. Now, at the end of the discussion, I wonder to what extent the consequences of these tensions for the character of sport are, in fact, uniquely American. I suspect that few of them are, and that they may be found in most of the nations we bring together in the application of that cumbersome concept, "Western civilisation". All these remarks attest to the lack of ease and the discomfort with which many of us view sport and leisure. Our arrangements and stylisations of sport and play do not permit us to look upon the game with the same understanding and sympathy that, let us say, Plato experienced in his view of play and the game:

> Though human affairs are not worthy of great seriousness it is yet necessary to be serious; happiness is another thing. . . . I say that a man must be serious with the serious, and not the other way about. God alone is worthy of supreme seriousness, but man is made God's plaything, and that is the best part of him. Therefore every man and woman should live life accordingly, and play the noblest games, and be of another mind from what they are at present. For they deem war a serious thing, though in war there is neither play nor culture worthy the name, which are the things *we* deem most serious. Hence all must live in peace as well as they possibly can. What, then, is the right way of living? Life must be lived as play, playing certain games, making sacrifices, singing and dancing, and then a man will be able to propitiate the gods, and defend himself against his enemies and win in the contest.[39]

I would doubt that Americans would be the only people today made uneasy by those words. But this in no way restricts the implications of our discussion. A social science of play *is* needed in America. Without its contributions the ways in which we spend our growing leisure time may never be ennobled.

NOTES

1 Above all, see Thomas S. Szasz, *The Myth of Mental Illness* (New York: Harper and Row, Inc., 1961). In a more popular vein, see Eric Berne, *Games People Play,* New York: Grove Press, Inc., 1964.

2 More than a decade has elapsed since this statement was written, and the situation remains pretty much unchanged. An excellent theoretical treatment has been provided by Roger Callois' *Man, Play,* and *Games,* New York: The Free Press of Glencoe, Inc., 1961, and highly important observations on various sports may be found in Robert H. Boyle, *Sport—Mirror of American Life,* Boston: Little Brown and Co., 1963. Psychiatry has also made some attempts to provide analyses of sport. Two recent books in this vein are Arnold R. Beisser, *The Madness in Sports,* New York: Appleton-Century-Crofts, 1967, and Ralph Slovenko and James A. Knight (eds.), *Motivation in Play, Games and Sport,* Springfield, Illinois: Charles C. Thomas Publishers, 1967. In addition, a first rate journalistic account of the transformation of professional boxing has appeared—Barney Nagler, *James Norris and The Decline of Boxing,* Indianapolis: The Bobbs-Merrill Co., Inc., 1964—and an economist has focused a very bright spotlight, indeed, on major league baseball—Ralph Andreano, *No Joy in Mudville,* Cambridge: Schenkman Publishing Co.,

Inc., 1965. As far as baseball is concerned, Jim Brosnan's and Bill Veck's books must also be cited for their excellence. In the major sociological journals, two articles have appeared. The first, Oscar Grusky, "Managerial Succession and Organizational Effectiveness", *American Journal of Sociology*, LXIX (July, 1963), pp. 21–31, aroused some controversy. See William A. Gamson and Norman A. Scotch, "Scapegoating in Baseball", *American Journal of Sociology*, LXX (July, 1964), pp. 69–72; and Grusky's "Reply", pp. 72–76. The second, "The Play World of Camping: Research into the Social Meaning of Outdoor Recreation", *American Journal of Sociology*, LXX (March, 1965), pp. 604–12, deals with forest camping, and, as the title suggests, takes us into the border area between sport and play. Play and recreation have received rather more extensive treatment in the last ten or fifteen years.

3 Jan Huizinga, *Homo Ludens: A Study of the Play Element in Culture*, London: Routledge and Kegan Paul, Ltd., 1949.

4 David Riesman, "Some Observations on Changes in Leisure Attitudes", *Individualism Reconsidered*, Glencoe, Illinois: The Free Press, 1954, p. 202.

5 Nelson Foote, "Comments on 'The Consumer in the New Suburbia', by William H. Whyte, Jr.", in Lincoln Clark (ed.), *Consumer Behaviour*, New York: New York University Press, 1954, p. 114. He says, "I am deadly serious about this. I would propose that there be a social science of play. On the level of empirical findings, Americans don't know what to do with themselves. When they have free time, they become frantic to kill it."

6 However, there is a powerful force of snobbery here. Certainly the serious analysis of popular sport is construed to be beneath the dignity of many academics.

7 U.S. Bureau of the Census, *U.S. Census of Population*, Vol. I: *Characteristics of the Population, Part 1, United States Summary*, Washington, D.C.: United States Government Printing Office, 1964, *passim*.

8 U.S. Bureau of the Census, Census of Business, 1963, *Selected Services, United States Summary* BC63-SA1, Washington, D.C., United States Government Printing Office, 1965, Table 2, pp. 1–8 and 1–9.

9 Wrestling provides an exception. However, whether pro wrestling is sport or drama is still argued by some. See my "Wrestling: the Great American Passion Play" (reprinted in Part III of this Reader).

10 There may be some exceptions to this statement. Wrestling is a lucrative side-line for football players, and popular wrestling champions may well rise to powerful controlling positions in the wrestling "game". Television and radio, too, hold out lucrative opportunities for handsome, colourful, or glib ex-athletes as announcers, commentators, or providers of "colour" for sportcasts. In addition, the career pattern, player to coach to athletic director or manager, that prevails in American football seems to be acquiring its counterpart in baseball. However, the career of Hank Greenberg in baseball remains the exception. Compare, for example, the work cycle of the professional athlete with that of the other professions. Even in the other "notorious professions", e.g. motion picture acting, the productive work life is considerably longer, as a listing of the ages of many Hollywood "glamour girls and boys" will testify. Moreover, the obsolete movie star can always be revived, while the obsolete athlete never can. The fate of a Gloria Swanson, whose early movie, *Indiscreet*, was shown the other evening on TV, may well be compared with the current plight

of a Joe Louis (undoubtedly more pre-eminent in his notorious profession than Gloria Swanson ever was in hers) who was faced with the possibility of dissolving trust funds established for his children to appease the government's demand for back taxes which can never be completely repaid. The myth that sport is a channel of social mobility for disprivileged ethnics may well be re-examined in this light. Notoriety and fame are short lived and differ radically from privilege and dignity.

11 David Riesman, Nathan Glazer, and Reuel Denney, *The Lonely Crowd*, New York: Doubleday Anchor Books, 1954, p. 154.

12 *Ibid.*, p. 84.

13 Kirson Weinberg and Henry Arond, "The Occupational Culture of the Boxer", *American Journal of Sociology*, LVII (March, 1952), p. 469, reprinted in Part III of this Reader.

14 *Ibid.*, p. 465.

15 Survey of Current Business. U.S. Department of Commerce. *National Income Number*, XLIV, No. 7, Washington, D.C.: United States Government Printing Office, July, 1964, Table 7, p. 13.

16 U.S. Bureau of the Census, *U.S. Census of Business*: 1948, Vol. VI: *Service Trade—General Statistics*, Washington, D.C.: United States Government Printing Office, 1952, Table 1B, p. 104; and U.S. Bureau of the Census, *Census of Business*, 1963, *op. cit.*, Table 1, pp. 1–6.

17 Note well that this is an underestimate for expenditures on recreation: expenditures for goods and paraphernalia are not included here. For the data in this and the following sentence, see U.S. Department of Commerce, *Survey of Current Business*, Vol. XLIV, No. 7, Washington, D.C.: United States Government Printing Office, July, 1964, Table 14, p. 16.

18 It certainly should be noted here that 258 column inches of the business pages were *solely* devoted to listings on the American Stock Exchange, the New York Stock Exchange, listings of Toronto stocks, grain futures, U.S. Treasury Notes, etc. Thus, 88 column inches were devoted to substantive accounts of news in the business world. Obviously nowhere near as great a proportion of the sports pages was devoted *solely* to the reporting of scores. My colleague in the sociology of sport, Günther Lüschen, of the University of Illinois, has always been amazed at the detail of American sportswriting.

19 James Reston, in a rare appreciative view of American sports, has written, ". . . sports in America are something more than a diversion. They are a unifying social force, and a counter to the confusion about the vagueness and complexities of our cities, our races, and in this long-haired age, even the confusion between our sexes." Minneapolis *Tribune*, 11 October, 1966, p. 6.

20 The involvement of Brooklyn fans has, of course, been legendary, and I naively predicted the Dodgers would not (indeed, *could not*) ever leave Brooklyn! To gauge the extent of involvement, let me cite the reminiscences of a younger colleague, Harvey Farberman. In high school, Farberman reports in conversation, baseball was *the* fundamental organising activity for his peers. Moreover, positions were not designated by title, but by the name of the Brooklyn Dodger player. Thus, Farberman, a portly man who played shortstop, was known as "Pee-wee". The centre-fielder was called "Duke", etc. Powerful identifications are required to transform names into titles, e.g. Christ to Christian, Marx to Marxist, or Luther to Lutheran. Arnold Beisser, a California psychiatrist, reports the case of a St. Louis Cardinal fan who, moving to Los Angeles, lost his

sense of identity, until he was able to re-establish an identification with the Los Angeles Dodgers, *op. cit.*, pp. 124–141. In this regard, the resentment of deserted fans is well attested to by the fact that the Milwaukee Braves were at the bottom of attendance figures in the National League, the year (1965) prior to their departure for Atlanta, Georgia. Finally, I can not refrain from commenting on the zeal of the New York Mets' fans. Today, it is unique in baseball, as though the Mets filled an "identity-void" left by the evacuation of the Dodgers and the Giants, "We must be doing something right!"

21 On the homogenisation of the sexes, see Charles Winick, "Dear Sir or Madam, as The Case May Be", *The Antioch Review* (Spring, 1963), pp. 37–49.

22 Indeed, current legislation seems to be abolishing Monday as a work day. Labour Day has always been celebrated on Monday, but the Congress completed legislation on 24 June, 1968, to insure that Washington's birthday, Memorial Day, Veterans Day, and Columbus Day be celebrated on Monday.

23 Huizinga, *op. cit.*, p. 8.

24 Foote, *op. cit.*, p. 114.

25 U.S. Bureau of the Census, Census of Business, 1963, *op. cit.*, Table 2, pp. 1–8 and 1–9. However, bowling remains a sport predominantly engaged in by lower status people.

26 In former days, in cricket matches played at the Lord's Ground in London, amateurs and professionals used to use different entrances and separate locker rooms. However, Peter McIntosh informed me in correspondence that this practice has ceased. "The separation of amateurs and professionals in the pavilion at Lords and at County Cricket Grounds survived for a few years after the war, but was abandoned about 1952. . . . When county teams travelled to 'away' matches, amateurs travelled first class, professionals third (now second) class. Two or three years ago, however, the world of cricket abandoned the distinction between amateur and professional. All cricketers are now just 'cricketers'. How they make a living is not reflected in their description or their locker rooms! You say you are interested in spectator sport. Cricket has almost ceased to deserve that name. The county grounds are full only when Australians or West Indians come. For most matches they are less than half full. Things have a way of surviving in Britain when they would die . . . anywhere else. Cricket—or county cricket—is just such a survival." Letter from Peter McIntosh, Senior Inspector of Physical Education for the London County Council, dated 18 December, 1965. In June 1968, the Wimbledon Tennis Tournament admitted professional participation.

27 I am extremely indebted to my colleague, Joanne Bubolz Eicher, now of Michigan State University, for preliminary insights into these transformations.

28 Gregory P. Stone, "Comments on 'Careers and Consumer Behaviour' ", in Lincoln H. Clark (ed.), *Consumer Behavior*, II, *The Life Cycle and Consumer Behavior*, New York: New York University Press, 1955, p. 26.

29 Huizinga, *op. cit.*, p. 186. See also Kenneth Burke's wonderful discussion of style in his *Permanence and Change*, Los Altos: Hermes Publications, 1954, pp. 50–8. Another, perhaps more significant conception of style would conceive stylisation as an individualisation of role performance.

30 David Riesman, "Some Observations on Changes in Leisure Attitudes", *op. cit.*, p. 218.

31 Here I am exaggerating somewhat for effect. Certainly there are female hunters and fisherwomen, but these seem still to be the exception. The "invasion" of females into such predominantly male play forms as hunting and fishing signals a phase of the "battle between the sexes" which I am unable to analyse here.

32 Detroit *Free Press*, 30 June, 1955, p. 33.

33 In a personal note to the author David Riesman has written, "It seems to me that both among men and women there is a growing fear of homosexuality and the avoidance of certain sports for women is a way of avoiding this fear." This provides an alternative explanation of some of our observations, but we would like to reiterate that the problem may also be aggravated by the *loss* of sexual identity precipitated by the "homogenisation of the sexes". Thus, rather than avoiding homosexuality, many Americans may be attempting to discover "who" they are in sexual terms.

34 Vance Packard, *The Hidden Persuaders*, New York: Pocket Books, Inc., 1957, p. 73.

35 Gregory P. Stone, *op. cit.*, see Part III of this Reader.

36 Nelson Foote, "Sex as Play", *Social Problems*, I (April, 1954), pp. 159–63.

37 This is not always the case. There are many positive functions of spectatorship.

38 Sports appear to vary in their resistance to spectator "heat". Baseball, to cite one instance, retains an impervious dignity. Thus, Juan Marichal's clubbing of John Roseboro in the hectic closing days of the 1965 season certainly did not rally the support of fans or his team-mates. In particular, Willy Mays, deplored the whole episode as "not good for baseball". The one thousand dollar fine and five-day suspension was a genuine penalty. Yet, Andreano (*op. cit.*) complains that baseball has become too dignified, lost its colour, and neutralised its heroes. Work, play, *and* drama, then, must be simultaneously present in all sports. The question is: which form dominates the contest and why.

39 Plato, *Laws*, vii, 796, cited in Jan Huizinga, *op. cit.*, pp. 211–12 and also, pp. 18–19.

CHAPTER 5

Dynamics of Sport Groups with Special Reference to Football*

Norbert Elias and Eric Dunning

It happens quite often in the development of a science, or of one of its branches, that a type of theory which has dominated the direction of research for some time, reaches a point where its limitations become apparent. One begins to see that a number of significant problems cannot be clearly formulated and cannot be solved with its help. The scientists who work in this field then begin to look round for a wider theoretical framework, or perhaps for another type of theory altogether, which will allow them to come to grips with problems beyond the reach of the fashionable type of theory.

What is called "small group theory" in contemporary sociology appears to be in that stage. It is fairly evident that a good many problems of small groups are beyond the reach of small group theory in its present form, to say nothing of its limitations as a model setting theory for the exploration of larger social units. It did not, at any rate, prove of great help to us when we tried to investigate problems of small groups engaged in sport-games such as football. Confronted with the study of sport groups *in vivo*, small group theory failed us.[1]

We therefore set out—in connection with a wider investigation of the long-term development of football—to explore some of the theoretical aspects of the dynamics of groups engaged in games of this type. It appeared to us that sport-games in general, football in particular, could serve as a useful point of departure for the construction of models of small group dynamics which are somewhat different from those offered within the framework of present-day small group theories. Some aspects of such a model are presented in this paper. Although it is built primarily with reference to football, the concepts derived from our analysis may perhaps be of wider use. They almost certainly apply not only to football, but also to other group games.

* Reprinted from *The British Journal of Sociology*, Vol. XVII, No. 4, December, 1966.

In studying football and other sport-games, one encounters from the start certain semantic difficulties. People often speak of a game of football as if it were something outside of, and apart from, the group of players. It is not entirely incorrect to say that a game such as football can be played by many different groups. As such, it is partly independent of any one of them. At the same time, the pattern of each individual game is itself a group pattern. In order to play a game, people group themselves in specific ways. As the game runs its course, they continually regroup themselves in a manner similar to the ways in which groups of dancers regroup themselves in the course of a dance. The initial configuration from which the players start changes into other configurations of players in a continuous movement. It is to this continuous movement of the configuration of players to which we refer when we use the term "game-pattern". The term can be misleading if it makes one forget what one actually observes when watching a game: one observes small groups of living human beings changing their relations in constant interdependence with each other.

The dynamics of this grouping and regrouping of players in the course of a game are fixed in certain respects and elastic and variable in others. They are fixed, because without agreement among the players on their adherence to a unified set of rules, the game would not be a game but a "free-for-all". They are elastic and variable, otherwise one game would be exactly like another. In that case, too, its specific character as a game would be lost. Thus, in order that group relations can have the character of a game, a very specific balance must be established between fixity and elasticity of rules. On this balance depend the dynamics of the game. If the relations between those who play the game are too rigidly or too loosely bound by rules, the game will suffer.

Take the initial configuration of players in Association Football. It is regulated by certain rules. Thus, the wording of one of the 1897 rules about the "kick-off" configuration, which with some qualifications is still valid, is this:

> The game shall be commenced by a place-kick from the *centre of the field of play* in the direction of the opponents' goal-line; *the opponents* shall not approach within ten yards of the ball until it is kicked off, nor shall any player on either side pass the centre of the ground in the direction of his opponents' goal until the ball is kicked off.[2]

It is easy to see how much room for manoeuvring this kind of rule leaves to the two sides—how elastic it is. Within the framework of the kick-off rules, players can group themselves in a "W-formation" (2—3—5) or in the form of a "horizontal H" (4—2—4). If they want to, the defending side may even mass themselves solidly in front of their own goal, although in practice this is rarely done. How the players actually position themselves at the kick-off is determined by formal rules as well as by convention, by their experience of previous games, and often by their own strategic plans coupled with their expectations of the intended strategy of their opponents. How far this peculiar characteristic, this blend of firmness and elasticity applies to the regulation of human relations in other spheres is a question which may deserve more attention that it has received so far.

From the starting position evolves a fluid configuration formed by both teams. Within it, all individuals are, and remain throughout, more or less interdependent; they move and regroup themselves in response to each other. This may help to explain why we refer to this type of game as a specific form of group dynamics. For this moving and regrouping of interdependent players in response to each other *is* the game.

It may not be immediately clear that by using the term "group dynamics" in this context, we do not refer to the changing configurations of each of the two groups of players as if they could be considered in separation, as if each had dynamics of its own. That is not the case. In a game of football, the configuration of players on the one side and that of players on the other side, are interdependent and inseparable. They form in fact one single configuration. If one speaks of a sport-game as a specific form of group dynamics, one refers to the overall change in the configuration of the players of both sides together. Few aspects of the group dynamics of football show as clearly as this the relevance of sport-games as models for the dynamics of groups in many other fields.

A fundamental characteristic, not only of football, but of practically all sport-games, is that they constitute a type of group dynamics which is produced by controlled tensions between at least two subgroups. For this reason alone, traditional sociological small group theory is not of very great help in the exploration of the sort of problems which confronted us here. These require specific concepts different from those used so far in the sociological study of small groups, and perhaps a little more complex than those commonly used in discussions about sport-games. According to present conceptual usage, one might be content with saying that a game of football is played by two different groups. This is one of those linguistic conventions which induce people to think and to speak as if the game were something apart from the human beings concerned. By stressing that the game is nothing but the changing configuration around a moving ball of the players themselves, one brings into focus at the same time that it is not the changing configuration of each of the two teams seen separately, but of the players of *both* teams together in their struggle with one another. Many people who watch a game of football may know that this is what they try to follow—not merely one team or the other, but the fluid pattern formed by both. This *is* the pattern of the game—the dynamics of a group in tension.

As such, this model of group dynamics has theoretical implications beyond the study of small groups. It may be of help for the study of such varied problems as, for example, that of marital tensions, or of union-management tensions. There, as in the case of sport groups, tensions are not extraneous, but intrinsic to the configuration itself; there too, they are to some extent controlled. How and to what degree they are, and how they came to be controlled, is a problem to be studied. Interstate relations are another example of a configuration with built-in tensions. But in that case, effective and permanent tension control has not yet been achieved and, at the present level of social development and of sociological understanding of groups-in-tension, perhaps cannot be achieved. Among the factors which prevent the achievement of better control is certainly the widespread inability to perceive and to investigate two states in tension or a multi-polar state system as a single configuration. One usually approaches such a system as the involved participant of one side and is therefore not quite able to visualise and to determine the paramount dynamics of the configuration which different sides form with each other and which determines the moves of each side. The study of sport-games like football can thus serve as a relatively simple introduction to a configurational approach to the study of tensions and conflicts—to an approach in which attention is focused, not on the dynamics of one side or the other, but of both together as a single configuration in tension.

Today, sociological thinking with regard to problems of this kind often seems to revolve around two alternatives: problems of group tension stand on one side, problems of group co-operation and harmony on the other. Group tensions appear to be one phenomenon; group co-operation and harmony another. Because one has different words, it appears almost as if the phenomena themselves were different and independent of each other. An analysis of sport-games illuminates the inadequacy of this approach. The group dynamics of a game presuppose tension and co-operation on a variety of levels at the same time. Neither would be what it is without the other.

Traditional small group theory is apt to lead attention away from problems of this type. Its representatives often select for study small group problems in which tensions play no part at all, or if they select for study problems of tension, they confine themselves to specific types of individual tension such as individual competition. In reading their arguments, one often has the feeling that their discussions on the subject of group tensions and conflicts are discussions about questions of political philosophy and political ideals rather than about conclusions derived from strictly scientific enquiries. In this case as in others, contemporary sociology appears at times to be threatened by a polarisation between those who are blind to the role of tensions in social groups—or at least who greatly underplay this role—and those who overplay the role of tensions and conflicts to the neglect of other, equally relevant aspects of group dynamics. Homans, for example, has developed a small group theory in which conflict and tension play at most a marginal part. It is probably not unfair to suggest that this harmonistic tendency is connected with a pre-established scheme of values, a kind of sociopolitical *Weltanschauung* which sets the course for theoretical arguments and empirical observations alike. It almost appears as if Homans has developed an emotional allergy to the discussion of tensions and conflicts. Thus, he wrote:

> . . . if we confine ourselves to behaviour . . . (concerned with the exchange of rewarding activities), we are sure to call down upon our heads the wrath of the social scientists who make a profession of being tough-minded. "Never play down conflict," they would say. "Not only is conflict a fact of social life, but conflict has positive virtues and brings out some of the best in men." It turns out that these very scientists are no more willing than is the rest of mankind to encourage conflict within any body of men they themselves are responsible for. Conflict is good for other people's subordinates, not their own. But we must refrain. It is all too easy to ask men to practise what they preach. A trap that none can escape is no fun setting.[3]

This, as one can see, is an emotionally charged argument. It shows how greatly Homans himself misunderstands the character of sociological analysis. Without doubt, some writers who focus attention on problems of conflict, do so because they wish to encourage conflict— that is, for reasons extraneous to the sociological study of such problems. But to suggest, as Homans seems to do, that the encouragement of conflict is the only reason why sociologists try to determine the nature of tensions and conflicts in the social life of man implies a fundamental misunderstanding of the task of sociological analysis. Although Homans writes, "no one can deny . . . that conflict is a fact of social life", he obviously finds it difficult to deal with this fact simply as such, as one fact of life among others.

In this respect, the study of sport-games can be of considerable help. A specific type of tension plays a significant part in such games. In studying them, one cannot overlook tensions whether one likes them or not. It seemed useful to determine the character of sport-games like football as configurations with tensions of a specific type and we thought that "groups-in-controlled-tension" would be an appropriate term to express it.

At the present stage of theoretical development one is confronted by a dilemma in these matters which, in a somewhat different context, has been most clearly formulated by Dahrendorf. We have already referred to the tendency to treat conflict and co-operation as independent phenomena and to form different and separate theories, one for each of them. Dahrendorf encountered a similar problem with regard to integration and coercion, and posed in this connection a significant question:

> Is there, or can there be, [he asked] a general point of view that synthesises the unsolved dialectics of integration and coercion? So far as I can see there is no such general model; as to its possibility, I have to reserve judgment. It seems at least conceivable that unification of theory is not feasible at a point which has puzzled thinkers ever since the beginning of Western philosophy.[4]

The same might be said with regard to tensions and co-operation. Some sociological theories are woven around problems of conflict and tension without much regard for those of co-operation and integration; others pay regard above all to problems of co-operation and integration, treating conflict and tension more or less as marginal phenomena. From closer range, it is easy to see the reason. Both procedures are based on a reification of values: because one attaches different values to conflict and co-operation, one is apt to treat these phenomena as if they had a separate and independent existence.

A study of sport-games is thus a useful point of departure for an approach to these problems which may allow the passions to calm down. It is easier in this field to move outside the battle of extraneous evaluations and to keep in close touch with testable, factual evidence in framing theoretical propositions. It is less difficult, therefore, to move towards a unified theoretical framework within which both tension and co-operation can find their place as interdependent phenomena. In football, co-operation presupposes tension, and tension co-operation.

However, one can clearly perceive their complementary character only if one studies how the game has developed to its present form where tensions and co-operation are related to each other through firm types of control. The study of the long-term development of football enabled us, in fact, to see in a limited field, one aspect of the interplay between tension and tension-control without which the relevance of sport-games as a theoretical model cannot be fully understood. It showed how tensions which were at one time uncontrolled and probably uncontrollable were gradually brought under control.

In its present form, one of the central characteristics of Association Football and many other sport-games is certainly the manner in which the often fairly high group tensions engendered in the game are kept under control. But this is a fairly recent attainment. In former days, tensions between players, which were and are at all times characteristic of games, were often far less well controlled. This transformation, the development of a highly regulated, relatively non-violent form of group tension, from an earlier stage where the corresponding tensions were much more apt to discharge themselves in one or another form of violence, is at the core of the long-term dynamics of the game of football. It is representative—one might almost say symbolic—of certain aspects of the long-term development of European societies. For within many of these societies the general level of overt violence has diminished over the ages. There, too, one encounters, as one does in the development of football, both a higher level of organisation and higher levels of self-restraint and of security compared with the past. How and why this long-term development towards more "civilised" standards of human relations occurred in society at large need not concern us here.[5] But we were able to find out, and we shall indicate in our forthcoming book on that subject some of the reasons why a game like football developed, in connection with similar trends in society at large, from a more to a less violent and uncontrolled form and correspondingly to a different form of game-pattern—of group dynamics. This understanding of the long-term dynamics of football greatly assists that of the short-term dynamics of the game as played today.

As played in earlier ages, not only in England but also in many other countries, football, like most ball games, was a very wild game indeed.[6]

Centuries later, between 1845 and 1862, when the playing of football, at least in some of the leading public schools, had become much more highly regulated, the level of permitted violence was still very much higher than it is today and the dynamics of group tensions were therefore rather different.[7]

As late as 1863, the incipient Football Association split because the majority proposed to eliminate "hacking" altogether from the game, while a minority of the founder members held to the view that the abolition of hacking would make the game "unmanly" and opposed it. This was not the only, but certainly one of the major points which led to the development of two types of football in England. Association Football, or "soccer", on the one hand, and Rugby Football, or "rugger", on the other. It is interesting to note that even in the rugby game, although the general level of violence remained somewhat higher than in Association Football, hacking was also "outlawed" not very long after the break occurred.

The problem we encountered here—a problem not entirely without theoretical significance—was that of the reasons why one of the two types of football, namely "soccer", gained very much wider recognition and success than the other, not only in England but almost the world over. Was it because the level of violence in soccer was lower than in rugby? In order to answer questions such as this one needs a very clear idea of at least one of the central problems that resulted from the lowering of violence for the whole pattern of the game, for its group dynamics. The danger of this decrease of permitted violence was quite obviously that the game in its changed form would become uninteresting and dull. The survival of the game evidently depended on a peculiar kind of balance between, on the one hand, a high control of the level of violence, because without it the game was no longer acceptable to most players and most spectators in accordance with the now prevailing standards of "civilised" behaviour, and on the other hand, the preservation of a sufficiently high level of non-violent fighting without which the interest of players and public alike would have flagged. The whole development of most sport-games, and certainly that of football, centred to a very large extent on the solution of this problem: how was it possible to maintain within the set game-pattern a high level of group tension and the group dynamics resulting from it, while at the same time keeping recurrent physical injury to the players at the lowest possible level. The question was and still is, in other words, how to "steer the ship", as it were, between the Scylla of disorderliness and the Charybdis of boredom. People who have acted as coaches or managers in the game may appreciate that this is a problem of great practical significance. A good number of people in that position are used to thinking in terms of configurations as a matter of course if they plan ahead; for that is the most realistic way of envisaging a game and most appropriate for the working out of strategies. Thus, in preparing his team for a game, a manager may say that the opponents are likely to use a "4-2-4 system", that their own task is to prevent the opponents from dominating the mid-field play; in order to achieve this, he may assign to two of his players the task of "blotting out" the opponents' "link" men, so that the rest can concentrate on the task of attack. However, although trained by his immediate experience to envisage the game as a fluctuating configuration of players, it is neither his aim nor his task to stand back and to reflect on the characteristics and regularities of these configurations as such. The Committee of the Football Association who decided in 1925 to change the offside rule were probably aware that under the old rules the "tone" of the game had become too low, as people on other occasions noticed that the game had begun to stray from the middle course between disorderliness and dullness. But up to now the concepts available for dealing with such problems are not very articulate. In order to see their wider significance—their significance for a small group theory or for a sociological game theory in general—it is necessary to work out comparatively new concepts as a framework for observation and to change the meaning of some of those which already exist.

Let us start with the concept of configuration. It has already been said that a game is the changing configuration of the players on the field. This means that the configuration is not only an aspect of the players. It is not as one sometimes seems to believe if one uses related expressions such as "social pattern", "social group", or "society", something abstracted from individual people. Configurations are formed by individuals, as it were "body and soul". If one watches the players standing and moving on the field in constant interdependence, one can actually see them forming a continuously changing configuration. If groups or societies are large, one usually cannot see the configurations their individual members form with one another. Nevertheless, in these cases, too, people form configurations with each other—a city, a church, a political party, a state—which are no less real than the one formed by players on a football field, even though one cannot take them in at a glance.

To envisage groupings of people as configurations in this sense, with their dynamics, their problems of tension and of tension control and many others, even though one cannot see them here and now, requires a specific training. This is one of the tasks of configurational sociology, of which the present paper is an example. At present, a good deal of uncertainty still exists with regard to the nature of that phenomenon to which one refers as "society". Sociological theories often appear to start from the assumption that "groups" or "societies", and "social phenomena" in general, are something abstracted from individual people, or at least that they are not quite as "real" as individuals, whatever that may mean. The game of football—as a small-scale model—can help to correct this view. It shows that configurations of individuals are neither more nor less real than the individuals who form them. Configurational sociology is based on observations such as this. In contrast to sociological theories which treat societies as if they were mere names, a *flatum vocis*, an "ideal type", a sociologist's construction, and which are in that sense representative of sociological nominalism, it represents a sociological realism.[8] Individuals always come in configurations and configurations are always formed by individuals.

If one watches a game of football one can understand that it is the fluctuating configuration of the players itself on which, at a given moment, the decisions and moves of individual players depend. In that respect concepts such as "interaction" and its relatives are apt to mislead. They appear to suggest that individuals without configurations form configurations with each other a *posteriori*. They make it difficult to come to grips with the type of tensions one encounters in the study of football. These tensions are different in character from those which may arise when two formerly independent individuals, "ego" and "alter", begin to interact. As has already been said, it is the configuration of players itself which embodies a tension of a specific type—a controlled tension. One can neither understand nor explain its character from the "interaction" of individual players.

In societies such as ours, it is one of the characteristics of a game that the tension inherent in the configuration of players is neither too high nor to low: the game must last for a while, but must finally be resolved in the victory of one side or the other. There can be "drawn" games, but if they occur too often, one would suspect that something in the construction of the game was faulty.

Thus, in present-day industrial societies, a game is a group configuration of a very specific type. At its heart is the controlled tension between two sub-groups holding each other in balance. This is a phenomenon one can observe in many other fields. It appears to deserve a special name. We have called it a "tension-balance". Just as the mobility of a human limb is dependent on the contained tension between two antagonistic muscle groups in balance, so the game process depends on a tension between two at the same time antagonistic and interdependent sets of players keeping each other in a fluctuating equilibrium.[9]

The mechanics of configurations with a tension-balance at their centre are far from simple. Two examples may be enough to illustrate them: the flexible tension-balance in a game process cannot be produced and maintained at just the right level if one side is very much stronger than the other. If that is the case, the stronger side will probably score more frequently, the game tension—the "tone" of the game—will be relatively low, and the game itself will be slow and lifeless. But it would be a mistake to think that in studying the group dynamics of a game, one is mainly concerned with questions arising from the qualities of individual teams or of individual players.

What we have primarily studied is the development and the structure of the game-pattern as such. This pattern has at a given time a specific form maintained by controls at various levels. It is controlled by football organisations, by state and local authorities, by the spectators, by the teams mutually, by the players individually. One need not enumerate them all or analyse their interplay in this context. In theoretical discourse, one is apt to consider the controls preserving a particular configuration, and above all the tension-balance of a configuration, in terms of rules or norms only. But, as in other cases, rules and especially formal rules are only one of the "instruments" of control responsible for the relative stability of groups-in-controlled-tension. And, whatever they are, group rules or group norms, here as elsewhere, are no absolutes.

Rules or norms as devices for the control of tensions do not float outside and above social processes as is sometimes suggested in present discussions. The group dynamics which rules help to maintain may, on their part, determine whether rules persist or change. The development of football regulations shows very strikingly how changes of rules can depend on the overall development of that which they rule. The dynamics of such configurations have what one might call a "logic" of their own. Thus, in football the tension level may flag, not simply because of the distinguishing characteristics of individual playing groups or of their individual members, but because of set characteristics of the configuration which they form with one another. This is a phenomenon which one encounters again and again if one surveys the development of a game. In 1925, for example, the "offside" rule in soccer was changed. Until then, the rule was this: a player could only legitimately receive a ball passed forward to him by another member of his side if at least three members of the opposing team stood between him and their goal. If less than three were so positioned, he was ruled "offside" and a "free kick" was awarded to the opponents. In 1925, the number was reduced to two. The elasticity of the older rule, skilfully exploited, had led to a stage where stalemates had become increasingly frequent. What had happened was that the balance had moved too far in favour of the defence. Games tended to drag on without decision or scores were low. The reason was not any particular quality of individual players: the configuration of players as stabilised by a variety of controls, among which the formal rules held a key position, had itself proved deficient. Hence, the attempt was made, by means of a change of rules, to establish a more fluid configuration of the players which could restore the balance between attack and defence.

This is one example of a number of polarities which in football, and probably also in all other sport-games, are built into the established configuration of the game process. Such polarities operate in close connection with each other. In fact, a complex of interdependent polarities built into the game pattern provides the main motive force for the group dynamics of a football game. In one way or another they all contribute towards maintaining the "tone", the tension-balance of the game. Here is a list of some of them:

1. the overall polarity between the two opposing teams
2. the polarity between attack and defence
3. the polarity between co-operation and tension of the two teams
4. the polarity between co-operation and competition within each team.

Polarity, 4, can express itself in a variety of ways. One of them is that between individual team members and the team as a whole, shown in the following examples:

(a) In the 1860's and 70's, individual dribbling was the centre-piece of soccer. The fluctuating tension-balance between team interests and individual interests was geared in favour of the latter. This corresponded to the social characteristics of the game during that period. It was then a game primarily played by public school old-boys and by other middle- and upper-class people for their own enjoyment. In the last two decades of the nineteenth century, this technique gave way to a different manner of playing. Team co-operation became accentuated at the expense of opportunities for the individual to shine competitively within the team. Thus, the balance between individual and team interests changed. Individual dribbling receded and passing the ball from one member of a team to another came to the fore. It is possible to analyse the reasons for this change with considerable stringency. An increase in the number of teams, the establishment of formal competitions, increased competitive rivalry among teams, and the beginning of playing for a paying public were among them.

(b) Even after the balance between the team members' consideration for the team's interests and that for their individual interests had moved strongly in favour of the former, the polarity continued to play its part. Every game pattern leaves to some players considerable scope for decisions. In fact, without the capacity to take decisions quickly, an individual cannot be a good player. But again and again, in taking his decisions, the individual player must decide between the need for co-operating with other members for the team's sake and that for contributing to his personal reputation and advancement. The present conceptualisation in cases such as this is dominated by absolute alternatives such as "egoism" and "altruism". As

instruments of realistic sociological analysis they have little to re-
commend them. As one can see, thinking in terms of balances and
polarities makes it easier to come to grips with what one actually
observes.

Other polarities are of a slightly different type. These are a few
examples:

5. the polarity between the external controls of players on a
   variety of levels (by managers, captains, team-mates, referees,
   linesmen, spectators, etc.), and the flexible control which the
   individual player exercises upon himself
6. the polarity between affectionate identification and hostile
   rivalry with the opponents
7. the polarity between the enjoyment of aggression by the individual players and the curb imposed upon such enjoyment by
   the game pattern
8. the polarity between elasticity and fixity of rules.

These are some aspects of the theoretical model, and some
examples of the type of concepts which emerge from the study of
game configurations. They may help to bring into focus a few of the
distinguishing characteristics of this type of group. Such groups
differ from the types of groups usually employed as empirical evidence for small group studies not only because they are groups-in-
controlled-tensions, but also because they are more highly structured
and organised. Theories derived from studies of relatively loosely
structured, *ad hoc* groups specially formed for the purpose of studying groups are frequently marred by a confusion between properties
of groups which are mainly due to those of their individual members
and properties inherent in the configuration of people itself. In the
case of more highly structured and organised groups, it is easier to
determine the dynamics inherent in the configuration as such—and to
distinguish it from variations due to differences on the individual
level. It is easier, for instance, in the case of football to distinguish
the dynamics inherent in the game configuration as such from variations due to the characteristics of different nations, of different teams,
or of different players.

Ad hoc groups have little autonomy in relation to the society
where they are formed and this lack of autonomy can impair the
validity of the results derived from studies of such groups. Thus,
small groups formed in the United States with the aim of studying
problems of leadership generally, may in fact provide information
only about aspects of leadership in the United States. It is an open
question how far similar experiments undertaken, say in Russia or in
Ghana, would produce similar results.

Games such as football are played everywhere in the same manner and the basic configurational dynamics are everywhere the same. One can study them as such and one can study at the same time the variations which arise from the playing of different nationalities, of different teams, of different individuals.

Like *ad hoc* groups, sport groups have definite limitations as evidence for the study of small group problems or of problems of group dynamics in general. Among them are the limitations due to the fact that games are largely ends in themselves. Their purpose, if they have a purpose, is to give people pleasure. In that respect, they differ greatly from those groupings of men which are usually regarded as the centrepieces of social life and which hold a correspondingly central position in sociology from groupings such as factories with the purpose of producing goods, bureaucracies with that of administering states or other enterprises, and from other, equally useful configurations of men which are not normally regarded as ends in themselves or supposed to give people pleasure. It agrees with this scheme of values that sociologists often try to define organisations and social units in general, in the first place by means of their goals.

But if it is a limitation of the study of sport-games—compared with that of social units concerned with the serious business of life—that they have no purpose except perhaps that of providing enjoyment, and are often pursued as ends in themselves, it is also an advantage. It may serve as a corrective to the teleological fallacy still fairly widespread in sociological thinking. In a simplified manner, this can be described as a confusion between the individual level and the group level. With regard to games of football this distinction is fairly clear. Individual players and teams have aims, scoring goals is one of them. The enjoyment of playing, the excitement of spectators, the hope of rewards may be others. But the concatenation of purposeful actions results in a configurational dynamics—in a game—which is purposeless. One can determine it as such and to some extent that has been done here. But this could not have been done if one had attributed the aims of individual players to the changing configuration which the players form with each other.

How far this is true of other configurations of men need not be discussed here. But one can say that even state organisations, churches, factories, and other configurations of the more serious kind, whatever the aims of the people who form them, are at the same time ends in themselves with dynamics of their own. What, after all, are the purposes of nations? It is not entirely frivolous to say that even they resemble a game played by people with one another for its own sake. To neglect this aspect by focusing attention in the first place on their purposes, means overlooking the fact that, as in football, it is the changing configuration of people itself on which at any given time the decisions, the purposes, and the moves of individuals depend. This is particularly so in the case of tensions and conflicts. They are often explained only in terms of the intentions and aims of one side or the other. Sociologists would perhaps be better able to contribute to an understanding of those tensions and conflicts which have so far proved uncontrollable if they would investigate them as aspects of the purposeless dynamics of groups.

NOTES

1 We are referring here to small group theory in the sense in which this term is currently used in sociology. We are not referring to other theories of small groups, such as, e.g. those concerned with problems of group therapy, although in those cases, too, the configurational approach may be of help.

2 G. Green, *The History of the Football Association*, London, 1953.

3 G. Homans, *Social Behaviour: Its Elementary Forms*, London, 1961, p. 130.

4 R. Dahrendorf, *Class and Class Conflict in Industrial Society*, London, 1959, p. 164.

5 It has been dealt with extensively in N. Elias, *Über den Prozess der Zivilisation*, Basle, 1939. 2 vols; 2nd edn., Basle and Munich, 1969.

6 See Elias and Dunning "Folk Football in Medieval and Early Modern Britain", pp. 116–132.

7 See Dunning "The Development of Modern Football", pp. 133–151.

8 In order to avoid misunderstanding one has to add that the term "sociological realism" as used here does not mean what it means if it is applied to Durkheim's theory. Durkheim could not escape from a position where social phenomena appeared as something abstracted and apart from individuals. These abstractions he sometimes reified: he never got beyond a stage where "society" and "individuals" appear as separate entities which he tried to bring together again in the end by an almost mystical hypothesis. This criticism is perfectly compatible with the recognition of the intellectual calibre of his work and the scientific advances due to him.

9 There is one characteristic difference between the tension-balance of antagonistic muscles and that of antagonistic players in a game. In the case of muscles, one side relaxes when the other is tensed. In the case of players, the specific character of the tension-balance is due to the fact that both sides are "tensed".

PART II

THE DEVELOPMENT
OF SPORTS AND
GAMES

Introduction

Sports and games have not always existed in their present forms.
They have arisen in the course of long-term processes of social
development. The investigation of these processes forms an important area of research in the sociology of sport. Some of the issues
which are raised in this connection are explored in this section of the
Reader. More specifically, the articles in it are addressed to questions
of the following kinds: is sport a universal institution found in all
societies whatever their type and level of development, or are modern
sports a completely new, specifically modern social phenomenon?
If they are new, what characteristics distinguish them from the comparable institutions, the "sports" of societies at earlier stages? How
have modern sports arisen? In what ways has their development been
connected with processes of development in society at large such as
industrialisation and urbanisation? Can analysis of the development
of sports and games help to throw light on to processes of development at the wider, societal level?

The section begins with "The Genesis of Sport as a Sociological
Problem" by Norbert Elias. As the title indicates, the author's main
concern is not to undertake a substantive analysis of the genesis of
sport but to prepare the way for such an analysis by clarifying some
of the central sociological issues which the subject raises. Modern
sport, he suggests, is a wholly new phenomenon. On close inspection,
the widepread idea that it is the revival of an ancient Greek tradition turns out to be a myth. Ancient Greek sports were based on a
warrior ethos and involved traditions of "honour" rather than "fairness". There were no written rules and they embodied a high level
of socially tolerated physical violence. This, Elias suggests, corresponded to the fact that the ancient Greek city-states stood at a
relatively early stage in a "civilising process". They had not
achieved such a high degree of stable central, i.e. state control over
the means of violence as is characteristic of modern nation-states.
People were much more dependent on themselves and their kinsmen
for righting wrongs and prosecuting conflicts, than is the case in our
type of society. There was no relatively impersonal police force or
judiciary. People could not rely on the due processes of law. They

had to be more or less constantly ready to respond to attack with counter-attack. A strong conscience with respect to the exercise of aggression would have proved a disadvantage. Under such circumstances, life in general was much more violent and insecure than it is in modern nation-states. This violence was reflected in their sports. It follows that, according to Elias, the principal sociological problem posed by the genesis of modern sports is that of explaining their civilised character relative to the "sports" of earlier ages. Such relatively civilised sports, he notes, developed for the first time in England during the eighteenth and nineteenth centuries. The problem thus becomes that of discovering which characteristics in the social structure of England at that time account for the genesis of modern sports *there* rather than in some other society. Elias suggests that the process is probably connected with the nature of England's ruling elites in that period, particularly with the fact that they lacked strong military traditions. In this manner, besides formulating clearly and precisely the central sociological problem raised by the genesis of modern sports, he provides a useful guide to further research in this area. In addition, he discusses some of the implications of his analysis of Greek sports for traditional stereotypes of Greek society in general. In doing so, he shows why the sociological analysis of sports inevitably leads one into discussion of wider sociological issues and how the sociology of sport can contribute to our understanding of more than the subject to which it is principally directed.

The remaining essays in the section are concerned with various aspects of the development of football. All three of them are centred on problems suggested by Norbert Elias in the leading article to the section. In the first, "Folk Football in Medieval and Early Modern Britain", Norbert Elias and Eric Dunning discuss the traditional antecedents of the modern game and relate them to the wider structure of British society at that stage in its development. They show how very different these ancestral forms were from the contemporary game. They were played according to unwritten local rules which often differed markedly from each other. In fact, traditional football shaded into other folk-games which went by different names such as "hurling", "knappan" and "camp-ball". As the authors show, this is symptomatic of the fact that medieval folk-games generally were by no means as specialised as their modern counterparts have tended to become. Thus, elements of what we now call soccer, rugby, hockey, polo, wrestling and boxing were often embodied in a single game.

Standard limitations were rarely imposed on the size of pitches, the number of players or the duration of matches in these traditional folk-games. Sometimes hundreds, even thousands of people would take part in a single match. The goals were often as much as two or three miles apart and the game would last from sunrise until sunset, sometimes being played on two or three consecutive days. Few limitations, moreover, were placed on the tactics which the players might employ. Practically none at all were imposed to keep their passions in check. Nor were there referees, linesmen or other "external" agents of control. In this, traditional football and other related British folk-games were similar to the "sports" of Ancient Greece. They reflected the violent, relatively unregulated tenor of life in society at large. This in its turn, again similar to the situation in Ancient Greece, corresponded to the relatively low level of state-formation in medieval Britain. In fact, these traditional folk-games were not merely games in our sense of the term. As Elias and Dunning show, they were a form of semi-institutionalised fight, a violent but ritualised way of releasing the tensions which had arisen between local groups in the course of their day-to-day relations. They formed part of the traditional ritual and ceremonial of holy days such as Shrove Tuesday.

The development of more regulated and civilised forms of football out of these ancestral games is the subject of the next essay, "The Development of Modern Football" by Eric Dunning. He concentrates on developments in the middle of the nineteenth century which he regards as particularly decisive. In addition, he treats, in considerably less detail, the development of football as a mass commercial spectacle in the latter part of the nineteenth century. His analysis is modelled on the paradigm suggested by Norbert Elias in his theory of civilising processes. He accepts that the principal problem posed in connection with the development of modern sports is that of explaining their civilised character relative to the sports of earlier ages. As he shows, the development of modern football was not simply a process internal to the game. It came about in connection with a series of interconnected wider social changes on several levels. More specifically, it occurred because of the way in which increasing industrialisation and urbanisation led to certain changes in the public schools. It follows that a central sociological problem posed in connection with the development of modern football is that of explaining how and why these changes occurred in the public schools and how and why they came to be reflected in the development of newer forms of football.

In the late eighteenth and early nineteenth centuries, a state of near anarchy existed in the English public schools. Masters, who came for the most part from lower social strata, were unable to control their upper-class pupils largely because the latter resented being given orders by men whom they considered socially inferior. Rebellion against the authority of the masters was endemic at this stage in the development of the public schools. Control passed virtually into the hands of the oldest and most powerful boys. The "prefect-fagging" system, a system of customary domination of the younger and weaker boys by those who were older and physically stronger, was the result. Their way of playing football reflected this pattern of domination. It was one of the means whereby prefects asserted dominance over fags. In this way, the violence of traditional football was, if anything, reinforced.

Increasing industrialisation and urbanisation, however, led the middle classes to grow in wealth and power. By the 1840's, they were able to enforce reform of the public schools, in particular of the prefect-fagging system. At the same time, as a way of improving relations with their pupils, masters began to take a greater interest in games such as football. They also began to develop an ideology according to which team-games could act as useful instruments of character training. But the wild forms of football inherited from earlier times were unsuited to the educational aims of the masters. Therefore, they encouraged the boys to regularise their football, to commit the rules to writing. Many of the more brutal practices of earlier times were rooted out and the first significant step towards the development of modern football had been taken.

Many modern sports developed their specifically modern character first of all in England during the eighteenth and nineteenth centuries. In that period of its history, this country experienced a "sports revolution" as well as the "industrial revolution" which is so well known and so well-documented. Towards the end of the nineteenth century, these English sports began to be taken up in other societies in many different parts of the world. Usually, they did not change significantly in the course of their diffusion. This is sociologically problematic since changes normally occur when a cultural artefact is diffused from the society where it originated to others with a different social structure. The diffusion of rugby football from England to America comform to this more general pattern. This process is analysed in detail by David Riesman and Reuel Denney in their "Football in America: A Study in Culture Diffusion", the final article in this section. The changes which it underwent can be regarded, they suggest, as symptomatic of the type of changes which usually occur in connection with a process of diffusion.

Riesman and Denney begin by noting that forms of football had been played in America prior to the Civil War. It was not until the 1870's that the rugby game was taken up there. Characteristically enough, it was adopted first of all by members of the elite, specifically by students at the Universities of Yale and Harvard. Two sets of factors are singled out by Riesman and Denney to account for the changes which occurred in rugby in connection with its diffusion to the U.S.A.: firstly the fact that the English game was in a fluid state at the time of the diffusion: the rules had not yet reached a very high level of systematisation and rationalisation; and, secondly, the fact that this fluid game gradually came to be adapted more and more to the different social setting within which it was played in the United States.

There were numerous anomalies and ambiguities in the written rules which governed English rugby in the 1870's. Such anomalies, Riesman and Denney suggest, did not present serious obstacles to playing in an English context. Both players and spectators there had grown up with the game. They had learned the rich tradition of etiquette and informal rules which had arisen to cover any gaps or inconsistencies in the formal rules and to provide ways of coping with conflicts and disagreements. For example, deliberate heeling out from the scrum was taboo according to the formal rules but in practice it was tolerated: it had to be, otherwise scrummages would have lasted for far too long. The Americans, Riesman and Denney argue, could not understand that this was a characteristically English piece of "legal fiction", a way of changing the rules at the grass roots level without going through the lengthy and difficult process of changing them institutionally. Failing to see how the game could operate given such a rule, they changed it by instituting the practice of picking up the ball in the scrum and throwing it back. This led to the creation of the role of centre, thus sparking off the series of changes which eventually resulted in a markedly different, specifically American form of football. Among other features, it came to embody forward passing, a strict "yardage" rule which prevented either side from monopolising possession of the ball, highly formalised offensive and defensive tactics rationally worked out and practised prior to each game, the use of numerical codes for calling moves and a highly elaborate division of labour. A number of factors in American society contributed to these changes according to Riesman and Denney. Among them were the American spectators' taste for visible action in their sports, the widening ethnic base from which players and spectators came to be recruited following the expansion of college education and the fact that the game soon began to function both as a means of upward social mobility for boys from disadvantaged backgrounds and as a source of considerable revenue for the colleges.

CHAPTER 6

The Genesis of Sport as a Sociological Problem[1]

Norbert Elias

I

Many types of sports which, today, are played in a more or less identical manner all over the world originated in England. They spread from there to other countries mainly in the second half of the nineteenth and first half of the twentieth century. Football, in the form which became known in England as "Association Football" or, by a popular abbreviation, as "soccer", was one of them. Horse-racing, wrestling, boxing, tennis, foxhunting, rowing, croquet and athletics were others. But none of the others was quite as widely and, in many cases, quite as rapidly adopted and absorbed by other countries as their own as the soccer type of football. Nor did they enjoy quite as much popularity.[2]

The English term "sport", too, was widely adopted by other countries as a generic term for this specific type of pastimes. That "sports", the type of English pastimes which spread to many other countries mainly between 1850 and 1950, had certain distinguishing characteristics in common which justified their designation as such, i.e. as "sports", has probably been noted more in other countries than in England itself.

"As is well known," [wrote a German author in 1936], "England was the cradle and the loving 'mother' of sport ..." It appears that English technical terms referring to this field might become the common possession of all nations in the same way as Italian technical terms in the field of music. It is probably rare that a piece of culture has migrated with so few changes from one country to another.[3]

That "sport"—the social datum as well as the word—was initially a stranger in other countries can be shown from many examples. The timing of a process of diffusion and adoption is always a significant datum in the context of a sociological diagnosis. Thus in Germany in 1810, an aristocratic writer who knew England was still able to say, "Sport" is as untranslatable as "gentleman".[4] In 1844 another German author wrote with regard to the term "sports", "... we have no word for this and are almost forced to introduce it into our language".[5] The diffusion of the English term "sport" as an expression which German people could understand as a matter of course continued to be slow up to the fifties of the nineteenth century. It gradually gained momentum in conjunction with the increase in sports activities themselves. Finally, in the twentieth century, "Sport" became fully established as a German word.

In France, the *Larousse du XIX iéme Siécle* characterised the term "sport" thus, as an English word originally derived from the French. "Sport—sportt—English word formed from the old French 'desport', pleasure, diversion...." It complained about the importation of such terms "which obviously corrupt our language but we have no customs barriers in order to prohibit their importation at the frontier". Other imports from England to France, factual as well as verbal, were "turf", "jockey", "steeplechase", "match", "sweepstake" and "le boxe". Already under Louis XVIII horse-racing and betting became more regularised in France in accordance with English models. The fashion disappeared during the revolution but was revived with the re-establishment of a more or less aristocratic upper class. A jockey club was founded in Paris in 1833. In fact, the aristocratic or "Society" type of pastimes which dominated the meaning of the term "sport" in England itself in the first half of the nineteenth century, spread to other countries and were adopted there by corresponding social elites before the more popular types such as football, developed the characteristics of a "sport", were perceived as such in England itself and spread in that form to other countries, as a pastime of middle and working class groups. In Germany as in France, some English terms which belonged to the language of the upper-class type of sport were taken up as early as the eighteenth century. From about 1744 on an older term "baxen" appeared in the more literate form of "boxen". It is as significant for our understanding of the development of European societies as it is for that of sport itself that the first types of English sports which were taken up by other countries were horse-racing, boxing, foxhunting, and similar pastimes, and that the diffusion of ball games such as football, tennis and of "sport" generally in the more contemporary sense began only in the second part of the nineteenth century.

The transformation of a polymorphous English folk-game into Association Football or "soccer" was characterised by a fairly long development in the direction of greater regulation and uniformity. It culminated in the codification of the game more or less on a national level in 1863. The first German football club playing according to English rules was founded, characteristically enough in Hanover, in 1878. In the Netherlands, the first football club was founded in 1879/80, in Italy about 1890. In 1892, the first football match between a French team (Stade Français) and an English team (Rosslyn Park) was played in Paris under the auspices of the English ambassador, Lord Dufferin.[6] Football federations were founded in Switzerland in 1895, in Germany in 1900, and in Portugal in 1906 indicating the increase in the number of clubs in each country. In the Netherlands alone, twenty-five different football clubs with more than ten members each existed as early as 1900/1901. By 1910/11, the numbers had risen to one hundred and thirty-four. From 1908 onwards, football became—with interruptions—a regular part of the Olympic Games.

As the game spread to other countries, the term "football" itself, often suitably transformed and in most, though not in all cases, associated with the "soccer" type of English football, entered other languages. In France, it retained its original form. In Germany, it was transformed without great difficulty into "Fussball'. In Spain, it became "futbol" with characteristic derivatives such as "fut-bolero" and "futbolista". In Portugal, it became "futebol", in Holland "voetbal". In the United States, too, the term "football" was for a time connected with the soccer type of game but there the term changed its meaning in accordance with the changing fortunes of the game itself. The dominant American style of playing football gradually changed from the soccer type. Some of the leading American universities, so it seems, diverged from its rules, at first influenced by a Canadian variant of the English rival of soccer, "rugby" football or "rugger", which they then developed further in their own way. But the term "football" remained attached to the different style of playing the game which evolved gradually and finally became standardised in the United States. The Association type of game became known there purely and simply as "soccer" in contrast to the continued use of "futbol" and "futebol" for this form of the game in the Latin-American states.

One could give many other examples of this diffusion from England and of the absorption by other countries of sport and the terms associated with it. But as a first approach, these few may be enough to indicate the problem.

II

What accounts for the fact that, mainly in the nineteenth and twentieth centuries, an English type of pastimes called "sport" set the pattern for a world-wide leisure movement? Pastimes of this type evidently corresponded to specific leisure needs which made themselves felt in many countries during that period. Why did they emerge in England first? What characteristics in the development and structure of English society account for the development there of leisure activities with the specific characteristics which we designate as sport? What are these characteristics? and what distinguished pastimes which came to possess them from earlier pastimes?

At first glance, one may well feel that this array of questions is based on wrong assumptions. Surely, contemporary societies are not the first and not the only ones whose members have enjoyed sport? Did not people play football in England and in other European countries in the middle ages? Did not the courtiers of Louis XIV have their tennis courts and enjoy their "jeu de paume"? And above all the ancient Greeks, the great pioneers of "athletics" and other "sports". Did they not, like ourselves, organise local and inter-state game-contests on a magnificent scale? Is not the revival of the Olympic Games in our times a sufficient reminder of the fact that "sport" is nothing new?

It is difficult to clarify the question whether the type of game-contests which developed in England under the name "sport" during the eighteenth and nineteenth centuries and which spread from there to other countries was something relatively new or whether it was a revival of something old which had unaccountably lapsed, without looking briefly into the question of whether in fact the game-contests of ancient Greece had the characteristics of what we now regard as "sport". The term "sport" is at present often used rather loosely to cover game-contests of many kinds. Like the term "industry", it is used both in a wider and a narrower sense. In the wider sense, it refers, like "industry", to specific activities of pre-state tribal societies and pre-industrial state-societies as well as to corresponding activities of industrial nation-states. If one uses the term "industry" in this wider sense, one is at present nevertheless well aware of its narrower and more precise meaning, of the fact that the "industrialisation process" of the nineteenth and twentieth centuries is something rather new and that the specific types of production and work which have developed in recent times under the name "industry" have certain unique structures which can be determined sociologically with considerable precision and clearly distinguished from other types of production. If one speaks of "sport", however, one still uses the term indiscriminately in a wider sense in which it refers to the game-contests and physical exercises of all societies and in a narrower sense in which it refers to the specific type of game-contests which, like the term itself, originated in England and spread from there to other societies. This process—one might call it the "sportisation" of game-contests if that did not sound rather unattractive—points to a problem which is fairly clear: can one discover in the recent development of the structure and organisation of those leisure activities which we call "sport", trends which are as unique as those in the structure and organisation of work which we refer to when we speak of a process of industrialisation?

This is an open question. One can easily misread it. Given the prevailing evaluation of work as something of much higher value than leisure activities of all kinds, it can easily suggest that any transformation, whether of leisure activities in general or of game-contests in particular, which has taken place in the last two hundred years or so must have been the "effect" of which industrialisation was the "cause". The implicit expectation of causal connections of this type closes the issue before it has been properly opened. Can one not consider, for instance, the possibility that both industrialisation and the transformation of specific leisure occupations into sports are interdependent part-trends within an overall transformation of state societies in recent times? But only if one ceases to treat changes in social spheres which rate higher in the value scale of one's own society as "causes" and changes in lower ranking spheres as "effects", can one hope to clarify the problem which one encounters here. And the clarification of the problem itself—that of the genesis of sport—is the main task of this essay. In this as in other cases, it is easier to find solutions if one is quite clear what the problem is.

III

The following excerpt from the article on athletics in the most recent edition of the *Encyclopaedia Britannica* can probably be regarded as a reasonable summary of the conventional views on this problem:

> The earliest historical records of athletics are of the Grecian Olympic Games (*c.* 800 B.C.) ... terminated by order of the emperor Theodosius in A.D. 394. The history of athletics between the fall of Rome in the 5th century and the 19th century is quite sketchy. Religious festivals in the middle ages were often accompanied by crude ball games between rival towns or guilds.

These were the forerunners of the great spectator sports of the 20th century: soccer, baseball, tennis, football, etc. The coming of the Industrial Revolution in the mid-18th century and the later introduction of sports as a regular extra-curricular activity in public schools by Thomas Arnold (c. 1830) provided a spur which led to the great development of sport during the Victorian age of England. Capping the athletic revival of the 19th century was the restoration of the Olympic Games at Athens in 1896. As the 20th century dawned, interest in all competitive sports reached a peak and despite two world wars and numerous minor hostilities, this interest continues to grow.

This summary, as one can see, states a number of reasonably well-documented facts. It occasionally hints at an explanation such as the spur supposedly given to sport through the initiative of Dr. Arnold. But it is hardly designed to open the eyes of a reader to the many unsolved problems buried under the smooth surface of the narrative. How, for instance, is it to be explained that the religious festivals of the middle ages were accompanied by games which were "crude" while the religious festivals in antiquity at Olympia and elsewhere were apparently less crude and thus more akin to those of the nineteenth and twentieth centuries? And how is it to be determined that these, too, are less crude? How can one determine with a reasonable degree of precision, variations in "crudeness", in civilising standards in the performance of games? And how can one explain them? How can one explain the "great development of sport", the "athletic revival of the nineteenth century"? If one remembers the tournaments of the middle ages or the innumerable folk-games of that age, unsuppressed and, in fact, unsuppressible even if the authorities disapproved of them as the recurrent edicts against playing football in England and other European countries indicate, one can hardly say that there was not a very lively interest in game-contests as such. Was the difference between the game-contests that people enjoyed prior to the eighteenth century and those which they enjoyed in the age of the "industrial revolution" simply a question of a higher or lower degree of "crudeness"? Was it due to the fact that the latter were less savage, that they were more "civilised"? And is that one of the distinguishing characteristics of "sport"? But in that case, is it justified to speak of a "revival"? Is the sports movement of the nineteenth and twentieth centuries another "Renaissance", an unexplained "rebirth" of something which existed in antiquity, perished in the Middle Ages and, for unknown reasons, was simply reborn in our time? Were the game-contests of antiquity less "crude" and less savage? Were they like ours, relatively restrained and representative of a comparatively high sensitivity against playfully inflicting serious injuries on others for the delight of spectators? Or is the tendency to present the modern sports movement as the revival of a similar movement in antiquity one of those benevolent ideological legends innocently used as a means for strengthening the unity of a movement that is full of tensions and conflicting tendencies and for heightening its glamour and prestige? In that case, would it not perhaps be preferable to examine realistically the specific conditions which account for the genesis and rise of the sports movement of our time, to face up to the fact that game-contests of the type which we call "sport", like the industrial nation-states where they take place, have certain unique characteristics which distinguish them from other types and to start the difficult task of enquiring into and explaining the nature of these distinguishing characteristics?

IV

On closer inspection, it is not difficult to see that the game-contests of classical antiquity, which are often represented as the great paradigm of sport, had a number of features and grew up under conditions which were very different from those of our own game-contests. The ethos of the contenders, the standards by which they were judged, the rules of the contests, and the performances themselves differed markedly in many respects from those characteristic of modern sport. Many of the relevant writings of today show a strong tendency to minimise the differences and to maximise the similarities. The result is a distorted picture of our own as well as of Greek society and a distorted picture of the relationship between them. The issues are confused not only by the tendency to treat the game-contests of antiquity as the ideal embodiment of contemporary sport but also by the corresponding expectation to find confirmation for this hypothesis in the writings of antiquity and the tendency to neglect contradictory evidence or to treat it automatically as a reference to exceptional cases.

It may be enough here to point to one of the basic features characteristic of the differences in the whole structure of game-contests in classical antiquity and those of the nineteenth and twentieth centuries. In antiquity, the customary rules of "heavy" athletic events such as boxing and wrestling admitted a far higher degree of physical violence than that admitted by the rules of the corresponding types of sport-contests. The rules of the latter, moreover, are very much more detailed and differentiated; they are not primarily customary rules but written rules, explicitly subject to reasoned criticism and revision. The higher level of physical violence in the games of antiquity itself was anything but an isolated datum. It was symptomatic of specific features in the organisation of Greek society, especially in the stage of development reached by what we now call the "state" organisation and by the degree of monopolisation of physical violence embodied in it. A relatively firm, stable and impersonal monopolisation and control of the means of violence is one of the central structural traits of contemporary nation-states. Compared with it, the institutional monopolisation and control of physical violence in the city-states of Greece was still rudimentary.

The clarification of problems such as these is not difficult if their investigation is guided by a clear theoretical model such as that provided by the theory of civilising processes.[7] According to it, one expects that state formation and conscience formation, the level of socially permitted physical violence and the threshold of repugnance against using it or witnessing it, will differ in specific ways at different stages in the development of societies. It is striking to find how fully the evidence in the case of classical Greece confirms these theoretical expectations. In this way, theory and empirical data together remove one of the main obstacles to the understanding of developmental differences such as those which exist between ancient and contemporary game-contests, namely the feeling that one casts a slur on another society, that one lowers its human value by admitting that the level of physical violence tolerated there, even in game-contests was higher, the threshold of revulsion against people wounding or even killing each other in such a contest to the delight of spectators, correspondingly lower than our own. In the case of Greece, one is thus torn between the high human value traditionally attached to its achievements in philosophy, the sciences, the arts and poetry and the low human value which one seems to attribute to the ancient Greeks if one speaks of their lower level of revulsion against physical violence, if one seems to suggest that they were, compared with ourselves, "uncivilised" and "barbarous". It is precisely the misunderstanding of the factual nature of civilising processes, the prevailing tendency to use terms like "civilised" and "uncivilised" as expressions of ethnocentric value judgments, as absolute and final moral judgments—"we are 'good', they are 'bad' " or *vice versa*—that leads our reasoning into seemingly inescapable contradictions such as these.

We ourselves are brought up, in accordance with the specific social organisation and control of the means of violence within the industrial nation-states of our time, with specific standards of self control with regard to impulses of violence. We measure transgressions automatically by these standards—whether they occur in our own or in other societies at a different stage of development. Internalised, these standards afford protection and strengthen our defences against lapses in a variety of ways. A heightened sensibility with regard to acts of violence, feelings of repugnance against seeing violence committed beyond the permitted level in real life, guilt-feelings about our own lapses, a "bad conscience", are symptomatic of these defences. However, in a period of incessant violence in inter-state affairs, these internalised defences against impulses to violence inevitably remain unstable and brittle. They are continuously exposed to conflicting social pressures—those encouraging a high level of self-control of violent impulses in human relations within one and the same state-society and those encouraging a loosening of the self-control of violent impulses and even a training for violence in the relations between different state-societies. The former account for the relatively high degree of physical security, though not, of course, of psychological and other forms of security, enjoyed by citizens of more developed nation-states within their own societies. They constantly conflict with the demands made on the citizens of these states as a result of the absence of any effective monopolisation and control of physical violence in inter-state relations. A double morality, a split and contradictory conscience formation is the result.

No doubt discrepancies of this type can be found at many stages in the development of societies. The level of violence control within social groups at the tribal stage is almost always higher than that of violence control between social groups of this type. It was certainly different in the case of the Greek city-states. But in their case, the disparity between the two levels was relatively small compared with that characteristic of our own time. There is a good deal of evidence to suggest that this gradient, the disparity between the level of physical security and of both social and self-control of violent impulses, with the corresponding conscience formation reached today in intra-state relations, and the level of physical security and social regulation of overtly violent feelings and—intermittently—of overt acts of violence in inter-state relations is greater today than ever before. The level of physical security within the more advanced industrial nation-states, though it may appear low enough to those who live in them, is, in all likelihood, normally higher than in less developed state societies while the insecurity in inter-state relations has hardly decreased. Violent inter-state conflicts at the present stage of social development are still as unmanageable for those involved in them as they always were. Standards of civilised behaviour, accordingly, are relatively low and the internalisation of social taboos against physical violence, the conscience formation, is in that respect transient and comparatively unsteady. That conflicts and tensions within industrial nation-states have become—normally—less violent and somewhat more manageable is the result of a long unplanned development; it is certainly not the merit of the present generations. But present generations are apt to regard it as such; they are inclined to sit in judgment over past generations whose conscience formation, whose level of revulsion against physical violence, for instance in the relations between ruling elites and ruled, was lower, as if their own higher level of revulsion were simply their own personal achievement.

The level of violence to be observed in the game-contests of past ages is often judged in this manner. We often fail to distinguish between individual acts of transgression against the standards of violence control within our own society and individual acts of a similar kind committed in other societies in accordance with *their* socially permitted level of violence, in accordance with the norms of *those* societies. Thus our immediate, our almost automatic emotional response often induces us to judge societies with different standards of violence control and of revulsion against violence as if the members of these societies had been free to choose between their standards and their norms and ours, and, having this choice, had taken the wrong decision. We enjoy, in relation to them, the same feeling of "being better", of moral superiority, often experienced in relation to individual offenders in our own society if we call their conduct "uncivilised" or "barbarous", in this manner expressing our feeling of moral superiority. We treat their adherence to social norms which permit forms of violence that are condemned as repulsive in our own societies, as a blot on their moral character, as a sign of their inferiority as human beings. Another society is thus judged and evaluated by us as a whole as if it were an individual member of our own. As a rule we do not ask, and as a result we do not know, how changes in the level of violence control, in the social norms regulating violence, or in the feelings associated with violence occur. Nor, as a rule, do we ask and therefore we do not know why they occur. We do not know, in other words, how they can be explained or, for that matter, how our own, higher level of sensitivity with regard to physical violence, at least in intra-state relations, can be explained. At the most, we explain them vaguely by the choice of our expressions rather than explicity and critically, for example as a "flow" in the nature of the groups concerned, as an unexplainable characteristic of their racial or ethnic make-up.

IV

The customary levels of violence used and permitted in the game-contests of societies at different stages of development thus illuminate a much wider and a very fundamental problem. A few examples may help to give it precision.

Take the case of wrestling as performed in our own days and in antiquity. Today, the sport is highly organised and highly regulated. It is governed by an International Wrestling Federation with headquarters in Switzerland. According to the Olympic rules of January, 1967, among the foul-holds of free-style wrestling are strangle-hold, half-strangle, double nelson with pressure applied straight down or with the use of legs. Punching, kicking, butting with the head are all forbidden. A bout, lasting not more than nine minutes, and divided into three periods of three minutes each with two intervals of one minute, is controlled by a referee, three judges and a time-keeper. In spite of these very tight regulations, free-style wrestling appears to many people today as one of the less refined, "cruder" types of sport. Performed as a spectator sport by professionals, a slightly rougher though often pre-arranged version is still highly popular. But the professionals rarely inflict serious injuries on each other. In all likelihood, the public would not enjoy seeing bones broken and the blood flow. But the performers make a good show of hurting one another, and the public seems to like the make-believe.[8]

Among the game-contests of the ancient Olympic Games was the "pancration", a kind of ground-wrestling which formed one of the most popular events. But the level of permitted violence represented by the customary duel of the pancration was very different from that permitted in contemporary free-style wrestling. Thus, Leontiskos of Messana who twice in the first half of the fifth century won the Olympic crown for wrestling, obtained his victories not by throwing his opponents but by breaking their fingers. Arrhachion of Phigalia, twice Olympic victor in the pancration, was strangled in 564 during his third attempt to win the Olympic crown but before being killed, he succeeded in breaking the toes of his opponent and the pain forced the latter to give up the struggle. The judges, therefore, crowned Arrhachion's corpse and proclaimed the dead man victor. His compatriots subsequently erected a statue of Arrhachion in the market place of their town.[9] This, apparently, was the customary practice. If a man was killed in a game-contest at one of the great festivals, the dead man was crowned victor. But apart from loss of the crown—a very severe loss—the survivor was not punished. Nor, as far as one can see, was any social stigma attached to his action. To be killed or to be very severely wounded and perhaps incapacitated for life was a risk a fighter in the pancration had to take. One can assess the difference between wrestling as a sport and wrestling as an "agon" from the following summary:

> In the pancration, the competitors fought with every part of their body, with their hands, feet, elbows, their knees, their necks and their heads; in Sparta they even used their feet. The pancratiasts were allowed to gouge one another's eyes out ... they were also allowed to trip their opponents, lay hold of their feet, noses and ears, dislocate their fingers and arms and apply strangle-holds. If one man succeeded in throwing the other, he was entitled to sit on him and beat him about the head, face and ears; he could also kick him and trample on him. It goes without saying that the contestants in this brutal contest sometimes received the most fearful wounds and that not infrequently men were killed! The pancration of the Spartan ephenoi was probably the most brutal of all. Pausanius tells us that the contestants quite literally fought tooth and nail and bit and tore one another's eyes out.[10]

There was a judge but no timekeeper and no time limits. The struggle lasted until one of the opponents gave up. The rules were traditional, unwritten, undifferentiated and, in their application, probably elastic. It seems that, traditionally, biting and gouging were forbidden. But before the judge could drive an offender who was caught up in the fury of the battle away from his opponent, the damage was probably done.

The old Olympic Games lasted for more than a thousand years. Standards of violence in fighting may have fluctuated throughout this period. But whatever these fluctuations were, throughout antiquity the threshold of sensitivity with regard to the infliction of physical injuries and even to killing in a game-contest and, accordingly, the whole contest ethos, was very different from that represented by the type of contest which we nowadays characterise as "sport". Boxing is another example. Like the pancration type of wrestling, it was very much less hedged in by rules and was therefore to a much higher extent dependent on physical strength, on spontaneous fighting passion and endurance, than sport boxing.

One did not distinguish between different classes of boxers. One did not try, therefore, to match people according to their weight either in this or in any of the other contests. The only distinction made was that between boys and men. Boxers did not only fight with their fists. As in almost all older forms of boxing, the legs played a part in the struggle. Kicking the shins of an opponent was a normal part of the boxing tradition in antiquity.[11] Only the hand and the upper parts of four fingers were bound with leather thongs fastened to the forearm. Fists could be clenched or fingers stretched and, with hard nails, rammed into the opponent's body and face. As time went on, soft leather thongs gave way to harder thongs specially made from tanned ox-hide.[12] These were then fitted with several strips of hard thick leather with sharp projecting edges. The statue of a seated boxer by Appolonius of Athens (first century B.C.), now in the Museo Nazionale delle Terme in Rome, shows the arrangement fairly clearly. But perhaps boxing is a misleading term. Not only the manner but also the aim and the ethos of this kind of fighting was different from those in sport boxing. Significantly enough, the fighting ethos of these pugilistic matches, like that of the Greek *agones* generally, was far more directly derived from the fighting ethos of a warrior aristocracy than is the case with the fighting ethos of sport contests. The latter stemmed from the traditions of a country which, more than most other European countries, developed a distinct organisation of sea-warfare, a naval organisation,[13] very different from that of land-warfare, and whose landowning upper classes, aristocracy and gentry developed a code of behaviour less directly concerned than that of most other European upper classes with the military code of honour of the officer-corps of land-armies.

Greek "boxing", in common with the other forms of agonistic training and practice in the Greek city-states, but unlike English boxing in the eighteenth and nineteenth centuries, was regarded as a training for warfare as well as for game-contests. Philostratos mentions that the fighting technique of the pancration stood the Greek citizen-armies in good stead in the battle of Marathon when it developed into a general mêlée and also at Thermopylae where the Spartans fought with their bare hands when their swords and spears had been broken.[14] In the time of Imperial Rome in which he wrote, wars were no longer fought by citizens' armies. They were fought by professional soldiers, by the Roman legions. The distance between military technique and the conduct of war on the one hand and the traditional agonistic technique of the game-contests on the other hand, had become greater. The Greek Philostratos looked back to the classical age with understandable nostalgia. Perhaps even there, in the period of the hoplite armies, the fighting techniques of war and those of the game-contests were no longer quite as connected with each other as he suggests, but their connection was very much closer than that between the fighting techniques of sport-contests and the fighting techniques of warfare in the age of industrial nation-states. Philostratos was probably very near the mark when he wrote that, in former days, people had regarded the game-contests as an exercise for war and war as an exercise for these contests.[15] The ethos of the game-contests at the great Greek festivals still reflected that of the heroic ancestors as represented in the Homeric epics and perpetuated to some extent from generation to generation by their use in the education of the young. It had many characteristics of the display ethos which rules the status and power rivalries of noble elites in a great number of societies. Fighting, in games as in war, was centred on the ostentatious display of the warrior virtues which gained for a man the highest praise and honour among other members of his own group and for his group—for his kin-group or his city—among other groups. It was glorious to vanquish enemies or opponents but it was hardly less glorious to be vanquished, as Hector was by Achilles, provided one fought with all one's might until one was maimed, wounded or killed and could fight no longer. Victory or defeat was in the hands of the gods. What was inglorious and shameful was to surrender victory without a sufficient show of bravery and endurance.

It was in line with this warrior ethos that a boy or a man killed in one of the Olympic boxing or wrestling matches was often crowned as victor to the glory of his clan and his city and that the survivor—"the killer"—was neither punished nor stigmatised. The Greek games were not ruled by a great concern for "fairness". The English ethos of fairness had non-military roots. It evolved in England in connection with a very specific change in the nature of the enjoyment and excitement provided by game-contests as a result of which the all too brief pleasure in the outcome of a sports battle, in the moment of consummation or victory, was extended and prolonged by the equal pleasure and excitement derived from what initially was foreplay, from participating in or from witnessing the tension of the game-contest itself. Greater emphasis on the enjoyment of the game-contests and the tension-excitement it provided as such, was to some extent connected with the enjoyment of betting which, in England, played a considerable part both in the transformation of "cruder" forms of game-contests into sports and in the development of the ethos of fairness. Gentlemen watching a game-contest played by their sons, their retainers or by well-known professionals, liked to put money on one side or the other as a condiment of the excitement provided by the contest itself which was already tempered by civilising restraints. But the prospect of winning one's bet could add to the excitement of watching the struggle only if the initial odds of winning were more or less evenly divided between the two sides and offered a minimum of calculability. All this required, and in turn was made possible by, a higher organisational level than that reached in the city states of ancient Greece:

> The boxers of Olympia were not classified according to weight any more than the wrestlers were. There was no boxing ring, the bouts being fought on an open piece of ground inside the stadium. The target area was the head and the face.... The fight went on until one of the two contestants was no longer able to defend himself or acknowledged defeat. This he did either by raising his index finger or extending two fingers towards his opponent.[16]

Representations on Greek vases usually show boxers in a traditional stance so close to each other that each stands with one foot forward next to or even behind that of the other. There was little scope for the footwork which enables modern boxers to move quickly, now to the right or left, now backwards, now forwards. To move backwards, according to the code of warriors, was a sign of cowardice. To avoid the enemy's blows by moving out of his way was shameful. Boxers, like warriors at close quarters, were expected to stand fast and not to give way. The defences of skilful boxers might be impenetrable; they might tire their opponents and win without receiving injuries. But if the fight took too long, a judge could order the two opponents to take and to give blow for blow without defending themselves until one of them was no longer able to continue the fight. This agonistic type of boxing, as one can see, accentuated the climax, the moment of decision, of victory or defeat, as the most important and significant part of the contest, more important than the game-contest itself. It was as much a test of physical endurance and of sheer muscular strength as of skill. Serious injuries to the eyes, ears and even to the skull were frequent; so were swollen ears, broken teeth and squashed noses. We hear of two boxers who agreed to exchange blow for blow. The first struck a blow to the head which his opponent survived. When he lowered his guard, the other man struck him under the ribs with his outstretched fingers, burst through his side with his hard nails, seized his bowels and killed him.[17]

V

"Of all the Olympic contests the one which is most alien to us today is boxing; no matter how hard we try we are still unable to conceive how a highly cultivated people with such discriminating aesthetic tastes could derive pleasure from this barbaric spectacle in which two men beat one another about the head with their heavily mailed fists . . . until one of them acknowledged defeat or was reduced to such straits that he was unable to continue to fight. For not only under the Romans, but under the Greeks as well this form of contest was no longer a sport; it was a deadly serious business. . . . More than one Olympic competitor lost his life in the stadium."

This critique, made in 1882 by Adolf Boetticher, one of the early Olympic scholars, is valid today. Like their colleagues in the wrestling and the pancration, the boxers were determined to win at all costs.[18]

The facts are not in doubt but the evaluation is. The quotation represents an almost paradigmatic example of the misunderstanding that results from the unquestioned use of one's own threshold of repugnance in the face of specific types of physical violence as a general yardstick for all human societies regardless of their structure, of the stage of social development they have reached, especially the stage they have reached in the social organisation and control of physical violence: this is as significant an aspect of the development of societies as the organisation and control of the "economic" means of production. One encounters here a very striking example of the barrier to the understanding of societies produced by the dominance of heteronomous[19] evaluations over the perception of functional interdependencies. Classical Greek sculpture ranks highly in the value scale of our time. The types of physical violence embodied in Greek game-contests such as the pancration, according to our own value scale, receive high negative marks. The fact that we associate with the one a high positive value, with the other a high negative value, makes it appear to those who allow their understanding to be guided by preconceived value judgments that these data cannot possibly be connected with each other. It confronts those who judge the past in terms of this type of evaluations with an insoluble problem.

However, if one is concerned with the sociological analysis of the connections between different aspects of the same society, one has no reason to assume that only those manifestations of that society to which, as an outsider observer, one attributes the same value, be it positive or negative, are interdependent. One can discover in all societies factual interdependencies between aspects to which an observer on the one hand and the people themselves who form these societies on the other, attach opposite values. The beauty of Greek art and the relative brutality of Greek game-contests are an example. Far from being incompatible, they were closely connected manifestations of the same level of development, of the same social structure.

The emergence of Greek sculpture from its archaic mould and the idealistic realism of the sculptures of the classical period remain incomprehensible without an understanding of the part which the physical appearance of a person played as a determinant of the social esteem in which he was held among the ruling elites of the Greek city states. In that society, it was hardly possible for a man with a weak or deformed body to reach or to maintain a position of high social or political power. Physical strength, physical beauty, poise and endurance played a very much higher part as determinants of the social standing of a male person in Greek society than they do in ours. One is not always aware that the possibility for a man who is physically handicapped to rise to, or to maintain, a position of leadership or high social power and rank is a relatively recent phenomenon in the development of societies. Because their "body image", their physical appearance ranks relatively low, much lower, for example than "intelligence" or "moral character", in the value-scale which, in societies such as ours, determines the ranking of men and the whole image we form of them, we often lack the key to the understanding of other societies in which physical appearance played a much greater part as a determinant of the public image of a man. In ancient Greece, this was undoubtedly the case. One can perhaps convey the difference by pointing to the fact that, in our society, physical appearance as a determinant of the social image of an individual still plays a very high and perhaps a growing part as far as women are concerned but with regard to men, although television may have some impact on the problem, physical appearance and particularly bodily strength and beauty do not play a very great part in the public esteem of a person. The fact that one of the most powerful nations of our time elected a paralysed man to its highest office is in this respect symptomatic.

It was different in the society of the Greek city-states. From childhood, human beings who were weak or deformed were weeded out. Weak babies were left to die. A man who was unable to fight counted for little. It was very rare for a man who was crippled, ailing or very old, to gain or to maintain a position of public leadership. The term "arete", used in classical Greek society as one of the expressions of its ideal, is often translated as "virtue". But in fact it did not refer, as the term "virtue" does, to any moral characteristics. It referred to the attainments of a warrior and a gentleman among which his body image, his qualification as a strong and skilled warrior, played a dominant part. It was this ideal which found expression in sculptures as well as in game-contests. Most Olympic victors had their statues erected in Olympia and sometimes also in their home town.[20]

It is merely another facet of the same distinguishing characteristic of Greek society during the classical age, that the social position of athletes was very different from that which they hold in our own society. The equivalent of sport, the "culture" of the body, was not to the same extent a specialism as it is today. In contemporary societies, a boxer is a specialist. If we apply the term to those who gained fame as "boxers" in antiquity, the mere use of the word is apt to conjure up in our minds a similar picture. But in fact, the men who proved their physical strength, their agility, their courage and their endurance through their victories in the great festivals, of which those at Olympia were the most famous, stood a very good chance of gaining a high social and political position in their home society if they did not already hold it. For the most part, the participants in the game-contests of Olympia probably came from "good families", from the relatively wealthy elites of their home towns, from groups of landowners and perhaps from wealthier peasant families. Participation in these game-contests demanded a long and arduous training which only relatively wealthy people could afford. A promising young athlete who lacked the money for such a training might find a wealthy patron; or a professional trainer might advance him the money. But if he gained a victory at Olympia, he brought fame to his family and his home town and had a strong chance of becoming a member of its ruling elites. Probably the most famous wrestler of classical antiquity was Milon of Croton. He gained a considerable number of victories at Olympia and other panhellenic festivals. He was a man of prodigious strength which in time became proverbial. He is also mentioned as one of the best pupils of Pythagoras and as commander of the army of his home town in its victorious battle against the Sybarites which ended in the furious mass-killing of the latter after their defeat. We find the same picture in reverse if we learn that men who, today, are remembered above all for their intellectual achievements, were often remembered in their own time also in connection with their attainments as warriors or athletes. Aeschilus, Socrates and Demosthenes went through the hard school of hoplite fighting. Plato had victories in some of the athletic festivals to his credit. Thus, the idealisation of the warrior in Greek sculpture, the representation even of the gods in accordance with the ideal physical appearance of the aristocratic warrior, and the warrior ethos of the game-contests were, indeed, not only compatible; they were closely connected manifestations of the same social groups. Both are characteristic of the social position, the manner of life and the ideals of these groups. But the understanding of this factual interdependence does not impair the enjoyment of Greek art. If anything, it enhances it.[21]

VI

A comparison between the level of violence represented by the game-contests of classical Greece, or for that matter, by the tournaments and folk-games of the middle ages, with those represented by contemporary sport-contests, shows a specific strand in a civilising process but the study of this strand, of the civilising of game-contests, remains inadequate and incomplete if one does not link it to that of other aspects of such societies. In short, the fluctuating level of civilisation in game-contests must remain incomprehensible if one does not connect it at least with the general level of socially permitted violence, of the organisation of violence-control and with the corresponding conscience formation in given societies.

A few examples may help to bring this wider context into focus. In the twentieth century, the mass slaughter of conquered groups by the German Nazis has aroused almost world-wide revulsion. The memory of it for some time tarnished the good name of Germany among the nations of the world. The shock was all the greater because many people had lived under the illusion that, in the twentieth century, such barbarities could no longer happen. They had tacitly assumed that men had become more "civilised", that they had become "morally better" as part of their nature. They had taken pride in being less savage than their forefathers or than other peoples that they knew without ever facing up to the problem which their own relatively more civilised behaviour posed—to the problem of why they themselves, why their behaviour and their feelings had become a little more civilised. The Nazi episode served as a kind of warning; it was a reminder that the restraints against violence are not symptoms of the superiority of the *nature* of "civilised nations", not eternal characteristics of their racial or ethnic make-up, but aspects of a specific type of social development which had resulted in more differentiated and stable social control of the means of violence and in a corresponding conscience-formation. Evidently, this type of social development could be reversed.

This does not necessarily imply that there are no grounds for evaluating the results of this development in human behaviour and feelings as "better" than the corresponding manifestations of earlier developmental stages. Wider understanding of the nexus of facts provides a much better, indeed provides the only secure basis for value judgments of this type. Without it, we cannot know, for example, whether our manner of building up individual self-controls against physical violence is not associated with psychological malformations which, themselves, might appear highly barbaric to a more civilised age. Moreover, if one evaluates a more civilised form of conduct and feeling as "better" than less civilised forms, if one considers that mankind has made progress by arriving at one's own standards of revulsion and repugnance against forms of violence which were common in former days, one is confronted with the problem of why an unplanned development has resulted in something which one evaluates as progress.

All judgments about standards of civilised behaviour are comparative judgments. One cannot say in any absolute sense: "we are civilised, they are uncivilised", but one can say with great confidence; "the standards of conduct and feeling of society A are more, those of society B, less civilised", provided one has worked out a clear and precise developmental gauge. The comparison between the Greek agon-contests and contemporary sport-contests provides one example. Standards of public revulsion in the face of mass murder provide another. As it showed itself in recent times, the almost universal feeling of repugnance against genocide, indicates that human societies have undergone a civilising process, however limited in scope and however unstable its results. Comparison with past attitudes shows this very clearly. In Greek and Roman antiquity, the massacre of the whole male population of a defeated and conquered city and the sale into slavery of its women and children, though they might have aroused pity, did not rouse widespread condemnation. Our sources are incomplete but even they show that cases of mass slaughter recurred with fair regularity throughout the whole period.[22] Sometimes the battle fury of a long threatened or frustrated army played its part in the wholesale massacre of enemies. The destruction of all the Sybarites they could lay their hands on by the citizens of Croton under the leadership of Milon, the famous wrestler, is a case in point. Sometimes, "genocide" was a calculated act aimed at destroying the military power of a rival state. The wholesale destruction of all men of Argos who could bear arms, by order of the Spartan general Cleomenes, which led to the more or less complete annihilation of the military power of Argos as a potential rival of Sparta is an example. The massacre of the male population of Melos by order of the Athenian Assembly of Citizens in 415, vividly described by Thucydides, resulted from a configuration very similar to that which led to the Russian occupation of Czechoslovakia in 1968. The Athenians regarded Melos as part of their empire. It had a specific strategic significance for them in their struggle with Sparta. But the inhabitants of Melos did not wish to become part of the Athenian empire. Therefore, the Athenians killed the men, sold the women and children into slavery and settled the island with Athenian colonists. Some Greeks regarded war as the normal relationship between city-states. It could be interrupted by treaties of limited duration. Gods, through the mouths of their priests, and writers might disapprove of massacres of this kind. But the level of "moral repugnance" against what we now call "genocide" and, more generally, the level of internalised inhibitions against physical violence, were decidedly lower, the feelings of guilt or shame associated with such inhibitions decidedly weaker than they are in the relatively developed industrial nation-states of the twentieth century. Perhaps they were entirely lacking.

There was no lack of compassion for the victims. The great Athenian dramatists, above all Euripides in his "Trojan Women", expressed this feeling with a vividness which was all the stronger because it was not yet overlaid by moral repugnance and indignation. Yet one can hardly doubt that the sale into slavery of the women of the defeated, the separation of mother and child, the killing of male children, and many other themes of violence and warfare in their tragedies, possessed very much greater actuality for an Athenian public in the context of their lives than they possess for a contemporary public in the context of ours.

Altogether the level of physical insecurity in the societies of antiquity was very much higher than it is in contemporary nation-states. That their poets showed more compassion than moral indignation is not uncharacteristic of this difference. Homer, already, disapproved of the fact that Achilles, in his grief and fury at the death of Patrocles, had not only sheep, cattle and horses but also twelve young Trojan nobles killed and burned on the funeral pyre of his friend as a sacrifice to his ghost. But again, the poet did not sit in judgment and condemn his hero from the high throne of his own moral righteousness and superiority because he had committed the barbarous atrocity of "human sacrifice". The poet's criticism of Achilles did not have the emotional colour of moral indignation. It did not cast doubt on what we call the "character" of his hero, on his value as a human being. People do "bad things"—"kaka erga"—in their grief and fury. The bard shakes his head but he does not appeal to the conscience of his listeners; he does not ask them to regard Achilles as a moral reprobate, a "bad character". He appeals to their compassion, to their understanding of the passion which seizes even the best, even the heroes, in times of stress and which makes them do "bad things". But his human value as a nobleman and a warrior is not in doubt. "Human sacrifice" did not have for the ancient Greeks quite the same odour as something horrible that it has for the more "civilised" nations of the twentieth century.[23] Every schoolboy of the Greek educated classes knew of the wrath of Achilles, of the sacrifices and the game-contests at the funeral of Patrocles. The Olympic game-contests stood in a direct line of succession from these ancestral funeral contests. It was a very different line of descent from that of contemporary sport-contests.

VII

Nor, as far as one can see, was the normal level of passion and violence of the Homeric heroes and gods or, expressed differently, their normal developmental level of built-in self-control, or "conscience", more than a few steps behind that reached in Athens during the classical period. The surviving stones, the temples and the sculptures of Greek gods and heroes have all contributed to the image of the ancient Greeks as a peculiarly even-tempered, balanced and harmonious people. The term "classical" itself, in phrases such as "classical antiquity", conjures up the picture of Greek society as a model of balanced beauty and equipoise which later generations can never again hope to emulate. This is a misconception.

One cannot set out here with the precision it deserves, the place of classical Greece in the development of "conscience", of internalised controls with regard either to violence or to other spheres of life. It must suffice to say that even classical Greece still represents the "dawn of conscience", a stage where the transformation of a self-controlling conscience represented by communal images of external superhuman persons, of commanding or threatening demon-gods who told human beings more or less arbitrarily what to do and what not to do—into a relatively impersonal and individualised inner-voice speaking in accordance with general social principles of justice and injustice, right and wrong, was still rather the exception than the norm. Socrates' "daimonion" was perhaps the closest approximation to our type of conscience-formation in classical Greek society but even this highly individualised "inner-voice" still had in some measure the character of a tutelary genius. Moreover, the degree of internalisation and individualisation of norms and social controls which we encounter in Plato's representation of Socrates was, in his time, without doubt a very exceptional phenomenon. It is highly significant that the classical Greek language lacked a differentiated and specialised word for "conscience". There are a number of words such as "synesis", "euthymion", "eusebia" and others which are occasionally translated as "conscience" but, on closer inspection, one soon becomes aware that each of them is less specific and covers a much broader spectrum such as "having scruples", "piety", and "reverence towards god". But a single concept as highly specialised as the modern concept of "conscience" denoting a highly authoritative, inescapable and often tyrannical inner-agency which, as part of his self, guides an individual's conduct, which demands obedience and punishes disobedience with "pangs" or "bites" of guilt-feelings, and which—unlike "fear of the gods" or "shame"—acts on its own, seemingly coming from nowhere, seemingly without deriving power and authority from any external agency, human or super-human—this concept of conscience is absent from the intellectual equipment of ancient Greece. The fact that this concept of "conscience" had not yet developed in Greek society can be regarded as a very reliable index of the fact that conscience-formation in that society had not yet reached a stage of internalisation, individualisation and relative autonomy in any degree comparable to our own.

If one wants to understand the higher level of violence embodied in Greek game-contests and the lower level of revulsion against violence in Greek society generally, this is one of the clues that one needs. It is symptomatic of the fact that, within the social framework of a Greek city-state, individuals were still to a much higher extent dependent on others, on external agencies and sanctions as a means of curbing their passions, that they could rely less on their own internalised barriers for controlling violent impulses, than people in contemporary industrial societies. One must add that they, or at least their elites, were already much more capable of restraining themselves individually than their forefathers in the pre-classical age had been. The changing images of Greek gods, the critique of their arbitrariness and ferocity, bear witness to this change. If one bears in mind the specific stage in a civilising process represented by Greek society in the days of self-ruling city-states, it is easier to understand that—compared with ours—the very high passionateness of the ancient Greeks in action was perfectly compatible with the bodily balance and equipoise, the aristocratic grace and pride in movement reflected in Greek sculpture.

As a last step, it may be useful to point briefly to one other link in the chain of interdependencies which connect the level of violence embodied in the Greek type of game-contests and of warfare with other structural characteristics of Greek society. It is quite significant for the stage which state organisation had reached in the period of the Greek city-states that the protection of the life of a citizen against attacks by others was not yet treated in the same way as it is treated today, as a monopoly concern of the state. Even in Athens, it was not yet treated in this manner. If a person was killed or maimed by a fellow citizen it was, even in classical times, still a matter for his kinsmen to avenge and settle the account. By comparison with our own time, the kin-group still played a much larger part in protecting an individual against violence. This meant at the same time, that every able-bodied male person had to be prepared for the defence of his kinsmen or, if it came to that, for an attack in order to help or to avenge his kinsmen. Even within a city-state, the general level of physical violence and insecurity was comparatively high. This, too, helps to account for the fact that the level of revulsion against inflicting pain and injuries on others, or of witnessing such acts was lower, and that feelings of guilt about acts of violence were less deeply bred into the individual. In a society so organised, they would have been a severe handicap.

A few sayings of a great Greek philosopher, of Democritus, may perhaps help to give a little more depth to the understanding of these differences. They are symptomatic of the common social experience of people in that situation. They show that—and they indicate why—"right" and "wrong" cannot mean quite the same thing in a society where every individual may have to stand up for himself and for his kinsmen in defence of his life as they do in a society such as ours. It is right according to the rules of custom, said Democritus, to kill any living thing which has done an injury; not to kill it is wrong. The philosopher expressed these views wholly in human and social terms. There is no appeal to the gods; nor to righteousness and holiness as can be found later in Socrates' dialogue with Protagoras if one can trust Plato. Nor, as one can see, is there any appeal for protection to law courts, to state institutions, to governments. Men were then far more on their own with regard to sheer physical survival than we are. This is what Democritus said:

68 (B257)

As to animals in given cases
of killing and not killing the rule is as follows:
if an animal does wrong
or desires to do wrong
and if a man kill it
he shall be counted exempt from penalties.
To perform this promotes well-being
rather than the reverse.

3 (B258)

If a thing does injury contrary to right
it is needful to kill it.
This covers all cases.
If a man do so
he shall increase the portion in which he partakes of right and security
in any (social) order.

5 (B256)

Right is to perform what is needful
and wrong is to fail to perform what is needful
and to decline to do so.

6 (B261)

If men have wrong done to them
there is need to avenge them so far as is feasible.
This should not be passed over.
This kind of thing is right and also good
and the other kind of thing is wrong and also bad.[24]

NOTES

1 This essay is based on the introduction to a larger, as yet unpublished enquiry, "An Essay on Sport and Violence". I am very grateful to Eric Dunning who read the first draft and made many helpful suggestions for improvements. The theoretical framework embodied in the essay

is closely connected with and in part represents an enlargement of the theory of civilising processes set out in my *Ueber den Prozess der Zivilisation,* 1st Edn., Basle, 1939; 2nd Edn., Basle and Munich, 1969.

2 It is not possible here to enquire in greater detail into the problem of why, in contrast to the almost world-wide diffusion and adoption of the "soccer" type of English football, the diffusion and adoption of the "rugger" type was far more limited in scope. But it may be worth mentioning that the exploration of problems such as this can provide a good deal of evidence and can serve as a test case for specific aspects of a sociological theory of sport.

3 Agnes Bain Stiven, *Englands Einfluss auf den deutschen Wortschatz,* Marburg, 1936, p. 72.

4 Prince Puechlser—Muskau, *Briefe eines Verstorbenen,* 9 October, 1810.

5 J. G. Kohl, quoted in F. Kluge, *Ethymologisches Wörterbuch,* 17th Edn., 1957, article on sport.

6 It is likely that this match was played according to "rugger"—or "rugby"—rather than "soccer" rules.

7 Norbert Elias, *op. cit.*

8 See "American Sports: Play and Dis-Play" and "Wrestling: The Great American Passion Play" by Gregory P. Stone, reprinted respectively in Parts I and III of this Reader, for a stimulating and highly original discussion of modern professional wrestling as a type of farce.

9 H. Foerster, *Die Sieger in den Olympischen Spielen,* Zwickau, 1891.

10 Franz Mezoe, *Geschichte der Olympischen Spiele,* Munich 1930, pp. 100–1: quoted in Ludwig Dress, *Olympia: Gods, Artists and Athletes,* London, 1968, p. 83.

11 Philostratos, *On Gymnastics (Peri Gymnastike),* first half of the third century A.D., Chapter II.

12 Philostratos mentions that thongs made from pigs' hide were forbidden because one believed that the injuries inflicted by them were too severe. Also that one should not punch with the thumb. It is perhaps worth mentioning these details. One should not think that the customary rules of game-contests in antiquity showed no regard at all for the participants. But rules such as these were simply handed on by oral tradition and thus still left a very wide scope for serious injuries.

13 See Norbert Elias, "Studies in the Genesis of the Naval Profession", *British Journal of Sociology,* Vol. 1, No. 4, December, 1950.

14 Philostratos, *op. cit.,* Chapter 11.

15 *Ibid.,* Chapter 43.

16 Ludwig Dress, *op. cit.,* p. 82.

17 Dress, *loc. cit.*

18 *Ibid.,* p. 81.

19 For an explanation of this term and for a discussion of problems of objectivity in sociology see Norbert Elias, "Problems of Involvement and Detachment", *British Journal of Sociology,* Vol. 7, September, 1956.

20 One does not need to discuss here the reasons for the wave of secularisation which shows itself, among other things, in the transition from the more solemn, more awe-inspiring, and perhaps more expressive representations of gods and heroes in the archaic period—an example is the Medusa from the pediment of the temple of Artemis at Coreyra, sixth century B.C.—to the idealising realism of the classical period where gods and heroes are represented as well-proportioned warriors, young or old, whose bodies speak, though their faces are perhaps a little empty even if,

as in the case of the Delphi charioteer, the inlaid eyes and part of the colour have been preserved.

21 The extent to which the characteristics of an earlier stage in the development of state organisation, especially in the monopolisation and control of physical violence, affects all human relationships, shows itself, among other things, in the frequency with which Greek legends refer to conflicts between father and son. So far, as Greek society is concerned, Freud was probably misled in his interpretation of the Oedipus legend or, at least, he saw only one side of the picture, that of a single individual, the son. In the context of Greek society, one cannot help but notice the specific social configuration reflected in this, as in other, related Greek legends. One cannot help questioning the relationship between the son and the father, the young king and the old king, from the father's side as well as from the son's side. From the son's side it may well be, as Freud said, tinged with jealousy over the father's possession of the wife—and, one may add, with fear of the father's physical strength and power. Seen, however, from the father's side, as reflected in Greek legends, the old king's fear and jealousy of the son plays an equal part in the relationship between the two. For inevitably, the father will grow older and physically weaker, the son, weak as a little child, will grow physically stronger and more vigorous. In ancient times, when the well-being of a whole community, of a clan or a house, was not only factually but—in the imagination of the members of such groups—magically bound up with the health and vigour of the king or the leader, the older man was often ritually killed when he grew older, when his strength and vigour departed, and replaced by one of his sons, the young king. Numerous Greek legends show that the young son, the future heir, had to be hidden from the wrath and persecution of his father while he was still young and that he usually had to be educated by strangers. Thus, "we know", according to a recent study (Edna M. Hooker, *The Goddess of the Golden Image, in Parthenos and Parthenon, Greece and Rome*, supplement to Vol. X, Oxford, 1963, p. 18) "that royal children in primitive agarian communities were in constant danger as a potential threat to the king's tenure of his throne or sometimes to a stepmother's ambition for her own sons. Few princes in Greek myth and legend were brought up at home. Some were sent to the Centaur, Cheiron; but most were exposed with tokens of their origin to be reared by strangers. King Lajos exposed his son Oedipus fearing that he would be killed by him. Zeus was reared by nurses and brought up in secrecy because his father, Kromos, felt that he was a menace and tried to kill him. Zeus himself, like Jahwe, was afraid that man would learn to participate in his magical knowledge and violently punished the younger man, Prometheus, who had dared to steal fire from heaven and to give it to men."

It may well be that the escalation of mutual rivalry and jealousy as one ingredient in the complex relationship between father and son, the peculiar process whose reflection we find in Greek and in many other legends, no longer plays the part in a society where even male relatives no longer endanger one another's lives, where the state has monopolised the right to use physical violence, that it once played in societies where fathers could kill or expose their children. It would require more configurational investigations of fathers and sons, in order to find out to what extent the son's feeling of rivalry and jealousy of the father, as discovered in his patients by Freud, is at the same time a reaction to the father's feeling of rivalry and jealousy of the son. But if one considers Greek legends, above all the Oedipus legend itself, one can hardly doubt the double-sidedness, the reciprocal feelings of rivalry which play a part in the relationship between father and son. The use made of this legend as a theoretical model seems incomplete as long as the part played by the dynamics of this configuration, by the reciprocity of feelings between a son who, from being weaker gets stronger, and a father who, from being strong gets weaker, is more fully investigated. In societies where physical strength and power played a much larger part than they do today in the relationships within as well as outside a family, this configuration must have had very great and by no means only unconscious significance. Seen in this context, the Oedipus legend reads like a legend designed to threaten the sons that they will be punished by the gods if they kill their father. However, the salient point about the legend is probably not, in the first place, the killing of the old king by or in favour of the younger king, but the breaking of the incest taboo, of the prohibiting of the son's intercourse with his mother which, of course, is a much older social prohibition than that against killing the father. In this respect, the Oedipus myth evidently symbolises a relatively late stage in the development of a society in which, at an earlier stage, neither the killing of the young son nor the killing of the old father was a crime. These legends, thus, can help us to understand a type of human relationship which existed at a stage of social development when the organisation which we now call "state" was still in its infancy and when the physical strength of a person, his capacity to ensure his survival through his own fighting power, was a major determinant of all types of human relationships, including that between father and son.

22 Pierre Ducrey, *Le Traitement de Prisonniers de Guerre dans la Grece antique*, Ecole Francaise d'Athenes, Travaux et Memoires Fas XVIII, Paris, 1968, p. 196 ff.

23 Fr. Schwenn, *Die Menschenopfer bei den Griechen und Romern*, Giessen, 1915.

24 I am quoting these fragments in the translation which Eric A. Havelock has published in his book *The Liberal Temper in Greek Politics*, New Haven and London, 1964, pp. 127 and 128.

I think his attempt at conveying to a contemporary English-speaking reader the meaning of these fragments, as far as that is possible, succeeds rather well. He also shows, more clearly perhaps than many other writers, that the stress which Plato and Aristotle laid on the central authority of the state as the primary issue of political problems is often wrongly regarded as characteristic of the ancient Greeks in general, while in fact, this stress is, at most, characteristic of a late and perhaps only the last phase in the development of the independent Greek city states. I cannot quite agree, however, with Professor Havelock's interpretation of the teachings of philosophers such as Democritus as "liberal". Liberalism as a political philosophy presupposes a very highly developed state organisation even though it is aimed at preventing too great an interference of the representatives of the state into the affairs of its individual members. The self-reliance of the individual which Democritus advocates, on the other hand, is characteristic of a stage of development in which an individual and his kin-group cannot yet count on the protection of a reasonably effective and impersonal state organisation. It is not really a "liberal" idea that men have a right and a duty to avenge themselves and to kill their own enemies.

CHAPTER 7

Folk Football in Medieval and Early Modern Britain*

Norbert Elias and Eric Dunning

Reasonably reliable references to a ball-game called "football" can be found in English sources from about the fourteenth century onwards,[1] but identity of the name does not in the least vouchsafe identity of the game itself. All that we know of the way in which it was played points to a very different type of game. The majority of references to football in medieval English sources come either from official prohibitions of the game in the edicts of kings and civic authorities or from reports of court cases against people who had broken the law by playing the game despite these official prohibitions. Nothing can be more revealing about the kind of game played at that time under the name of football than the constant and, by and large, apparently quite unsuccessful attempts of state and local authorities to suppress it. It must have been a wild game, suiting the temper of the people of that age. The comparative helplessness of those among the authorities who made themselves responsible for maintaining the peace of the land is extremely instructive for outlining the difference in the position of state and local authorities *vis-à-vis* ordinary citizens and above all in the effectiveness of the social machinery for the enforcement of laws in a medieval as opposed to a modern state.

One of the earliest prohibitions of the game occurred in London in a proclamation of 1314 issued in the name of King Edward II by the Lord Mayor. It reads as follows:

1314. Proclamation issued for the Preservation of the Peace. . . . Whereas our Lord the King is going towards the parts of Scotland, in his war against his enemies, and has especially commanded us strictly to keep his peace. . . . And whereas there is great uproar in the City, through certain tumult arising from great footballs in the fields of the public, from which many evils perchance may

---

* This article is an extract from Chapter I of a book, *The Making of Football: A Sociological Study* which the authors are currently preparing.

arise—which may God forbid—we do command and do forbid, on the King's behalf, upon pain of imprisonment, that such game shall be practised henceforth within the city. . . .[2]

An order from King Edward III to the Sheriffs of the City of London also illustrates how strongly the authorities disapproved of these unruly pastimes. They were evidently in their eyes a waste of time as well as a threat to peace and they wished to canalise the energies of the people into what they regarded as more useful channels. They wanted the people to train in the use of military weapons instead of indulging in these unruly games. But the people, already at that time, apparently preferred their games to military exercises:

1365. To the Sherriffes of London. Order to cause proclamation to be made that every able bodied man of the said city on feast days when he has leisure shall in his sports use bows and arrows or pellets and bolts . . . forbidding them under pain of imprisonment to meddle in the hurling of stones, loggats and quoits, handball, football . . . or other vain games of no value; as the people of the realme, noble and simple, used heretofore to practise the said art in their sports when by God's help came forth honour to the kingdom and advantage to the King in his actions of war; and now the said art is almost wholly disused and the people engage in the games aforesaid and in other dishonest, unthrifty or idle games, whereby the realme is likely to be without archers.[3]

However wild and riotous their traditional ball-games were, the people liked them. Their tug-of-war with the authorities in the matter of these pastimes continued intermittently for centuries. The reasons given by the authorities for their opposition to these sports vary. The danger to public order and the competition with military training in archery are among the most prominent.

The following selected list may give an idea of the frequency of these edicts. Their recurrence indicates the relative powerlessness of the authorities at that stage in the development of English society to enforce permanently the legal prohibition of what today we might perhaps call a form of "deviant behaviour". By applying this term to breaches of the law in a different age, one can see more clearly that, sociologically speaking, the concept of "deviant behaviour" is quite inadequate. The recurrence of special types of law-breaking implies not so much an accidental or arbitrary failure of individuals, as an inability of a society which is organised as a state to allow individual needs to be canalised in a way which is at the same time socially tolerable and individually satisfactory.

1314	Edward II	London	1471	James II of Scotland	
1331	Edward III	London			Perth
1365	Edward III	London	1474	Edward IV	London
1388	Richard II	London	1477	Edward IV	London
1409	Henry IV	London	1478		London
1410	Henry IV	London	1481	James III of Scotland	
1414	Henry V	London			Perth
1424	James I of Scotland		1488		Leicester
		Perth	1572		London
1450		Halifax	1581		London
1454		Halifax	1608		Manchester
1457	James II of Scotland		1609		Manchester
		Perth	1615		London
1467		Leicester			

Although it appeared as asocial behaviour to the authorities, it remained for centuries a favourite pastime of the people in many parts of the country to amuse themselves with a football, broken bones and bloody noses or not. As one can see, the state apparatus for the enforcement of such edicts was as rudimentary as their ability to find other, equally satisfying leisure outlets for the citizens. Some people were fined or sent to prison for taking part in one of these riotous games. Perhaps here or there the custom lapsed for a time. If so, it continued in other places. The exciting game itself did not die out.

We still have records of many court cases against offenders. Two selections from these records may be enough to show what often happened when the people of these times played with a football although, unfortunately, they do not show in detail the kind of game they played:

(1) *Middlesex County Records for 1576:* That on the said day at Ruyslippe, Co., Midd., Arthur Reynolds, husbandman, (with five others) all of Ruyslippe afsd., Thomas Darcye of Woxbridge, yeoman, (with seven others, four of whom were husbandmen, one a taylor, one a harnis maker, one a yeoman) all seven of Woxbridge afsd., with unknown malefactors to the number of one hundred assembled themselves unlawfully and played a certain unlawful game called football, by means of which unlawful game there was amongst them a great affray, likely to result in homicides and serious accident.

(2) *Middlesex County Records for 1581:* Coroner's inquisition—post mortem taken at Southemyms, Co., Midd., in view of the body of Roger Ludford, yeoman, there lying dead, with the verdict of the jurors that Nicholas Martyn and Richard Turvey both late

of Southemyms, yeomen, were on the third instant between three and four p.m. playing with other persons at footeball in the field called Evanses Feld at Southemyms, when the said Roger Ludford and a certain Simon Maltus, of the said parish, yeoman, came to the ground, and that Roger Ludford cried out, cast him over the hedge, indicating that he meant Nicholas Martyn, who replied, "come thou and do yt". That thereupon Roger Ludford ran towards the ball with the intention to kick it, whereupon Nicholas Martyn with the forepart of his right arm and Richard Turvey with the forepart of his left arm struck Roger Ludford a blow on the fore-part of the body under the breast, giving him a mortal blow and concussion of which he died within a quarter of an hour and that Nicholas and Richard in this manner feloniously slewe the said Roger.[4]

A number of reports show the recurrent tug-of-war between the people who clung to their violent customs and the authorities who tried to suppress or to change them. Thus, a document dated 10 January, 1540 issued by the mayor and corporation of Chester mentions that it was customary in that town on a Shrove Tuesday for the shoemakers to challenge the drapers to a match with a "ball of letter (leather), caulyd a foutbale". The mayor and corporation pronounced in the strongest terms against these "evill disposed persons" who caused such "grete inconvenience" in the city. They tried instead to introduce a footrace, supervised by the mayor, with what success we do not know.[5]

An order prohibiting football promulgated in Manchester in 1608 and repeated almost literally a year later shows very much the same picture. One reads there of the great harm done by a "company of lewd and disordered persons usinge that unlawfulle exercise of playing with the ffotebale in ye streets". The order mentions the large numbers of windows which they broke, how they wronged other inhabitants and committed many "great inormyties".[6]

It is probably useful to add at least one example not connected with football in order to show, in general, the relatively greater ease with which restraints were loosened in medieval England and accordingly, with which people, within their own country or town, behaved violently in relation to each other:

1339. The King having a resolve to go abroad in 1339 granted a commission to the mayor, aldermen and commonalty of London for the conservation of the peace in the city during his absence and invested them with power to cause due and speedy punishment to be done upon any malefactors and disturbers of the peace in the said city.[7] Soon after the King's departure, a contest arose between the Companies of the Skinners and Fishmongers which terminated in a bloody skirmish in the streets. The mayor with his officers hastened to the place of riot and apprehended several of the disturbers of the peace as required by his office and duty; but Thomas Hounsard and John le Brewerer, with some of their accomplices, resisted the power of the magistrates, and not only rescued the malefactors, but Thomas, with a drawn sword, violently assaulted Andrew Aubrey, the mayor, and endeavoured to overthrow him; and in the meanwhile, the said John grievously wounded one of the city officers. They were, after a struggle secured and conveyed without delay to the Guildhall where they were indicted and tried before the mayor and aldermen, having severally pleaded guilty, they were condemned to die and being forthwith conveyed to West Cheape or Cheapside were there beheaded. This sovereignty of the mayor was so well timed for the preservation of peace within the city and for preventing the riots and outrages so frequent in those days ... that it gave great satisfaction to the King, who, by his writ dated 4th June '15 Edward III at the tower, not only pardoned the mayor for beheading the above parties, but also approved and confirmed the same.[8]

The chronicles of medieval England, like those of other medieval societies, describe many scenes such as this. Without reference to the frequency of outbreaks of uninstitutionalised violence in the middle ages one cannot understand the more institutionalised forms of which football was one.[9] Semi-institutionalised fights between local groups arranged on certain days of the year, particularly on Saints' Days and Holy Days, were a normal part of the traditional pattern of life in medieval societies. Playing with a football was one of the ways of arranging such a fight. It was, in fact, one of the normal annual rituals of these traditional societies. To remember this institution helps us to see their manner of life in better perspective. Football and other similar encounters in those times were not simply accidental brawls. They constituted an equilibrating type of leisure activity deeply woven into the warp and woof of society. It may seem incongruous to us that, year after year, people engaged in a kind of fight on Saints' Days and Holy Days. Our forefathers, at a different stage in the civilising process,[10] evidently experienced it as a perfectly obvious and obviously enjoyable arrangement.

People today, preoccupied with the disagreeable sides of life in big towns and with the disadvantages of living in a mass society, occasionally look back nostalgically to the times when most men lived in small communities which resembled in character and social structure what we would call large villages or small market towns. There were, of course, exceptions of which London is perhaps the most outstanding example. But, even in the sociological literature, a notion persists about the way of life in these "traditional" or "folk" societies according to which they were permeated by feelings of great "solidarity". This can easily be interpreted and is, in fact, quite often taken to mean, that tensions and conflicts were less strong and harmony greater within them than is the case with our own societies.[10] The difficulty about the use of such categories is not that they are wrong but that all such general terms as "solidarity" applied to a different kind of society are apt to mislead the reader. Types of institutions and of conduct which appear to be incompatible in contemporary industrial societies are by no means always equally incompatible in the eyes of people accustomed to the life in societies of a different type. Our language, therefore, when applied to other societies reflects our own distinctions which may not be applicable to societies at a different stage of development. Thus, the term "solidarity" evokes in us the impression of permanent unity, of friendliness and the absence of strife. "As they intimately communicate with each other, every member (of a folk society) claims the sympathy of all the others", as a writer on the subject put it.[11] One can, indeed, often observe expressions of strong and spontaneous "fellow feeling" in traditional societies. But such expressions of what we might conceptualise as "strong solidarity" were perfectly compatible with equally strong and spontaneous enmities and hatreds. What was really characteristic, at least of the traditional peasant societies of our own middle ages, was the much greater fluctuation of feeling of which men were then capable and, in connection with this, the relatively greater instability of human relationships in general. In connection with the lesser stability of internalised restraints, the strength of passions, the warmth and the spontaneity of emotional actions were greater in both directions: in the direction of kindness and readiness to help as well as in that of unkindness. callousness and readiness to hurt. That is why terms such as "solidarity", "intimacy", "fellow-feeling", and others like them used to describe attributes of pre-industrial folk-societies are rather inapt. They only show one side of the picture.

Even many institutional traditions were "double-faced" in our sense of that term. They allowed for the expression of intimate unity and solidarity and for the expression of equally intimate and intense hostility, without giving the slightest impression that the participants themselves saw anything contradictory or incompatible in these fluctuations.

Shrove Tuesday football, a ritualised and, according to our notions, fairly savage brawl between neighbouring groups is a striking example of this compatibility between emotionally charged activities which seem to be incompatible according to present standards. As we have seen, the secular authorities tried, fairly early and for a long time without much success, to suppress these riotous fighting games of the people. But one cannot wholly understand the strong survival power of such customs if one sees in them merely games in our sense of the word. Medieval football formed part of a traditional ritual. It belonged to the Shrove Tuesday ceremonial which was to some extent a Church ceremonial and was closely linked to the whole cycle of Saints' Days and Holy Days. In this respect, too, a differentiation which appears almost self-evident to us, the differentiation between religious and secular activities in medieval society, had not reached the same stage as in contemporary societies. One can occasionally read that everything medieval people did was "steeped in religion". The same writer has even gone so far as to say that one can express "the essence of a folk-society by applying to it the term 'sacred society' ".[12] This sort of statement can easily give the impression that everything done in these societies had the character of earnest and highly disciplined solemnity which prevails in Church services today. The truth is that even Church services in the middle ages were often noisier, less disciplined and far less removed from people's daily lives than is the case today. On the other hand, people's daily lives were permeated to a higher extent, for better or for worse, by beliefs in the nearness of God, the Devil, and their various helpers —saints, demons, spirits of all kinds, good or bad—which they hoped to influence by various forms of prayer as well as by white or black magic. With regard to this field, too, the application of abstract terms such as "religious" or "secular" which appear to us as exclusive alternatives, blocks the understanding of a kind of life which does not conform to our standard of institutional and conceptual differentiation into religious and secular activities. If one must express the lesser degree of differentiation in our terms, one can only say that, in the folk societies of the middle ages, secular activities were more religious and religious activities more secular than in contemporary societies.

The same applies to the medieval folk game of football. It reflected potential for greater solidarity as well as for conflict and strife. Frictions between neighbouring communities, local guilds, groups of men and women, young married and younger unmarried men were often endemic. If tempers ran high, they could, of course, lead at any time to outbreaks of open fighting. But in medieval society, in contrast to ours, there were traditional occasions when some of these tensions between groups within a community or between neighbouring village communities could find expression in a form of fighting which was sanctioned by tradition and probably also for a considerable time by the Church and local magistrates. Again and again the old reports show that fighting between representatives of local groups, with or without a football, formed part of an annual ritual. One gets the feeling that the young members of such groups were often spoiling for a fight and, unless the tension exploded beforehand, waited with pleasurable anticipation for the coming of Shrove Tuesday or for any other day in the year which was earmarked for such a public encounter. Throughout this period, the game of football provided one of these outlets for standing tensions between local groups. The fact that such a game formed part of a traditional ritual did not prevent one side or the other from bending the traditions in its own favour if their feelings against the other side ran high enough. In the year 1579, for example, a group of Cambridge students went, as was customary, to the village of Chesterton to play "at foteball". They went there, so we are told, peacefully and without any weapons but the townsmen of Chesterton had secretly hidden a number of sticks in the porch of their church. After the match had started, they picked quarrels with the students, brought out their sticks, broke them over the heads of the students and gave them such a severe beating that they had to run through the river in order to escape. Some of them asked the Constable of Chesterton to keep the "Queene's peace" but he was among those playing against them and, in fact, accused the students of being first to break the peace.[13]

This is a good example of the way in which football was used as an opportunity for paying off old scores. If we speak of traditions, of rules and rituals, these words can easily conjure up the picture of regulative institutions which work in a fairly strict and impersonal manner, for that is the connotation of these words in our own time. But if one uses the same words with reference to medieval societies one must not lose sight of the fact that the regulative institutions to which they refer and among them what we call "traditions", although people clung to them more firmly than we do to ours, were at the same time far more dependent in their actual working on the changeable personal feelings of people and on passions of the moment. This explains on the one hand the extraordinary tenacity with which the people of medieval England played their Shrove Tuesday games year after year in the traditional manner despite all the proclamations of kings and fulminations of local magistrates against them, while they were quite capable at the same time of breaking the traditional conventions when their feelings ran high and of playing a trick or two on their opponents as they did in Chesterton.

A report from Corfe Castle, Dorsetshire, dated 1553, shows in

greater detail some aspects of the type of folk ritual which was embodied in a game of football. The Company of Freeman Marblers
or Quarriers played annually with a football as part of a whole series
of Shrovetide ceremonies. First, the company officers were elected,
then the apprentices were initiated. Each member of the company
who had married in the previous year paid a "marriage shilling"
which gave his wife the right to have apprentices work for her in the
case of his death. However, the man who had married last was
excused from payment of the shilling. Instead, he had to provide a
football. Then, on the next day, Ash Wednesday, the football was
carried to the Lord of the Manor and a pound of pepper was given
to him as a customary payment for an ancient right of way which the
Company claimed. When the gift of pepper had been delivered, a
game of football was played over the ground for which the company
claimed this right.[14] An example such as this, and there are many
others, shows very clearly that the people of this age saw nothing incongruous in the fact that a wild and riotous customary game should
form part of a solemn ritual. Official solemnities and uproarious
celebrations often shaded into each other as a matter of course.

Closely connected with the less impersonal character of all activities and with the higher levels of open emotionality was a peculiar
variability of traditional customs, including games. People were
deeply attached to their traditional ways of life. One reason for this
was because a great many of the tension and conflict situations which
today are formally regulated by a unified code of laws discussed and
executed in relatively impersonal law courts, were then still the subjects of often highly personal decisions in the context of the local
group. But the unwritten customary traditions, although they had
to some extent, similar regulative functions to the written laws of
our time, were by no means as completely immutable as they appear
from a distance today. They could change, either imperceptibly if
the group relations with which they were concerned changed, or
perhaps more radically under the impact of wars, civil strife, epi-
demics and other events which often deeply disturbed the life of
medieval communities. People would then develop new customs.
They soon came to regard them as their traditions, whether or not
they were identical with those which they had possessed before the
disturbances. The greater part of these medieval folk traditions were
handed on from one generation to another by word of mouth. They
were oral traditions. The majority of the people concerned with them
were non-literate. It was not customary to put any of the rules of
games such as football formally in writing. The sons played as the
fathers played or, in the case of disturbances, as they thought their
fathers had played.

As there were neither written rules nor any central organisations to unify the manner of playing, references to football in medieval documents do not imply, as similar references would in the documents of our own time, that the game played with a football in different communities was everywhere the same. How people actually played was dependent on local customs not on common national rules. The organisation of the game was much looser than it is today. The emotional spontaneity of the struggle was much greater; traditions of physical fighting and the few restraints—imposed by custom rather than by highly elaborate formal regulations which require a high degree of training and self-control—determined the manner of playing and made for a certain family likeness among all these games. The differences between games which were differently named were not necessarily as sharply drawn as they are between different sport-games today. It is not unlikely that the reason why medieval documents referred to some of these local games as "football" while others were known by different names was primarily the fact that they were played with different implements. Indeed, references to "football" usually appear quite literally to be references to a particular type of ball and references to a type of game only in so far as a different kind of ball or of playing implements in general might dictate a different manner of playing. Some medieval documents do in fact refer to playing "with a football" and not to "playing football".[15] And, as far as one can see, the ball which was called a "football" had this in common with that used in football games today: it was an inflated bladder sometimes, but not always, encased in leather. Peasant communities the world over have used such balls as a device for their amusement. Records of their use certainly exist for most parts of medieval Europe. If it has the right size and resilience, and is neither too small nor too large, such an inflated animal bladder, whether encased in leather or not, probably lends itself better than a small solid ball to kicking with the feet. But there is no reason to assume that the medieval "football" was only propelled by foot or, conversely, that the medieval "handball" was only propelled by hand. Again, the primary reason for such differences in the names of these games may simply refer to the fact that they were played with balls which were different in size and shape or that they were played with sticks or with other implements of a similar kind. But the elementary characteristics, the character of the game as a struggle between different groups, the open and spontaneous battle-enjoyment, the riotousness and the relatively high level of socially tolerated physical violence, as far as one can see, were always the same. And so was the tendency to break whatever customary rules there were, if the passions moved the players. Thus, since the family likeness of all these games in some of their aspects was very great, one can gain a vivid impression of the manner in which people played with a football, of which we have no really detailed report, from the few more extensive reports that have come down to us from this period even though they were not actually played with a football but with other implements.

One of these more extensive reports which is well worth reading is that of a Cornish game which had the still familiar name of "hurling". It shows very vividly how much less strict, how much more personal and informal the handling of traditional customs and rules was in medieval societies than the handling of rules and even of customs and traditions is in our own time.

The report speaks for itself. No paraphrase can emulate the impression of the game and of its atmosphere which it conveys:

Hurling

Hurling taketh his denomination from throwing of the ball, and is of two sorts, in the East parts of *Cornwall*, to goales, and in the West, to the countrey.

Hurling to goales.

For hurling to goales, there are 15, 20 or 30 players more or lesse, chosen out on each side, who strip themselves into their slightest apparell, and then joyne hands in ranks one against another. Out of these ranks they match themselves by payres, one embracing another, and so passe away: every of which couple, are specially to watch one another during the play.

After this, they pitch two bushes in the ground, some eight or ten foote asunder; and directly against them, ten or twelve score off, other twayne in like distance, which they terme their Goales. One of these is appoynted by lots, to the one side, and the other to his adverse party. There is assigned for their gard, a couple of their best stopping Hurlers; the residue draw into the midst betweene both goales, where some indifferent person throweth up a ball, the which whosoever can catch, and cary through his adversaries goale, hath wonne the game. But therein consisteth one of *Hercules* his labours: for he that is once possessed of the ball hath his contrary mate waiting at inches, and assaying to lay hold upon him. The other thrusteth him in the breast, with his closed fist, to keepe him off; which they call Butting, and place in weldoing the same, no small poynt of manhood.

If hee escape the first, another taketh him in hand, and so a third, neyther is hee left, untill having met (as the Frenchman sayes) *Chaussera son pied*, hee eyther touch the ground with some part of his bodie, in wrastling, or cry, Hold; which is the word of

yielding. Then must he cast the ball (named Dealing) to some one
of his fellowes, who catching the same in his hand, maketh away
withall as before; and if his hap or agility bee so good, as to shake
off or outrunne his counter-wayters, at the goale, hee findeth one
or two fresh men, readie to receive and keepe him off. It is therefore a very disadvantageable match, or extraordinary accident,
that looseth many goales; howbeit, that side carryeth away best
reputation, which giveth most falles in the hurling, keepeth the
ball longest, and presseth his contrary nearest to their owne goale.
Sometimes one chosen person on eche party dealeth the ball.

The Hurlers are bound to the observation of many lawes, as,
that they must hurle man to man, and not two set upon one man
at once: that the Hurler against the ball, must not *but*, nor hand-
fast under the girdle: that hee who hath the ball, must *but* onely
in the others brest: that he must deale no Fore-ball, *viz.* he may
not throw it to any of his mates, standing neerer the goale, than
himselfe. Lastly, in dealing the ball, if any of the other part can
catch it flying, between, or e're the other have it fast, he thereby
winneth the same to his side, which straightway of defendant becommeth assailant, as the other, of assailant falls to be defendant.
The least breach of these lawes, the Hurlers take for a just cause
of going together by the eares, but with their fists onely; neither
doth any among them seek revenge for such wrongs or hurts, but
at the like play againe. These hurling matches are mostly used at
weddings, where commonly the ghests undertake to encounter all
commers.

Hurlinge to the countrie.

The hurlinge to the Countrey, is more diffuse and confuse, as
bound to few of these orders: Some two or more Gentlemen doe
commonly make this match, appointing that on such a holyday,
they will bring to such an indifferent place, two, three, or more
parishes of the East or South quarter, to hurle against so many
other, of the West or North. Their goales are either those Gentle-
mens houses, or some townes or villages, three or four miles
asunder, of which either side maketh choice after the neernesse to
their dwellings. When they meet, there is neyther comparing of
numbers, nor matching of men: but a silver ball is cast up, and
that company, which can catch, and cary it by force, or sleight, to
their place assigned, gaineth the ball and victory. Whosoever get-
teth seizure of this ball, findeth himselfe generally pursued by the
adverse party; neither will they leave, till (without all respects) he
be layd flat on Gods deare earth: which fall once received, dis-
ableth him from any longer detayning the ball: hee therefore

throweth the same (with like hazard of intercepting, as in the other hurling) to some one of his fellowes, fardest before him, who maketh away withall in like maner. Such as see where the ball is played, give notice thereof to their mates, crying, Ware East, Ware West, etc. as the same is carried.

The Hurlers take their next way over hilles, dales, hedges, ditches; yea, and thorow bushes, briers, mires, plashes and rivers whatsoever; so as you shall sometimes see 20, or 30 lie tugging together in the water, scrambling and scratching for the ball. A play (verily) both rude and rough, and yet such, as is not destitute of policies, in some sort resembling the feats of warre: for you shall have companies layd out before, on the one side, to encounter them that come with the ball, and of the other party to succor them, in the maner of a foreward. Againe, other troups lye hovering on the sides, like wings, to helpe or stop their escape: and where the ball it selfe goeth, it resembleth the joyning of the two mayne battels: the slowest footed who come lagge, supply the showe of a rere-ward: yea, there are horsemen placed also on either party (as it were in ambush) and ready to ride away with the ball, if they can catch it at advantage. But they must not so steale the palme: for gallop any one of them never so fast, yet he shall be surely met at some hedge corner, crosse-lane, bridge, or deep water, which (by casting the Countrie) they know he must needs touch at: and if his good fortune gard him not the better, hee is like to pay the price of his theft, with his owne and his horses over-throwe to the ground. Sometimes, the whole company runneth with the ball, seven or eight miles out of the direct way, which they should keepe. Sometimes a foote-man getting it by stealth, the better to scape unespied, will carry the same quite backwards, and so, at last, get to the goale by a windlace: which once knowne to be wonne, all that side flocke thither with great jolity: and if the same bee a Gentlemans house, they give him the ball for a *Trophee*, and the drinking out of his Beere to boote.

The ball in this play may bee compared to an infernall spirit: for whosoever catcheth it, fareth straightwayes like a madde man, strugling and fighting with those that goe about to holde him: and no sooner is the ball gone from him, but he resigneth this fury to the next receyver, and himselfe becommeth peaceable as before. I cannot well resolve, whether I should more commend this game, for the manhood and exercise, or condemne it for the boyster-ousnes and harmes which it begetteth: for as on the one side it makes their bodies strong, hard, and nimble, and puts a courage into their hearts, to meete an enemie in the face: so on the other

part, it is accompanied with many dangers, some of which do ever
fall to the players share. For proofe whereof, when the hurling is
ended, you shall see them retyring home, as from a pitched battaile,
with bloody pates, bones broken, and out of joynt, and such bruses
as serve to shorten their daies; yet al is good play, and never
Attourney nor Crowner troubled for the matter.[16]

Such a description, as one can see, is of very great help if one
wants to form a reasonably clear idea of the distinguishing characteristics—of the different "structure"—of games in an earlier, in the
late medieval and early modern stages in the development of English
society. It also helps to illuminate differences in the wider structure
of English society at that stage in its development. In some respects,
a folk-game tradition as it has been described here must have been
affected by one very influential characteristic of British society,
though it is not possible to know exactly in what ways. Only comparative studies of other societies and the structure of their games
could reassure us in this respect. The folk-game as we see it here reflects a very specific relationship between landowners and peasantry.
As one can see, the landowners themselves made it their business to
organise, to act as patrons of folk-games of this kind. The game as
we see it here, brutal and disorderly as it may appear to us, is not
simply a game played between villagers and townsmen without any
reference at all to people of higher authority who could check what,
according to the standards of that time, might have appeared as
excessive violence. It is, as one knows, characteristic of the pattern
of social development on these islands, that on the one hand, a rural
population which consisted of peasants living in varying degrees
of serfdom transformed themselves into a rural population of more
or less free peasants; and that on the other hand, side by side with
a class of landowning noblemen, there emerged a class of landowners
who were untitled, a class who were only "gentlemen". This, as
far as one can make out, is the setting of the game as we see it here:
a local amusement for a population of more or less free peasants
promoted by local landowners who often, though perhaps not always,
were non-nobles. If some bones were broken in the course of the
game, if perhaps occasionally someone died as a result of injuries
received in the game, if in short the whole affair infringed the king's
laws and was frowned on by the king's representatives, the local
people, peasantry and gentry together, enjoyed it and were, as one
can see, quite prepared to snap their fingers at them. One can still
hear the sly undertones in the voice of Carew when he spoke of
pitched battles, bloody pates and bones broken—yet, "... never
Attourney nor Crowner troubled for the matter". This was a local

tradition. Both peasantry and gentry meant to keep it up and to enjoy it.

Its violence was by no means unmitigated and completely lawless, however. There were in fact already, as we learn from this account, customary "laws" or more strictly speaking, rules. A rudimentary sense of what became known as "fairness" was already there and it is most likely that this peculiar social setting, relatively free peasants and middle class landowners, had something to do with it. If there was a fight between the man with the ball and his opponents, the "laws" stipulated that only one should attack him at a time, not two. Another rule decreed that players should not hit each other below the belt: the chest was the only legitimate target. However, there was no formal organisation outside and apart from the players themselves to ensure that the rules were obeyed. There was no referee, no outside arbiter in the case of disputes. In some respects, this manner of playing a game shows us an aspect of the social life of early communities which is otherwise difficult to grasp. As we have seen already, it is often said of them that they were more closely integrated or had a special kind of solidarity feeling compared with ours. However, these peasant communities had their conflicts, either within their own ranks or with neighbouring communities. The manner of settling them was considerably more violent as a rule than became the case at a later stage. And football and other folk-games, as we have seen, were one way of releasing the tension. But the fact that there were no written rules or central authorities and no referees to supervise the players or to arbitrate did not mean that they played without any rules at all. Traditional rules, customary regulations, as one can see, which had developed over the centuries as a kind of communal self-restraint took the place of our more elaborate and often more carefully thought-out institutional rules and it may well be that people in these earlier societies clung to their traditions and among them to the few customary restraints of tensions and conflicts as tenaciously as we know they did, precisely because to lose them would often have meant to lose a very essential part of such restraints against their own passions as were available to them. But if these customary restraints were broken they had no one but themselves to keep the offenders in check. What one encounters here is a very early type of democracy—a kind of village democracy. The manner of punishing offenders against the "laws" of the game as Carew describes it, is a small-scale paradigm of this self-regulating peasant democracy, with relatively little supervision by outside officials. One has the impression that by our standards this way of preventing people from breaking the customary rules was perhaps not very efficient. A breach of the rules, as Carew describes it, was often enough just another occasion for a fairly violent fight—probably with few holds barred.

One can also see fairly clearly from Carew's description that the traditions of what are today two different and, apparently, quite unrelated types of sports still formed an undifferentiated game-pattern in some of these ancestral folk-games. Hurling, in fact, contained elements of a ball-game on the one hand, and of unarmed mock- or display-combat on the other. In such a folk-game it was quite evidently accepted by all participants and spectators as a normal element of the game and as part of the fun that people engaged in some kind of physical fighting with each other. However, even hand-to-hand fighting in societies of the "medieval" type followed some sort of regulating tradition which provided both a mutual attunement of the movements of the combatants and some limitation on the injuries they inflicted on each other. In Cornwall at the time of this hurling game, one type of mock and display fighting, called wrestling, still formed one of the standing amusements of village life. The ordinary Cornish wrestlers proclaimed each other locally the best and most famous in the country. It is not surprising to see, therefore, that wrestling techniques played a part in the ball-game of hurling. One of the factors taken into account in determining the winner of a game, as Carew describes it, was the number of "falles" inflicted on the other side; and "to give a falle", to put an opponent on his back and make him touch the ground with a shoulder on one side and with a heel on the other was in fact one of the main aims in hurling. Skill and success in this respect enhanced the reputation of a village team. One can imagine how the teams and the communities which they represented must have afterwards discussed who got the better of the other in this respect and that they sometimes had an extra row about it.

Even in "hurling to goales", however, the more regulated of the two types of hurling described by Carew, the criteria for winning were not as clearly defined and as calculable as the winning of sport-games is in our own time, for the latter is usually connected with some unequivocal measurement such as the "goal", the "point" or the "run". The determination of the winner in a folk-game such as hurling, as one can see from Carew's description, was far less precise and sharply regulated and, in a way, this is symptomatic of the distinguishing character of these traditional folk-games with modern sport-games generally. Even at the turn of the sixteenth century, European societies were not yet "measuring" societies. What is most important to note, however, is that, while compared with our sport-games, the hurling game, including its wrestling component, was far less highly regulated, it was certainly not completely anarchic. Our conceptual vocabulary is not yet developed enough, our perception not yet trained enough to enable us to distinguish clearly and precisely between different degrees and types of regulation. It is clear that a series of detailed comparative studies both with other folk-games in our own society and with the folk-games of different societies at a comparable stage of social development would perform a useful service in this respect.

NOTES

1 Many historians of football treat earlier references to the game as equally reliable. We think that this confidence is not wholly justified and have given some of our reasons for this scepticism in an earlier part of this chapter.

2 H. T. Riley (ed.), *Munimenta Gildhallae Londoniensis*, Rolls. Ser., No. 12, London 1859–62, Vol. III, Appendix ii, extracts from the *Liber Memorandum*, pp. 439–41, Latin and Anglo-French text, with English translation of the Anglo-French.

3 Cal. of Close Rolls, Ed. III (1910), pp. 181–2.

4 J. C. Jeafferson (ed.), *Middlesex County Records*, London 1886–7, p. 97.

5 See a contemporary account published in D. Lysens, *Magna Britannia*, London, 1810; it is also quoted in T. F. T. Dyer, *British Popular Customs*, London, 1900, pp. 70–72.

6 J. F. Earwaker (ed.), *The Court Leet Records of the Manor of Manchester*, London, 1887, p. 248.

7 "The mayor was at the time Andrew Aubrey of the Pepperer's Company, a very wealthy man".
The Chronicles of London, Collectanea Adamantea X, Edinburgh, 1885, from 44, Henry III to 17, Edward III, p. 27.

8 *Ibid.*, p. 27.

9 There is every reason to believe that relatively uninstitutionalised forms of football existed side by side with the more ritualised forms in medieval England. In this context, the important thing to grasp is the relatively high level of violence in the latter.

10 See, e.g. Robert Redfield who has written, "Thus we may characterise the folk society as small, isolated, nonliterate and homogeneous, with a strong sense of group solidarity"; "The Folk Society", *American Journal of Sociology*, No. 52, 1947, pp. 292–308.

11 Redfield, *loc. cit.*

12 Redfield, *loc. cit.*

13 C. H. Cooper, *Annals of Cambridge*, Cambridge, 1843, p. 71.

14 O. W. Farrer, *The Marblers of Purbeck*, papers read before the Purbeck Society (1859–60), pp. 192–7.

15 e.g. the Manchester decrees promulgated in 1608 and 1609. See p. 119.

16 Richard Carew, *A Survey of Cornwall*, London, 1602, pp. 73–5.

CHAPTER 8

The Development of Modern Football*

Eric Dunning

The subject of this essay is the development of modern football. Four early stages can be distinguished in this process of development. Each of them was characterised by more orderly and elaborate behaviour and by more complex, more formal organisation than its predecessors. The transition between the first and second stages and that between the third and fourth also involved changes in the social context of the game which proved significant for its further development.

The first of these stages lasted from at least the fourteenth until well into the nineteenth century when football was a relatively simple, wild and unruly folk game played according to unwritten, customary rules. Considerable local variation existed within the overall pattern of the game at this stage. It will not be treated here since it was discussed at length in the preceding essay.

The approximate duration of the second stage was from 1750 to 1840, when the game in its rough, relatively simple folk-forms was taken up by the public schools, elaborated in certain respects and adapted to their characteristic forms of social organisation, particularly to their systems of authority.

The third stage lasted from about 1840 to about 1860 when the game in the public schools began to be subjected to more formal organisation, when the rules were written down for the first time and when the players were required to exercise a higher degree of self-control in their play than had previously been demanded of them.

The fourth stage occurred when football in its public school forms was diffused into society at large and when organisations began to be set up in order to promote its further development and to organise and regulate it on a national level. In the course of this stage, the game began to develop a mass spectator following for the first time and the possibility emerged of men working as full-time pro-

---

* It is proposed to include the material presented in this essay in a forthcoming book by the author and Norbert Elias. Its prospective title is *The Making of Football: A Sociological Study.*

fessional players. This was the last pre-modern stage in the development of the game. It lasted from about 1850 to about 1890.

These four stages were relatively distinct as far as the ways of playing characteristic of each of them were concerned but, like stages in the development of society at large, they overlapped in a temporal sense. There were no clear-cut dividing lines between them at specific dates; that form of the game which was dominant at one stage did not disappear immediately or entirely as soon as newer forms emerged: it ceased merely to be the dominant form. Thus, the folk forms of football played before the nineteenth century did not disappear when, in the course of the nineteenth century, newer forms emerged in the public schools. Nor did the game as played in the second and third stages disappear when rules on the national level were successfully instituted. Indeed, modified versions of most of these forms continue to be played in certain areas and among certain social groups right up to the present day. Traditional football is still played at Ashbourne in Derbyshire and at Kirkwall in the Orkneys; "hurling" is still played in certain parts of Cornwall and the Eton "wall" and "field" games are good examples of "survivals" of the forms played in the second and third stages. These two latter stages represent crucial transitional phases in the development of the game. Attention in this essay, therefore, will be focused mainly on them. Stage one has already been discussed in the previous essay, and stage four can only be treated here in cursory fashion. To accord it the space which its importance really merits would require at least another essay. Discussion of it is included solely in order to indicate some of the direct links between football in the public schools and the modern type of game.

From the second half of the eighteenth century onwards, traditional forms of football began gradually to decline. More or less directly, increasing industrialisation and urbanisation were the major causes. At the same time, newer models of the game, more appropriate to an urbanising, industrialising society were beginning to emerge in the public schools.[1] The public schools in question were the following seven: Charterhouse, Eton, Harrow, Rugby, Shrewsbury, Westminster and Winchester, the only seven schools generally recognised as "public schools" throughout the period under consideration. In many respects, the games played by students at these schools during the eighteenth and early nineteenth centuries did not differ greatly from traditional forms. The rules were still oral, local differences continued to prevail, and football retained the wild and unruly character of former times. Nevertheless, in the structural context of the public schools, the game began to develop in ways which were significant for the future. It was played, for example, for the first time on a regular weekly or bi-weekly basis with its own specific "season" which lasted through the autumn and spring terms. At the public schools, also for the first time, it was played regularly by members of the upper and middle classes though not as yet by adult members of them. This, in time, was to prove of considerable importance. The boys at the public schools came mainly from aristocratic, gentry and professional backgrounds. The former association of football with lower status groups was a stigma which led them to elaborate and refine what had previously been a relatively crude and simple game. There was in England at that time a much more distinct "status hierarchy" of sports than that which exists at present. Football stood at the bottom of this hierarchy. Thus, an Old Etonian wrote in 1831, "I cannot consider the game of football at all gentlemanly. It is a game which the common people of Yorkshire are particularly partial to . . ."[2] As is often the case with social developments, a process of diffusion—in this case between groups in the same society—played an important part in the early development of football.

The feature that most strongly differentiated the public school football of this stage from traditional forms in society at large was connected with the specific social structure of the schools. In each case, the game was closely bound up with the "prefect-fagging" system, a nearly all-encompassing system of power relations among the boys which, since these were boarding schools, covered the whole of life outside the classroom. The development of football in the second half of the eighteenth and the first half of the nineteenth century can only be understood in connection with the development of the prefect-fagging system. As the structure of this system changed, so did the pattern of the game.

The public schools were initially founded in order to provide free education for boys from the poorer classes.[3] During the eighteenth century, however, they began to draw their membership increasingly from the ranks of the landed gentry, the aristocracy and associated professional groups. By 1780, they had become essentially upper-class institutions with the poor virtually excluded. As a result, the existing system of authority broke down[4] largely because the boys resented being given orders by those who came from lower social strata than themselves. Control of the schools, especially outside but even inside the classroom to some extent, passed into the hands of the oldest and most powerful boys. Frequently, when masters tried to assert their authority and establish order, overt conflict and even rebellion ensued. Each of the seven public schools considered here experienced rebellion during the latter part of the eighteenth and early part of the nineteenth centuries. At Winchester, no less than six are recorded for the period between 1770 and 1818. The revolt at that school in 1818 reached such serious proportions that it could only be quelled by the militia using bayonets. At Rugby in 1797, when the boys burned books and smashed windows, the army was called in and the riot act was read. Rebellions such as these were endemic in the public schools. They were symptomatic of the deep-seated conflict between masters and boys.

The limited power of the school authorities in the late eighteenth and early nineteenth century public schools was not without effect on relations among the boys themselves. The strongest held sway and, as one might expect of boys of that age untrammelled by adult control, they often exercised their power cruelly and without mercy. Bullying and cruel practical jokes were the order of the day. The older boys forced their juniors to perform all sorts of menial services for them. Their way of playing football corresponded to these power relations It was one of the means whereby prefects asserted their dominance over younger boys. They made football compulsory for all. The prefects could call on the younger boys to play at any time and one of the duties of a "fag" was to "fag out" at football. The fags, sometimes as many as two hundred on a side, were forced to "keep goal" for their seniors. They were ranged along the base line where they were expected to prevent the ball from being driven across. This defensive role was compulsory for them and inherent in their status as fags. The prefects retained for themselves the prerogative of attack Thus, at Rugby in the early part of the nineteenth century:

> All fags were stopped on going out after three o'clock calling over ... and compelled to go into the Close ... (Then) two of the best players in the school commenced choosing in about a score on each side. A somewhat rude division was made of the remaining fags, half of whom were sent to keep goal on the one side, the other half to the opposite goal for the same purpose.[5]

A similar system operated at the other schools. At Westminster, for example:

> All boys were compelled to take part and were divided roughly into two sides. The small boys, the duffers and the funksticks were the goalkeepers, but by skilful and heroic action might qualify for a more active role.[6]

It was by no means uncharacteristic of this stage that the name given to football at Shrewsbury, "douling"—derived from the Greek word for "slave"—was the same as they used for "fagging".[7] Of course, a fag who showed exceptional pluck or skill at the game was sometimes allowed to play a more central part, as the example from

Westminster shows. He was probably also accorded higher esteem among the boys in general than his less able fellows. In fact, one can detect here in embryo the beginnings of the system of choosing the leading pupils of a public school—the prefects or praepostors—principally from among the boys who were good at games. It was not until the 1840's and 50's, however, that this system became more or less formally established and operated with the full approval of the majority of masters.

The boys themselves were responsible for running their football at this stage. Masters were hostile or indifferent to the game. According to Samuel Butler, headmaster of Shrewsbury from 1798 to 1836, it was "fit only for butcher boys", "more fit for farm boys and labourers than young gentlemen".[8] Butler attempted to suppress football at Shrewsbury but the boys continued to play in defiance of his ruling. Their ability to do so was deeply rooted in the characteristic structure of the late eighteenth and early nineteenth century public schools.

As far as one can tell, few other masters followed Butler in his attempt to abolish football entirely. But even if they were not hostile, they tended to be indifferent towards the game. In any case, their limited power did not enable them to exercise much influence over the leisure activities of the boys. Left largely to their own devices, the games of the boys tended to be disorderly and not highly regulated. At Charterhouse, for example, they played a rough, unrestrained game called "football in the cloisters". The cloisters in question were seventy yards long by twelve feet wide, paved with smooth flagstones and surrounded by walls lined with sharp, jagged flints. A number of buttresses protruded into the cloisters, providing further hazards for the players and determining some of the characteristics of the game. E. P. Eardley-Wilmot and E. C. Streatfield have vividly described some of its main features:

> ... the ball very soon got into one of the buttresses, when a terrific squash would be the result, some fifty or sixty boys huddled together, vigorously "rouging", kicking and shoving to extricate the ball. A skilful player, feeling that he had the ball in front of his legs, would patiently bide his time until, perceiving an opportunity, he would dexterously work out the ball and rush wildly with it down the cloisters towards the coveted goal. The squash would then dissolve and go in pursuit. Now was the time for the pluck and judgment of the fags to be tried. To prevent the ball getting in amongst them at the goal, one of the foremost of the fags would rush out and engage the onset of the dribbling foe, generally to be sent spinning head over heels for five yards

along the stones. It served a purpose, however, for it not only gave his side time to come up, but also encouragement to his fellow fags to show a close and firm front. If the boy with the ball happened to be backed up by his own house, they would launch themselves right into the middle of the fags, when a terrific scrimmage would ensue. The fags would strive their utmost to prevent the ball being driven through, and hammer away with fists at hands grasping the corners of the wall to obtain a better purchase for shoving. One of these scrimmages sometimes lasted for threequarters of an hour. Shins would be kicked black and blue; jackets and other articles of clothing almost torn to shreds; and fags trampled under foot. At the end, amid shouts of "Through", "Through", nearly the whole contending mass would collapse upon the ground, when the ball would be discovered under a heap of prostrate antagonists, all more or less the worse for the fray.[9]

Such roughness did not result simply from the character of the playing area but also from the lack of stringent and enforceable regulations governing conduct in the game. At this stage in its development, football at all the public schools was similarly loosely regulated and rough, whether played under similar conditions as for example in the Eton Wall Game or on an open field. Thus, at Westminster, "when running . . . the enemy tripped, shinned, charged with the shoulder, got you down and sat upon you . . . in fact might do anything short of murder to get the ball from you".[10] At Rugby, players even wore special iron-clad boots called "navvies" for purposes of hacking. "Navvies", according to an Old Rugbeian, had "a thick sole, the profile of which at the toe much resembled 'the ram of an ironclad".[11]

The type of football played was essentially similar in all the public schools in the latter part of the eighteenth and early part of the nineteenth centuries. In each case, it had close functional connections with the prefect-fagging system. The rules were customary and the game was rough and wild. No formal limits were placed on the numbers of participants or on the duration of matches. Handling as well as kicking the ball was regarded as a legitimate practice but running with it in one's arms was forbidden. Recognition of the underlying similarities among the games of the various public schools, however, should not allow attention to be diverted from the very real differences which existed between them. The structure of society at large did not yet require or lend itself to a unification of the type which was to come later. There were no inter-school competitions and means of transport and communication were still in a relatively undeveloped state. Consequently the game was played at each school under conditions of relative isolation and there was ample room for the occurrence of new waves of local differentiation within the general model. The rules exhibited that mixture of fixity and fluidity which is characteristic of oral traditions in general. It seems likely that new rules and new techniques and ways of playing would have cropped up again and again and become established customs once they had been recognised as legitimate by the most powerful boys.

The bifurcation process in which the game split into its modern "rugger" and "soccer" forms seems to have begun in this manner. Some time during the 1820's, carrying, which forms such a central part of modern rugby, emerged as a legitimate practice at Rugby school. The circumstances surrounding its introduction remain obscure but it is usually attributed to the action of a single boy, William Webb-Ellis, who is said, in 1823, to have picked up the ball and run with it in defiance of the then existing rules. This story is probably apocryphal if only because it would be extremely difficult if not, perhaps, impossible, for a single individual to change the traditional way of playing a game so profoundly by a single act. It seems fairly certain that the practice of "running in", as it was then called, did become a firmly established part of football at Rugby School at some time during the 1820's and 1830's, thus for the first time differentiating the game there from the forms played at the other public schools in a marked way. Initially, it was probably just one of those fluid local customs which are frequent at such a stage in the development of rules. Its wider significance was to come only later at a time when local customs underwent a process of codification and unification because only then did the question arise as to which local models were either to form or to be incorporated in the model for acceptance on a national level. For the moment, it remained just one local custom among many.

The seven public schools which have so far formed the subject of this essay, were also the social loci of the next significant stage in the development of football. During the 1830's and 1840's, largely in response to outside pressure, the school authorities were forced to undertake reform, especially of the prefect-fagging system. At the same time, as part of a general effort to improve relations with their pubils, they came to accord games a central part in the official educational life of their schools. Such changes made possible for the first time the emergence of more civilised kinds of football in the public schools and hence, through a process of diffusion which was to occur somewhat later, also in society at large.

During the first three decades of the nineteenth century, reform of the public schools became the subject of increasingly intense debate among members of the upper and middle classes. Opinion on the issue ranged between extremes of traditionalism and liberal radicalism. Extreme traditionalists, who were mainly members of the aristocracy and gentry, argued strongly in favour of preserving the system as it then existed. The large measure of autonomy which the boys enjoyed, their struggles for power within the schools and the fact that, as prefects, they became accustomed to the exercise of power at an early age all combined, they felt, to make the public schools a useful training ground for young members of their class. The effect of the prevailing instability on the academic education of the boys was of little concern to them. The future of their sons as members of the aristocracy and gentry was secure: they would inherit titles, land, money, prestige and political influence. Of course, the position of younger sons was somewhat less secure but even they, for the most part, were guaranteed remunerative sinecures in the Church or in the army through the nepotism which was such a strongly established feature in the structure of British society at that time.

More moderate traditionalists on the other hand, though mainly from similar social backgrounds as far as one can see, appear to have been more acutely aware of the growing power of the middle classes and saw that concessions would almost certainly have to be made. They tended to adopt a conciliatory position with respect to political issues in general, probably because some sort of compromise was the only way they saw of preserving their social position with all that it entailed in terms of values and entrenched privileges. As far as the public schools were specifically concerned, they advocated measures to increase the power of the masters. Like their more extreme counterparts, however, they, too, regarded the prefect-fagging system as a useful elite-training instrument and wished to see some degree of self-rule preserved.

Liberals of all shades attacked the existing system. Most of them had connections with the rising business and professional strata. As they grew richer with the gathering momentum of industrialisation, more and more members of these groups came to desire a public school education for their sons but the general disorder in the schools was not conducive to the kind of education they desired. It was to the prefect-fagging system that they traced most of the disorder. They proposed that it be reformed yet even they did not argue in favour of its total abolition since self-rule acorded to a high degree with the *laissez-faire* principles which most of them adhered to. What they demanded were modifications of a kind that would enable their sons to get down to the serious business of preparing for their careers under more stable conditions and which would help them to learn ways of behaving appropriate for converting the newly-won economic status of their families into more general social status.[12]

By the 1830's, the balance of power in the struggle for reform of the public schools had reached a stage where change had to come but the situation was conducive to compromise. Extreme traditionalists, the only group wholly resistant to change, were outnumbered by moderate traditionalists and liberals; both these groups desired only moderate reforms. In the event, the prefect-fagging system was retained but in a formalised, legitimised form. Some degree of autonomy was preserved for the boys, but the masters increased their control.

Rugby, the first school where reform designed to deal with the endemic crises inherent in the earlier system was successfully undertaken, illustrates particularly well the kind of changes that were made. Thomas Arnold, headmaster there from 1828 to 1842 is generally seen as the main agent. The prevalence of bullying, drinking and disorderly behaviour in the schools concerned him greatly. The main function of the public schools, as he saw it, was to train an enlightened ruling class thoroughly imbued with Christian values. The endemic disorderliness in the schools, he felt, was not conducive to the performance of this function. He traced it largely to the existing form of the prefect-fagging system. This, he felt, allowed the boys far too much freedom, yet he chose the prefect-fagging system itself as a major instrument for countering the disorder, partly, of course, because the balance of external opinion in favour of self-rule by the boys acted as a constraint which limited his freedom of manoeuvre. Briefly, the course of action which he undertook at Rugby in order to achieve a form of organisation more conducive to performance of the functions he considered appropriate for a public school was this: he transformed the sixth form into a kind of "moral elite" whose example was to impress the rest of the school with the ideals of the "Christian Gentleman". The roles of prefects and fags and the rights and duties associated with these roles were much more explicitly and formally defined and henceforth, the prefects were appointed and controlled by Arnold personally. Previous headmasters, not only at Rugby, had tended to accept as prefects those who had risen to the top in the struggle for power, prestige and influence among the boys themselves. Now, prefects became to a large extent lieutenants of the headmaster who could be used by him in order to achieve his educational aims.

Such was Arnold's success and so great the need for reform in the other public schools that they soon followed suit and made similar modifications in their own versions of the prefect-fagging system. The changes made differed somewhat from school to school, but the overall result was everywhere the same: masters increased their control over the boys but did not at the same time abolish their autonomy entirely. The anarchic prefect-fagging system of the late eighteenth and early nineteenth centuries, perhaps best described as a system of customary domination of the older and stronger boys over those who were younger and physically weaker, was transformed into a much more formal system of indirect rule. What had in the past been conducive mainly to disorder became, in its new form, a useful instrument for maintaining discipline in a school.

Around the time that successful reform of the prefect-fagging system was accomplished, many public school masters came to recognise that organised games played with their approval might prove useful in the attainment of certain educational ends. One of these was essentially preventive: masters came to sanction games as a leisure activity because participation in them would help to stop boys engaging in undesirable pursuits on half- and whole holidays such as breaking bounds, drinking, poaching and destroying the property of neighbours. The school authorities also came to regard games as a useful instrument for promoting communication and understanding between boys and masters and for breaking down the barriers that existed between them. To this end, they started to help with the organisation of games and some even began themselves to play alongside the boys. Perhaps most important, however, they came to feel that team games might represent a useful instrument for character training, that they might help to impart such desirable traits as loyalty to one's group, co-operativeness, the willingness to subordinate individual aims to the achievement of group goals, the ability to compete according to rules, the capacity to make quick decisions, physical and moral courage, leadership ability and so on. This change in attitude can be illustrated in part from the Clarendon Commission on the public schools which reported in 1864. The following extract illustrates very well the games "ideology" which was developing in that period.

> ... bodily training ... is imparted at the English schools, not by the gymnastic exercises ... employed ... on the continent ... but by athletic games, which, while they serve this purpose well,

serve other purposes besides . . . The cricket and football fields . . .
are not merely places of exercise and amusement: they help to
form some of the most valuable social qualities and manly
virtues . . . They hold . . . a distinct and important place in public
school education.[13]

A passage from *Tom Brown's Schooldays* by Thomas Hughes in
which Tom and a group of his school fellows are discussing cricket
with a master provides a further illustration:

> "The discipline and reliance on one another which it teaches
> is so valuable . . ." went on the master. "It ought to be such an
> unselfish game. It merges the individual into the eleven; he
> doesn't play that he may win but that his side may."
> "That's very true," said Tom, "and that's why football
> and cricket . . . are so much better games than fives or hare and
> hounds, or any other where the object is to come in first, and
> not that one's side may win."[14]

In connection with this change in their attitude towards games
and the development of the "games ideology", masters in the
public schools began to take a much more active part in the
organisation and playing of games. Their influence, however, remained indirect. In no case did they usurp the power of the leading
boys as far as games were concerned: they acted merely as advisers
and intervened directly only in cases of serious difficulty or dispute.
Nevertheless, by virtue of the greater power which reform of the
prefect-fagging system had conferred upon them, they were able
from that time onwards to exercise a much greater influence on
the way of playing games such as football.

The wild forms of football inherited from the past, however,
were ill-suited to the performance of the educational functions
masters now expected of them. They needed to be "domesticated",
to become far more orderly and controlled. Therefore, the masters
encouraged the leading boys to regularise their football, to commit
the rules to writing and to develop more regular procedures for
settling disputes. Between 1845 and 1862, each of the public
schools considered here committed its football rules to written
form. That Rugby again took the lead brings out very clearly the
close connection between the development of the game at this
stage and the development of the prefect-fagging system.

The kinds of rules formulated in connection with the masters'
drive to establish forms of football, more compatible with the
educational aims implicit in their developing games ideology, can

be illustrated by four of the rules produced at Rugby in 1845:

(i)   No player being off his side shall hack, charge, run in, touch down in goal or interrupt a catch.

(ii)   A player standing up to another may hold one arm only but may hack him or knock the ball out of his hand if he attempt to kick it or go beyond the line of touch.

(iii)   No hacking with the heel or above the knee is fair.

(iv)   No player may wear projecting nails or iron plates on the soles or heels of his shoes or boots.[15]

Thus, the types of force pronounced legitimate in the game began to be hedged around with explicit conditions and prohibitions. Many of the more brutal practices of earlier times were rooted out but the chances for satisfaction from participation in a physical struggle were by no means entirely eliminated. Football remained for at least another two or three decades a rougher, wilder game than is the case with the modern Rugby and Association forms. At this stage, however, the "mock-fight" component in the game began to increase at the expense of the "real-fight" component. Football began to become a form of group contest which provided as much as possible the pleasures of a real fight without its risks and dangers, a form of struggle regulated in such a way that the contestants had much less chance than formerly to inflict serious injury or to use physical violence on each other in earnest. Pleasure in playing began to be enhanced by the fact that the "battle" was fought less and less by brute force alone and more and more by force transformed by specific skills. Football had taken a major step in the development towards its modern form, towards a type of game structured in such a way that it is relatively spontaneous yet highly controlled. Ample room was left for inventiveness and the expression of individuality but barriers—in the form of explicit rules—were being set up to ensure that the excitement of the struggle did not carry the players too far. These barriers made the game more conducive to the attainment of the educational aims of the masters and began to bring it into line with the more civilised standards that had been developing for some time and were now beginning to spread in society at large.

It was by no means accidental that, in the course of the general reform of conduct in the public schools, greater stress was laid, not merely on making the rules of football more refined, more elaborate and more conducive to greater restraint, but also on making them more explicit, on writing them down. In that way, boys were no longer bound simply by the often arbitrary influence they exercised upon each other. In the previous stages of more fluid, oral rules, those practices were considered legitimate which were sanctioned by the most powerful boys. Now they were all, even the prefects, subject to written rules which possessed an objectivity that removed them from the caprice of the most powerful. Behind these written rules, serving to bolster their objectivity, stood the newly-gained authority of the masters. The older and stronger boys were no longer able to dominate the fags in their football as and how they pleased.

Even though the game at this stage was developing towards stricter control, however, emphasis continued to be laid on internalisation of the rules, upon self-imposed rather than external restraint. Not until the foundation of the F.A. Cup Competition in 1871, when the game began to become intensely competitive and players from different social class and regional backgrounds regularly played together, did it become necessary to introduce external agents of control in the form of referees and linesmen as a regular feature of the game. Of course, in its emphasis on self-control, public school football in the 1840's, '50's, and '60's was dependent partly on the absence of really stringent competition but it also reflected the recently reformed system of indirect rule in the public schools. It seems plausible to suggest that such a game could only have developed within a social structure of that type. The Prussian schools of that time provide an illuminating contrast. They were highly authoritarian institutions in which the main parallel of organised football was "drill", a highly regimented activity in which a master barked orders at a group of boys which they mechanically obeyed. Drill reflected the authoritarian structure of the Prussian schools and indeed of Prussian society as a whole. Duelling in the German universities provides a further contrast. It represented a far more open outlet for sadistic and aggressive urges: death or serious injury and disfigurement were its frequent accompaniments. Football as it developed in the English public schools came to represent a far more socially constructive means of satisfying the need for excitement by providing it in the form of an orderly, relatively harmless, spontaneous yet controlled type of "mock-fight".

It is appropriate to conclude the consideration of this stage in the development of football by discussing a further process of local differentiation which occurred within it. At Eton in 1849, rules were laid down enjoining that "the ball may not be caught, carried, thrown, nor struck by hand" and that "a goal is gained when the ball is kicked between (the goalposts), provided it be not above them".[16] Eton was the only school where the use of hands was forbidden outright at this stage and where the rules distinctly stated that goals were to be scored by kicking the ball between rather than above the goalposts. It seems plausible to maintain that these two rules were a direct response to the development of differentiating marks in the game at Rugby where the distinctive practices of carrying the ball and of scoring above the cross bar had been introduced somewhat earlier. It can be imagined how all this must have incensed the boys at Eton who felt their own school to be the leading public school in all respects. By placing an absolute taboo on handling in their own game they were, one might suggest, attempting to put the upstart Rugby in its place.

Thus, a further important driving force in the early development of football appears to have been a struggle between the leading public schools for the status of "model-making centre" for the game on a national level. The absolute taboo on the use of hands imposed at Eton is an example of how the game probably developed under the impetus of such competitive pressure. Such a prohibition represented a very severe imposition of self-control upon the players. Only in a society which already imposed a high degree of self-control on its members could such a game—the prototype of modern soccer—have developed and spread. Like the Rugby game, however, the newly evolving model of football at Eton was to receive its wider significance only when football was diffused into society at large and when, in consequence, the struggles for dominance on a national level between the exponents of rival models increased in their intensity.

By about 1850, because of its more civilised character and because acceptance by the public schools had given it the stamp of "respectability", football became, for the first time, a socially permissible activity for young adult "gentlemen". Numbers of independent clubs were founded, mainly by old boys from the public schools. For the most part, they continued to play according to the traditions of their various schools. On this account, very great difficulties were posed for playing and organising inter-club matches but the demand for these was growing. The development of railways and improved means of transport and communication meant that inter-club matches were now a much more feasible proposition than had previously been the case. Moreover, matches now began to be reported in the newspapers and a specific sporting press had begun to emerge. Skill at football was beginning to be regarded as a desirable accomplishment in the young gentleman. Under these conditions, it became increasingly possible for individual players and for teams to gain a national rather than simply a local reputation at the game. In this manner, their status as gentlemen could be accorded wider recognition. In addition, the more effective national unification which was now becoming possible enabled class, regional and other group rivalries to be extended, symbolically, to a test of strength and skill on the football field. In any case, inter-club matches would introduce elements of uncertainty into football competitions which were not possible with intra-school and intra-club matches. In this way, they increased the potential for generating excitement in the game.

Under these circumstances the demand for unified rules soon arose. A series of stormy meetings were held in London in the autumn of 1863 which resulted in the formation of the Football Association. A set of rules was adopted in which handling, carrying and "hacking"—the deliberate kicking of an opponent's shins—were prohibited. As a result of their opposition to the elimination of hacking which they felt would render the game "unmanly", but also because they favoured a game in which handling and carrying played a central part, a number of clubs refused to join. In 1871, they formed their own association, the Rugby Football Union, thus perpetuating on a national level the bifurcation of football which appears to have originally resulted from public school rivalry during the 1840's. Interestingly enough, one of the first acts of the new Union was to prohibit hacking. They were forced to by a growing body of public opinion which considered the practice barbaric. Indeed, the strength of this opposition to hacking was itself one of the major reasons why the rugby clubs were forced to unite.

During the 1870's, the new models of football forged in the public schools ceased to be monopolised by the middle and upper classes. With the gradual shortening of working hours, members of the urban working classes, at first mainly in the North and Midlands, began to form clubs, too. "Muscular Christian" and "Christian Socialist" priests, many of them educated at public schools, played a central role in the diffusion of Rugby and Association Football to the working classes. They regarded them as means of moral and physical salvation, as activities which would help the denizens of slums to become strong and physically healthy and to develop traits of character which would enable them to improve their miserable lot. Indeed, many of the new, working-class clubs founded after 1870—some of them the ancestors of present-day professional teams—were founded by Muscular Christian and Christian Socialist priests in association with church or chapel.

In 1871 the F.A. Cup, the first football competition to be operated on a national level, was founded. At first, the public school old boy clubs reigned supreme but in 1883, Blackburn Olympic, a team of Lancashire mill workers, defeated Old Etonians in the final by two goals to nil. This marked the end of the public schools and their old boys' teams as significant agents in the game's development. The transition to the modern situation where the game is dominated by professional clubs playing to vast paying audiences was soon to follow.

While the old boys were in the ascendant, football drew comparatively few spectators. During the first eight years of the F.A. Cup Competition, for example, the crowd at the final never exceeded 5,000. As the social origin of the players changed, however, and the centre of the game moved north, so the numbers who watched rather than played increased. In 1885, 27,000 saw the cup tie between Aston Villa and Preston. The cup final in 1893 was watched by 45,000 and 80,000 was the average number of spectators over the next ten years.

The reasons why spectators were attracted to the game in such large numbers are not difficult to find. As the nineteenth century wore on and the length of the working week decreased, large sections of the working classes found themselves with increased spare time at their disposal. Some, by pooling their resources, were able to rent grounds where they could play football. Those who could not and those who were too old to play themselves—still by far the majority—came to watch. But there was more to it than this. In the dingy nineteenth century towns, the proletariat found little opportunity for communal enjoyment, for enjoyable excitement in company with others or for ritual identification with some larger group. The urban working classes in the later nineteenth century were still to a considerable extent drawn from rural backgrounds. The impersonality of life in towns and the need to adjust to secondary forms of social control were conducive to high rates of alienation and anomie amongst them. Gradually, however, the ceremonial battles of the local football team came to form a major outlet for the need for leisure-time excitement and to provide a partial focus for the regular and ritualised expression of identity with the community, thus helping to counter alienation and anomie.

Encouraged by the numbers of spectators, some clubs began to charge admission. When Aston Villa first adopted the practice in 1874, the takings amounted to 5s. 3d. Only thirty years later, the same club took £14,329 at a single match. With such pickings to be had, a number of clubs formed themselves as limited companies. They became commercial concerns with profit as a major yardstick of success. This implied the need to maintain high playing standards in order to attract the largest possible crowds. The obvious development was to pay players in order to attract and retain those with the highest ability and to free them from the necessity to work full time so that they could train properly and develop their skills. A further consequence followed in 1888. Twelve leading clubs, six from Lancashire and six from the Midlands, entered an agreement to play one another regularly following a fixed programme and always fielding their strongest sides. They called themselves the Football League.

The Football Association and the Rugby Football Union, however, were still dominated by middle and upper class groups. That a sport could become a type of work ran counter to their entire system of values. While they stressed individual competition in the sphere of work, in the sphere of leisure they emphasised "team spirit", "fair play", and co-operation. Professionalism entailed an intensification of competition and a dependence on success which they abhorred. They saw their lives as sharply divided between a work sphere and a play sphere. As a sport, they felt, football should be played entirely for its own sake. To play for money was to make it work.

The hostility of such groups towards professionalism led them to declare it illegal. The dependence of the northern and midland clubs on revenue from the gate continued, however, to grow. In order to attract and retain high calibre players, they were forced to adopt underhand methods of payment. "Shamateurism", as it was later called, became the norm among the leading clubs in the north and midlands during the 1880's. In order to force the hand of the Football Association, several northern soccer clubs stated their intention to break away and form a rival association of their own should professionalism not be granted full recognition. The status of the Football Association as sole legislator for the game on a national level was threatened, but a compromise solution was worked out in 1885. Professionalism was legalised under "stringent conditions". Ten years later, despite the fact that many northern rugby clubs were as deeply involved in shamateurism as their soccer counterparts, the Rugby Football Union rejected a proposal to legalise professionalism and precipitated the split between themselves and the Northern Union which set the pattern for the future development of the rugby game along class and regional lines: mainly middle class and amateur in the South, and working class and professional in the North.

NOTES

1 In some respects, the following discussion of public schools in the late eighteenth and early and middle nineteenth centuries consists of working hypotheses rather than established facts. Such hypotheses have not been presented in the form of separate, formal propositions in the interests of ensuring brevity, readability and textual continuity.

2 An Etonian, *Reminiscences of Eton*, London, 1831, p. 47.

3 Thus, at Winchester and Eton provision was made for seventy poor students and at Westminster for forty. Charterhouse, Harrow, Rugby and Shrewsbury were all originally open to the poor of their respective communities.

4 E. C. Mack, *Public Schools and British Opinion*, Vol. I.

5 M. Bloxam, *Meteor* (The Rugby School Magazine), No. 157, 1880.

6 F. Markham, *Recollections of a Townboy at Westminster*, London, 1903, pp. 92–9.

7 J. B. Oldham, *A History of Shrewsbury School*, London, 1952, p. 231.

8 G. W. Fisher, *Annals of Shrewsbury School*, 1899, p. 313.

9 E. P. Eardley-Wilmot and E. C. Streatfield, *Charterhouse, Old and New*, London, 1895, pp. 74–6.

10 Markham, *loc. cit.*

11 An Old Rugbeian, *The Cornhill Magazine*, London, 1922, p. 295.

12 It is important to note that the actual numbers of middle class boys who gained access to the public schools during the period under consideration was relatively small. (See T. W. Bamford, "Public Schools and Social Class", *British Journal of Sociology*, Vol. XII, No. 3, September, 1961, pp. 224–35.) Their parents' aspirations in that direction were satisfied far more by independent action on their part in securing the foundation of new boarding schools modelled on the reformed versions of the existing public schools, especially on Rugby. Such schools came, for the most part, eventually to be accorded the high prestige which attaches generally in England to the public schools. The main point to grasp for present purposes, however, is that, despite their failure to gain a firm foothold in the existing public schools, middle class pressure for reform appears to have played an important part in securing and determining the character of the changes that were made during this period. The school authorities were forced to act, however, not only on account of the power of public opinion explicitly critical of the existing situation, but also on account of the fact that dissatisfaction on the part of many upper class parents who already sent their sons to the schools was growing. Many of them expressed their dissatisfaction in the most direct way open to them: by withdrawing their sons from the schools. Of all the seven public schools considered here, only Eton and Rugby continued to attract large numbers of pupils in the first four decades of the nineteenth century and even they experienced a decline of moderate proportions during that period.

13 *Royal Commission on the Public Schools*, London, 1864, 4 vols., Vol. 1, p. 56.

14 Thomas Hughes, *Tom Brown's Schooldays*, 1857 (edn. cited, London, 1902), p. 289. As can be seen, this and the extract from the Clarendon Commission Report quoted before it, refer to football after it had already become a much more civilised type of game. It will be shown in the next section how the development of the "games ideology" of which

they are representative played an important part in the emergence of more civilised kinds of football.

15 *The Rules of Football as Played at Rugby School* (pamphlet), Rugby, 1845.

16 G. Green and H. Fabian (eds.), *Association Football*, London, 1959, Vol. I, p. 140.

CHAPTER 9

Football in America: A Study in Culture Diffusion

David Riesman and Reuel Denney*

I

On 9 October, 1951, Assistant Attorney General Graham Morrison instituted an anti-trust action against a number of universities on account of their efforts to limit TV broadcasts of their games—efforts dictated by the terrible burdens of what we might speak of as "industrialised football". This action occurred only a few weeks after the scandal of the West Point student firings, which, along with the William and Mary palace revolution, indicated that football was indeed reaching another crisis in its adaptation to the ever-changing American environment. Small colleges such as Milligan— a church-supported school in the mountains of Eastern Tennessee— were discovering that football was now so mechanised that they could no longer afford the necessary entry fee for machinery and personnel. Last year, Milligan spent $17,000, or two-thirds of its whole athletic budget—and did not get it all back in the box-office net. Football had come to resemble other industries or mechanised farms, into which a new firm could not move by relying on an institutional lifetime of patient saving and ploughing back of profits, but only by large corporate investment. The production of a team involves the heavy overhead and staff personnel characteristic of high-capital, functionally rationalised industries, as the result of successive changes in the game since its post-Civil-War diffusion from England.[1]

It would be wrong, however, to assert that football has become an impersonal market phenomenon. Rather, its rationalisation as a sport and as a spectacle has served to bring out more openly the part it plays in the ethnic, class, and characterological struggles of our time—meaning, by "characterological struggle", the conflict between different styles of life. The ethnic significance of football is immediately suggested by the shift in the typical origins of player-

* Reprinted from David Riesman, *Individualism Reconsidered*, Glencoe, Ill., 1954.

names on the All-American Football Teams since 1889. In 1889, all but one of the names (Heffelfinger) suggested Anglo-Saxon origins. The first name after that of Heffelfinger to suggest non-Anglo-Saxon recruitment was that of Murphy, at Yale, in 1895. After 1895, it was a rare All-American team that did not include at least one Irishman (Daly, Hogan, Rafferty, Shevlin); and the years before the turn of the century saw entrance of the Jew. On the 1904 team appeared Pierkarski, of Pennsylvania. By 1927, names like Casey, Kipke, Oosterbaan, Koppisch, Garbisch, and Friedman were appearing on the All-American lists with as much frequency as names like Channing, Adams, and Ames in the 1890's.

While such a tally does little more than document a shift that most observers have already recognised in American football, it raises questions that are probably not answerable merely in terms of ethnic origins of players. There is an element of class identification running through American football since its earliest days, and the ethnic origins of players contain ample invitations to the making of theory about the class dimensions of football. Most observers would be inclined to agree that the arrival of names like Kelley and Kipke on the annual All-American list was taken by the Flanagans and the Webers as the achievement of a lower-class aspiration to be among the best at an upper-class sport. The question remains: what did the achievement mean? What did it mean at different stages in the development of the game? Hasn't the meaning worn off in the fifty-odd years, the roughly two generations since Heffelfinger and Murphy made the grade?

There are many ways to begin an answer to such questions, and here we can open only a few lines of investigation. Our method is to study the interrelations between changes in the rules of the game (since the first intercollegiate contest: Rutgers, six goals—Princeton, four goals in 1869) and to analyse the parallel changes in football strategy and ethos. All these developments are to be seen as part of a configuration that includes changes in coaching, in the training of players, and in the no less essential training of the mass audience.

Since football is a cultural inheritance from England, such an analysis may be made in the perspective of other studies in cultural diffusion and variation. Just as the French have transformed American telephone etiquette while retaining some of its recognisable physical features, so Americans have transformed the games of Europe even when, as in track or tennis, the formalities appear to be unaltered. Even within the Western industrial culture, there are great varieties, on a class and national basis, in the games, rules, strategy, etiquette, and audience structures of sport. In the case of college football—we shall leave aside the symbolically less important professional game—the documentation of sportswriters (themselves a potent factor in change) allows us to trace the stages of development.

II

A study of Anatolian peasants now under way at the Bureau of Applied Social Research indicates that these highly tradition-bound people cannot grasp the abstractness of modern sports. They lack the enterprise, in their fatalistic village cultures, to see why people want to knock themselves out for sportmanship's remote ideals; they cannot link such rituals, even by remote analogy, with their own. These peasants are similarly unable to be caught up in modern politics, or to find anything meaningful in the Voice of America. Nevertheless, football itself, like so many other games with balls and goals, originated in a peasant culture.

Football, in its earliest English form, was called the Dane's Head and it was played in the tenth and eleventh centuries as a contest in kicking a ball between towns. The legend is that the first ball was a skull, and only later a cow's bladder. In some cases, the goals were the towns themselves, so that a team entering a village might have pushed the ball several miles en route. King Henry II (1154–89) proscribed the game, on the ground that it interfered with archery practice. Played in Dublin even after the ban, football did not become respectable or legal until an edict of James I reinstated it. The reason was perhaps less ideological than practical: firearms had made the art of bowmanship obsolete.

During the following century, football as played by British schoolboys became formalised, but did not change its fundamental pattern of forceful kicking. In 1823, Ellis of Rugby made the mistake of picking up the ball and running with it towards the goal. All concerned thought it a mistake: Ellis was sheepish, his captain apologetic. The mistake turned into innovation when it was decided that a running rule might make for an interesting game. The localism, pluralism, and studied casualness of English sports made it possible to try it out without securing universal assent— three or four purely local variants of football, football-hazing and "wall games" are still played in various English schools. Rugby adopted "Rugby" in 1841, several years after Cambridge had helped to popularise it.[2]

This establishment of the running or Rugby game, as contrasted with the earlier, kicking game, had several important results. One was that the old-style players banded themselves together for the defence of their game, and formed the London Football Association (1863). This name, abbreviated to "Assoc", appears to have been the starting point for the neologism, "Soccer", the name that the kicking game now goes by in many parts of the English-speaking world. A second result was that the English, having found a new game, continued to play it without tight rules until the Rugby Union of 1871. As we shall see, this had its effects on the American game. The third and most important result of Ellis' "mistake", of course, was that he laid the foundations for every-thing fundamental about the American game between about 1869 and the introduction of the forward pass. (The forward pass is still illegal in Rugby and closely related football games.)

III

In the colonial period and right down to the Civil War, Ameri-cans played variants on the kicking football game on their town greens and schoolyards. After the war, Yale and Harvard served as the culturally receptive importers of the English game. Harvard, meeting McGill in a game of Rugby football in 1874, brought the sport to the attention of collegiate circles and the press—two identifications important for the whole future development of the game. But if Harvard was an opinion leader, Yale was a techno-logical one. A Yale student who had studied at Rugby was instru-mental in persuading Yale men to play the Rugby game and was, therefore, responsible for some of Yale's early leadership in the sport.

It happened in the following way, according to Walter Camp and Lorin F. Deland.[3] The faculty in 1860, for reasons unknown, put a stop to interclass matches of the pre-Rugby variety. "During the following years, until 1870, football was practically dead at Yale. The class of '72, however, was very fond of athletic sports, and participated especially in long hare and hound runs. The revival of football was due in a large measure to Mr. D. S. Schaft, for-merly of Rugby School, who entered the class of '73 and succeeded in making the sport popular among his classmates, and eventually formed an association which sent challenges to the other classes."

Soon after the period described by Camp, it became clear that American players, having tasted the "running" game, were willing to give up the soccer form. It became equally clear that they either did not want to, or could not, play Rugby according to the British rules. "The American players found in this code [English Rugby Rules] many uncertain and knotty points which caused much trouble in their game, especially as they had no traditions, or older and more experienced players, to whom they could turn for the necessary explanations", says Camp. An example of such a problem was English rule number nine:

A touchdown is when a player, putting his hand on the ball in touch or in goal, stops it so that it remains dead, or fairly so.

The ambiguity of the phrase "fairly so" was increased by the statement in rule number eight that the ball is dead "when it rests absolutely motionless on the ground".

Camp's description of these early difficulties is intensely interesting to the student of cultural diffusion not only because of what Camp observed about the situation, but also because of what he neglected to observe. Consider the fact that the development of Rugby rules in England was accomplished by admitting into the rules something that we call a legal fiction. While an offensive runner was permitted to carry the ball, the condition of his doing so was that he should happen to be standing behind the swaying "scrum" (the tangled players) at the moment the ball popped back out to him. An intentional "heel out" of the ball was not permitted; and the British rules of the mid-nineteenth century appear to take it for granted that the difference between an intentional and an unintentional heel-out would be clear to everyone. Ellis' mistake became institutionalised—but still as a mistake. This aspect of Rugby rule-making had important implications for the American game.

British players, according to tradition as well as according to rules, could be expected to tolerate such ambiguity as that of the heel-out rule just as they tolerated the ambiguity of the "dead" ball. They could be expected to tolerate it not only because of their personal part in developing new rules but also (a point we shall return to) because they had an audience with specific knowledge of the traditions to assist them. In America it was quite another matter to solve such problems. No Muzafer Sherif was present[4] to solidify the perceptions of "nearly so", and the emotional tone for resolving such question without recurrent dispute could not be improvised. Rather, however, than dropping the Rugby game at that point, because of intolerance for the ambiguities involved, an effort was undertaken, at once systematic and gradual, to fill in by formal procedures the vacuum of etiquette and, in general, to adapt the game to its new cultural home.

The upshot of American procedure was to assign players to the legalised task of picking up and tossing the ball back out of scrimmage. This in turn created the role of the centre, and the centring operation. This in turn led to a variety of problems in defining the situation as one of "scrimmage" or "non-scrimmage", and the whole question of the legality of passing the ball back to intended runners. American football never really solved these problems until it turned its attention, in 1880, to a definition of the scrimmage itself. The unpredictable English "scrum" or scramble for a free ball was abandoned, and a crude line of scrimmage was constructed across the field. Play was set in motion by snapping the ball. Meanwhile Americans became impatient with long retention of the ball by one side. It was possible for a team that was ahead in score to adopt tactics that would ensure its retention of the ball until the end of the period. By the introduction of a minimum yardage-gain rule in 1882, the rule-makers assured the frequent interchange of the ball between sides.

The effect of this change was to dramatise the offensive-defensive symmetry of the scrimmage line, to locate it sharply in time ("downs"), and to focus attention not only on the snapping of the ball, but also on the problem of "offside" players. In the English game, with no spatially and temporarily delimited "line of scrimmage", the offside player was penalised only by making him neutral in action until he could move to a position back of the position of the ball. In the American game, the new focus on centring, on a scrimmage line, and on yardage and downs, created the need for a better offside rule. From that need developed offside rules that even in the early years resembled the rules of today. American rulemakers were logically extending a native development when they decided to draw an imaginary line through the ball before it had been centred, to call this the "line of scrimmage", and to make this line, rather than the moving ball itself, the offside limit in the goalward motion of offensive players. At first, lined-up players of the two sides were allowed to stand and wrestle with each other while waiting for the ball to be centred; only later was a neutral zone introduced between the opposing lines.

Even with such a brief summary of the rule changes, we are in a position to see the operation of certain recurrent modes or patterns of adaptation. The adaptation begins with the acceptance of a single pivotal innovation (running with the ball). The problems of adaptation begin with the realisation that this single innovation has been uprooted from a rich context of meaningful rules and traditions, and does not work well in their absence. Still more complex problems of adaptation develop when it is realised that the incompleteness of the adaptation will not be solved by a reference to the pristine rules. In the first place, the rules are not pristine (the English rules were in the process of development themselves). In the second place, the tradition of interpreting them is not present in experienced players. In the third place, even if it were, it might not be adaptable to the social character and mood of the adapters.

Let us put it this way. The Americans, in order to solve the heel-out problem, set in motion a redesign of the game that led ultimately to timed centring from a temporarily fixed line of scrimmage. Emphasis completely shifted from the kicking game; it also shifted away from the combined kicking and running possible under Rugby rules; it shifted almost entirely in the direction of an emphasis on ball-carrying. Meanwhile, to achieve this emphasis, the game made itself vulnerable to slowdowns caused by one team's retention of the ball. It not only lost the fluidity of the original game, but ran up against a pronounced American taste for action in sports, visible action. There is evidence that even if players had not objected to such slowdowns, the spectators would have raised a shout. The yardage rule was the way this crisis was met. This, in turn, led to an emphasis on mass play, and helped to create the early twentieth-century problems of football. But before we consider this step in the game's development we must turn to examine certain factors in the sport's audience reception.

IV

A problem posed for the student of cultural diffusion at this point can be stated as follows: What factor or factors appear to have been most influential in creating an American game possessing not only nationally distinct rules, but also rules having a specific flavour of intense legality about many a point of procedure left more or less up in the air by the British game?

We can now go beyond the rule-making aspect of the game and assert that the chief factor was the importance of the need to standardise rules to supply an ever-widening collegiate field of competition, along with the audience this implied. The English rule-makers, it appears, dealt with a situation in which amateur play was restricted to a fairly limited number of collegians and institutions. The power of localism was such that many an informality was tolerated, and intended to be tolerated, in the rules and their interpretation. American football appeared on the American campus at the beginning of a long period in which intercollegiate and interclass sportsmanship was a problem of ever-widening social participation and concern. Football etiquette itself was in the making. Thus, it appears that when early American teams met, differences of opinion could not be resolved between captains in rapid-fire agreement or penny-tossing as was the case in Britain. American teams did not delegate to their captains the role of powerful comrade-in-antagonism with opposing captains, or, if they did, they felt that such responsibilities were too grave.[5]

Into just such situations football players thrust all of the force of their democratic social ideologies, all their prejudice in favour of equalitarian and codified inter-player attitudes. Undoubtedly, similar considerations also influenced the audience. Mark Benney, a British sociologist who is familiar with the games played on both sides of the Atlantic, points out that, whereas the American game was developed in and for a student group, the English game was played before quite large crowds who, from a class standpoint, were less homogeneous than the players themselves, though they were as well informed as the latter in the "law" of the game. Rugby football was seldom played by the proletariat; it was simply enjoyed as a spectacle.

Held by the critical fascination the British upper strata had for the lower strata, the audience was often hardly more interested in the result of the game than in judging the players as 'gentlemen in action". "The players", Mr. Benney writes, "had to demonstrate that they were sportsmen, that they could 'take it'; and above all they had to inculcate the (politically important) ideology that legality was more important than power." The audience was, then, analogous to the skilled English jury at law, ready to be impressed by obedience to traditional legal ritual and form, and intolerant of "bad form" in their "betters". The early Yale games, played before a tiny, nonpaying audience, lacked any equivalent incentive to agree on a class-based ritual of "goodform", and when the audiences came later on, their attitude towards upper-class sportsmanship was much more ambivalent—they had played the game too, and they were unwilling to subordinate themselves to a collegiate aristocracy who would thereby have been held to norms of correctness. The apparent legalism of many American arguments over the rules would strike British observers as simply a verbal power-play.

Such differences in the relation of the game to the audience, on this side of the Atlantic, undoubtedly speeded the development of the specifically American variant. Native, too, are the visual and temporal properties of the game as it developed even before 1900: its choreography could be enjoyed, if not always understood, by non-experts, and its atomistic pattern in time and space could seem natural to audiences accustomed to such patterns in other foci of the national life. The mid-field dramatisation of line against line, the recurrent starting and stopping of field action around the timed snapping of a ball, the trend to a formalised division of labour between backfield and line, above all, perhaps, the increasingly precise synchronisation of men in motion—these developments make it seem plausible to suggest that the whole procedural rationalisation of the game which we have described was not unwelcome to Americans, and that it fitted in with other aspects of their industrial folk-ways.

Spurred by interest in the analysis of the athletic motions of men and animals, Eadweard Muybridge was setting out his movie-like action shorts of the body motion (more preoccupied even than Vesalius or da Vinci with the detailed anatomy of movement)[6] at about the same time that Coach Woodruff at Pennsylvania (1894) was exploring the possibilities for momentum play: linemen swinging into motion before the ball is snapped, with the offensive team, forming a wedge, charging towards an opposition held waiting by the offside rule. In Philadelphia, the painter Eakins, self-consciously following the tenets of Naturalism and his own literal American tradition, was painting the oarsmen of the Schuylkill. Nearby, at the Midvale plant of the American Steel Company, efficiency expert Frederick Winslow Taylor was experimenting with motion study and incentive pay geared to small measurable changes in output—pay that would spur but never soften the workman.[7]

Since we do not believe in historical inevitability, nor in the necessary homogeneity of a culture, we do not suggest that the American game of football developed as it did out of cultural compulsion and could not have gone off in quite different directions. Indeed, the very effectiveness of momentum play, as a mode of bulldozing the defence, led eventually to the rule that the line must refrain from motion before the ball is snapped. For the bulldozing led, or was thought to lead, to a great increase in injuries. And while these were first coped with by Walter Camp's training table (his men had their choice of beefsteak or mutton for dinner, to be washed down with milk, ale, or sherry), the public outcry soon forced further rule changes, designed to soften the game. After a particularly bloody battle between Pennsylvania and Swarthmore in 1905, President Roosevelt himself took a hand and insisted on reform.[8]

Camp's colleague at Yale, William Graham Sumner, may well have smiled wryly at this. Sumner was exhorting his students to "get capital", and cautioning them against the vices of sympathy and reformism—a theme which has given innumerable American academics a good living since—while Camp was exhorting his to harden themselves, to be stern and unafraid. In spite of them both, the reformers won out, but the end of momentum play was not the end of momentum. Rather, with an ingenuity that still dazzles, the game was gentled and at the same time speeded by a new rule favouring the forward pass. But before going on to see what changes this introduced, let us note the differences between the subjects of Sumner's and Camp's exhortations on the one hand, and Taylor's on the other.

Frederick Taylor, as his writings show, was already coming up against a work force increasingly drawn from non-Protestant lands, and seeking to engender in them a YMCA-morality, whereas Camp was inculcating the same morality into young men of undiluted Anglo-Saxon stock and middle- to upper-class origins. Not for another fifty years would the sons of Midvale prove harder, though fed on kale or spaghetti, and only intermittently, than the sons of Yale. Meanwhile, the sons of Yale had learned to spend summers as tracklayers or wheat harvesters in an effort to enlarge their stamina, moral toughness, and cross-class adventures.

Nevertheless, certain basic resemblances between the purposes of Taylor and those of Sumner and Camp are clearly present. In contrast with the British, the Americans demonstrated a high degree of interest in winning games and winning one's way to high production goals. The Americans, as in so many other matters, were clearly concerned with the competitive spirit that new rules might provoke and control. (British sports, like British industry, seemed to take it more for granted that competition will exist even if one does not set up an ideology for it). Much of this seems to rest in the paradoxical belief of Americans that competition is natural—but only if it is constantly recreated by artificial systems of social rules that direct energies into it.

Back of the attitudes expressed in Taylor, Sumner, and Camp we can feel the pressure not only of a theory of competition, but also a theory of the emotional tones that ought to go along with competition. It is apparent from the brutality scandals of 1905 that President Roosevelt reacted against roughhouse not so much because it was physical violence, but for two related reasons. The first and openly implied reason was that it was connected with an unsportsmanlike attitude. The second, unacknowledged, reason was that Americans fear and enjoy their aggression at the same time, and thus have difficulty in pinning down the inner meanings of external violence. The game of Rugby as now played in England is probably as physically injurious as American football was at the turn of the century. By contrast, American attitudes towards football demonstrate a forceful need to define, limit, and conventionalise the symbolism of violence in sports.

If we look back now at England, we see a game in which shouted signals and silent counting of timed movements are unknown—a game that seems to Americans to wander in an amorphous and disorderly roughhouse. Rugby, in the very home of the industrial revolution, seems pre-industrial, seems like one of the many feudal survivals that urbanisatiaon and industrialisation have altered but not destroyed. The English game, moreover, seems not to have produced anyone like Camp, the Judge Gary of football (as Rockne was to be its Henry Ford): Camp was a sparkplug in efforts to codify inter-collegiate rules; he was often the head of the important committees. His training table, furthermore, was one of the signs of the slow rise in "overhead" expense—a rise which, rather like the water in United States Steel Stock, assumed that abundance was forthcoming and bailing out probable, as against the British need for parsimony. But at the same time the rise in costs un-doubtedly made American football more vulnerable than ever to public-relations considerations: the "gate" could not be damned.

V

This public relations issue in the game first appears in the actions of the rules committee of 1906—the introduction of the legalised forward pass in order to open up the game and reduce brutal power play. Between 1906 and 1913 the issue was generally treated as a problem centred about players and their coaches, and thus took the form of an appeal to principles rather than to audiences. How-ever, the development of the high audience appeal that we shall show unfolding after 1913 was not autonomous and unheralded. If public relations became a dominant factor by 1915, when the University of Pittsburgh introduced numbers for players in order to spur the sale of programmes, it had its roots in the 1905–13 period. The rules committee of 1906, by its defensive action on roughhouse rules, had already implicitly acknowledged a broad public vested interest in the ethos of the game. Let us turn to look at the speed with which football was soon permeated by broad social meanings unanticipated by the founders of the sport.

By 1913, the eve of the First World War, innovation in American industry had ceased to be the prerogative of Baptist, Calvinist, and North of Ireland tycoons. Giannini was starting his Bank of America; the Jews were entering the movies and the garment hegemonies. Yet these were exceptions, and the second generation of immigrants, taught in America to be dissatisfied with the manual work their fathers did, were seldom finding the easy paths of ascent promised in success literature. Where, for one thing, were they to go to college? If they sought to enter the older eastern institutions, would they face a social struggle? Such anxieties probably contributed to the fact that the game of boyish and spirited brawn played at the eastern centres of intellect and cultivation was to be overthrown by the new game of craft and field manoeuvre that got its first rehearsal at the hands of two second-generation poor boys attending little-known Notre Dame.

The more significant of the two boys, Knute Rockne, was, to be sure, of Danish Protestant descent and only later became a Catholic.[9] During their summer vacation jobs as lifeguards on Lake Michigan, Rockne and Gus Dorais decided to work as a passing team. Playing West Point early in the season of 1913, they put on the first demonstration of the spiral pass that makes scientific use of the difference in shape between the round ball used in the kicking game and the oval that gradually replaced it when ball-carrying began. As the first players to exploit the legal pass, they rolled up a surprise victory over Army. One of the effects of the national change in rules was to bring the second-generation boys of the early twentieth century to the front, with a craft innovation that added new elements of surprise, "system" and skull-session to a game that had once revolved about an ethos of brawn plus character-building.

With the ethnic shift, appears to have come a shift in type of hero. The work-minded glamour of an all-round craftsman like Jim Thorpe gave way to the people-minded glamour of backfield generals organising deceptive forays into enemy territory—of course, the older martial virtues are not so much ruled out as partially incorporated in the new image. In saying this, it must not be forgotten, as sports columnist Red Smith has pointed out, that the fictional Yale hero, Dick Merriwell, is openly and shamelessly represented as a dirty player in the first chapters of his career. But the difference is that his deviation from standard sportsmanship consisted largely of slugging, not of premeditated wiliness. In fact, the Yale Era, even into Camp's reign, was characterised by a game played youthfully, with little attention to the players' prestige outside college circles. Again, the second-generationers mark a change. A variety of sources, including letters to the sports page, indicate that a Notre Dame victory became representational in a way a Yale or Harvard victory never was, and no Irish or Polish boy on the team could escape the symbolism. And by the self-confirming process, the Yale or Harvard showing became symbolic in turn, and the game could never be returned, short of intramuralisation, to the players themselves and their earlier age of innocent dirtiness.[10] The heterogeneity of America which had made it impossible to play the Rugby game at Yale had finally had its effect in transforming the meaning of the game to a point where Arnold of Rugby might have difficulty in drawing the right moral or any moral from it. Its "ideal types" had undergone a deep and widespread character-ological change.

For the second-generation boy, with his father's muscles but not his father's motives, football soon became a means to career ascent. So was racketeering, but football gave acceptance, too—acceptance into the democratic fraternity of the entertainment world where performance counts and ethnic origin is hardly a handicap. More-over, Americans as onlookers welcomed the anti-traditional inno-vations of a Rockne, and admired the trick that worked, whatever the opposing team and alumni may have thought about the effort involved. One wonders whether Rockne and Dorais may not have gotten a particular pleasure from their craftiness by thinking of it as a counter-image to the stereotype of muscle-men applied to their fathers.

It was in 1915, at about the same time that the newcomers per-fected their passing game, that the recruitment of players began in earnest. Without such recruitment, the game could not have served as a career route for many of the second generation who would not have had the cash or impetus to make the class jump that college involved.[11]

The development of the open and rationalised game has led step by step not only to the T formation, but also to the two-platoon system. These innovations call for a very different relationship among the players than was the case under the older star system. For the game is now a co-operative enterprise in which mistakes are too costly—to the head coach, the budget, even the college itself—to be left to individual initiative. At least at one institution, an anthropologist has been called in to study the morale problems of the home team, and to help in the scouting of opposing teams. To the learning of Taylor, there has been added that of Mayo, and coaches are conscious of the need to be group-dynamics leaders rather than old-line straw bosses.

Today, the semi-professionalised player, fully conscious of how many people's living depends on him, cannot be exhorted by Frank Merriwell appeals, but needs to be "handled". And the signals are no longer the barks of the first Camp-trained quarterback—hardly more differentiated than a folkdance caller's—but are cues of great subtlety and mathematical precision for situations planned in ad-vance with camera shots and character fill-ins of the opposing team. James Worthy and other advocates of a span of control beyond the usual half-dozen of the older military and executive manuals might find support for their views in the way an eleven is managed. Industrial, military, and football teamwork have all a common cultural frame.

Yet it would be too simple to say that football has ceased to be a game for its players, and has become an industry, or a training for industry. In the American culture as a whole, no sharp line exists between work and play, and in some respects the more work-like an activity becomes, the more it can successfully conceal elements of playfulness.[12] Just because the sophisticated "amateur" of today does not have his manhood at stake in the antique do-or-die fashion (though his manhood may be involved, in very ambivalent ways, in his more generalised role as athlete and teammate), there can be a relaxation of certain older demands and a more detached enjoyment of perfection of play irrespective of partisanship.

The role of football tutor to the audience has been pushed heavily on to radio and TV announcers (some of whom will doubtless be mobile into the higher-status role of commentators on politics or symphony broadcasts). The managerial coalescence of local betting pools into several big oceans has also contributed to the audience stake in the game. Yet all that has so far been said does not wholly explain alumnus and subway-alumnus loyalties. It may be that we have to read into this interest of the older age groups a much more general aspect of American behaviour: the pious and near-compulsory devotion of the older folks to whatever the younger folks are alleged to find important. The tension between the generations doubtless contributes to the hysterical note of solemnity in the efforts of some older age groups to control the ethics of the game, partly perhaps as a displacement of their efforts to control youthful sexuality.

And this problem in turn leads to questions about the high percentage of women in the American football audience, compared with that of any other country, and the high salience of women in football as compared with baseball imagery (in recent American football films, girls have been singled out as the most influential section of the spectators). The presence of these women heightens the sexual impact of everything in and around the game, from shoulder-pads to the star system, as the popular folklore of the game recognises. Although women are not expected to attend baseball games, when they do attend they are expected to understand them and to acquire, if not a "male" attitude, at least something approaching companionship on a basis of equality with their male escorts.[13]

For all its involvement with such elemental themes in American life, it may be that football has reached the apex of its audience appeal. With bigness comes vulnerability: "inter-industry" competition is invited, and so are rising costs—the players, though not yet unionised, learn early in high school of their market value and, like Jim in Huckleberry Finn, take pride in it.[14] The educators' counter-reformation cannot be laughed off. With the lack of ethnic worlds to conquer, we may soon find the now-decorous Irish of the Midwest embarrassed by Notre Dame's unbroken victories. Perhaps the period of innovation which began in 1823 at Rugby has about come to an end in the United States, with large changes likely to result only if the game is used as a device for acculturation to America, not by the vanishing stream of immigrants to that country, but by the rest of the world that will seek the secret of American victories on the playing fields of South Bend.

NOTES

1 The growing scale of college football is indicated by its dollar place in the American leisure economy. In 1929, out of $4.3 billion recreation expenditures by Americans, the college football gate accounted for $22 million. In 1950, out of $11.2 billion on such expenditures, it accounted for $103 million. While something less than 1% of the total United States recreation account, college football had ten times the gross income of professional football. The 1950 gate of $103 million suggests that a total capital of perhaps $250 million is invested in the college football industry. The revenue figures, above, of course, do not include the invisible subsidisation of football, nor do they hint at the place that football pools occupy in the American betting economy.

2 A commemorative stone at Rugby reads as follows:

> THIS STONE
> COMMEMORATES THE EXPLOIT OF
> WILLIAM WEBB ELLIS
> WHO WITH A FINE DISREGARD FOR THE RULES OF
> FOOTBALL, AS PLAYED IN HIS TIME,
> FIRST TOOK THE BALL IN HIS ARMS AND RAN WITH IT,
> THUS ORIGINATING THE DISTINCTIVE FEATURE OF
> THE RUGBY GAME
> A.D. 1823

3 Walter Camp and Lorin F. Deland, *Football*.

4 Cf. his *An Outline of Social Psychology*, pp. 93–182.

5 "Fifty years ago arguments followed almost every decision the referee made. The whole team took part, so that half the time the officials scarcely knew who was captain. The player who was a good linguist was always a priceless asset." John W. Heisman, who played for both Brown and Penn in the 1890's, quoted in Frank G. Menke, *Encyclopedia of Sports*, p. 293.

6 Sigfried Giedion, *Mechanization Takes Command*, pp. 21–7.

7 In view of the prejudice against "Taylorism" today, shared by men and management as well as the intellectuals, let us record our admiration

for Taylor's achievement, our belief that he was less insensitive to psychological factors than is often claimed, and more "humane" in many ways than his no less manipulative, self-consciously psychological successors.

8 "In a 1905 game between Pennsylvania and Swarthmore, the Pennsy slogan was 'Stop Bob Maxwell', one of the greatest linemen of all time. He was a mighty man, with amazing ability to roll back enemy plunges. The Penn players, realising that Maxwell was a menace to their chances of victory, took 'dead aim' at him throughout the furious play.

"Maxwell stuck it out, but when he tottered off the field, his face was a bloody wreck. Some photographer snapped him, and the photo of the mangled Maxwell, appearing in a newspaper, caught the attention of the then President Roosevelt. It so angered him, that he issued an ultimatum that if rough play in football was not immediately ruled out, he would abolish it by executive edict." Frank G. Menke, *Encyclopedia of Sports.*

Notice here the influence of two historical factors on football development: one, the occupancy of the White House in 1905 by the first President of the United States who was a self-conscious patron of youth, sport, and the arts; two, the relative newness in 1905 of photographic sports coverage. Widespread increased photographic coverages of popular culture was the direct result of the newspaper policies of William Randolph Hearst, beginning about 1895.

9 "After the church, football is the best thing we have", Rockne.

10 One of us, while a Harvard undergraduate, sought with several friends to heal the breach between Harvard and Princeton—a breach whose bitterness could hardly be credited today. The Harvards believed Princeton played dirty—it certainly won handily in those years of the 20's—while Princetonians believed themselves snubbed by Harvard as crude parvenus trying to make a trio out of the Harvard-Yale duo. The diplomatic problems involved in seeking to repair these status slights and scars were a microcosm of the Congress of Westphalia or Vienna—whether the Harvard or Princeton athletic directors should enter the room first was an issue. A leak to the Hearst press destroyed our efforts, as alumni pressure forced denials of any attempt to resume relations, but the compromise formulas worked out were eventually accepted, about the time that the University of Chicago "solved" the problem of the intellectual school by withdrawing from the game altogether.

11 See George Saxon, "Immigrant Culture in a Stratified Society", *Modern Review*, II, No. 2, February 1948.

12 See Riesman's discussion in his essay "The Themes of Work and Play in the Structure of Freud's Thought", *Individualism Reconsidered*, Glencoe, Ill., 1954, pp. 310–33.

13 Anthropologist Ray Birdwhistell convincingly argues that football players play with an eye to their prestige among teammates, other football players, and other men.

14 Their pride varies to some extent with their place on the team. Linemen, with the exception of ends, have lower status than backfield men. Many players believe that backfields are consciously and unconsciously recruited from higher social strata than linemen.

PART III (A)

SPORTS AND SOCIALISATION

Introduction

It has been recognised for a long time now that play and games perform important functions in socialisation, the process during which the asocial baby is gradually moulded into a social human being. George Herbert Mead, for example, has shown how they assist in the emergence of self-identity and in the capacity to interact with others.[1] Jean Piaget has explored some of the relations between the play of children and the development of moral judgment.[2] By and large, however, the complex relations between participation in sports and late childhood and adolescent socialisation are virtually unexplored. This is surprising, in view of the claims and counter-claims which are sometimes made on behalf of sport as an agency for character training.

It has only been possible, to include two articles on sports and socialisation in this book of readings. Each of them tackles a different aspect of the subject and approaches it from a different angle. Each of them, furthermore, is suggestive of further lines of research. The first is a comparative study by Zurcher and Meadow in which they use a largely neo-Freudian model to explore the way in which the different patterns of socialisation and resultant character structures of people in Mexico and the United States have led them to espouse characteristically different national sports. The second, by Schafer and Armer, discusses a survey which they have carried out on some of the relations between participation in sports and educational attainment in the typical American high school.

Zurcher and Meadow's essay is entitled "On Bullfights and Baseball". It begins with a discussion of the way in which socialisation frustrates the natural impulses of children. They are forced, for example, to learn to do all sorts of things that they would not naturally do. Such frustrations generate hostility, but the children cannot express it directly against their parents, the main frustrating agents, because they are too powerful. They fear the punishment that would almost certainly ensue. The result is a reservoir of hostility towards authority which can neither be completely repressed nor rendered ineffective. However, the individual has to deal with it in some way or another if he is not to become neurotic.

What he does is to seek sources for discharging it in a socially
approved manner. One such outlet, according to Zurcher and
Meadow, is provided by the national sport. It is an institutionalised
means for dealing with this problem. It symbolises, they argue, "in
its structure and function the processes in the modal family that
both engender and restrict hostility towards authority . . . and exemplifies a socially legitimised means for expression of that hostility".

After their preliminary discussion, Zurcher and Meadow compare
patterns of socialisation in Mexico with those in the United States
in order to show how they lead on the one hand to people with a
different type of character structure and on the other to correspondingly different national sports. Thus, there is a strong emphasis on
virility in Mexican culture (the *macho* complex). This is reflected in
the family which is male-dominated and severely authoritarian. It
serves as a proving ground for the dominance needs of the father.
Young boys typically react to the tyranny of their fathers by
trying to emulate them. They attempt to dominate their younger
and their female siblings, fight a lot and are sexually boastful and
promiscuous as soon as this is possible. For their part, wives and
daughters react by forming a "female mutual protection society".
They wait patiently to seize control whenever the father's dominance
shows signs of faltering. Such a family climate tends to produce over-
compensating sons, highly ambivalent towards their fathers, and
women who profoundly distrust all men. The bullfight, Zurcher and
Meadow suggest, relives aspects of this frustration engendering
family situation and provides an outlet for the resultant aggression.
The bull, with his flagrant masculinity, is symbolic of the father. The
frail matador is symbolic of the son. His apparent helplessness *vis-
à-vis* the bull symbolically emphasises the helplessness of the son in
relation to the father. Yet the whole affair is constructed in such a
manner that the "son" typically emerges as triumphant. In this way,
according to Zurcher and Meadow, by watching the struggle between the matador and the bull, the Mexican male is able to
compensate symbolically but uninhibitedly and with all the hate and
invective he can muster for the deprivations suffered during childhood and adolescence at the hands of his tyrannical father. Mexican
women spectators, as an expression of their generalised hostility towards men, may unconsciously desire the matador to be killed as
well as the bull.

The American family, Zurcher and Meadow argue, particularly
the culturally ideal family of people of Anglo-Saxon descent, provides a striking contrast to its Mexican counterpart. Here, the ideological byword is equality and this leads authority to be muted in
an unrealistic manner. Parents are expected to be the "pals" or

"buddies" of their children but at the same time to socialise them into the dominant values of society. This requires authority and its use necessarily leads to frustration. Hostility and aggression are thus engendered in the children but they are faced with a peculiar dilemma: how can one overtly show hostility towards a "pal" or a "buddy"? In such a family situation, Zurcher and Meadow suggest, hostility tends to be intellectualised and displaced. The Mexican acts out his hostility but the American rationalises his and elaborately disguises it with verbal repartee. Just as the authoritarian Mexican family reflects authority patterns in Mexican society however, so, too, the ideologically egalitarian, intellectualising American family reflects the abstract, bureaucratic, impersonal and ideologically egalitarian character of the overall culture of the United States. Again, Zurcher and Meadow suggest, this pattern is reflected in the national sport. Baseball is a highly elaborate, abstract game in which equality is a central ethic. It mutes aggression in a masterful way behind its reciprocity, rules, records and rituals. In this, they argue, it duplicates the vagueness and intellectualisation of conflict in the American family and provides a markedly abstract and controlled means for expressing hostility towards authority.

"On Scholarship and Interscholastic Athletics" by Walter E. Schafer and J. Michael Armer tackles a vastly different but none the less interesting and important problem. Unlike Zurcher and Meadow who are concerned with the way in which patterns of socialisation lead people in different countries to espouse characteristically different types of sport, they are concerned with the reverse equation: with the effects of sport in a limited area of socialisation, that of educational attainment. Numbers of people have argued that the great emphasis on sports in American high schools militates against the achievement of strictly academic goals. Similar arguments are frequently propounded in this country, too. Schafer and Armer decided to subject them to empirical test. They designed a questionnaire and systematically gathered data on a sample of 585 boys attending or who had recently left two Midwestern senior high schools. What they discovered was this: that there is a slight *positive* correlation between participation in sports and academic performance (i.e. the sportsmen in their sample performed on average *better* academically than non-sportsmen): that the positive relationship increases with greater participation; and that there are no significant differences between major and minor sports in this respect. They also found that boys otherwise least likely to succeed academically such as those from working class backgrounds and those with no aspirations for a college education appear to benefit most from participation in sports. Their data, they conclude, although the positive relationship is slight and the size of the sample small, indicates that, far from exercising a damaging effect, participation in sports is conducive to higher levels of academic attainment. Why this should be the case cannot be deduced from their data but Schafer and Armer propose a number of hypotheses which may help to explain it. Among the more interesting of them are these: that the "achievement motivation" necessary for successful participation in sports may reflect a more general pattern which makes itself felt in the field of study also or that the prestige accorded to successful sportsmen may heighten their self-esteem and give them confidence which is transferred to other areas of behaviour including that of their schoolwork. Of course, as Shafer and Armer note, it may simply be the case that teachers mark their work more leniently than they do that of non-sportsmen. At present, one cannot tell. Schafer and Armer's study, however, even though it is inconclusive in this vital respect, is based on a precise and systematic methodology and can serve as an excellent model for further research in the field. It would be interesting to discover whether similar relationships can be found in countries other than the U.S.A. It would also be interesting to discover the precise nature of the causal links which are involved. Comparative studies, in fact, might prove to be the best way of getting at the aetiological roots of this interesting and important problem.

NOTES

1 See his *Mind, Self and Society*, Chicago, 1934.
2 See *The Moral Judgement of the Child*, London, 1932.

CHAPTER 10

On Bullfights and Baseball: An Example of Interaction of Social Institutions[1]*

Louis A. Zurcher and Arnold Meadow

Los toros dan y los toros quitan.
Mexican proverb

The typical American male strikes
out the Yankee side before going
to sleep at night.
James Thurber

A "social institution", typically considered, is "a comparatively stable, permanent, and intricately organised system of behaviour formally enforced within a given society and serving social objectives regarded as essential for the survival of the group".[2] Four major social institutions are found very widely in human society: 1. economic, 2. familial, 3. political, and 4. religious. Through these the society strives to achieve material well-being, an adequate population, organisation, and some feeling of control over the unknown or unexpected. As a society becomes more urbanised, more "highly developed", it may evolve additional institutions, such as the recreational, the educational, and the aesthetic, which take over functions no longer adequately performed by the basic four.

Since individuals have overlapping roles in a number of the society's institutions, and since each institution is a functional segment of the total, ongoing society, the interaction of institutions presents itself as a fruitful area for study. This interaction is a key variable in the process of social change and highlights cultural themes running through the structures of a society.

The central institution of a society and its primary agent of socialisation is the family—which interacts in various degrees with

* Reprinted from *The International Journal of Comparative Sociology*, Vol. VIII, No. 1, March, 1967.

other institutions. Whiting and Child, for example, have described the impact of values learned in the family upon behaviour in other social institutions.[3] Kardiner has written of the ways in which the religious institution is shaped by family patterns.[4] Tumin has described the interaction between the family and the economic institution.[5]

In this paper the authors will focus their attention on some aspects of the interaction between two social institutions: 1. the family and 2. the institutionalised recreation form known as the "national sport". It is hypothesised that the national sport symbolises in its structure and function the processes in the modal family that both engender and restrict hostility towards authority, and that it also exemplifies a socially legitimised means for the expression of that hostility.

As Dollard has described it, the socialisation process itself engenders hostility towards authority. The demands of socialisation, which of course have their focal point in the family, conflicts in many instances with the child's own behavioural choices. The child is thus frustrated and desires to move against the restrictive figure but does not do so because he fears punishment. This fear acts as a catalyst, inciting further aggressive feelings towards the frustrating agent. Repression of this aggression is not complete and the individual seeks sources for its legitimised expression.[6]

Hostility towards authority is especially generated in the authoritarian family milieu, or when some characteristics of the parents create for the child an uncertainty of or rejection of his or the parent's familial role. Situations such as this not only arouse keen hostility but are also usually unyieldingly restrictive and harshly punitive of any demonstration of that hostility.

From another view, it is quite possible that hostility towards authority is a lesson of, as well as a reaction to, socialisation. That is, the characteristics of the society may be such that a general distrust for or hatred of authority has become part of the cultural value system. This is particularly the case in those societies which have undergone long periods of manipulation and oppression under a tyrannical or exploitative power structure.

Since every society depends, from the family up, on authority to maintain relative consistency of behaviour, and since not all the members of the society will take well to that restrictive authority, it follows that the society must provide as a further means of control some outlet for the resultant hostility towards authority—not only that incited in the family situation or learned in socialisation, but also the generalised forms of hostility that are re-awakened and intensified by the demands of interpersonal relations. The provisions for such expression, as well as the degree to which it is controlled, vary from society to society. As Dollard points out, "Each society standardises its own permissive patterns, and differs from the next in the degree to which hostility may be expressed."[7]

In the terminology of modern dynamic psychiatry, it can be said that the defence processes which societies employ to channel hostility differ from culture to culture. These defence processes will be differentially manifested not only in the families of different societies, but also, as we hypothesise, in their "national sports", since both are institutions of these societies.

PLAY, THE GAME, THE SPORT

Play has been considered by a number of social scientists to be of major importance in the socialisation and personality formation of the individual. Other writers have seen the various forms of play as reflecting the particular traits, values, expectations, and the degree of social control in a given culture. In addition to the foregoing, play is a "permissive pattern", a "channel" serving as a legitimised means for the symbolic demonstration of hostility towards authority figures.

There is a hierarchy of play extending from seemingly purposeless, repetitive movements in the crib, through games (with competition, an "ethic" of some sort, elaborate rules and regulations, mutual player expectations, and an ostensible purpose), up to the highest level of complexity, the "organised sport" (with schedules, painstaking record keeping, large audiences, governing bodies supplying officials and dispensing rules, "seasons", recruiting, training, and if professional, the paying of participants). The "national sport" is an organised sport that has been adopted by a nation as its own special "home-owned" variety. When, for example, the "American Way" is alluded to, it implies, among other things, apple pie, hot-dogs, mother, Disneyland, and baseball.

It is hypothesised, then, that the national sport, as the epitome of institutionalised recreation, maximally reflects that aspect of the "social character" of a society which establishes the degree of tolerance for the expression of hostility towards authority. Furthermore, it is hypothesised that the national sport replicates, on the playing field or in the arena, the family processes which engender, exacerbate, or restrict that hostility, and will manifest the "societal ideal" for its expression.

Baseball is the national sport of the United States of America. Its counterpart in the United States of Mexico is the *corrida de toros*, the bullfight.[8] An analysis of baseball and the bullfight, and of the modal family patterns in their respective societies, should reveal, especially with regard to the dynamic of hostility towards authority, a facet of the interaction between the social institutions of family and recreation. In addition to the formation and legitimised expression of hostility, the analysis should reveal, as they appear in both the family and the sport, some of the characteristic defence mechanisms, values, and social relationships shared by members in each of the two societies.

ANALYSIS OF FAMILY PATTERNS

The Mexican family typically is described as a proving ground for the dominance needs of the father. Though the family structure is essentially mother centred, the father compulsively strives to maintain his *macho* (manly) role and to prove that he has *huevos largos* (large "eggs"), *muy cojones* (abundant testicles) or "hair on his chest" by playing the role of the emotionally detached but severally authoritarian head of the household. He overtly disparages the achievements of, violently disapproves of any show of independence in, and physically punishes any demonstration of hostility by his wife or children. Often, the children are punished by their father for sins (especially sexual) projected upon them from his own guilt-ridden repertoire. Drunkenness, promiscuity, and abandonment, as components of *machismo*, further compound the overpowering image of father. This pattern of behaviour has been detailed in the literature by Lewis, Gillin, Meadow *et al.*, and Diaz-Guerrero.[9]

The question then arises, how do the children, especially the males, handle the hostility that they cannot direct against the mitigated feudalism of such an unyielding socialisation figure as the Mexican father? It appears that the son attempts to recoup his identity by emulating the father's example, but he does so in other quarters (dominating his younger sisters and brothers, fighting, being sexually promiscuous). The wife and daughters seem to develop a solidly female "mutual protection society", adopt a passively controlling "martyr" role, and wait patiently to seize control whenever the father's dominance falters. Thus exists a climate which fosters over-compensating sons, with ambivalence (passive-aggressive) towards the father, and daughters who, because of hostility towards a punishing father, distrust all men.

A safe but indirect manner for the Mexican male to express hostility against his father, then, seems to be one of "showing the old boy that I am as much, or more, man than he is". This, however, cannot be done in direct confrontation. Rather it is done in spheres away from the father's bailiwick—away from his watchful eye. As Jesus Sanchez puts it, "to grow up away from your parents helps you to become mature".[10] The son can't compete with the father directly, so he acts out his hostility guided by his father's example, but on his own terms in his own battle field.

The family is, of course, a reflection of and the basis for culture. Mexican culture is, as is the family, authoritarian and hierarchial in structure.[11] Though Mexican citizens have a general distrust of and disregard for the "officials" in government, church, and other large-scale organisations, they are most hesitant to directly or overtly criticise them. This passiveness in the face of authority has, as the passiveness to the father, an aggressive counterpart. As a matter of fact, Meadow et al.,[12] in depth studies of Mexican psychopathology, cite different degrees of passive-aggressiveness as a central feature of the modal personality of the Mexican. Does this aggressive component demonstrate itself in a socially acceptable manner in a Mexican institution? The premise here is that the bullfight will relieve aspects of the frustration engendering conflict and provide an outlet for the resultant aggression. It would be expected, from observations of the Mexican family and from examination of the symptom-formation in Mexican psychopathology, that the legitimised expression would be of a type allowing "acting out" of hostility. But first, before considering the bullfight itself, let us examine by contrast the situation in the Anglo-American family.

If the Anglo-American father were to attempt to follow the dominance pattern of his Mexican counterpart, he would posthaste be imprisoned, divorced with the condemnation of the court, or at best, socially ostracised.

In the Anglo nuclear family, as in the Anglo culture, the ideological byword is equality. Mother, father, son and daughter are "members of the group" and have a right to be heard, to voice their opinion, and to register their vote around the family conference table. Everyone "shares the responsibility" and "pulls his weight" in the "togetherness" of the family.

The Anglo ethic, loaded as it is with the popular meaning of "democracy" encourages an unrealistic muting of authority as it exists in the society. Fathers and mothers are not supposed to be authority figures but "pals", "buddies", "good heads", and "regular guys". They are still, however, expected to be the prime socialisation agents of Anglo society, and as such, must impress upon the child an awareness of behaviour which is accepted and expected by that society. This cannot be done without the exertion of authority. Socialisation makes demands that often are contrary to the child's own preferences. Thus, the frustration-aggression cycle is manifested. But how can the child demonstrate overt hostility to a "pal", a "buddy" or an equal. Furthermore, the vagueness of the parental role in the Anglo family presents the child with a mercurial identification model. Should he be dependent upon or independent of his parents—and when? Mother preaches togetherness, but usually agrees with the television and movie stereotype of the well-meaning, bungling father who needs her subtle domination.

Authoritarianism from people who are not supposed to be authoritarian, vagueness of or conflict in role expectations, obscure role models, plus the restrictions of socialisation set the stage for hostility towards authority in the Anglo family. Typically, however, this hostility, and in fact most familial conflict, is intellectualised and abstracted into elaborate displacements and doublebind communications.

The Mexican child seems to have clear reason for hostility, but can't reveal it to the father because he may be beaten. He can't be hostile to the mother because she is a "saint". The Anglo child has difficulty showing overt hostility in his family because, first, he has a hard time tracing the basis for his frustration, and second, he can't be aggressive to two "buddies". But the hostility from socialisation and role conflict is still there and needs expression.

The Mexican is forced to be passive to the frustrating agent, but along with this passiveness rides an aggressive component. If the Mexican has been shaped into a passive-aggressive, then it seems feasible to posit as a central feature of the Anglo modal personality the defence mechanism of intellectualisation. The Anglo child learns from his parents to intellectualise conflict, to abstract hostility, to disengage it from painful affect, and to deal with it in a symbolic, ritualistic fashion. Whereas the Mexican acts out his hostility, the Anglo rationalises it and elaborately disguises it with verbal repartee.[13] Manuel Sanchez observed "life in the United States is too abstract, too mechanical. The people are like precision machines".[14]

As does the Mexican family in the Mexican culture, the Anglo family reflects and maintains the Anglo culture. Anglo society has been characterised by a plethora of writers as being abstract, universalistic, materialistic, impersonal, unemotional, and bureaucratic. One would expect, then, the ideal legitimised outlets for hostility to be similarly complex, elaborately diffuse, and intellectualised, impersonalised and de-affected after a bureaucratic fashion. The national sport of the United States, baseball, we have hypothesised, should fully reflect this pattern.

THE BULLFIGHT

Aficionados who are of a mind to describe the essence of the bullfight do so in terms that parallel the *corrida* with a Greek drama. Robinson writes that the theme of the bullfight lies "somewhere between the themes of fate and death".[15] Allen proclaims the bullfight to be "the last drama of our times that has death as an immediate object".[16] In *The Brave Bulls*, two of Lea's Mexican characters discuss the *fiesta brava* as follows:

> It is a form of drama as certainly as the works of Sophocles. But what a difference between the happenings on a stage or in a poem, and the happening in a plaza!
> ... The festival of bulls is the only art form in which violence bloodshed, and death are palpable and unfeigned. It is the only art in which the artist deals actual death and risks actual death that gives the art its particular power ...[17]

Who, then, do the principals in this drama represent? Who is killing, and who is being killed? We have hypothesised that the events in the bullfight will provide a socially legitimised, symbolic, vehicle for the aggression towards authority which has been developed mainly in and by the Mexican family situation.

Since the reader may be unfamiliar with the structure of the bullfight, we shall undertake here a brief description before proceeding to the analysis.

Prior to the appearance of any of the principals in the *corrida*, the *alguacil*, a mounted bailiff, rides across the bull ring and, with a bow and a flourish, renders his respect to the *Presidente* (a national, state, or local official), who is in charge of the conduct of the bullfight. The *alguacil* will thereafter be the courier for the *Presidente*, and will transmit orders from him to the principals in the *corrida*. Thus is the hierarchial nature of Mexican society represented in the bullfight. No major shift in action, no new sequence is attempted without first gaining the nod of the *Presidente*. It is he who will pass final judgment upon the performance of the *matador*. He, and only he, can decide that the bull shall live (on rare occasions), or die. In essence he has the power of life and death. It is interesting to note that, though disapproval in the highly emotional framework of the *corrida* may incite the crowd eloquently and thoroughly to curse and insult the *matador*, his assistants, his mother, father, *compadres*, lovers, children, and future children, there is seldom a harsh word directed towards the sacrosanct *Presidente*. This respect remains, ironically, while symbolically authority is about to be murdered in the ring!

Upon receiving the nod from the *Presidente*, the *alguacil* rides out of the ring to lead back the *paseo*, or parade, which consists of, in splendid order, the *matadors*, their *banderilleros* (assistants), the *picadors*, the ring attendants, and the harnessed team whose task it will be to remove the dead bull from the ring. The *matadors* halt directly beneath the *Presidente* and bow their respect. Following this, all the principals, usually with the exception of a *banderillero*, leave the ring. The *Presidente* gives permission for the bull to be released, and the assistant receives the bull.

The bullfight itself consists of three major parts (*Los Tres Tercios de la Lidia*). In the first, the *banderilleros* work the bull with the cape, thus allowing the *matador* to observe the *toro's* idiosyncracies (direction of hook, favoured eye, and straightness of charge). Then the *picadors pic* the bull, this to demonstrate the bull's courage (by his charge to the horse) and to lower his head. Following this, the ring is cleared—the bull remains, having "conquered", for a moment, all his antagonists. The *banderilleros* (sometimes the *matador*), in the second major part, place the *banderillas* (barbed sticks), these to correct for the bull's tendency to hook in one or the other direction. The third part consists of *brindis*, or formal dedication of the bull to the *Presidente* (then to anyone else in the crowd the *matador* chooses), the work with the *muleta* (small red cloth), and, finally, the sword.

Since there are two bulls for each *matador*, and two or three *matadors* in each bullfight, these three segments are repeated from four to six times in an afternoon.

Such is the bare structure of the bullfight. This tells nothing of the key to, the vitality of, the drama in the ring, the feeling in the crowd, or the symbolic expression of hostility.

Perhaps a discussion of this can best be introduced by quoting the *matador* protagonist in Ramsey's *Fiesta* as he describes, when facing the bull, "a fear that never quite left him, and that encompassed others too indefinite for him to understand or even name, a fear of authority, of the powerful, the *patron* . . ."[18]—of the father! Freedom from this authority is granted, he contends, in those rare moments when fear is combated and overcome.

Characteristically, the Mexican son profoundly fears his father. Manuel Sanchez testifies that in order to become a man, the individual must escape his father. Yet it was not until he, himself, was twenty-nine years old that he smoked in his father's presence. At that time, Manuel, though fearful, felt himself to be acting most bravely by showing his father that he was a man—at twenty-nine years of age!

This need for "manhood" (courage, domination, sexual prowess) which we have mentioned many times above is crucial enough in the Mexican culture to claim a syndrome entity all its own—the *machismo*. *Macho* connotes maleness—demonstrable and blatant maleness. The individual who is *macho* is *muy hombre* (much man), abundantly endowed with sexual organs, and fears nothing. The most grave and threatening insult to the Mexican male is one that challenges his masculinity.

What more natural pre-occupation could one expect from a son who has been subject to an emasculating father—to a father whose own fear of male competition has led him to use his physical size to dominate his son? We have mentioned that one way the son can compensate for his subordinate role is to emulate his father in another sphere, and later in his own home with his own wife and children. But through the bullfight another compensation is offered. As a spectator (or better, a principal) he can compensate symbolically, uninhibitedly, with all the hate, insult, and invective that he can muster. What clearer representative of the father than the bull with his flagrant masculinity, awesome power, and potential to maim and kill? What clearer representative of the son than the delicate, almost fragile, *matador* whose protection obviously cannot be strength but must be courage? See how the bull charges the *banderilleros*! See how he hurls himself against the *pic* and the horse! How can the *matador* stand up to the bull? How can the son stand up to the father? Aha! *Toro*! Aha!

The *matador* provides the spectator with an amazingly flexible psychological figure. He can identify with the *matador's* courage, with his expertise, with his skill, and yet he can project upon the *matador*, especially in a bad performance, accusations of cowardice and powerlessness he has experienced himself in the constantly losing battle with his father. It is interesting that many bullfighters take nicknames with diminutive denotations—Joselito, Armillita Chico, Amoros Chico, Gallito, Machaquito, etc. Similarly, well over three hundred *matadors* whose names have been entered in the records have somewhere in their nickname the word *nino* (child)— El Nino de la Palma, etc. Thus is emphasised their smallness, their fragility *vis-à-vis* the bull. Thus is emphasised symbolically the helplessness of the child *vis-à-vis* the father. Strength is not nearly so valued an attribute of the *matador* as is demonstrable courage. The great *matadors* are not remembered for their muscle, but for their *macho*. Belmonte was sickly, Maera had wrists so fragile that he often dislocated them in a *faena* (series of passes), Manolete was painfully thin. In fact, size and strength may be a disadvantage. Joselito, a tall, athletic, and graceful man, often complained that he had to take more chances with the bull than the physically struggling Belmonte in order to make his *faenas* appear as difficult. When asked how he developed strength for the *corrida*, Gallo is said to have replied, "I smoke Havana cigars", adding that one cannot possibly match the bull for strength, but he can for courage. The *matador* must, then, appear finite when facing the awesome power of the bull. A sign of fear is acceptable, even desirable, if the *faena* is good. Thus is highlighted the fact that the *matador* has in spite of his fears faced, dominated, and killed the bull. A too calm, too nonchalant, too perfect *matador*, without the emotion of fear (and pride in controlling that fear), who cannot convey to the crowd that his is in fact a struggle in which he has faced, averred, and administered death to an over-powering force, may be viewed as a *matador* without *salsa*—without "sauce". The fact of the matter is that the Mexican father is threatening, does physically hurt, and does strike fear in the heart of his sons. To dominate and destroy him would be a remarkable feat. If the bullfight is to provide symbolically a resolution of this one-sided affair then it must be representative of its acts, events, and especially of its emotions.

We have mentioned earlier that the passive role forced upon the Mexican child brings with it an aggressive component—a dynamic seen again and again in the Mexican personality structure. This interaction is beautifully manifested in the three commandments for the *matador's* conduct in the bullfight—*Parar! Templar! Mandar!* (Keep the feet quiet! Move the cape and *muleta* slowly! Dominate and control the bull!) The central feature is, in the modern bullfight, the domination of the bull.[19] But domination is expressed in the *bonita corrida* with a studied parsimony of movement, with a deliberately slow tempo. Boyd writes that "the *matador* gains mastery by his cunning awareness of the power of the absence of movement".[20] The most valued placing of the *banderillas* and the most honoured kill both consist of the *matador* performing these tasks while passively standing his ground and receiving the charge of the bull. The *matador's* knees may knock together with fright, and the crowd will understand—as long as he continues to *parar*.

Kluckhohn sees this passive element in another Mexican institution, religion. She describes the Mexican's dependence upon the Saints and submissive and accepting attitude towards the supernatural.[21] Since the basic cultural values run through all of a society's institutions, it is not surprising to find this same passivity modifying the legitimised expression of hostility towards authority in the bullfight.

The *matador* demands submissive behaviour from his own assistants. Traditionally, the latter have not been allowed to eat at the same table with the *matador*, must obey his orders immediately and without question and, regardless of the amount of the *matador's* income, are paid very poorly. Hemingway writes ". . . a *matador* feels that the less he pays his subordinates the more man he is and in the same way the nearer he can bring his subordinates to slaves the more man he feels he is".[22] Thus, out of the ring as well as in, the *matador* perpetuates the *machismo*. This is also observed in the sexual exploits of *matadors*, and highlighted especially by their blatant disregard for and high incidence of syphilis. "You cannot expect", Hemingway says, "a *matador* who has triumphed in the afternoon by taking chances not to take them in the night."[23]

Often the *matador* will single out a woman in the crowd and dedicate the kill to her, expecting, of course, some token of appreciation in return. One of the authors witnessed a *matador* leaving the *Plaza de Toros* after a successful *corrida* survey a bevy of adoring females, make his selection with a toss of the head and beckoning gesture with his blood-stained arm, and walk off hand-in-hand with the amazed and grateful girl to her car.

It would seem from the *matador's* point of view that the crowd is symbolically female. The *matador* (son) looks for approval to the crowd (mother) when he demonstrates his domination, his superiority over, the bull (father). The crowd continually calls on the *matador* to work closer to the bull. It demands that he take chances and promises in return to give him manifestations of approval. In his study of Mexican psychopathology, Meadow has observed that the Mexican mother subtly encourages the son to compete with the father, thus providing her an added element of control. It is not surprising, then, to see this dynamic represented in the *corrida*. The crowd (mother) calls for the *matador* (son) to challenge, to' dominate, the bull (father), and offers love as a reward. *Matadors* who have been gored when responding to the crowd's urges have been reported to turn to the crowd, blaming it, shouting, for example, "See what you have done to me! See what your demands have done!" It may well be that the females in the crowd would enjoy seeing both the *matador* and the bull destroyed, thus expressing the generalised hostility that Mexican women have towards men. For the Mexican female, the *corrida* may be a legitimised way of acting out aggression towards dominating husbands, fathers, and lovers.

A famous breeder of *toros* writes that ". . . certain of their (the fighting bulls) number will stay home to take care of the cows and carry on the breed with those formidable sacs that swing between their legs. But not our fighters to the death. They are virgins. It is a curious thing, our festivals."[24] The bull has not experienced mating, and never will, because the *matador* will kill him. Perhaps the son will have dominated and killed that symbolic father before he can mate with the mother (the *matador* prays before each fight to the Virgin Mother).

In *Capeas*, or informal street bullfights, the bull may be slaughtered by many people (if the town can afford the loss) and often the testicles will be cut off, roasted, and devoured. At one time it was customary in the *corrida* to remove the testicles (*criadillas*) of the first killed bull of the afternoon and serve them as a prepared meal to the *Presidente* during the killing of the fifth bull. Thus with one symbolic move were expressed and satisfied two needs— to dominate and render forever impotent the father and to incorporate the "source" of his strength. In the same vein, small children are often seen flooding the ring after the last kill, dipping their fingers in the fallen bull's blood and licking their fingers of this fluid of courage. If the *matador* has performed well and is acclaimed by the crowd the *Presidente* may award him the bull's ear, two ears, or two ears and a tail, in that ascending order of honour.

Thus through the *corrida* does the Mexican spectator, identifying with the *matador* and re-enacting the family situation, not only symbolically dominate and destroy the unyielding and hated authority figure, but he captures some of that figure's awesome power.

The bullfight itself has undergone considerable change. What exists now, as "modern bullfighting", began with Belmonte in the early 1930's, and according to the *aficionado*, is considerably different from its earlier stages. Hemingway writes,

> As the *corrida* has developed and decayed, there has been less emphasis on the form of the killing, which was once the whole thing, and more on the cape work, the placing of the *banderillas*, and the work with the *muleta*. The cape, the *banderillas*, and the *muleta* have all become ends in themselves rather than means to an end . . .[25]

A bullfighter is now judged, and paid much more on the basis of his ability to pass the bull quietly and closely with the cape than on his ability as a swordsman. The increasing importance and demand for the style of cape work and work with the *muleta*, that was invented or perfected by Juan Belmonte; the expectation and demand that each *matador* pass the bull, giving a complete performance with cape, in the *quites*; and the pardoning of deficiency in killing of a *matador* who is an artist with the cape and *muleta*, are the main changes in modern bullfighting.[26]

Pre-Belmonte, then, the "kill" was the focal point of the bull-fight. The matador who could kill with lust and enjoyment was admired and loved. The earlier phases of the *corrida* were to demonstrate the bull's courage and power and to prepare him for the kill. The essence of the bullfight was the final sword thrust, the actual encounter between man and bull where for an interminable moment they became one figure and was called the "Moment of Truth". Now, to accommodate the emphasis on the cape and *muleta* work, the bulls are smaller and killing is barely a "third of the fight"[27] and anticlimactic to the cloth work. As Boyd points out, the "Moment of Truth" is now at the highlight of domination with the cape and *muleta*, not at the kill.[28] Hemingway agrees, writing that the emphasis in the modern *corrida* is upon dominance rather than killing and that this has gone hand-in-glove with the padding of the horses, the smaller bulls, and the changing of the *picador's* function for lowering the bull's head and showing his courage to weakening him.[29] There are, say the older *aficionados*, no longer *matadors*, but now only *toreadors*.

Mexico has been gradually evolving from the feudal social structure and caste system imposed by the Conquistadors towards urbanisation and industrialisation. The reference group emulated in this transition is, of course, the "advanced" Western world, especially the United States. The trend towards urbanisation brings with it more emotionally restrictive patterns of socialisation and more abstract channels for the expression of hostility.[30] Western Europeans and Anglo-Americans are usually "shocked", for example, by the "brutality" of the bullfight and tend to dub cultures of which it is a part as "primitive". The more urbanised cultures do not, however, deny the need for legitimised expression of hostility. Kemp, a leading opponent of the bullfight, writes: "One of the functions of civilisation is to direct the expression of one's desires by early training and social pressures so that, ideally, we will receive the minimum harm and maximum value from that expression."[31] He admits to the need for satisfaction of the appetite for violence in all members of society but thinks that they must be satisfied less grossly than in the bullfight.

The general disapproval of Western Europe and the United States concerning the "barbarism" of the bullfight certainly must have had considerable influence on its conduct. (The padding of the horses was instigated by the English-born wife of a King of Spain, following promptings from her own country.) Since the institutions of a society reflect its culture, since the culture is influenced by the demands of other more powerful societies, and since urbanisation itself accounts in part for change in cultural patterns, we would expect to see corresponding changes in all of the subject society's institutions, including the bullfight. Thus is seen the shift in emphasis from the "primitive" killing of the bull to the more abstract, more aesthetic, and certainly more "acceptable" domination with the cape and *muleta*. Thus is seen the complete elimination of the kill in Portugal and Switzerland, and in Spain and Mexico, its secondary, almost apologetic status.

Urbanisation not only demands more intellectualised dealing with hostility but also brings with it a need for task specialisation. This too is reflected in the modern *corrida*. The well rounded "generalist" *matador* is rare. Most are specialists—cape men, *muleta* men, and a few who are known for their work with the *banderillas*.

The shift in emphasis in the bullfight (some say, the emasculation of the bullfight) has not affected the average American spectator's reaction of being revolted, disgusted, even sickened by the *corrida*. In sounding the reactions of some American college students to their first (and usually last) attendance at a bullfight, the authors have noted the recurring theme: "It's too much", "too blatant", "overpowering". Robinson writes "the bullfight allows the American, protected from reality all his life by the palliation of modern American society, to face up to the real thing".[32] And the "real thing" is "too much".

No doubt the highly "civilised" Anglo-American is threatened by such a direct acting out of hostility and violence as is manifest in the bullfight. But in addition to this he is very likely frightened by such a direct confrontation with death. Americans tend to deny death, even avoiding it in their speech (he "passed away", was "laid to rest", etc.). In Mexico, according to Robinson, "the bullfight spectacle is only one of the forms through which Mexicans make their obeisance to death".[33] Brenner noted that concern for death is "an organic part of Mexican thought".[34] The possibility of early or violent death is much greater for the average Mexican than for the average Anglo. To see death averted by the *matador* is pleasing to the Mexican, giving him some feeling of control over an event that he witnesses, not atypically, taking place in the streets. To the American the drama is a grim reminder of the inevitability of an event he seldom sees and chooses to deny. Hemingway writes, "We, in games, are not fascinated by death, its nearness and avoidance. We are fascinated by victory and we replace the avoidance of death by the avoidance of defeat."[35] The symbolic "victory" over another team is certainly at a higher level of emotional abstraction than the symbolism of the domination of and bloody killing of a bull.

Anglo-Americans, the authors have observed, tend to "root" for the bull during a *corrida*. The *picadors* are soundly hooted (Mexicans only demonstrate disapproval if the bull is "ruined"), and a tremendous barrage of invective pummels the *matador* if it takes him more than one sword to make a kill (even if all his swords are perfectly "over the horns"). This may be the result of the proclivity of the American to identify with the underdog, or the revulsion at seeing an animal (who, in the American ethic, is also a "buddy") killed. This seemingly irrational preference to see the man rather than the bull killed may also be influenced by a degree of prejudice in the ethnocentric Anglo towards the Mexican *matador*. It may also be that the *corrida* does not present to the Anglo a perception of two "evenly matched" antagonists. The opponents are not "equal"—few *matadors* are killed, but the bull rarely lives. This may run counter to the "fair play" ethic of the Anglo.

If the bullfight's overt display of hostility with its overriding components of inevitable death, animal suffering, and inequality, is not acceptable as a suitable means for the expression of aggression to the Anglo, what does he prefer? As mentioned earlier, the Anglo, too, is subject to socialisation, and he, too, experiences conflict situations which engender hostility towards parents and parent surrogates. How, then, as reflected in the Anglo national sport of baseball, is the expression of hostility towards authority legitimised?

BASEBALL

It was presented above that the Anglo child is prevented from directly manifesting hostility towards parents by their representation as "good guys" and "pals". Verbal aggression, elaborately intellectualised, is usually the most overt form of hostility allowed to the child. Whereas the Mexican seems painfully aware of conflict, hates his father, and acts out his hostility (displaces, projects), the Anglo appears hopelessly ambivalent towards the vague "buddy" father, and represses the fact that conflict exists. A good part of his psychic life is spent sustaining this repression compulsively and obsessively. In general, the legitimised means of expressing hostility are just as subtle as is the subtlety of the hostility generating conflict situation—this muteness is manifest as we shall see in the national sport.

The *matador*'s servile bow to the *Presidente* is an obvious and undisguised move of deference. In the prelude to a baseball game, however, the players line up, facing the flag, and stand quietly during the playing of the National Anthem. Tribute to authority here certainly is less direct than in the bull ring. A flag is a considerably more abstract and less threatening symbol than the pompous gentleman in the priviliged box. The government official who, as *Presidente*, attends the *corrida*, controls its conduct, and can directly interfere in the performance. Government officials who attend baseball games are in no way able to interfere with play—at most, they throw in the first ball.

While the observer need only take a quick glance at the "barbaric" *corrida* to see a dramatically overt display of violence and aggression, he is hard pressed, after considerable observation, to see any marked degree of hostility in the structure of the "good clean sport" of baseball. He looks out over the field and sees two teams (composed of an equal number of similarly uniformed men), patiently and systematically taking an equal number of turns (innings) in the attempt to score. The field is elaborately chalked, demarcating those areas of "fair" from "foul" play, and an elaborate system of rules dictates when a player can get a "hit", take or advance a base, score a run, be "safe" or "out". The observer becomes aware of the game's dramatic emphasis on numbers (the most abstract of symbols)—the scoreboard, the batting averages, the earned-run averages, the team win percentages, and even the players, who are granted relative impersonality by the numbers on their backs.

Unlike the *matador,* who constantly communicates with the crowd, the baseball players are seen to remain distinctly aloof from them. The player's allegiance is to the team, and he who performs ostentatiously for the crowd is ostracised as a "grandstander". Contrast, for example, the baseball player's downcast eye and turf-kicking toe after an outstanding move with the *matador's* haughy glance and proud posture following a good series of passes. Contrast the convertible or television set given ritualistically by the crowd to the ball player on "his day" with the immediate, spontaneous, and extremely emotional reaction of the crowd following an appreciated *corrida*—they clamour for the *Presidente* to give him awards, throw him wine flasks, *sombreros,* and often rush into the ring to carry him about on their shoulders. It might be said that in baseball, the crowd is expected to observe, in a relatively detached way, the spectacle being performed for them on the field. At the bullfight, however, the crowd is expected to be one with the *matador,* to participate, fully, in the emotions of the fight.

There is, by contrast to the *corrida*, a noticeable lack of heterosexuality in the game of baseball. While the *matador* often dedicates his bull or tosses an ear to a *senorita,* the baseball player, on the field anyway, limits his interaction to male teammates, chattering to them, shaking their hands in success, slapping their buttocks in encouragement, and mobbing and hugging them for superlative feats of play.

There is, of course, competition taking place in the game—but nothing that can parallel the direct, individual confrontation of the *matador* with the bull. In baseball, two "teams" meet and the more evenly matched they are, the better the "contest" is. There are fans for both sides, each rooting for his team, hoping that it will win the "contest". After the game is over, there will be a winner, and a "good loser". (It is interesting that the participants in baseball are called "players". The *matador* is not "playing" at the *corrida*—it is a fight.) The aggressive component that one would expect in competition is muted by the rules governing the conduct of play and by the expectations of the crowd. There are occasional emotional outbreaks between rival players, between players and umpires, and between managers and umpires, but these "rhubarbs" are ephemeral and seem somehow distant and artificial. The shouts and jeers of the crowd, with an occasional "murder the bum", lack the emotional punch and especially the personal reference of the venomous insults hurled by the displeased Mexican *aficionado*.

Some psychoanalytically oriented behavioural scientists have written vividly of the symbolic castration represented in the baseball games. Stokes, for example, calls baseball "a manifest exercise in phallic deftness".[36] Petty sees the contest as a safe re-creation of the battle between father and son for the sexual favours of the mother.[37]

However, if hostility generated in a father-son competition is manifested here, how safe, how muted, is its expression. Its release is legitimised only under the restrictions of elaborate rules, omnipresent umpires, and with the insistence that each team systematically take turns playing one role or the other. It is diffused throughout a "team", no one man taking full responsibility and is submerged in a morass of batting and pitching rituals and superstitions that are unsurpassed by the most extreme of religion and the military. Batters will use only certain bats, stand a certain way, pound home plate a certain number of times, spit, rub dust, rub resin (or all three) on their hands, pull their clothing into a certain position before batting, wear lucky numbers, lucky charms, lucky hats, lucky socks, or use a lucky bat. Many pitchers have elaborate series of movements before delivering the ball—touch cap, rub ball, grab resin bag, scuff dirt, adjust glove, re-touch hat, re-rub ball. . . . Professional pitcher Lew Burdette has taken as long as a full minute to complete a series of irrelevant gestures, ticks, clutches, and tugs before throwing the ball. Similarly, an observer would be hard pressed to find a baseball player who doesn't ritualistically chew gum.

Furthermore, the conduct of the game, and therefore any expression of hostility, is closely scrutinised by at least three umpires. Interestingly enough, the word umpire is derived from the Latin, meaning not equal. Thus, on a playing field where equality is a central ethic, the umpires are unique. They are the only personnel on the field who even during inning intermissions cannot sit down or relax. Like the "super ego" theirs is an unrelenting vigilance. Their word is law, and disrespect for them can bring an ousting from the game. But how different is the player-umpire relationship from that of the *matador-Presidente*. The *Presidente* is treated with deference, and the interaction between authority and *matador* is seen to be personal and direct. As in the Mexican society at large, the authority figure, though he may be hated, is shown the utmost respect.[38]

The umpire, on the other hand is an impersonal figure. How many "fans" know the names of big league umpires? So abstract is the black-suited authority that "kill the umpire" can be vociferously and safely shouted. How non-threatening is the typical reaction of the umpire to the complaints, admonishments, and verbal aggressions of the players and managers—he turns his back and slowly walks away. Authority is challenged—and with impunity![39]

Another phenomenon, certainly cultural in nature, is the ritual hypochondriasis of baseball players. *Matadors* traditionally disregard wounds (the *macho* does not fear, avoid, or show disability because of pain), and have even fought with assistants who tried to carry them out of the ring after a serious goring. Baseball players leave the field for a simple pulled muscle. Yards of tape, gallons of ointment, heat treatments, vitamin pills, "isometrics", "training rules", arm warmers, whirlpool baths, and rub-downs pamper the ball player. Pitchers are carefully protected from the wind, rain, and cold "dugout" seats, and can ask to be relieved if they are feeling tired.

As the conduct of the bullfight has changed with the increasing urbanisation in Mexico, so also has the conduct of baseball changed with the increasing bureaucratisation in the United States. In the early twentieth century, fines for insulting (or even striking) the umpire were non-existent. The crowd very often displayed displeasures by throwing bottles and cushions at specific individuals in the fields. In general, the level of expression of hostility was more direct and involved somewhat more acting out. The farm club system, its scouting ties with organised collegiate athletics, and the bureaucratic "front office" were far less expansive. Rules and regulations were less restricting, and the tobacco chewing, swearing, sweating player was typical as contrasted with the "gentleman players" who grace our fields and television commercials today. Nine innings then took about two-thirds the time they do now, the ball was "dead", and the number of players on the team's roster was smaller. There were fewer substitutes, and pitchers as a rule stayed in for the entire game.

In the present situation even the abstract "team" concept has been made obsolete by increased bureaucratisation. The authors witnessed members of the winning (1963) Los Angeles Dodgers speaking proudly of the "Dodger Organisation", and the good job the "front office" had done.

In a television interview, Bill Veeck, an ex-professional manager, expressed dismay with the unnecessary "dragging out" of the game by prolonged warm-up pitches, drawn-out sessions of verbal haranguing, "long" walks to the dugout, and summit meetings of the pitcher, catcher, and manager. He complained about the time-wasting rituals of motion indulged in by both pitcher and batter. Veeck thus testifies to the increasing obsessive quality in the game, as its emphasis shifts to more and more diffuse, indirect, and disguised means for expressing hostility.

One wonders, in fact, if the restrictions in baseball are too many, if the fans aren't growing dissatisfied. The increasing public attendance at professional football games, reaching a point where some sports analysts predict that it will replace baseball as the National sport, may be an indication of the demand for a less abstract expression of hostility in spectator sports. Nevertheless, from the point of view of social control, baseball masterfully mutes aggression behind its reciprocity, rules, records, and rituals. It duplicates the vagueness and intellectualisation of the conflict situation in the American family and provides a markedly abstract and controlled expression of hostility towards authority. Macoby, et al, write that baseball represents the ideal of American society.[40] It remains to be seen whether or not this ideal can, in the face of a need for a clearer expression of hostility, remain intact.

SUMMARY

The passive-aggressive component of the Mexican modal personality can be traced to the dominant and harshly punitive role of the father and to the general authoritarian nature of the Mexican culture. This passive-aggressiveness is perpetuated in the *macho* pattern of the Mexican male, and in the "martyr" pattern of the Mexican female. Any acting out of the resultant hostility to authority must be carried out in spheres safely distant from that authority's immediate control.

The bullfight is seen to depict, symbolically, the power of the father, the subtle demands of the mother, and the fear of the child. Unlike the family situation, the awesome authority does not prevail, but rather is dominated and destroyed through the courage and daring of the *matador*. He, however, acting for the spectator, must accomplish this hostile act in a framework of "respect" for authority, and with a studied passiveness in and control of movement.

By contrast, the "intellectualisation" component of the Anglo modal personality can be traced to the superficial ethic of "equality" among family members and to the general intellectualised nature of highly urbanised societies. The attempt to mute authority by a pseudo-philosophy of togetherness, when authority is in fact assumed by the father, the mother, and by the society, engenders a vagueness in role definitions, confusion in behavioural expectations, and an intellectualisation of the resultant conflict. Hostility towards this intangible yet frustrating authority figure is expressed by the individual in a manner as abstract and as ritualised as its causative factors.

The national sport of baseball is set in a framework of equality. Hostility towards authority takes the symbolic form of competition and desire to win, and is smothered under a covering of rules, regulations, and player rituals. Guided by the authority of umpires (who are sufficiently impersonal to be challenged with relative impunity), and protected in the safety of numbers as a member of a team, the players systematically alternate roles, allowing each to have an equal opportunity to "be aggressive".

Spectators of the baseball game view two similarly uniformed teams consisting of the same number of players vying for an abstract "victory". The spectators' emotional participation in the game is distant and safe—"murder the bum" or "kill the umpire" does not have enough of a personal referent to arouse guilt or anxiety. They can take sides in occasional and severely regulated conflicts on the field, because such conflicts have "meaning" only in the game, and are forgotten when the game is over.

Since 1920, the bullfight has gradually been modified to accentuate domination rather than the kill. Paralleling this, the position of the father in the Mexican family has, with gradual urbanisation, come more closely in line with that of the "advanced" Western model. He is less threatening, less fearsome, and can be dominated to a degree sufficient to reduce the importance of his symbolic destruction.

Baseball, since 1920, has similarly undergone significant changes. With the increasing bureaucratisation of Anglo society, and with the increasing emphasis upon "equality" and impersonality in the family have come the more complex bureaucratisation and the more elaborate ritualisation of baseball.

The family, and the institutionalised recreation form known as the National Sport, mutually reflect, as they appear in Mexico, the cultural centrality of death, dominance, "personal" relationships, respect for and fear and hatred of authority, and the defence systems of the passive-aggressive character structure.

In the Anglo culture, these two institutions mutually reflect the cultural importance of equality, impersonality, and the defence mechanism of intellectualisation.

Both national sports provide a socially acceptable channel for the expression of hostility towards authority. This channel is modified by other cultural values and expectations, and is framed in an activity which duplicates, symbolically, aspects of the hostility generating familial situation.

NOTES

1 This research was supported by Public Health Service Mental Health Project Grant 5-R11-Mh-544-2, Arnold Meadow, Director.

2 Lundberg, G. A. Schrag, L. C. and Larsen, O. N., *Sociology*, New York: Harper and Bros., 1958, 757.

3 Whiting, J. W. and Child, I. L., *Child Training and Personality: A Cross Cultural Study*, New Haven: Yale University Press, 1953.

4 Kardiner, A., *The Individual and His Society*, New York: Columbia University Press, 1939.

5 Tumin, M. M., "Some Disfunctions of Institutional Imbalances", *Behavioural Science*, July, 1956, 218–23.

6 Dollard, J., "Hostility and Fear in Social Life", *Social Forces*, XLII, 1938, 15–25.

7 Dollard, *op. cit.*, 16.

8 It should be mentioned here that the *aficionado* (dedicated fan) would object to the association of the bullfight with the term "sport", and there are good arguments in support of his opinion. For the sake of parsimony, however, and since the bullfight approaches the criteria established in this paper, it will be considered, for analysis, the equivalent of a national sport.

9 Lewis, Oscar, *Children of Sanchez*, New York: Random House, 1961. Gillin, John P. "Ethos and Cultural Aspects of Personality", in Yehudi Cohen (Ed.) *Social Structure and Personality*, New York: Holt, Rinehart, & Winston, 1961; Meadow, Arnold, Zurcher, Louis and Stoker, David, "Sex Role and Schizophrenia in Mexican Culture", *International*

Journal of Social Psychiatry, In Press; Diaz-Guerrero, *Rogelio Estidios de Psichologia del Mecicano*, Mexico, Antigua Libreria Robredo, 1961; Diaz-Guerrero, Rogelio, "Socio- Cultural Premises, Attitudes, and Cross-Cultural Research", Invited Paper, Section 17, Cross-Cultural Studies of Attitude Structure and Dimension.[5] Seventeenth International Congress of Psychology, Washington, D.C., 1963.

10 Lewis, *op. cit.*, 8.

11 Lewis, *op. cit.*, xxiii.

12 Meadow, Arnold and Stoker, David, "Symptomatic Behaviour of Mexican-American and Anglo-American Child Guidance Patients", Unpublished paper, University of Arizona, Tucson, Arizona.

13 Family dynamics are most certainly influenced by socio-economic class. Mexico generally is viewed by social scientists to be a "poverty" culture, and the United States to be a "middle class" culture, though interpretations always must allow for cultural heterogeneity. The present authors wish to utilise the concepts "modal family" and "modal personality" as bases for discussion, but with caution against over-generalisation and stereotypy.

14 Lewis, *op. cit.*, 338.

15 Robinson, C., *With the Ears of Strangers: The Mexican in American Literature*, Tucson, University of Arizona Press, 1964, 173.

16 Allen, J. H., *Southwest*, New York: Bantam, 1953, 113–14.

17 Lea, T., *The Brave Bulls*, Boston: Little, Brown and Co., 1949, 199–200.

18 Ramsey, R., *Fiesta*, New York: John Day, 1955, 24.

19 Based upon records from cases under intensive psychotherapy, Meadow reports the recurrently expressed need of the Mexican-American patient to dominate during inter-personal relations. A person who is easily dominated is considered by the Mexican-American to be *controlado* (controllable). The same word is used to refer to manageable horses.

20 Boyd, G. in M. Wright (Ed.), *The Field of Vision*, New York: Harcourt-Brace, 1956, 192.

21 Kluckhohn, Florence and Strodbeck, F. L., *Variations in Value Orientations*, New York: Row, Peterson, 1961, 235.

22 Hemingway, E., *Death in the Afternoon*, New York: Scribner's and Sons, 16, 1945, 82.

23 Hemingway, *op. cit.*, 104.

24 Lea, *op. cit.*, 87.

25 Hemingway, *op. cit.*, 67.

26 Hemingway, *op. cit.*, 175.

27 Hemingway, *op. cit.*, 180.

28 Boyd, *op. cit.*, 192–93.

29 Hemingway, *op. cit.*, 176.

30 The position of father in the Mexican family has, with urbanisation, also begun to shift towards the "advanced" Western model. It might be said that as the father figure becomes less fearsome, less overpowering, there is less need to "kill" him symbolically—domination alone is an adequate expression of hostility.

31 Kemp, L., *The Only Beast*. New York: Pocket Books (Discovery No. 4), 1954, 46–56.

32 Robinson, *op. cit.*, 250.

33 Robinson, *op. cit.*, 257.

34 Brenner, Anita, *Idols Behind Altars*, New York: Payson and Clarks, 1929, 21.

35 Hemingway, *op. cit.*, 22.

36 Stokes, A. "Psychoanalytic Reflections on the Development of Ball Games", *International Journal of Psycho-Analysis*, 1956.

37 Petty, T. A., Address to the American Psychoanalytic Association, 1963.

38 Mexican patients have described their fathers as drunkards, brutes, etc., but always add that they "respect" them. Tucson, Arizona school teachers often report that the behaviour of the Mexican-American students *vis-à-vis* the teacher is exemplary, though their dropout and absentee records indicate a low value for education.

39 There is, however, a carefully defined limit to the amount of abuse the umpire is expected to endure. Physical violence, and certain profanities bring not only a removal from the game, but severe fines to the offender. Since there are fixed fines for specific obscenities, angry players will often turn to the umpire and, escaping the fine by ascending a rung on the abstraction ladder, declare, "You're that five hundred dollar word!"

40 Macoby, M., Modiano, Nancy, and Lander, P., "Games and Social Character in a Mexican Village", *Psychiatry*, December, 1964, 50–60.

CHAPTER 11

On Scholarship and Interscholastic Athletics*

Walter E. Schafer and J. Michael Armer

One of the central interests of high school students in the United States is interscholastic athletics. Although several studies show that less than one-quarter of high school boys participate, the importance of competitive sports can be fully seen only by taking account of the vast amount of time, energy, and attention given athletic teams and contests by non-participants as well.[1] The pep rallies, the marching band, the cheerleading squads, the team managers, the large and expensive stadiums and gymnasiums, high attendance at football and basketball games, the visibility and high status accorded athletic stars—all are indicative of the central place of interscholastic sports among large numbers of American high school students.

A continuing controversy among parents, educators, and social scientists is whether this emphasis on competitive sports interferes

* Considerable portions of this essay are drawn from two other papers. The first was presented at the World Congress of Sport and Physical Education in Madrid in September, 1966. Different versions of the second, co-authored by Schafer and Richard A. Rehberg, were presented at the International Seminar on Leisure Time and Recreation in Havana in December, 1966, and at the annual meetings of the American Sociological Association in San Francisco in August, 1967. Yet another version of the paper appeared in the November, 1968, issue of *Transaction* under the title, "Athletes are Not Inferior Students", pp. 21–6, 61–2. We are indebted to Professor Rehberg for several of the ideas in this essay. Gregory P. Stone provided helpful substantive and editorial suggestions during several extended conversations, for which we are grateful. Various parts of the research have received support from the following sources: The Co-operative Research Programme of the Office of Education, U.S. Department of Health, Education and Welfare; The Centre for Advanced Study of Educational Administration, University of Oregon; a curriculum development grant from the office of Juvenile Delinquency & Youth Development, Welfare Administration, U.S. Department of Health, Education & Welfare in Co-operation with the President's Committee on Juvenile Delinquency & Youth Crime; the Centre for Research on Social Organization, University of Michigan; and the Office of Scholarly and Scientific Research, Graduate School, University of Oregon.

with the intellectual or academic objectives of the school. As James S. Coleman has noted, contrasting positions are often voiced.

Athletics is castigated as the antithesis of scholastic activity by intellectuals—many of whom have never taken part in inter-scholastic sports. It is defended and praised as the builder of men by coaches and athletes—most of whom have a vested interest in this proposition.[2]

Officially, high school sports are supported by school boards, administrators, and teachers because of their presumed contribution to the physical, psychological, moral, and social development of youth. Perhaps the best statement of the educational justification for high school athletics is contained in the Educational Policies Commission's 1954 pronouncement:

Participation in sound athletic programmes, we believe, con-tributes to health and happiness, physical skill and emotional maturity, social competence and moral values.

We believe that co-operation and competition are both im-portant components of American life. Athletic participation can help teach the values of co-operation as well as the spirit of competition.

Playing hard and playing to win can help to build character. So also do learning to "take it" in the rough and tumble of vigorous play, experiencing defeat without whimpering and vic-tory without gloating, and disciplining one's self to comply with the rules of the game and of good sportsmanship.

Athletics may also exemplify the value of the democratic process and of fair play. Through team play the student athlete often learns how to work with others for the achievement of group goals. Athletic competition can be a wholesome equaliser. Individuals on the playing field are judged for what they are and for what they can do, not on the basis of the social, ethnic, or economic group to which their families belong.[3]

Important as such presumed benefits might be, it is generally accepted that the main educational objective of the school is intel-lectual or academic growth. Athletics, like other extracurricular activities, are intended to develop youth in secondary ways. How-ever, any organisation risks interference with its primary goals and activities when it creates programmes to achieve ancillary goals. For example, the contemporary church faces the continuing risk that members will become more interested in ladies circles, monthly parties, or church basketball teams than in religion itself.

Similarly, the school faces the danger that extracurricular activities such as athletics will interfere with its central intellectual or academic goals.

Several observers contend that in many high schools, athletics in fact have partly displaced intellectual development as the primary objective and activity.[4] They argue that, whatever the contribution of athletic programmes to character development, to sportsmanship or to physical fitness, an excessive amount of time, energy, and attention is diverted from academic activities. This view is illustrated by Coleman's observation that a stranger in an American high school might well suppose, by looking and listening, that ". . . more attention is paid to athletics by teenagers, both as athletes and as spectators, than to scholastic matters".[5]

Alleged over-emphasis on interscholastic sports and resulting interference with scholarship are often explained by the fact that athletics are one of the only symbols towards which school and community identification and loyalty can be directed. Several sociologists have commented on the importance of sports in generating school and community cohesion. Coleman, for example, has remarked:

> . . . the importance of athletic contests in both high schools and colleges lies in part in the way the contests solve a definite problem for the institution—the problem of generating enthusiasm for and identification with the school and of drawing the energies of the adolescents into the school.[6]

Willard Waller, in his classic book of 1932, *The Sociology of Teaching*, came to a similar conclusion.

> It is perhaps as a means of unifying the entire school group that athletics seems most useful from the sociological point of view—athletic games furnish a dramatic spectacle of the struggle of picked men against the common enemy, and this is a powerful factor in building up a group spirit which includes students of all kinds and degrees and unifies the teachers and the taught. In adult life we find the analogue of athletics in war: patriotism runs high when the country is attacked.[7]

Several community studies have provided evidence of this integrative function of interscholastic sports. In their study of Middletown, the Lynds made the following observation.

> An even more widespread agency of group cohesion is the high school basket-ball team. In 1890, with no school athletics,

such a thing as an annual state high school basket-ball tournament was undreamed of ... Baseball received much newspaper space, but support for the teams had to be urged. Today more civil loyalty centres around basket-ball than around any other one thing. No distinctions divide the crowds which pack the school gymnasium for home games and which in every kind of machine crowd the roads for out-of-town games.[8]

At the same time that athletics serve as "... a great machine for generating communal Selfhood[9]...," critics contend there are at least five different ways in which athletics, as a secondary activity, interfere with the more central academic objectives of the school. First, it is argued that an excessive amount of resources, personnel, and facilities is diverted from "more fruitful" academic activities. Second, some critics argue that although sports direct the attention of large numbers of parents and other adults towards the school, this support is not channelled towards primary educational goals, but towards a marginal activity. Third, pep rallies, trips, attendance at games, preparation of floats and displays, and frequent conversations are thought to combine to draw the time, energy, and attention of student fans away from studies. Fourth, critics claim that many potentially good students are discouraged from the serious pursuit of academic goals because the rewards of popularity and status go to athletes and cheerleaders instead. Moreover, the serious student may be subjected to scorn and ridicule. Fifth, the scholastic performance of participating athletes is said to suffer because direct involvement in sports demands excessive time, energy, and attention. This is especially true since athletic participation is so necessary for the acquisition of status in the high school.

Whether athletics in fact do interfere in each of these ways with the academic objectives of the school is, of course, an empirical question. During the remainder of this essay, we will review previously reported evidence and present new data on this problem.

EVIDENCE FROM THE ADOLESCENT SOCIETY

Evidence on the relationship between athletics and academic pursuits is very sparse. By far the most important study, in terms of scope and recognition, is reported by James Coleman in *The Adolescent Society*.[10] In this section, we will review and assess available data, especially from Coleman, as they touch on each of the above possible types of athletic-academic conflict.

Diversion of Resources. To our knowledge, no studies have been conducted on the extent to which the present allocation of resources, personnel, and facilities to interscholastic sports in fact creates a drain away from the academic mission of the school. Clearly, studies are needed to investigate the relationship between financial resources, staff man-hours, and facilities given to athletics and level of academic achievement. Such investigations, of course, would be extremely difficult to carry out, because of the problem of holding constant other relevant factors such as size, location, and social class composition of the school.

Diversion of Parental Support. Coleman's investigation of teenage culture in ten midwestern high schools mainly focused on the attitudes, values, and norms of students themselves. One of the few uses made of a parental questionnaire was the response pattern to the following question: "If your son or daughter could be outstanding in high school in one of the three things listed below, which one would you want it to be?" Choices for parents of boys were brilliant student, athletic star, and most popular. For girls, leader in activities was substituted for "athletic star".[11] The choice of more than three-fourths of the parents of both boys and girls was brilliant student, suggesting that most parents value scholarship far more highly than athletics.

Coleman points out, however, that "... these values may not be those they express day by day to their children".[12] In fact, responses of students themselves to a related set of questions suggest such a discrepancy. When each student was asked how his parents would feel if he were asked to be a biology assistant, 60.2% of the boys responded "both would be very proud of me", while 63.5% of the girls gave that response. However, when asked how their parents would react if they unexpectedly made the basketball team (or cheerleading squad), 68.2% of the boys and 77.0% of the girls said they would both be very proud.[13]

These data provide slight support, then, for the position that, in practice, parental support of scholarship is diverted to some extent by greater interest in athletic accomplishment. More direct evidence, however, is still needed. For instance, it would be well to know from parents themselves how proud they would be if their son or daughter were made biology assistant or a member of the basketball team or cheerleading squad. Perhaps they would stress the academic alternative here as well, and students simply attributed their own attitudes or those of their peers to their parents. On the other hand, maybe students were accurate in their reports, and parents in fact stress non-academic values most. Further, it is possible that even if a higher percentage of parents had indicated they would be more proud of their son or daughter being made biology assistant, the actual academic achievement of students would be unaffected.

It must be noted that by interpreting this student report of greater parental support for athletic than academic success as he does, Coleman contradicts one of his own central arguments. He maintains throughout the book that youth subculture, emphasising athletics, cars, good looks, and popularity, conflicts with adult values and school doctrines which emphasise intellectual growth, academic achievement, and serious preparation for adulthood. He argues that the development and expansion of a separate educational institution for youth has created a peer society in which teenagers interact mainly among themselves. As a result, the adult society is losing its influence over the values, norms, and energies of youth.[14] Yet, his interpretation of the data just cited support his own contention that ". . . it is the adult community that fixes the activities of the adolescent community".[15] In short, the emphasis among youth on athletics and non-academic activities *reflects,* and does not contradict adult interests.

Thus, he simultaneously argues that youth subculture is contradictory to adult values but that adults support adolescent activities and values. Perhaps this serious inconsistency arises from his failure to make clear that the adolescent subculture may be opposed to adult values and official goals of the school, but not to "practical norms" and *actual* behaviour of adults which openly, or not so openly, support athletics, appearance, and popularity.

Diversion of Energy Among Student Fans. Proof that support of school teams by student fans interferes with their academic performance would have to demonstrate that, other things being equal, the greater the time and energy devoted to the support of athletics, the lower the academic achievement. Although such interference may well occur, there seems to be no evidence in the literature one way or the other, even in Coleman's research. Therefore, it is premature to accept the position of the critics, although it does remain plausible.

Discouragement of Scholarship. As formulated by Coleman, this kind of erosion of scholarship operates in the following way. Since popularity and prestige are accorded more readily for athletic achievement, academic achievement remains a relatively unrewarded activity. In fact, high scholastic performance is likely to bring negative sanctions in the form of exclusion, scorn, or ridicule. As a result, many able students either are not attracted to academic pursuits in the absence of potential payoffs in popularity and status, or they deliberately avoid the image of "intellectual' because of the fear of being labelled as "square" or "out of it".[16]

But again, Coleman's data are inconclusive. The main evidence presented is that the less the importance of good grades for membership in the leading crowd in a school, the lower the average IQ of "top scholars" in that school.[17] Coleman writes:

> ...where [academic] achievement brings few social rewards, those who are motivated to "go out" for scholarly achievement will be few. The high performers, those who receive good grades, will not be the boys whose ability is greatest, but will be a more mediocre few. The "intellectuals" of such a society, the best students, will not in fact be those with most intellectual ability. The latter, knowing where the social rewards lie, will be off in the directions that bring social rewards.[18]

In short, potentially able students are discouraged from trying very hard scholastically by the absence of positive social rewards for academic achievement. Several criticisms can be made of this interpretation. First, there is not a perfect inverse rank order correlation between the school's emphasis on academics and athletics. In fact, secondary analysis reveals a *positive* rank order correlation of 0.70 and 0.20 in the five small schools and the five large schools in terms of the importance of scholarship and athletic stardom for membership in the elite group.[19] In short, schools that emphasise athletics do not necessarily do so at the expense of academic pursuits. Rather, the above correlations suggest that the two emphases often go together. By itself, then, the negative relationship between academic emphasis and the average IQ of "top scholars" says nothing about the extent to which *athletics*, as opposed to other factors, divert high ability students from top academic performance.

Coleman also argues that anti-academic norms and sanctions partly result from the interpersonal structure of academic competition: high grades for some automatically result in low grades for others. Thus, high performance is negatively sanctioned by other students.[20] This argument strongly suggests that the structure of academic competition itself, rather than interference by athletics, accounts for the aversion of many students to full academic effort and achievement. If, then, athletics were highly rewarded and academic competition were carried on between schools rather than between individuals, social rewards for academic achievement and, hence, actual scholastic performance would be high.[21] On the other hand, if interscholastic athletics were eliminated or very much de-emphasised while academic competition remained inter-individual, the rewards for scholastic performance would remain low, as would actual levels of academic achievement.

Further, Coleman assumes that peer rewards are the sole or at least the most important factor determining the positive or negative attitudes of students towards intellectual or academic achievement. However, he ignores the real possibility that, even in the absence of high social gains among peers, many high school students probably are motivated towards academic pursuits because of a concern with other rewards—qualifying for college, making the honour roll, the satisfaction of excellence, qualifying for jobs, gaining the approval of parents, or the inherent excitement in learning.

In short, Coleman's data do not directly confirm that potentially high scholastic achievers are discouraged from trying because of the diversion of social rewards towards athletics. Though this type of interference might well operate, the data are inconclusive.

Diversion of Energy Among Athletes. A clear implication of Coleman's writings is that athletic participation interferes with scholastic performance. When he refers to the relative "flow of energy" into athletics and academics,[22] he implies that athletics "recruit" many boys who might have become top students and that, once "recruited", they are induced by the lure of popularity, publicity, and prestige to give as much of their limited time and energy as possible to athletics even at the expense of scholastic endeavour. He contends that this has adverse consequences for the larger society.

> The implications for American society as a whole are clear. Because high-schools allow adolescent societies to divert energies into athletics, social activities, and the like, they recruit into adult intellectual activities many people with a rather mediocre level of ability, and fail to attract many with high levels of ability.[23]

No evidence is presented, however, about the proportion of boys with high IQs who in fact are "drained off" into athletics or about the proportion of boys in athletics (or other extra-curricular activities) who are and are not recruited into "adult intellectual activities". In fact, Coleman studiously avoids direct analysis of this type of possible athletic-academic conflict. Although he presents grade point averages of top athletes and all boys at different points in the book he never compares them in a single table. When these tables are combined, however, we find that athletes fall below all boys in their school in academic achievement in only three of the ten schools (see Table 1).

Studies by Biddulph, Keating, Eidsmore, Whitten and others have also reported a positive relationship between athletic participation and scholastic grades.[24] Although we know nothing about the background, ability, or prior motivation of athletes and non-athletes in any of these studies, they suggest that athletic participation might not interfere with academic performance and in fact might enhance it.

TABLE 1

Average Grades of Top Athletes and All Boys
In Schools in *The Adolescent Society*

School	Mean GPA*		
	Top Athletes†	All Boys‡	Difference
Maple Grove	5.6	4.3	1.3
Elmtown	5.0	4.2	.8
Executive Heights	4.8	4.0	.8
Midcity	4.5	3.6	.9
Newlawn	4.3	3.5	.8
St. John's	4.1	3.7	.4
Green Junction	4.0	4.0	.0
Millburg	3.3	3.7	−.4
Marketville	3.2	3.7	−.5
Farmdale	3.0	4.1	−1.1

* Coleman used the following point system in computing GPA: $A = 8$, $B = 6$, $C = 4$, $D = 2$, $F = 0$.
† Figures in this column are taken from Tables 60 and 61, pp. 274–75.
‡ Figures in this column are from Table 54, p. 252. GPAs for all boys were rounded from two decimal points to one in this combined table so they would be equivalent with those of athletes.

NEW EVIDENCE

Despite the limitations in Coleman's research discussed above, there are other data and conclusions in *The Adolescent Society* that are more compelling. Some of these provide a basis for the prediction that, other things being equal, participation in interscholastic athletics exerts a detrimental effect on scholastic achievement. If it is indeed true: (1) that informal social rewards, such as popularity, prestige, and leadership, are more readily accorded by peers and adults for athletic success than for academic achievement; (2) that most high school athletes are boys;[25] and (3) that boys value such informal social rewards more than formal system rewards (e.g. grades, promotions, honours) or long-term gains (e.g. qualifying for college or a job) that accompany academic achievement;[26] then boys can be expected to give as much time, energy, and attention as possible to athletic endeavours. And if we add a fourth assumption, that time, energy, and attention are limited resources, then it follows that academic achievement should be lower if boys participate than if they do not.

Three testable hypotheses can be derived from these assumptions. First, athletes should not perform as well scholastically as non-athletes, other things being equal. Second, the greater the amount of participation in sports, the greater the detrimental effect on academic performance. Third, participation in sports that receive greater attention and recognition in the high school, such as football and basketball, should have a greater negative effect on academic achievement than participation in less recognised sports, since, in the former, the potential payoff in social rewards is greater warranting a greater investment of time, attention, and energy. Data have been gathered to test each of these hypotheses.

The Data. During the summer of 1964, complete high school records were examined for all 585 who began as tenth graders three years earlier in two midwestern senior high schools.[27] At the time the records were examined, most of the class had already graduated from high school. One of the three year high schools had a total enrolment of 2,565 in the fall of 1963 and was located in a predominantly middle class, university community of about 70,000. The other school had a total enrolment of 1,272 and was located in a nearby, predominantly working class, industrial community of about 20,000. For purposes of this study, boys from the two schools are treated as a single sample.

Of the 585 in the total sample, 164 (24%) were classified as athletes. These boys completed at least one full season in an interscholastic sport (varsity or junior varsity) during the three years of high school. Any given boy could participate in three seasons each year; for example, football in the fall, basketball in the winter, and track in the spring. Thirty per cent of the athletes completed one season during the three years, 34% completed two or three seasons, 21% four or five seasons, and 15% six to nine seasons.

Academic achievement was measured by obtaining each boy's grade point average (GPA) for all major courses during their six semesters of senior high school. (Physical education, which might inflate the GPAs of athletes, is not a major course). Scholastic grades were translated into numeric scores ranging from 4.00 (all A's) to 0.00 (all F's). GPAs were based on as many semesters as the student stayed in school.

Athletic Participation and Academic Achievement. Table 2 shows the gross differences in GPA between athletes and all other boys in the two schools. As may be seen, athletic participation is positively related to academic achievement (2.35 average GPA for athletes versus 1.83 for non-athletes). This finding, which is inconsistent with the first hypothesis derived from Coleman's work, suggests that athletic participation might exert a positive, rather than a negative, influence on scholastic performance.

Certainly, this does not *prove*, however, that athletic participation has a positive effect, since it is possible that athletes *began* high school with greater academic ability or achievement motivation than non-athletes and attained higher grades *despite* the

TABLE 2

Mean GPA for Athletes and All Boys
In Their Class

	Mean GPA*	N
Athletes†	2.35	164
All Other Boys	1.83	421

* Grade point averages are based on the following scale: A = 4.0, B = 3.0, C = 2.0, D = 1.0, F = 0.0. Each student's GPA is based on his final marks in all major courses during the six semesters of high school. Physical education is not included as a major course. GPAs may be based on anywhere from one to six semesters, depending on how long the student remained in school.

† Boys who completed at least one full season as a member of an interscholastic athletic team are classified as athletes.

"interference" of sports. It is necessary, then, to control for important confounding variables in order to isolate the effect of participation. Among the variables that might confound the relationship between participation and academic achievement are father's occupation, intelligence test score, and curriculum location, since each has been found in past research to exert an independent influence on academic achievement and might also be related to athletic participation.[28] Table 3 shows that each factor in fact is associated with both participation and achievement in this sample as well. By controlling these variables, then, we are able to reduce the possibility that the relationship in Table 2 is spurious.

There is still the chance, however, of residual, uncontrolled motivational or ability differences between athletes and non-athletes. In order to decrease this possibility still further, academic performance for the final semester of junior high school, which Table 3 also shows is associated with both participation and achievement, is introduced as a fourth control. In doing this, we assume that most residual differences between athletes and non-athletes will already have affected ninth grade performance and that, by controlling for this factor, we are eliminating the effects of many other determinants of academic achievement. Of course, the possibility remains that still other uncontrolled factors exert

TABLE 3

Relationship of Father's Occupation, Intelligence Test Score, Curriculum and GPA for Final Semester of Junior High School to High School Athletic Participation and Grade Point Average

Characteristic	Per cent Participating	Mean GPA	Total N
Father's Occupation*			
White Collar	33	2.28	(310)
Blue Collar	22	1.65	(250)
Farm	27	1.68	(11)
Intelligence Test Score†			
High	35	2.44	(383)
Low	22	1.58	(289)
Curriculum Location‡			
College Preparatory	36	2.30	(373)
Non-College Preparatory	14	1.40	(221)
GPA for Final Semester of Junior High Schools§			
High	37	2.48	(291)
Low	18	1.42	(270)

* Census occupational categories were collapsed as follows:
White Collar: Professional, Technical, and Kindred Workers; Managers, Officials, and Proprietors; Clerical and Kindred Workers.
Blue Collar: Craftsmen; Foremen and Kindred; Operatives and Kindred; Private Household; Service Workers and Labourers.
  † Scores in the larger school are based on the California Test of Mental Maturity; those in the smaller school are based on the Lorge-Thorndike. Since both the median and means were virtually the same in both schools, it is legitimate to combine them. The cutting point, which represents the median for both schools, is as follows:
High—109 and above
Low —108 and above
  ‡ Curriculum location is based on tenth grade English. Although there are finer curriculum distinctions in both schools, these distinctions are ignored in the present study.
  § Cutting points are as follows:
High—2.25 and above
Low —2.24 and below

an influence on scholastic performance after the ninth grade, though we may assume for purposes of our analysis that such factors are randomly distributed between athletes and non-athletes.[29]

Control of these four confounding factors was accomplished by matching each athlete with a non-athlete on all four variables.[30] Table 4, which contains the academic performance averages of the resulting 152 matched pairs of athletes and non-athletes, indicates that the average GPA remains slightly higher for athletes than for matched non-athletes (2.35 versus 2.24), a difference attributable to the fact that somewhat more than half the athletes (56.6%) exceed their matches on GPA.

TABLE 4

Mean GPA for Athletes and Matched Non-Athletes and
Percentage of Athletes Who Exceed Their Match in GPA*

	Mean GPA	Per cent of Athletes Higher Than Match	N
Athletes	2.35		152
		56.6	
Matched Non-Athletes	2.24		152

* Below are the percentages of athletes exceeding their matches, by within-school and across-school matching:

	Percentage of Athletes Higher Than Match	Number of Pairs
Within Large School	52	(80)
Within Small School	46	(24)
Mixed-athlete in Large School	71	(21)
Mixed-athlete in Small School	67	(27)

These figures reveal that athletes who are matched with a non-athlete in the other school exceed their matches considerably more often than do athletes who are matched with a non-athlete within the same school.

Since both "mixed" percentages are higher, however, there is no reason to believe that they result from anything other than chance. That is, the findings are not affected by the fact that high achieving athletes in one school are matched with low achieving non-athletes in another.

Athletic participation does not appear to have an overall detrimental effect on academic performance. In fact, the relationship suggests that participation might exert some *positive* effect, although such a conclusion must be viewed with caution, because of the small size of the sample, the weakness of the positive relationship, and the possibility that athletes still exceed non-athletes in previous achievement motivation or ability.

Variation by Amount of Participation. Earlier, we suggested that the greater the amount of participation in sports, the greater the detrimental effect on academic performance. In Table 5, athletes are divided into those who completed one or two seasons and those who completed three or more. This indicator of participation is relatively crude, of course, since there are only two categories and there is no distinction between participation in the same sport for two or three years and participation in two or three sports during the same year. Nevertheless, it provides a gross measure of overall athletic participation.

TABLE 5

Mean GPA For Athletes and Matched Non-Athletes and Percentage of Athletes Who Exceed Their Match in GPA, by Amount of Participation

Amount of Participation	Mean GPA	Per cent of Athletes Higher Than Match	N
Three Seasons or More			
Athletes	2.42		86
		60.4	
Matched Non-athletes	2.24		86
Two Seasons or Less			
Athletes	2.26		66
		51.5	
Matched Non-athletes	2.23		66

Again, the results do not support the hypothesis. In fact, they suggest the opposite. The more they participate, the more the athletes exceed their matches in GPA. Whereas the difference in average GPA between "low" participants and their non-athlete matches is 0.03, it increases to a difference of 0.18 between "high" participants and their matches. Viewed another way, 51.5% of the "low" participants exceed their matches, compared to 60.4% of the "high" participants. These data suggest that, rather than "eroding" academic performance, extensive participation in interscholastic sports slightly enhances a boy's chances for scholastic success.

Variation by Type of Sport. It was also predicted that participation in football or basketball would have a more adverse effect on academic performance than participation in minor sports such as track, swimming, wrestling, and gymnastics. Table 6 clearly shows that, while participants in the two major sports are somewhat lower in average GPA than participants in minor sports,[31] those in major sports exceed their matches to a greater extent than do those in minor sports. Whereas participants in major sports exceed their controls in GPA by 0.18 (2.20 versus 2.02), participants in minor sports exceed theirs by the smaller margin of 0.03 (2.53 versus 2.50). This pattern is also reflected in the percentage of athletes who exceed their matches in scholastic performance: 60.2% of the "major" participants, compared to 52.1% of the "minor" participants.[32]

TABLE 6

Mean GPA for Athletes and Matched-Non-Athletes and Percentage of Athletes Who Exceed Their Match in GPA, by Type of Sport

Type of Sport	Mean GPA	Per cent of Athletes Higher Than Match	N
Major Sport*			
Athlete	2.20		83
		60.2	
Matched Non-athlete	2.02		83
Minor Sport†			
Athlete	2.53		69
		52.1	
Matched Non-athlete	2.50		69

* Major sports include football and basketball, according to our coding criteria. Participants in major sports sometimes participated in one or more minor sports also, but the reverse is never true.

† Minor sports in both schools include baseball, track, cross-country, swimming, wrestling, tennis and golf; the larger school also fields teams in gymnastics and in hockey.

Contrary to the prediction, participation in the more highly rewarded sports has no greater adverse scholastic effect than participation in the less rewarded ones. In fact, if we assume equally close matching for both categories of athletes, participation in football and basketball appears to have a greater positive effect on academic performance than participation in minor sports.

Variation Among Types of Boys. Having found no support in the sample as a whole for the various "interference" hypotheses, we next raise the question whether the major prediction holds among any of the various sub-samples within the control variables. For instance, does athletic participation have a greater positive effect on academic achievement among white collar than blue collar boys, among high IQ than low IQ boys, among college-bound than work-bound boys, or among high than low achievers in junior high school? Further, does the general relationship between athletic participation and academic achievement conceal a slight negative relationship among certain types of boys?

Data in Table 7 reveal two clear patterns. First, the slight positive association between participation and achievement persists in *all* sub-groups. In no case is the relationship negative. Rather, more than half the athletes in each category exceed their matches, and the average GPA of athletes is always higher than that of matched non-athletes. Moreover, on every variable except previous GPA, the athletes in the lower category exceed their matches by a greater margin than do those in the higher category. This can be seen, for example, in the fact that greater percentages of blue collar athletes than white collar athletes exceed their matches in GPA (63.0% versus 53.7%). An even greater spread separates non-college preparatory from college preparatory athletes (69.0% versus 53.7%). In short, boys otherwise least likely to succeed academically appear to benefit most from participation in sports.

Interpretation. These findings tell us nothing, of course, about the first four possible types of "erosion" of the academic or intellectual objectives of the school by interscholastic sports. That is, they shed no light on whether athletics divert resources, staff man-hours, and facilities at the expense of the scholastic programme; whether parental support is channelled away from academics; whether the academic achievement of student fans suffers from their support of school teams; or whether potentially top students are discouraged from trying because social rewards go to athletes instead.

These data do bring into serious question, however, the notion prevalent among many teachers, parents, and social scientists that the supposed over-emphasis of athletics in the American high school results in the lowering of academic achievement among participants. At the very least, the data cast doubt on the validity of Jules Henry's irate judgment that "athletics, popularity and mediocre grades go together with inarticulateness and poor grammar". Tentative as the findings are, in fact—because of the small size of the differences, the small size and non-randomness of the sample, the absence of a longitudinal design, and the possibility of initial differences remaining between the athletes and their controls in motivation or academic ability—they *suggest* that participation in sports exerts a positive influence on academic achievement, especially among boys who complete several seasons,

TABLE 7

Mean GPA for Athletes and Matched Non-Athletes and Percentage of Athletes Who Exceed Their Match in GPA, by Father's Occupation, Intelligence Test Score, Curriculum, and GPA for Last Semester of Junior High School

Characteristic	Mean GPA	Per cent of Athletes Higher Than Match	N
Father's Occupation*			
White Collar			
Athlete	2.53		95
		53.7	
Matched Non-athlete	2.48		95
Blue Collar			
Athlete	2.05		54
		63.0	
Matched Non-athlete	1.84		54
Intelligence Test Score			
Upper Half of Class			
Athlete	2.64		94
		56.4	
Matched Non-athlete	2.55		94
Lower Half of Class			
Athlete	1.88		58
		56.9	
Matched Non-athlete	1.74		58
Curriculum			
College Preparatory			
Athlete	2.47		123
		53.7	
Matched Non-athlete	2.40		123
Non-college preparatory			
Athlete	1.85		29
		69.0	
Matched Non-athlete	1.56		29
GPA for Last Semester of Junior High School			
Upper Half of Class			
Athlete	2.82		78
		57.7	
Matched Non-athlete	2.70		78
Lower Half of Class			
Athlete	1.85		74
		55.4	
Matched Non-athlete	1.75		74

* The three "farm" pairs are not included in the "Father's Occupation" section of the Table.

participate in a major sport, are in the lower half of their class in IQ, and are not doing college preparatory work.

In interpreting these findings, we will first re-examine the assumptions from which the "interference" hypotheses were derived. Then we will suggest several possible explanations for the consistent contradictions of the hypotheses.

The first assumption stated earlier is that informal social rewards, such as popularity, prestige, and leadership, are more readily accorded by peers and adults for athletic success than for academic achievement. One reason for the absence of a negative relationship might be that, in contrast to the schools in Coleman's study, social rewards are not given more for athletic achievement than for academic achievement in the schools in the present study. As a result, boys might not be attracted to athletic endeavours at the expense of academic effort. We have no way of directly testing this assumption, but the schools in this study do not appear to stress athletics any less than Coleman's schools.

A second assumption underlying the "interference" hypotheses is that boys value informal social rewards more than formal school rewards, such as grades, promotions, or honours, and more than long-term gains, such as qualifying for college or a job, that accompany high academic achievement. Perhaps the first assumption is valid but this one is not. That is, athletes in this sample might value informal social rewards less than academically-related formal or post-high school gains. In the competition for energies, the publicity and prestige of athletic participation might fail to outweigh the immediate preference among athletes for high grades or the broader concern with qualifying for college or a good job. Again, there is no way with our data to test this assumption.

The final assumption is that time, attention, and energy are limited resources. Perhaps both the above assumptions are valid but this one is not. While youth obviously have only a limited supply of time, attention, and energy, it is possible—and in fact likely—that the supply devoted to athletics does not create a serious diversion away from studies. Rather, it might be that most youth have a "pool" of time and energy sufficient for both athletics and studies.

Lack of validity of one or more of these three assumptions, which cannot be tested with available data, would help account for the absence of a *negative* relationship between athletic participation and academic performance, but not for the appearance of a slight *positive* association. To the extent that there is a positive influence of participation on scholarship, it might operate either directly or indirectly.

Directly, such an effect could take several forms. First, some have suggested that the exposure in sports to an emphasis on effort, hard work, persistence, and self-improvement results in higher aspirations and performance in other activities, including scholastics. Certainly, this is one of the first arguments likely to be expressed by coaches and other apologists of competitive sports.[33] Systematic evidence on such a "carry-over effect", however, seems to be non-existent.

Second, others have pointed out that the superior physical condition of athletes is likely to facilitate mental discipline and academic achievement. Again, cause and effect data are lacking, although athletes, coaches, and other advocates of physical fitness argue strongly for the mental and behavioural benefits of good body health.[34]

Third, it is possible that the requirement that athletes maintain a certain level of academic performance in order to remain eligible, motivates many athletes to achieve higher than they otherwise would.[35] This interpretation, of course, applies especially to boys who are marginal in grades. The performances of middle or high achieving boys are not likely to be very much influenced by the fear of losing their eligibility, unless they drop below their usual level in a particular class or two. Nevertheless, the boost given marginal athletes by the eligibility requirement might well account for the overall positive relationship described earlier. This interpretation might also account for the fact that non-college preparatory athletes, who are marginal in GPA, exceed their matches more than do college preparatory athletes (Table 7).

Fourth, it is frequently contended that boys are forced to make more efficient use of their limited study time when participating in sports, resulting in heightened achievement. Therefore, boys who participate perform higher in their school work than those who do not, other things being equal, accounting in part at least for the positive relationship described earlier. Indirect support for this interpretation comes from the fact that athletes exceed their matches slightly more often during the season of competition than during the off-season, although the difference is a small one.[36]

Finally, it is possible that many athletes are spurred to higher achievement by the hope of qualifying for college or even receiving an athletic scholarship in order to continue their athletic careers. This interpretation is especially plausible for accounting for the relatively strong relationship among athletes from blue collar backgrounds who otherwise are not very likely to attend college. In a later section, data from another sample are presented showing that athletes, especially from working class backgrounds, in fact expect to attend and graduate from college more often than non-athletes.

The positive influence of athletic participation might also operate in several *indirect* ways. Participation in sports usually results in high status among peers and adults which in turn might lead to higher achievement. First, high status might in turn result in a heightened self-concept and in higher aspirations in other activities, including schoolwork.[37] In other words, accomplishment in sport, when reinforced by social rewards, might give the athlete a sense of confidence and competence which he generalises to other arenas of behaviour such as the classroom. This outcome of sport involvement, which would be expected to increase with athletic success, is especially likely to occur during the teenage years when the self-concept is still being shaped. There is less likely to be a similar effect from collegiate or professional participation, since the self-concept is already shaped to a greater extent.

Second, high status from athletic participation might result in more academic assistance from peers, teachers, or parents than comparable non-athletes receive. Special help in schoolwork might be expected to be given especially to successful athletes and to those in danger of losing their eligibility.

Third, athletic involvement might be associated with lenient grading. That is, teachers might give easier grades to athletes than to non-athletes performing at the same level because of a "halo effect" whereby athletes are seen as more special or deserving than the ordinary student. The chances of this happening are greatest for top stars, especially if they are in danger of failing a course and losing their eligibility. Of course, the reverse could just as well be true: anti-athletic teachers might be harder than usual in their grading of athletes.

All three of these *indirect* effects of athletic participation are mediated by the high visibility and social status of athletes among peers and adults. Therefore, they are especially plausible ways of accounting for the findings that the greater the participation, the more positive the effect, and that the positive effect is greater for participants in major sports (football and basketball) than for those in minor sports, since extensive participation and involvement in major sports are likely to result in greater visibility and prestige.

There is yet another possible way to account for the major-minor sport difference. The same assumptions stated at the beginning of the chapter could generate the opposite hypotheses: participants in minor sports might be expected to exceed their matched non-athletes to a greater extent than would athletes in major sports, since the latter are relatively assured of high rewards by the mere fact of participating, while minor sport athletes have to "win" their visibility and prestige through accomplishment and not mere participation. This alternative hypothesis would help account for the fact that minor athletes exceed their matches more than do major athletes.

We have seen that athletic participation appears to have its greatest positive effect on the academic performance of boys with blue collar backgrounds, low IQs, and a non-college preparatory label. A plausible interpretation of these findings is that, compared to non-athletes with the same characteristics, blue collar and non-college bound athletes are more likely to associate and identify with white collar and college-bound members of the school's leading crowd. Illustrative cases are abundant of blue collar boys who were not at all academically or college-oriented until they began to "make it" in sports and to be increasingly influenced by white collar boys (and girls) with whom they would not otherwise have associated or identified. For them, then, "upward mobility" in the peer system might exert an "upward pull" in aspirations and achievement.

OTHER EDUCATIONAL EFFECTS OF ATHLETIC PARTICIPATION

The above data and discussion relate to one educational effect of athletic participation—scholastic performance. Data from the same sample, together with information from a separate study, make it possible to examine two other educational effects of athletic participation: persistence in high school and expectations for attending college. The findings are briefly reviewed below.

Athletic Participation and Persistence in School. Does participation in interscholastic sports keep boys in school? Data presented in Table 8, which are from the same sample as above, strongly suggest an affirmative answer. Whereas 9.2% of the matched non-athletes dropped out of school before graduating, less than one fourth that number (2.0%) of the athletes failed to finish. These figures do not include boys who transferred to another school.

This finding suggests that athletics exert a "holding influence", which might operate in four different ways. First, the high prestige that athletes are likely to receive probably creates a positive attraction to school. Second, athletes who are potential dropouts are likely to associate and identify with college-oriented or at least graduation-oriented boys more often than are non-athletes who are potential dropouts. As a result, athletes who are potential dropouts are likely to be "pulled" towards graduation by peer influences.

Third, some athletes might stay in school simply to be able to participate in high school sports or even sports at the college or professional level. Fourth, potential dropouts who are athletes are likely to benefit from the encouragement and counselling of coaches, while potential dropouts who are not participants are likely to receive less attention of this kind.

TABLE 8

Percentage of Athletes and Matched Non-Athletes Who
Dropped Out Before Graduation

	per cent	N
Athletes	2.0	152
Matched Non-athletes	9.2	152

Whatever the reasons for greater persistence among athletes, it is clear that, while all dropouts in this sample manifest low levels of academic performance prior to exit from school, athletic participation exerts a "holding influence" over some boys who, on the basis of their low achievements, would have been expected to drop out. This is illustrated by the fact that, of the nine matched non-athletes who dropped out after attaining GPAs of less than 2.0, eight were paired with an athlete who ended up with an equal or lower GPA but did not drop out. This finding provides limited support for Coleman's suggestion that ". . . if it were not for interscholastic athletics . . . the rate of dropout might be far worse . . ." Athletics appear to serve as an important mechanism for committing boys to the socially valued pathway to adulthood.[38]

Athletic Participation and College Plans. An assertion often heard but little studied is that competitive sports serve as an important vehicle for upward mobility. Numerous examples can be cited, of course, of college or professional athletes having risen above their fathers in income and status solely or primarily because of their athletic prowess and achievements. We know of no systematic studies in the United States, however, to determine how often athletic participation is associated with mobility. One study providing a lead in this direction is Guenther Lueschen's, which reports higher rates of upward mobility for participants in German sport clubs than for non-participants.[39]

Information about the relationship between interscholastic athletic participation and college expectations is of interest in this chapter for two reasons: first, it provides a basis for understanding the role of athletics in upward mobility, in so far as mobility is dependent on college attendance and graduation; second, it provides additional data about the extent to which athletics impede or facilitate attainment of one of the school's educational goals; to send a maximum number of youth to college.

Pertinent data on this point have been gathered from question-naires administered to 785 twelfth grade boys in three public and three Catholic high schools in three middle-sized (50,000 to 100,000) Pennsylvania cities during the spring of 1965.[40] For pre-sent purposes, all respondents are treated as a single sample. Among other things, boys were asked to name the extra-curricular activities in which they participated during their senior year, how far they expected to go in college, their father's education and occupation, and the frequency of parental encouragement to go to college. In addition, rank in graduating class was obtained from school records.

TABLE 9

College Expectation of Athletes and All
Other Boys in Their Class

| | Per cent Who Expect to Complete: | | Total |
	At Least Two Years of College	At Least Four Years of College	N
Athletes	82	62	284
All Other Boys	75	45	490

Table 9 shows that, in comparison with non-athletes, athletes are slightly more likely to expect to complete at least two years of college (82% versus 75%) and are considerably more likely to expect to complete at least four years of college (62% versus 45%). Of course, this relationship could result from the fact that athletes are more "disposed" towards college on the basis of their background or earlier ability or aspirations. Therefore, it was decided to re-examine the relationship controlling for the following three potential confounding factors: social status (measured with the Hollingshead Two-Factor Index of Social Position), parental encouragement to go to college, and rank in graduating class. The controlling procedure used is the Rosenberg technique of test factor standardisation, which permits the controlling of tabular data in a fashion analogous to partial correlation with continuous data.[41]

The figures in Table 10 clearly indicate that, even when the three factors are controlled, participation continues to be associated with a slightly higher expectation of completing at least two years of college (80% versus 76%) and a considerably higher expectation of at least graduating from college (61% versus 46%). In fact, the original relationship, before controls, remains virtually undiminished. The extent to which athletic participation *causes* higher educational expectation is, of course, still open to question, since not all potential confounding factors are controlled and the design is cross-sectional rather than longitudinal.

TABLE 10

College Expectations of Athletes and All Other Boys
In Their Class, Controlling for Social Status, Parental
Educational Encouragement, and Rank In Graduating Class*

	Per cent Who Expect to Complete:		
	At Least Two Years of College	At Least Four Years of College	Total N
Athletes	80	61	284
All Other Boys	76	45	490

* The three variables are controlled by means of the Rosenberg technique of test factor standardisation. See note 41.

In the earlier analysis of the academic effects of athletic participation, it was noted that higher scholastic achievement was especially marked among athletes who were from working class backgrounds and who were non-college bound. That finding raises the additional question of whether college expectations are relatively more frequent among athletes who are less, rather than more, "disposed" towards college. Table 11 shows that the answer to this question appears to be affirmative. When social status, parental encouragement, and class rank are all dichotomised, the difference in percentage of athletes and non-athletes expecting to graduate from college is greater in each case in the "lower" category (except for the two categories of "two years of college or more" where the differences are virtually identical). That is, a greater percentage of athletes than non-athletes expect to complete at least four years of college among working rather than middle status boys, among boys with less rather than more parental encouragement, and among boys in the lower rather than the upper half of their graduating class. It would seem, then, that interscholastic athletics serve a "democratising" or "equalising" function in the sense that they represent a vehicle for upward mobility, especially for youth otherwise not likely to complete college. Further, the data suggest that, at least as far as participants are concerned, athletics enhance rather than interfere with the educational goal of sending a maximum number of youth to college.

TABLE 11

College Expectations of Athletes and All Other Boys in Their Class, by Social Status, Parental Educational Encouragement, and Rank in Graduating Class

	Per cent Who Expect to Complete:		
	At Least Two	At Least Four	Total
Characteristic	Years of College	Years of College	N
Social Status			
Middle			
Athletes	91	78	90
All Other Boys	89	87	144
Working			
Athletes	78	55	194
All Other Boys	69	36	346
Parental Educational Encouragement			
High			
Athletes	90	68	208
All Other Boys	88	56	298
Low			
Athletes	58	46	66
All Other Boys	55	26	164
Rank in Graduating Class			
High			
Athletes	94	85	116
All Other Boys	89	78	205
Low			
Athletes	74	46	164
All Other Boys	66	21	280

As in the earlier analysis, the data themselves do not tell us *why* athletic participation exerts a positive influence on college expectations, if in fact it does. Thus, we are forced to speculate. Does participation in athletics enhance the chances of obtaining a college education because athletes are more likely to associate and identify with college-bound students; because of a "transfer effect" of the emphasis in sports on success, achievement, and self-improvement; because athletes are more likely to be accorded status and prestige by their peers and to raise their own personal self-concepts and aspirations as a result; because many athletes want to go to college to continue their athletic careers; because athletes more often receive college scholarships; or because athletes receive more counselling, encouragement, and "sponsorship" from teachers, counsellors and coaches? Answers to these questions await further research.

CONCLUSIONS AND IMPLICATIONS

Although interscholastic sports might erode the educational objectives of the high school in other ways, the findings reported here suggest they do not interfere with academic achievement, persistence in school, or college expectations of athletes. On the contrary, participation in sports appears to enhance slightly each of these outcomes. Thus, interscholastic sports are probably an important mechanism for tying boys into those career channels defined as legitimate and desirable by the school. Future research is needed, of course, to determine the extent to which such a conclusion is warranted.

There are numerous additional problems for investigation suggested by this discussion. Perhaps the most important is determination of the social and psychological processes mediating between athletic participation, on one hand, and academic achievement, persistence in school, and college attendance, on the other. In addition, the question needs to be asked, what effects do school and community context have on the relationships between athletic participation on the one hand, and academic achievement, persistence in school, and college attendance, on the other. For instance, a school or community with a great deal of emphasis on sports might have a lower dropout rate but also a lower achievement average among athletes than a school or community that places less value on sports. What difference do size, location, and social class composition of the school make?

Another highly interesting question is the relationship between athletic participation and the academic achievement, dropout rate, and college attendance rate among Negro boys. Although it is well known that sports represent an important channel to success for many Negroes, little is known about the extent to which this is true or about the conditions under which it varies.

A variable that was referred to several times in the above discussion but for which data were unavailable is degree of success in sports. Clearly, the effects of participation are likely to be different for a successful than an unsuccessful athlete. For instance, greater success probably is associated with greater prestige, which in turn might result in an improved self-concept, higher aspirations generally, and better academic performance.

There are a series of interesting questions about other consequences of participation in interscholastic sports. To what extent do athletics deter deviance within the school and delinquency in the wider community? More than three decades ago Willard Waller remarked on teachers' deliberate support of interscholastic sports because of their presumed usefulness in harnessing teenage energies.

> The theory which is perhaps most in vogue with the school men is that athletic activity makes students more teachable because it drains off their surplus energies and leaves them less inclined to get into mischief. This we may call the physical-drain justification of athletics . . . Part of the technique, indeed, of schools and teachers who handle difficult cases consists in getting those persons interested in some form of athletics.[42]

The actual role of athletics as a mechanism for social control seems to have escaped the attention of social scientists. Although some suggest a positive role and others contend athletic participation is probably unrelated to deviant behaviour, nobody seems to have systematically investigated the problem.[43]

One of the striking features of interscholastic (as well as intercollegiate) sports is the great amount of authority of the coach in prescribing off-the-field behaviour of athletes. The coach usually has the unquestioned authority to suspend or expel a boy from the team if he is found smoking, drinking, staying out too late, or violating a law. Beyond this, the coach often controls the hair style, dress, friendship patterns, and language of his boys. Although some "training rules" are laid down for the sake of physical conditioning and efficiency, others are quite unrelated to the sport itself and can best be understood as part of the "moralism" associated with athletics in the school. The high school athlete is supposed to practice—privately as well as publicly—all the virtues associated with the "good" American boy. A fascinating question for research is the extent to which this rigid and often puritanical control by coaches over the off-the-field appearance, demeanour, and conduct of their athletes has general and lasting effects.

A related problem is the validity of the common belief among coaches and others that the playing field, court, or track serves as a valuable training ground for the development of co-operativeness, competitiveness, leadership, and an attitude of fair play. Put another way, to what extent do high school sports contribute to so-called "character development"?[44]

Finally, what is the effect of participation and success in sports on occupational outcomes after high school and college. Again, numerous examples can be cited in which men have "made it" as a direct result of their athletic careers. However, the generality and mediating processes involved in this relationship have yet to be systematically studied.

These are all empirical matters, calling for careful and rigorous study. Clearly, sport plays a far more significant role in the educational process—for good or evil—than social scientists seem to recognise. Hopefully, the research reported in this chapter will stimulate new investigations that will yield a greater understanding of the individual and the social functions of interscholastic athletics in particular and competitive sports in general.

NOTES

1 James S. Coleman, *The Adolescent Society*, New York: Free Press, 1961, p. 148; David Matza, "Position and Behaviour Patterns of Youth", in R. E. L. Faris (editor), *Handbook of Modern Sociology*, Chicago: Rand McNally, 1964, p. 204; Joseph H. Fichter, *Parochial School: A Sociological Study*, Garden City, New York: Anchor Books, 1958, p. 216 (data are on athletes at upper elementary level); Roger G. Barker and Paul V. Gump, *Big School, Small School*, Stanford, California: Stanford University Press, 1964, pp. 54–5, 64, 69, 80.

2 James S. Coleman, "Athletics in High School", *Annals of the American Academy of Political and Social Science*, 338 (November, 1961) p. 34; reprinted in Coleman's *Adolescents and the Schools*, New York: Basic Books, 1965, pp. 35–51.

3 Educational Policies Commission, *School Athletics: Problems and Policies*, Washington, D.C., 1954, p. 1.

4 See, for example, Coleman, *The Adolescent Society*, *op. cit.*, "Athletics...", *op. cit.*, Jules Henry, *Culture Against Man*, New York: Vintage Books, 1963, pp. 186–92.

5 Coleman, "Athletics...", *ibid.*, p. 34.

6 *Ibid.*, p. 39.

7 Willard Waller, *The Sociology of Teaching*, New York: John Wiley, 1932, 1965, pp. 115–16.

8 Robert S. Lynd and Helen M. Lynd, *Middletown*, New York: Harcourt, Brace and World, Inc., 1929, 1956, p. 485. For other discussions of the role of athletics in generating school and community cohesion, see A. B. Hollingshead, *Elmtown's Youth*, New York: John Wiley, 1949, 1961, pp. 193; Grace Graham, *The Public School in the American Community*, New York: Harper and Row 1963, p. 122; Fichter, *op. cit.*, p. 213, 227–30; David Gottlieb and Charles Ramsey, *The American Adolescent*, Homewood, Illinois: Dorsey, 1964, pp. 39–41.

9 Henry, *op. cit.*, p. 190.
10 *op. cit.*, For Coleman's other writings on high school sports, besides the two already cited, see "Academic Achievement and The Structure of Competition", *Harvard Educational Review*, 29 (1959), No. 4, pp. 339–51; "The Adolescent Sub-culture and Academic Achievement"; *The American Journal of Sociology*, 65 (1960), pp. 337–47; "The Competition for Adolescent Energies", *Phi Delta Kappan* (March, 1961), pp. 231–36 (also reprinted in *Adolescents and the Schools*). For critiques of Coleman's research, see Bennett M. Berger, "Adolescence and Beyond", *Social Problems* (Spring, 1963), pp. 394–400; Matza, *op. cit.*, pp. 203–7; Lucius Cervantes, *The Dropout: Causes and Cures*, Ann Arbor: The University of Michigan Press, 1965, Chapter IV; David Gottlieb, "Youth Subculture: Variations on a General Theme", in Muzafer Sherif and Carolyn Sherif (editors), *Problems of Youth: Transition to Adulthood in a Changing World*, Chicago: Aldine, 1965, pp. 28–45; Marie Jahoda and Neil Warren, "The Myths of Youth", *Sociology of Education*, 38 (Winter, 1965) pp. 138–49; D. C. Epperson, "A Reassessment of Indices of Parental Influence in 'The Adolescent Society' ", *American Sociological Review*, 29 (February, 1964), pp. 93–6.
11 *The Adolescent Society*, pp. 32–3.
12 *Ibid.*, p. 32.
13 *Ibid.*, pp. 32–3.
14 *Ibid.*, especially Chapters 1 and 11.
15 *Ibid.*, p. 305.
16 *Ibid.*, Chapters 4, 5 and 9.
17 *Ibid.*, pp. 260–6.
18 *Ibid.*, p. 260.
19 These and several other very useful rank order correlations on Coleman's data were done in a term paper by James Stolzman, a graduate student at the University of Oregon.
20 Coleman, *The Adolescent Society*, Chapter 11, and his "Academic Achievement and the Structure of Competition", *op. cit.*
21 Interscholastic competition in academic pursuits would have to occur between entire schools in order to avoid a new form of interpersonal competition that would result from efforts to make elite scholastic teams.
22 Coleman, *The Adolescent Society*, op. cit., p. 301.
23 *Ibid.*, p. 266.
24 See, for example, Walter T. Keating, "Scholarship of Participants in High School Football", *The Athletic Journal*, Vol. 41 (Feb. 1961), p. 11; Russell M. Eidsmore, "The Academic Performance of Athletes", *School Activities*, Vol. 32, pp. 105–6; C. W. Whitten, "The Academic Achievement of the Participants of the State-Wide Basketball Tournament", *Journal of the National Educational Association* (for 1925), pp. 618–28; Lowell G. Biddulph, "Athletic Achievement and the Personal and Social Adjustment of High School Boys", *The Research Quarterly*, Vol. 25, pp. 1–7; Roy Pangle, "Scholastic Attainment and the High School Athlete", *The Peabody Journal of Education*, pp. 360–4; Russell M. Eidsmore, "High School Athletes are Brighter", *School Activities*, November, 1963, pp. 75–7. A recent study shows that University of Minnesota athletes (classes of 1960 and 1961) entered with higher average rankings in their high school classes than non-athletes. Again, however,

there were no controls for possible confounding variables. See John E. Stecklein and Logan D. Dameron, *Intercollegiate Athletes and Academic Progress: A Comparison of Academic Characteristics of Athletes and Non-Athletes at the University of Minnesota*, Minneapolis: University of Minnesota Bureau of Institutional Research, Report Series No. 3, 1965, p. 14. At the upper elementary level, Fichter (*op. cit.*, p. 225) found that athletes spent slightly more time per week in homework than no-athletes and more often graduated from the eighth grade with a high academic record.

25 Coleman, "Athletics...", *op. cit.*, pp. 37–8; Coleman, *The Adolescent Society*, Chapters 2 and 3.

26 Coleman, *The Adolescent Society*, Chapters 2 and 3.

27 For a more complete description of the sample and for the results of a more extensive study of the careers of these boys, plus their female classmates, see Walter E. Schafer, *Student Careers in Two Public High Schools*. (Unpublished doctoral dissertation, University of Michigan, 1965).

28 For illustrative studies on the relationship between social class and academic achievement, see Hollingshead, *op. cit.*, p. 168; Stephan Abrahamson, "Our Status System and Scholastic Rewards", *Journal of Educational Sociology* (April, 1952), 25:8, pp. 441–50; Wilbur B. Brookover and David Gottlieb, *A Sociology of Education*, second edition, New York: American Book Company, 1964, p. 172; Patricia Sexton, *Education and Income*, New York; Viking, p. 163; for a review of such studies, see Peter H. Rossi, "Social Factors in Academic Achievement; A Brief Review", in A. H. Halsey, Jean Floud, and C. Arnold Anderson, editors, *Education, Economy and Society*, New York: Free Press, 1961, pp. 269–72.

For illustrative studies on the association between intelligence test scores and academic achievement, see Albert J. Reiss, Jr. and Lewis Rhodes, *A Sociopsychological Study of Adolescent Conformity and Deviation*, U.S. Office of Education, Co-operative Research Project No. 507, (1959); *The Adolescent Society, op. cit.*, p. 255; Leona E. Tyler, *The Psychology of Human Differences*, third edition, New York; Appleton-Century-Crofts, 1965, pp. 72–81.

For illustrative studies on the relationship between curriculum location and achievement, see Aaron V. Cicourel and John I. Kitsuse, *The Educational Decision-Makers*, Indianapolis: Bobbs-Merrill, 1963, p. 53; Kenneth Polk and Lynn Richmond, "Those Who Fail" (unpublished paper, University of Oregon, Eugene, Oregon); Walter E. Schafer and J. Michael Armer, "High School Curriculum Placement: A Study of Educational Selection", paper presented at the Annual meeting of the Pacific Sociological Association, Vancouver, B.C., April, 1966.

29 It should also be noted that although participation in athletics before high school may well affect academic achievement, this earlier effect should show up in ninth grade GPA. Therefore, we are interested in and in fact are measuring only the effect of *high school* athletic participation.

30 On the first three factors, athletes and non-athletes were matched within the following categories: white collar, blue collar, farm; high intelligence, low intelligence; and college preparatory, non-college preparatory. On ninth grade GPA, each athlete was matched to within plus or minus 0.25 of a non-athlete. Using these procedures, it was possible to locate matches for 152, or 93%, of the original 164 athletes.

31 The lower GPAs of athletes in major sports, compared with those in minor sports, results from the fact that football and basketball players are more often from blue collar backgrounds than are participants in other sports.

32 An alternative way of classifying sports is by "team" and "individual" or "dual" sports. Here ice hockey and baseball are combined with football and basketball. Using this division, 50% of the boys who participated primarily in a "team" sport exceeded their matches, compared with 55.8 of those who participated primarily in an "individual" or "dual" sport. Below are the average high school GPAs and number of participants exceeding their match for each sport for which there were five or more boys. A boy who participated more in one sport than in any other was chosen to represent that sport in the table. Since many boys completed an equal number of seasons in two or more sports, the total N is less than 152. These, and other interesting computations not presented here, were carried out by a graduate student at the University of Oregon, Hans Buhrmann.

Sport	GPA	No. of athletes exceeding their match
Tennis	2.84	6 of 10
Swimming	2.74	12 of 17
Wrestling	2.35	4 of 7
Track and Field	2.27	13 of 23
Basketball	2.26	2 of 5
Baseball	2.17	9 of 19
Football	1.97	17 of 32

33 This is suggested by the Educational Policies Commission, *op. cit.*, and by Eidsmore, *op. cit.*

34 This interpretation is suggested by several studies showing a relationship between physical and mental performance. See, for example, Frank Kobes, "Predictive Values of Initial Physical Performance Levels of Freshmen at USMA", paper presented at the World Congress of Sports and Physical Education, 13–18 September, 1966; Jack Schendel, "Psychological Differences Between Athletes and Non-participants in Athletics at Three Educational Levels", *The Research Quarterly*, 36:1 (March, 1965), pp. 52–75; J. Burton Merriman, "Relationship of Personality Traits to Motor Ability", *The Research Quarterly*, 31:2 (1960), 163–73; Ernst Jokl and others, "Sports Medicine", *Annals of the New York Academy of Sciences*, Vol. 134 (February, 1966), pp. 908–35.

35 In the state where this study was carried out, a boy becomes ineligible for participation in interscholastic athletes when he fails three courses.

36 The study cited earlier on the achievement of University of Minnesota athletes found no consistencies in athletes' grades during on-season and off-season teams. Even this finding, however, calls into question the common belief that involvement in sports is certain to lessen academic achievement. See Stecklein and Dameron, *op. cit.*, Chapter 6.

37 This interpretation is suggested by Coleman's finding that . . . "it is the best athletes who have the most positive feeling about themselves . . ." (*The Adolescent Society*, p. 232). Although Coleman presents data on the linkages between participation, prestige and self-evaluation, he does not have information on the connection between self-evaluation and subsequent aspirations. On the other hand, Matza points out that, for

a number of reasons ... "high standing attributed to athletic youth does not necessarily result in a subjective feeling of satisfaction and contentment ...", especially, we might add, among unsuccessful athletes. (Matza, *op. cit.*, p. 207).

38 In a recent report to the President's Crime Commission, one of the authors has noted the potential of athletics for dealing with the dropout problem. See Walter E. Schafer and Kenneth Polk, "Delinquency and the Schools", Appendix M, *Task Force Report on Juvenile Delinquency and Youth Crime*. The President's Commission on Law Enforcement and Administration of Justice, Washington, D.C.; U.S. Government Printing Office, 1967.

39 Guenther Lueschen, "Soziale Schichtung Und Soziale Mobilität Bei Jungen Sportlern", *Kölner Zeitschrift Für Soziologie Und Sozial-Psychologie*, 15, Jahrgang, 1963, Heft 1, pp. 74–93. Also see S. Kirson Weinberg and Henry Arond, "The Occupational Culture of the Boxer", *American Journal of Sociology*, 1952, 57:460–9; David Riesman and Reuel Denney, "Football in America: A Study of Culture Diffusion", in Riesman's book, *Individualism Reconsidered*, Glencoe, Illinois, 1954. These papers are all included in this Reader, those by Lueschen, Weinberg and Arond in Part III, that by Riesman and Denney in Part II.

40 This section is drawn from a more extensive analysis, reported by Richard A. Rehberg and Walter E. Schafer in "Participation in Interscholastic Athletics and College Expectations", *A.J.S.*, LXXIII, 1965, pp. 732–40.

41 Morris Rosenberg, "Test Factor Standardization as a Method of Interpretation", *Social Forces*, (October, 1962), pp. 53–61.

42 Waller, *op. cit.*, 114–15.

43 For discussions suggesting that athletic participation is likely to deter delinquency, see Matza, *op. cit.*, p. 206; Coleman, "Athletics ...", *op. cit.*, p. 39; Waller, *ibid.*, pp. 112–17; Fichter, *op. cit.*, p. 214; James B. Nolan, "Athletics and Juvenile Delinquency", *Journal of Educational Sociology*, Vol. 28 (1954–1955), pp. 263–5; Schafer and Polk, *op. cit.* On the other hand, at least two criminology texts take the position that athletic participation is not likely to deter delinquency. See Paul W. Tappan, *Juvenile Delinquency*, New York: McGraw-Hill, 1949, p. 150; and Edwin H. Sutherland and Donald R. Cressey, *Principles of Sociology*, 6th Edition, Chicago: Lippincott, 1960, p. 169.

44 Matza, *ibid.*, pp. 206–7; Fichter, *ibid.*, p. 226; Educational Policies Commission, *op. cit.*, pp. 15–17; Gordon L. Larson, "Athletics and Good Citizenship", *Journal of Educational Sociology*, Vol. 28 (1954–55), pp. 271–4; Charles C. Noble, "The Moral and Spiritual Implications of School Athletics", pp. 260–2; R. Helanko, "Sports and Socialization", in Neil J. Smelser and William T. Smelser (editors), *Personality and Social Systems*, New York: John Wiley and Sons, 1963, pp. 238–47.

PART III (B)

CLASS AND RACE IN SPORT

Introduction

Class inequalities are a ubiquitous and all-pervasive feature of human societies. They raise significant moral, political and sociological issues of many kinds. Racial inequalities are a special type of class inequality which is growing in importance in the modern world. They involve the domination of one racial group by another and are a source of particularly explosive social and political problems. They, too, represent an important area of sociological investigation.

Numerous questions are posed for the sociology of sport in this connection. One of the most interesting and important of them concerns the widespread idea that sports represent a means of transcending class and racial barriers. Sport, according to this view, is a fundamentally egalitarian institution which helps to promote social harmony and integration by increasing friendly contacts across class and racial lines. It has even been seen as a means of ridding us of these divisions altogether. Each of the two articles in this section is more or less explicitly concerned with this idea. They suggest that, in fact, it is largely a myth and that sport, rather than acting as a means for transcending class and racial barriers, tends to become accommodated to the existing structure of class and racial inequalities in the societies where it is played.

"Social Stratification and Social Mobility Among Young Sportsmen" by Günther Lüschen reports a test of the "embourgeoisement thesis" as applied to the field of sports. According to this thesis, the increasing affluence of modern industrial societies is leading class differences to diminish in all spheres of life within them. One part of the thesis is the frequent contention that sports, because they are now played by members of all classes, represent a particularly striking symbol of decreasing class inequality. Lüschen found this not to be the case in West Germany. His findings are probably typical in most respects for Britain and other highly industrialised countries, although one must await the results of further research in order to be sure. He carried out a survey of active sports club members between the ages of fifteen and twenty-five and found that playing sport as a leisure occupation, though fairly widespread, is primarily an activity of upper and middle class youth and of young skilled workers for whom the middle classes act as a "reference group" (i.e. those who try to model themselves on the middle classes and who aspire to membership of them). His data also indicate that there is a distinct "status-hierarchy" of sports in West Germany. Higher status people tend to go in for newer sports, those which are most competitive and those which are highly organised. Thus, tennis, hockey and skiing are the sports most favoured by the middle and upper classes; handball, boxing, wrestling and association football are those most favoured by the working classes.

Because of the class-bound nature of their sports, young West Germans mainly come into contact with members of their own class in the course of pursuing them. In this respect, Lüschen suggests, sports appear to function as a means of socialisation into "class-specific" norms and values. They probably also serve, he argues, to a limited extent as a "lever" which facilitates upward social mobility for a small number of young people from working-class backgrounds who might otherwise be denied the chance of exposure to middle class norms and values. This interpretation is supported by the fact that, according to Lüschen's data, the rate of upward social mobility among sportsmen is higher and their rate of downward mobility lower, than either of these two rates for members of the West German population at large. Nonetheless, Lüschen's main conclusion is that sports reflect by and large the patterns of inequality in West German society as a whole. His survey did not yield any data which supports the "embourgeoisement thesis" as applied to sports. Nor does it suggest that sports serve to increase to any significant extent friendly relations between the members of different social classes.

A similar conclusion is reached by Robert H. Boyle in his essay on "Negroes in Baseball". It can serve as a fruitful source for generating hypotheses about the role of sports in promoting the integration of minority groups into the wider societies of which they are members. In particular, it makes one aware of the dangers of making facile generalisations in this respect. Boyle shows quite clearly that whites and Negroes can play together in a game such as baseball without producing any significant effects on patterns of racial segregation. Negroes played professional baseball in America as early as the 1860's. During the 1880's and 1890's, however, they were driven increasingly from the major leagues. Only afer World War II did they begin to gain a foothold once again. The breakthrough came in 1946 when Jackie Robinson became the first Negro in modern times to be signed on by a major league "ball club". By 1959, the number had risen to 57 out of an overall total of 400, a number proportionately higher than the ratio of Negroes to whites in the American population (about one tenth). Their relative success in this respect may be symptomatic of the way in which the members of a disadvantaged minority group strive for high achievement in such channels of social advancement as are open to them. As Boyle shows, however, it is not indicative of any significant increase of equality between whites and Negroes in the United States. Negroes have rarely been employed in baseball on equal terms with whites. Their "signing-on" fees are usually lower and, as is typical of Negroes in America generally, they tend to be the last to be hired and the first to be fired. The salaries they obtain are higher than the national average for Negroes—sometimes very much so. This places them squarely in the middle classes. But the patterns of *de facto* racial segregation which operate in many of the towns where they train and play, especially but not solely in the "deep South", mean that they often cannot share hotel accommodation with their white colleagues or go to the same places of entertainment. They are forced to restrict themselves to the Negro sections of a town. Faced with these circumstances, they have tended to maintain themselves as a separate, highly cohesive group. They have developed their own slang and an informal code of rules which facilitates adjustment to prejudice and discrimination. By and large, they get on better with southern than with northern white players because the former are used to the "interracial etiquette" which has developed in the South as a means of minimising friction in day-to-day relations between the races. Not all of their white colleagues are prejudiced against them—close, co-operative "work" relations of the type involved in baseball serve to some extent as a means of reducing racial prejudice—but they generally refuse invitations from whites as a means of avoiding tension. Above all, they scrupulously avoid contact with white women because sexual relations between Negroes and whites form the greatest area of tension in American race relations. Their lack of full integration with their white colleagues is typical of the fact that the "black bourgeoisie" in America—the Negro upper and middle classes—is generally a "marginal" group, cut off on the one hand from the majority of Negroes by virtue of their income and their style of life and on the other from whites of similar social standing because the latter refuse to admit Negroes into their circles on equal terms. Thus, even though professional baseball allows a small number of Negroes to rise into the middle classes, it does not serve to integrate them into American society as a whole. They are forced to become members of the socially isolated Negro middle and upper class. In this respect, the game functions as an avenue of upward social mobility within the *separate* class structure of American Negro society. It does not function as a mobility channel which permits them to cross the "caste" or "colour line" which separates whites from Negroes.

CHAPTER 12

Social Stratification and Mobility Among Young German Sportsmen*

Günther Lüschen

(translated from the original German by Eric Dunning)

During the last decade, social stratification and mobility have formed a specially favoured area of research in German sociology. Most attention, however, has been devoted to problems of occupations, occupational groups, and stratification at the community level. The relations between social stratification and leisure have hardly been discussed at all. This is all the more surprising since, apart from problems of the family and of youth, leisure has been the foremost area of interest in post-war German sociology.

It has been usual in the sociology of leisure, to remain content with descriptions of various activities. Variations in behaviour have often been assumed by posing questions which are ultimately pedagogic in nature. Whether there is a relationship between social stratification and leisure has, for the most part, not been discussed, and when it has come up for debate, it has frequently been argued that leisure is not characterised by structures which are class specific. On the contrary, it is maintained that, in an age of general affluence, conspicuous consumption in leisure has become the dominant pattern of behaviour. This is seen most clearly in the position adopted by Helmut Schelsky, following David Riesman. He can be taken as a typical proponent of the thesis that we now live in an "undifferentiated middle status society". According to Schelsky, for example, "it seems as if, in place of social class status, consumer status is becoming the central determinant of all behaviour, whether in the education of children, in politics, or in the cultural spheres, so that the negative process of levelling class differences could be positively seen as having the effect of bringing about the leisure and consumption oriented society of advanced industrialisation".[1] Following the appearance of Schelsky's work,

* The German version of this essay appeared in the *Kölner Zeitschrift für Soziologie und Sozialpsychologie*, Vol. 15, No. 1, 1963, pp. 74–93.

the theory of conspicuous consumption, which conveniently supports the arguments of the critics of "mass culture", was surely overdone in the work of H. J. Knebel on modern tourism.[2]

Yet, since the publication of *Leisure: A Suburban Study*[3] by George Lundberg, Mirra Komarowsky and Mary A. McInery, and the work of the Warner school, enquiries into the relationship between stratification and leisure have become common in American Sociology. The scientific validity of the findings on the relationship between leisure activities and social stratification made by August B. Hollingshead[4] and Leonard Reissman,[5] for example, based as they are on discriminating analysis of empirical material, is at least as great as those of the followers of Thorstein Veblen. In Germany, however, they went unnoticed for a long time and were only paralleled in scientific publications in the work of Renate Mayntz[6] when she discussed participation in leisure organisations. Even Ralf Dahrendorf, influenced by the theory of conspicuous consumpt on, speaks of the "typical leisure activities of men of all classes" when discussing the entertainment industry.[7] Sport, too, tends to be seen in close connection with the entertainment industry. It conflicts, however, more than any other leisure occupation with stated opinions. At least from the point of view of personal and mass communication, sport has become the most important sphere of leisure.

The theory of mass consumption has also been applied particularly to sport. Hans-Joachim Knebel, who defines sport merely as a form of "tourist behaviour",[8] maintains in this connection that it is characterised by the "consumption of means in the form of tools, space, and clothes".[9] Referring to Dahrendorf, sport, along with cinema and television, appears to be a typical leisure activity of men of all classes. The figures and cautiously drawn conclusions produced by Karl-Gustav Specht appear to lend strong support to all of this.[10] If one can really believe the critics of mass culture, however, then, sport is to be seen as the most striking symptom of the massification of our culture and is associated *ergo* with the lower classes.[11]

METHODOLOGICAL NOTES

It is important in the first place, to distinguish clearly between active and passive participation in sport. Different attitudes and modes of behaviour obtain in this connection as is shown in a study by Gregory P. Stone undertaken in Minneapolis, U.S.A.[12] In what follows, only the class membership and mobility of *active* sportsmen will be discussed. The group we studied consisted of young people between fifteen and twenty-five years of age who were members of organised sports clubs.[13] It is important to note that this research, undertaken in 1958, was modelled on the type of studies of youth carried out around that time. It was concerned chiefly with the leisure activities of sportsmen and only touched on indices of social class as a matter of routine—at any rate, the primary theoretical objective of the study was not related to problems of social class. Therefore, only objective criteria of social class could be used. Problems of self-evaluation, attitudes towards stratification and class specific modes of behaviour in relation to sports remain to be investigated in the future.

The objective criteria used were occupation, occupational status, and educational level both of the young people themselves and of their fathers and eventually also of mothers. Data on fathers' income were not sought because members, especially of the younger age groups, often did not know their father's income. Hans-Jürgen Daheim stresses the rising significance of occupational roles as indices of personal achievement.[14] Talcott Parsons[15] has shown how social status in Western societies is a function of evaluation and reward by others. If they are right, then it follows that occupational role is by itself almost sufficient as an index of social class in achievement oriented systems in which only achieved statuses are important. However, most young people in the age groups studied by us have not yet achieved their final occupational positions. Many of them cannot even be guessed at. Education, therefore, is indispensable as an index for the classification of young people according to social class. Of course, in unclear cases one can always take account of the father's social characteristics. Such a procedure, however, would not account for the social mobility relative to their fathers which many young people experience after leaving school. One cannot for one moment deny that the measurement of social status in the age-group studied here poses numerous problems. In our society, social status tends only to be established finally after the age of thirty. In the interests of reliability, therefore, we will discriminate strictly in any doubtful cases.[16]

SOCIAL STRATIFICATION AMONG YOUNG SPORTSMEN

The following class divisions emerged among our research population (young sportsmen between fifteen and twenty-five years of age). We used the indices referred to in the note and drew heavily on the methods employed by Morris Janowitz.[17]

In many cases, the young people did not give completely clear answers concerning whether their fathers worked in a skilled or an

	%
Lower class	32.5
Lower middle class	35.0
Middle middle class	21.0
Upper middle class	11.0
(Unclassifiable)	0.5
N = 1880	100

unskilled occupation. Therefore, the lower class was not subjected to any further break down. At a rough estimate, however, the lower lower class—with a share of around 5% appears to be poorly represented among young sportsmen.

In order to compare the pattern of social stratification among young sportsmen with the pattern of social stratification discovered by Janowitz for the total population, one has to take into account the fact that he classified skilled craftsmen (*Meister*), employed by others—who form 3% of our sample—among the lower class. In addition, it emerges from our investigation that young people from the lower classes join several sports clubs much less, those of the upper middle class much more, than the average. The method of selection used, therefore, means that the upper middle class is over-represented by 1%, whilst the lower class is under-represented by that amount. Allowing for this bias, the following figures compare the pattern of social stratification among young sportsmen with that in the whole of Federal Germany: [18]

	Sportsmen	*All of Federal Germany*
	%	%
Lower class	36.5	57.9
Lower middle class	53.0	38.6
Upper middle class	10.0	4.6
(Unclassifiable)	0.5	4.9
	N = 1880	N = 3385

From these figures one can discern a progressive increase in the numbers of young sportsmen as one ascends the social class hierarchy. Given the small proportion of sportsmen in the lower class and the concentration of them in the lower middle class—divided for purposes of this analysis into a lower- and a middle-middle section—it is clear that sport in general can in no way be seen as a leisure pursuit of all social strata. Despite what its critics have said, it emerges primarily as an activity of those very social class groupings to which these critics themselves for the most part belong. However, in order to avoid a one-sided interpretation, it must be stated firmly nevertheless that sport is socially very widespread and that it is by no means the exclusive domain of a leisure class as Thorstein Veblen maintained.[19] The great number of skilled workmen whose sporting interests are oriented to those of the middle class is unmistakable.

Whether in the future the pattern of social stratification in sport will come to approximate more closely to that in the wider society remains a question and cannot be determined from our data. It does emerge, however, that sport was probably much more highly stratified in the previous generation. Since only 6% of lower class parents played a part in the sports socialisation of their children while the corresponding figures for the three middle classes were 12, 17, and 15% respectively, it seems reasonable to suppose that lower class parents of the group studied are involved in sport to a lesser degree than is the case with their middle class counterparts. The objection that relations between children and parents might be worse among the lower class does not hold. On the contrary, while the data collected by EMNID for the whole of Germany show the opposite tendency,[20] it emerges from our study that the family relationships of young sportsmen, measured by trust in parents and number of conflicts in the home, improve as one goes down the social class hierarchy. Bearing in mind all reservations with respect to this comparison, it seems also reasonable to suppose that the majority of lower class youths who are accepted into sports clubs come from stable families. If that is so, then the often repeated assertion that sport functions as an *ersatz* form of social work and as an agency of re-socialisation can hardly be regarded as valid.

The pattern of stratification for the two sexes is also very instructive:

	Sportsmen	
	Male	Female
	%	%
Lower class	37.5	15.5
Lower middle class	33.5	39.5
Middle middle class	18.0	32.0
Upper middle class	10.5	13.5
(Unclassifiable)	0.5	0.5
	N = 1474	N = 405

For lower class girls there apparently still exists a steep social barrier, which gives some indication of the fact that female roles are hardly defined as equal in the lower class and points to a host of prejudices, particularly in orthodox religious circles.

Nothing of significance can be said with respect to variations among the strata by age group, although it is likely that there are class specific variations as one ascends the age-scale.[21]

It seems reasonable to suppose that the high social status of young sportsmen is solely a result of the fact that we are here dealing with a leisure occupation that is tied to an organisation. The high social status of sportsmen would then only be a special case of the well-known fact that the number of members of voluntary organisations from the middle and upper classes exceeds that from the lower classes.[22] Doubtless, the organisation of sports in Germany could produce such a pattern. The possibility of such an influence must certainly be borne in mind, as the findings of Erich Reigrotzki lead one to expect.[23] Enquiries undertaken by the DIVO in 1960, however, lead one to suppose that, at least in the case of sports, leisure activities pursued independently of club organisations are also more frequently undertaken by members of the middle and upper classes.[24] The rising positive correlation found by them between sports participation, of an informal as well as a formal kind, and education and income, points to an equally strong relationship with class as holds in our figures for social stratification among organised sportsmen. The relationship between high achievement motivation and social class[25] also suggests that a system as dependent on the achievement principle as sport will, correspondingly, manifest relations which are class specific in this respect. That this, indeed, is so, is shown by our figures. The correlation between class and achievement is direct. The simple numerical majority of people with high achievement motivation are found in the already achievement-motivated "middle mass" (skilled workers, and the lower middle class).

SOCIAL STRATIFICATION, TYPES OF SPORT, AND THEIR SOCIAL RANK-ORDER

If, from one point of view, sport in general can be defined as a leisure activity of the middle classes and of those skilled workers for whom the middle class acts as a reference group, from another, one cannot avoid the fact that, despite this relative closure, single sports are highly differentiated along class lines. The young people in this research were asked to name their "favourite sport". This question, of course, brought the possibility of the class affiliations of particular sports fully into the open. The results obtained from the responses to it yield the following pattern of stratification among particular sports:

In %	Lower Class	Lower Middle	Middle Middle	Upper Middle	Unclass- ifiable	Totals	Cases N=100
Football	53	29	12	5	1	100	470
Wrestling, weight lifting, etc	51	26	14	9	—	100	35
Field handball	43	31	19	6	1	100	158
Badminton	27	46	24	3	—	100	33
Gymnastics (with apparatus)	31	39	23	7	—	100	279
Table Tennis	23	44	24	8	1	100	73
Canoeing	21	41	38	—	—	100	34
Gymnastics	16	43	41	—	—	100	44
Riding	18	49	15	18	—	100	33
Swimming	17	41	31	11	—	100	143
Athletics	19	40	24	17	—	100	231
Rowing	12	47	26	14	—	100	57
Skiing	11	33	20	36	—	100	72
Hockey	3	26	53	18	—	100	34
Tennis	2	27	28	42	1	100	101

The "status hierarchy of sports" reported by Carl Diem and Gerda Engelhardt is here unmistakable.[26] In order to investigate this hierarchy more closely, a numerical index of social status was worked out for each sport in terms of the numbers from each stratum who participated in it.[27] The individual sports can be divided into the following four groups on the basis of this index.

		Index
I	Tennis	209
	Hockey	186
	Skiing	181
II	Rowing	141
	Athletics	139
	Swimming	136
	Riding	133
III	Gymnastics	125
	Canoeing	117
	Table Tennis	116
	Gymnastics with apparatus	106
	Badminton	103
IV	Handball	87
	Field athletics, etc.	81
	Football	68

Using Janowitz's data, the index for the general population is around 70.[28] Football, therefore, approximates most closely to the index for the general population as far as its relationship to patterns of social stratification is concerned. This fact, by itself, explains much about the popularity of this sport. Since Group IV corresponds in large measure to the general pattern of social stratification in the Federal Republic, we can refer to it as "the sports of the common man". Group III corresponds to the average index for young sportsmen which amounts to 110. This group, therefore, can be referred to as "middle class" sports. Group II can be called "upper middle" and Group I "elite" sports.

The class affiliations of particular sports indicated by these data reveal a number of surprises. Along with Diem and Engelhardt, one would certainly have expected riding to come out on top. They refer to it as an "aristocratic" sport.[29] The number of riders from the gentry is small, however, compared to the great number of riders in rural areas who are small, independent farmers belonging overwhelmingly to the lower middle class. Their ranks also contain a number of skilled workers and farm labourers. Besides this, one has to take account of the rural/urban division in order to understand the pattern of social stratification among horsemen, since patterns of social stratification differ between rural and urban areas.[30] The small number of cases in this study, however, did not permit such a breakdown to be made. One must have certain reservations, therefore, with respect to the inclusion of riders in the upper middle category.

Types of sports not included here were all mentioned by less than thirty people as their favourite sport. Perhaps a fifth category should be added in which, for example, boxing and cycling would be included. The high average social status of the basketball players is interesting to note. In the United States, the country where this sport originated, there is no such clear-cut relationship with membership of higher social classes. This allows one to formulate our first proposition with respect to the differential patterns of social stratification in the various sports: *the newer a sport, the higher its social position; distinct fashion cycles can be discerned in sport.*[31] In terms of such fashion cycles, the striking fall in the social status of football and even of gymnastics since the turn of the century becomes, in part at least, explainable. In addition, Naumann's highly controversial thesis about "cultural traits of diminished value" (*gesunkenes Kulturgut*) can be applied in some areas of sport. In order to explain differential patterns of stratification in sport, one can formulate a second proposition: *that the social·status of a sport form rises as the importance of individual achievement within it increases,* a proposition which is applicable to the diminished status of relatively non-competitive football and gymnastics, since individual achievement has become more highly valued in society at large since the turn of the century. A third proposition also suggests itself: *the more a sport is organised along club lines, the higher its social status in terms of the class membership of those who practise it.*[32]

The division of sports into four social categories on the basis of our empirical enquiry is provisional in nature, above all as a classificatory scheme for the whole population. Nevertheless, these categories are not without relevance as far as the behaviour of young people is concerned. The sportsmen who practise sports included in Group I did not choose a single sport in Group IV as their second favourite sport. And vice versa, in no case, did a person in this group choose, for example, tennis as the sport he liked best after football. If, however, one takes those sports into consideration which are practised by young people along with their favourite sports (secondary sports), then the hierarchy which emerges on the basis of favourite sports is in part obliterated. Informal sports, that is those practised outside the framework of organised clubs, and those practised at school tend not to be differentiated along class lines. In like manner, badminton, table tennis, and skiing are very frequently the second or third sport both of lower class and of upper middle class people. Only relatively rarely, however, are they chosen as the favourite sport if they are not typical of one's own class. This is clear confirmation of the class-bound nature of particular sports, a finding which is valid not only for Germany, but, according to the figures of Roland von Euler, for Sweden also.[33] Both sport in general and particular sports are class-bound in the U.S.A. as well, although extensive research into the problem still remains to be carried out in that country.[34]

From these findings concerning organised youth between fifteen and twenty-five, an age-group which represents more than a third of the combined active and passive membership of German sports clubs, it is clear that the practise of sport in our society is a general symbol of relatively high social status and that participation in particular sports, especially those in the "common man" and "elite" categories, is an extensively used criterion for membership in a particular social stratum. They show that differentiation in sport is at least as strong as the class divisions which are evident in the wider society. It is true that, using objective criteria, no great difference in the social status of football and gymnastics was apparent. Nevertheless, people who play these sports feel themselves to be sharply discriminated against socially. From this fact, and taking into consideration the findings on stratification among particular sports, the sociological question arises whether the models of social stratification used up until now can adequately reflect such differences or whether there are not forms of differentiation and barriers in the social rank hierarchy which cannot be adequately comprehended, even with a six or seven stratum model —measured in terms of objective and not of behavioural characteristics—as is suggested for America by Werner S. Landecker in his article on "Class Boundaries".[35]

In terms of these findings, it can also be affirmed that the choice of a sport is not to be explained solely in psychological terms as has usually been the case up to now among those concerned with physical education. There are also sociological factors connected with social stratification which have to be taken into account. In some sports even, such as tennis and boxing, for example, they are of primary importance. From the relationship both of sports in general and of particular sports to social stratification, two main consequences follow for young people in the age group investigated:

1.   Participating in sport as the member of a club serves a social integration function beyond the level of the sport itself. In his club, the young sportsman comes into contact with other members of his class who practise that sport and with a system of norms and values which conform to those of his class. Sport is, therefore, an important factor in class specific socialisation. The significance of sports for socialisation into the general norms and values of a culture has been treated in another context through the example of competitive sports,[36] and Rafael Helanko[37] has discussed the significance of sports for socialisation into the basic rules of social behaviour. His data show that sport retains its importance in this respect longer than any of the other group activities of young people.[38]

That sport during youth can in no way be seen as a leisure activity free from obligations, but, on the contrary, is viewed by young people themselves, if perhaps unconsciously, as performing important functions for social integration in the widest sense, does implicitly emerge from research into leisure[39] by the fact that such studies have shown the high "value" generally accorded to sport. In fact, they have shown that, next to reading, sport is the "hardest" of our leisure occupations, though, of course, research using time-budget methodology probably would not lead one to accord such a high position to active sports-participation.

2. From its significance for social integration, follows a second consequence of the class-bound nature of sport: that it can act as a lever for socially mobile people in their climb up the social ladder. The degree to which this is the case will be discussed in the following section.

SOCIAL MOBILITY AMONG YOUNG SPORTSMEN

Two thirds of the young people investigated, reported that they were striving for a "better position" than their parents. However, only 35% indicated a high degree of certainty concerning their mobility expectations. Twenty-nine per cent reported that they might "perhaps" achieve a high position relative to their parents. Clear variations between classes emerged in this respect.

Expected mobility relative to parents' social status by social class

(Question: Do you think you will achieve this position?)

	Lower lower class	Lower class	Middle middle class	Upper class
Yes	32	43	38	30
Perhaps	41	28	27	17
No expectation of mobility	27	27	39	53
N=	613	655	394	208

Certainty with respect to mobility expectations is most frequently found among track and field athletes (47%) and among top level athletes (44%). In connection with the possibility that an achievement oriented system such as sport might have an effect on personal achievement motivation, it is instructive to note that more Catholics (39%) reported expectations of certain mobility than Protestants (33%) ($p < 0.1$).

To make definite statements about the extent of intergenerational mobility for young sportsmen, that is of upward and downward movement from at least one class to another, and to compare them with general mobility rates is, of course, not possible, since the final social position of these young people has not been established yet.[40]

The differences between young males in manual and non-manual occupations with respect to final mobility, however, are relatively clear-cut. In the age-group studied here (15.7 to 25.7 years: average age, exactly 20) those in manual occupations have nearly all reached their final positions. The few "drop-outs" still to be expected from schools leading on to higher education who will become workers are statistically insignificant. One would not expect those children attending such schools who have reached at least the middle forms to take up manual occupations. Accordingly, it is possible to make a statement about the mobility of those in manual and non-manual occupations in which the only uncertainty factor relates to those young men in manual occupations who will later become self-employed or reach managerial positions by studying at advanced technical institutes.

In contrast with the data cited by Seymour Martin Lipset and Reinhard Bendix[41] from three German investigations of mobility between manual and non-manual occupations which reported very different rates of downward mobility (between 20 and 38%), one can suggest from the data presented here that young people who participate in sport show a comparatively lower rate of downward mobility from non-manual to manual occupations. With the further

Intergenerational mobility of manual and non-manual workers

	Father's occupation	
Son's occupation*	Non-manual	Manual
	%	%
Non-manual	76	33.5
Manual	23	64.5
Unclear	1	2.0
N =	901	496

development of their careers this is certain to be the case, because, on the one hand, the already mentioned tendency for some to climb to positions as engineers and architects or to become self-employed, and on the other, the generally stronger rate of intragenerational mobility into non-manual occupations, have to be taken into account. Taking these factors into consideration, one can say with certainty that the number of young sportsmen whose fathers work in manual occupations and who themselves enter non-manual occupations is higher than the corresponding rate in the population at large which, according to Lipset and Bendix, stands at an average of 29%.[42] To be sure the difference at present discernible is not very significant. The whole question might, in fact, become clearer if one could control for age-group. However, data of that kind are not available at present.

According to Renate Mayntz, more than a quarter of the sons of skilled workers end up in non-manual occupations.[43] This would confirm the slight positive tendency among young sportsmen.

Quite a number of the young people investigated here, then, are mobile from one stratum to another. Taking into account the education, occupation, and occupational status both of the young people themselves and of their fathers, the following figures on intergenerational mobility emerge:

Upwards	14%
Downwards	7%
N=	1880

Because rigorous distinctions have been made here once again, borderline cases have not been included in the upwardly mobile group. It is likely, however, that quite a number of doubtful cases would have to be classed as upwardly mobile. Bearing this in mind, it still seems reasonable to maintain that the ratio of upward to downward mobility is favourable, since the data of both Janowitz[44] and of Lipset and Bendix[45] show a somewhat higher rate of downward intergenerational mobility for the Federal Republic as a whole. Apart from that portion of the group investigated whose intragenerational mobility is not yet ascertainable, there is strong reason to believe that the positive relationship holds good, since young sportsmen have relatively higher than average chances of downward mobility on account of their high social position relative to the average in the population at large. In addition, for the reasons already mentioned, mobility within the lower class is not taken into account in the figures 14% and 7%. Because of the very small numbers of unskilled and semi-skilled workers among these young people it is probably mainly upward.

UPWARD AND DOWNWARDLY MOBILE SPORTSMEN

The attitudes and modes of behaviour of upward and downwardly mobile young sportsmen were analysed in greater detail in order to draw inferences concerning the general social function of sport. This, for a long time, has been a controversial question in which, it is true, both friends and critics of sport have been able to illustrate their arguments with examples, but have seldom been in a position to evaluate these examples and to undertake to prove the extent to which sport is, in fact, a "useless and parasitic cultural phenomenon",[46] or "the great hope for the future".[47]

Our first question concerns the relationship between high achievement in sport and social mobility. As indices of high achievement, we took, for individual sports, at least second place in an area championship, and for team sports, first place in such a championship. The following rates for high sports achievers, grouped in terms of their mobility patterns, were found in our data:

	%	N
Upwardly mobile	25	263
Downwardly mobile	7	133
Non-mobile	15	1484
Totals	16	1880

From these data, one can state with certainty that, for young people in the age-group considered here, sport only performs in small degree a compensatory function for poor performance at work or school. That it does, nevertheless, perform such a function for a small group, is shown by the 7% of high-achievement sportsmen among those who were downwardly mobile. However, they represent only 0.5% of the total sample. Much more important numerically are the group of upwardly mobile, high-achievement sportsmen, who constitute 3.5% of the total and are a reference group who act as models for the behaviour of others. About half of them occupy leadership positions, while not one important office (membership of an executive committee, coach, youth leader) was occupied by any of those who were downwardly mobile.

Essential in order to comprehend the norms and values current among young sportsmen, are the conceptions about "the most important characteristics of a gymnast and a sportsman" held by those who are upwardly in contrast to those who are downwardly mobile. Two groups of value orientations can be distinguished in this connection:

1. Orientation to persons and partnership. (Comradeship, fairness, honour, team-spirit, self-control.)

2. Impersonal orientation to sport as such (endurance, performance, physique, industry in training, love of sport).

Values and norms of upward and downwardly mobile sportsmen:
Mobiles

	Upwards	Downwards
	%	%
Orientation to persons and partnership	67	47
Impersonal orientation to sport as such	26	47
Other	7	6
N=	263	133

The number of replies, however, was greater for those who were upwardly mobile. In order to effect comparability, the total number of responses was expressed in percentages. The resultant calculation yielded a significant correlation between upward mobility and orientation to persons and partnership ($x^2 = 25.6$, 2 degrees of freedom. $p > 0.001$). This may be quite instructive with respect to the general relationship between n—achievement and n—affiliation which, according to McClelland, is by no means clear-cut and in part negative, since the person—and partnership orientated values and norms of young sportsmen can be defined as allied to the "affiliation" syndrome.[48] According to our findings, however, this holds for the whole norm and value system of young sportsmen, so that one is led to expect that, through its person and partnership-oriented norms and values, sport will have an influence on achievement striving in the wider society. The dangers of socialisation into questionable, one-sided norms often attributed to sport on account of its achievement-oriented character must, therefore, be regarded as slight, since sportsmen have their own self-regulating system of norms and values.

The achievement-ability of the whole upwardly mobile group manifested both in their sport and in their upward mobility, shows itself in many areas compared with the total sample and with the downwardly mobile group. As a group, they show above average interest in politicis, and in reply to the question. "What in politics causes you most concern?", gave for the most part coherent and intelligent answers on the East-West conflict and on domestic and party politics, while fully one half of the downwardly mobile sportsmen gave no indication of political interests at all. Interestingly enough, no great differences between those who were upwardly and downwardly mobile emerged with regard to attitudes towards work. To be sure, job-satisfaction is significantly higher among the upwardly mobile, but the difference between 66 and 50% for those who indicated unqualified satisfaction and 29 and

30% who said they were satisfied but with reservations, is smaller than one might have expected. One should also note in this connection, the small extent to which sport performs a compensatory function for "social failure". It is significant that the downwardly mobile young people in our sample report human relations at work which are equally as good as those of the rest of the sample and that members of the sample for the most part report better relations with work colleagues than do young people in the population as a whole.

If our demonstration of the influence of sport on the relationship between achievement and person-partnership oriented norms and values has any validity, then, on account of the relationship between achievement in sport and upward social mobility, it is perhaps reasonable in that connection to suppose that sport, in fact, serves as a stimulus for upward mobility. However, more penetrating analysis than is possible with the data available at present would be required to establish whether this is so. The degree to which participation in different sports is correlated with mobility is shown in the following table:

%	Mobiles Upwards	Downwards	Direction of Difference	Significance of Difference
Football	18	25	negative	$p < 0.10$
Drill	15	16	negative	none
Gymnastics	8	9	negative	none
Athletics	19	11	positive	$p < 0.05$
Swimming	4	11	negative	$p < 0.01$
Handball	8	9	negative	none
Tennis	6	4	positive	none
Table tennis	6	3	positive	$p < 0.2$
Skiing	5	3	positive	none
Badminton	2	4	negative	none
Hockey	1	5	negative	$p < 0.01$
Rowing	4	–	positive	$p < 0.005$
Boxing	–	4	negative	$p < 0.01$
Riding	0.5	5	negative	$p < 0.01$
Cycling	1	3	negative	none
Other	15	13	positive	none
N=	263	133		

From this table, it can be seen that those who are downwardly mobile are more frequently players of team sports. Moreover, those who are downwardly mobile are only represented slightly in those individual sports in which achievement in competition plays a great

part (track and field athletics, skiing, tennis, and also rowing).
The downwardly mobile are to be found much more frequently in
less competitive individual sports (gymnastics, apparatus gymnastics, badminton). For men who take part in drill, the difference is
even more significant (11% of the upwardly, 16% of the downwardly mobile.) Swimming, of course, is competitive, but this is
not the case with "bathing" which has been included in the category "swimming". That the downwardly mobile tend also to be
found frequently in boxing and cycling is probably a consequence
of the low social status of these sports. Besides this, of course, it is
likely that participation in boxing on the part of downwardly
mobile people can be explained to a large extent in terms of the
frustration-aggression hypothesis (destructive character of aggression). With respect to riding, account has once more to be taken
of the different types of rural situations. According to Janowitz's
findings,[50] two-thirds of the non-inheriting sons of independent
farmers are downwardly mobile, while only 4% are mobile in an
upwards direction. That such downwardly mobile sons of farmers
are easily able to practise riding in their youth is sufficient to
explain the correlation.

It comes as no surprise that the upwardly mobile mainly practise
sports which are typical of their reference group. However, it was
somewhat surprising to find that the downwardly mobile have their
own reference group, too, and that they devote themselves to a
large extent to the "common man" sports, even though one would
expect from their fathers' status that sport groups I and II would
act as their reference groups. But the chances of becoming upwardly mobile from these groups are not great, so that the relationship is only logical. Both trends, however, show the significance
of sports for socialisation into the class of which one is currently
a member.

It is relevant to conclude by comparing young people and their
fathers with respect to education. From such a comparison it
emerges that those young people who are more definitely upwardly mobile retain their membership in sports clubs longer. The
following table contains the numbers in each age group who
attended a school which prepares one for higher education.

| | Age | | |
	15–18	19–21	22–25
Fathers	44.5	32	31
Young people	50.5	51	45
N=	787	554	539

The number of young people attending high schools or schools which lead on to higher education but whose fathers had only been educated to the primary school level is highest in the 19–21 age-group and lowest in the 15–18 age-group. It is clear that sport and membership of a club give these young people a sense of security in their behaviour which, in striving to climb up the social hierarchy, they do not find in their families. In fact, it is possible that such a function of sport is most important in the 19–21 age group since the transfer to college and university occurs at that time and since it is a period in which the mobile youngster from a lower social stratum is most in need of some kind of support in his mobility strivings. The clear disparity with the first age group indicates the extent to which sport is important for socialisation into the norms and values of a higher class.

SUMMARY

On the basis of this investigation of organised sportsmen between fifteen and twenty-five years of age it has been possible to show that sport in general is primarily a spare-time occupation of the middle classes and of those skilled workers for whom the middle classes act as a reference group. At the same time, nevertheless, a pattern of stratification in terms of sports practised at least as differentiated as the pattern of stratification among the population at large was discovered within sport itself. Using a simple index of status, four groups of sports were isolated whose relevance for the behaviour of young sportsmen was shown and which themselves can be used as secondary indices of social status. The class-bound character of sport was found to have consequences for socialisation into class-specific norms and values. Their class-bound character, however, can also act as a lever in upward social mobility. Many young sportsmen are upwardly mobile, and both their sport and their membership in a sports club are important sources of support for them in their mobility striving.

The respect for other people which is so necessary in modern society with its general emphasis on achievement-striving, is in part produced by the system of norms and values of young sportsmen, as was seen in the correlation between the achievement principle, which is of fundamental importance in sport, and partnership-oriented norms and values. Although to be sure, one or two of the conclusions presented here still have the character of hypotheses, it is already possible to define active sport during youth (in contrast with the cultural destructiveness it is often charged with) as contributive to the solution of many of the "structural problems inherent in mass society".[51]

It is true that a tendency towards conspicuous consumption can be seen in some areas of sport, but it cannot be interpreted as dominant among the mass of the people as one was led to expect from some of the views discussed at the beginning. On the contrary, sport must be understood in the first instance as a stratified area of social structure. It may, of course, perform physiological functions. It is seen, for example by sportsmen themselves, as a source of relief from tension, and to some extent also performs social functions of a compensatory kind. But it has to be defined above all in terms of its functions for security and advancement in social life. Work and sport, therefore, are not polar opposites, but stand in close relationship to one another.[52] This may hold good only for this particular area of leisure. It seems likely, however, that similar structures will be found in other areas, too.[53] Indeed, it also seems likely that, in a society in which social stratification is determined more and more by achieved status, sport (and particularly active sport) will become more and more significant.

NOTES

1 Helmut Schelsky, "Gesellschaftlicher Wandel", *Offene Welt*, 1956, 41.
2 Hans-Joachim Knebel, *Soziologische Strukturwandlungen im Modernen Tourismus*, Stuttgart, 1960.
3 George A. Lundberg, Mirra Komarowsky and Mary Alice McInery, *Leisure: A Suburban Study*, New York, 1934.
4 A. B. Hollingshead, *Elmtown's Youth*, New York, 1949.
5 Leonard Reissmann, "Class, Leisure and Participation", *A.S.R.*, 1954, 1, Vol. 19.
6 Renate Mayntz, *Soziale Schichtung und Sozialer Wandel in einer Industriegemeinde*, Stuttgart, 1958, p. 241 ff. See also, H. Meier, *Freizeit und soziale Schicht* (unpublished M.A. thesis), Cologne, 1957.
7 Ralf Dahrendorf, *Soziale Klassen und Klassenkonflikt in der industriellen Gesellschaft*, Stuttgart, 1957, p. 69.
8 H. J. Knebel, *op. cit.*, p. 163.
9 *Ibid.*, p. 160.
10 K. G. Specht, "Sport in soziologischer Sicht", *Studium Generale*, 1960, 1.
11 The many sided value-judgments about sport, which are oriented particularly towards spectators, records and mass-media coverage, are treated by the author in: *Kölner Zeitschrift für Soziologie und Sozialpsychologie*, 1960, 3, "Prolegomena zu einer Soziologie des Sports".
12 Gregory P. Stone, "Some Meanings of American Sport", Proceedings of the College of Physical Education Association, 60th Annual Meeting, Columbus, Ohio,. 1957, p. 6 ff.
13 Two stage random sample, representative for fifteen to twenty-five year old members of sports clubs in the Federal Republic and West Berlin. The sample covered 1,880 cases drawn from 121 clubs, and was stratified for size of club, types of sports, sex, and county. (Land.)

14 Hansjürgen Daheim, "Die Vorstellungen vom Mittelstand", *Kölner Zeitschrift für Soziologie und Sozialpsychologie*, 1960, 2.
15 Talcott Parsons, "An Analytical Approach to the Theory of Social Stratification", *Essays in Sociological Theory*, Glencoe, Ill., 1958, p. 69 ff.
16 The following were taken into consideration:

(i) occupation and occupational status of the young people, provided that occupational roles were already determined or future position was clearly recognisable.
(ii) educational level of the young people.
(iii) occupation and occupational status of the fathers. Principally for those still at school or in those cases where occupation and occupational status were not yet clearly recognisable.
(iv) fathers' educational level.
(v) mothers' occupation and occupational status, in case she were the main breadwinner.

The lower class and the middle class were distinguished in terms of manual and non-manual occupations. Skilled craftsmen (*Meister*) employed by others were placed in the lower middle class.

Examples of class placement

Upper middle class (including middle upper class)	Professionals, higher executives, managers, high-level self-employed.
Middle middle class	Middle level executives, qualified employees, middle level self-employed.
Lower middle class	Lower officials, employees, low level self-employed, employed, farmers.
Lower class	Skilled workers, semi-skilled and unskilled workers, farm labourers.

17 Morris Janowitz, "Social Stratification and Mobility in West Germany", *Kölner Zeitschrift für Soziologie und Sozialpsychologie*, 1958, 1.
18 *Ibid*, p. 10. Farmers were classified by us as lower middle class. For purposes of this comparison, the lower middle class, which we had divided into two sections, was taken as a whole.
19 Thorstein Veblen, *Theory of the Leisure Class*, Chicago, 1896.
20 Question: "To whom can you speak openly about anything that worries you?" (sports youth).
"Do you have anyone with whom you can discuss your trouble and worries?" EMNID (Institut für Markt und Meinungsforschung Bielefeld—Institute of Market and Public Opinions Research), young people between fifteen and twenty-four, Bielefeld 1955, p. 149.

Father or mother named (including mention of both)

Sports Youth	%	All youth (by father's occupation)	%
Lower class	97	Workers	49
Lower middle class	89	Employees	60
Middle middle class	90	Clerks	59
Upper middle class	81	Self-employed	55
		Farmers	52

21 Measured by father's education, the proportion of higher class young people decreases as one ascends the age-scale. This is not cancelled out to any significant degree, however, since the proportion of self-employed fathers rises somewhat.

22 cf. Reissman, op. cit. and Murray Hausknecht, The Joiners, New York, 1962, p. 15 ff.

23 Erich Reigrotski, Soziale Verflechtungen in der Bundesrepublik, Tübingen, 1956, p. 173 ff.

24 DIVO (German Institute for National Questions; Institute of Economic Research, Social Research and Applied Mathematics). Press release, May, 1960, II.

25 David C. McClelland, The Achieving Society, New York and London, 1961, p. 324.

26 Carl Diem and Gerda Engelhardt, "Sport", in W. Bensdorf and F. Bülow (eds.), Wörterbuch der Soziologie, Stuttgart, 1955, p. 313 ff.

27 In constructing this index, the lower class was given a score of 0, the lower middle class of 1, the middle middle class of 2, and the upper middle class of 3.

28 According to our own rough calculation.

29 Carl Diem and Gerda Engelhardt, op. cit.

30 cf. Karl Martin Bolte, Sozialer Aufstieg and Abstieg, Stuttgart, 1959, p. 49 ff.

31 cf. in this connection, Rene König, "Die Mode in der menschlichen Gesellschaft", in Rene König and Peter Schupisser (eds.), Die Mode in der menschlichen Gesellschaft, Zürich, 1957, p. 3 ff.

32 That a corresponding pattern of stratification can be discerned in a city in the Eastern Zone, emerges from the not very sophisticated analysis by H. Perleberg, Über die soziale Schichtung der Sporttreibenden in den einzelnen Sportarten, Dissertation, Griefswald, 1955.

33 Roland von Euler, "Yrhe och Socialgrupp", in Sten Svensson (ed.), Svensk Idrott, Malmö, 1953, p. 212 ff.

34 American sport is clearly stratified already at college in that the upper stratum practice sport, while the lower, non-academic stratum work in their spare time. On the other hand, the number of sports clubs is small. Only denominational youth groups faintly approximate the German club pattern and allow one to suppose that a similar pattern of stratification might prevail. cf. the passive interest and attitudes to particular sports of different educational and socio-economic strata reported by Stone, op. cit.

35 Werner S. Landecker, "Class Boundaries", A.S.R., Vol. 25, 1960, 6.

36 Günther Lüschen, "Der Leistungssport in seiner Abhängigkeit vom socio-kulturellen System", Zentralblatt für Arbeitswissenschaft, 1962, 12.

37 Rafael Helanko, "Sports and Socialisation", Acta Sociologica, Vol. 2, 1957, p. 229 ff.

38 Rafael Helanko, op. cit., p. 232.

39 cf. Viggo Graf Blücher, Freizeit in der industriellen Gesellschaft, Stuttgart, 1956.

40 The comparability of mobility rates is limited in any case, since such rates are dependent upon the number of strata employed in any study.

41 Seymour M. Lipset and Reinhard Bendix, Social Mobility in Industrial Society (2nd edition), Berkeley and Los Angeles, 1960, p. 17 ff.

42 Lipset and Bendix, op. cit., p. 25.

43 R. Mayntz, op. cit., p. 164.

44 M. Janowitz, op. cit., p. 12.

45 Lipset and Bendix, *op. cit.*, p. 25.
46 Alfred Peters, *Psychologie des Sports*, Leipzig, 1927, p. 58.
47 Heinz Risse, *Soziologie des Sports*, Berlin, 1921, p. 5.
48 cf. D. C. McClelland, *op. cit.*, p. 159 ff.
49 cf. EMNID, *op. cit.*, p. 236. Here, too, a somewhat differently formulated question was used, so the meaning attributed to the scores for young sportsmen must remain hypothetical.
50 M. Janowitz, *op. cit.*, p. 15.
51 Rene König, "Gestaltungsprobleme der Massengesellschaft" in Franz Greiss and Fritz W. Meyer (eds.), *Wirtschaft, Gesellschaft und Kultur, Festgabe für Alfred Müller-Armack*, Berlin, 1961, p. 559 ff; cf. also Rene König, "Die Freizeit als Problem des heutigen Menschen", *Universitas*, 1961, 5.
52 On the basis of a preliminary analysis of the data collected in connection with the study we are at present carrying out on "Leisure and the Working Class" it emerges that sportsmen in North Rhine-Westphalia for the most part engage in types of sports which are appropriate for their work.
53 cf. in connection with this very fundamental question, see Harold L. Wilensky, "Work, Careers, and Social Integration", special issue of the *International Social Science Journal*, October, 1960; cf. also Max Kaplan, *Leisure in America*, New York, 1960, p. 21 ff.

CHAPTER 13

Negroes in Baseball*

Robert H. Boyle

Sport has often served minority groups as the first rung on the social ladder. As such, it has helped further their assimilation into American life. It would not be far-fetched to say that it has done more in this regard than any other agency, including church and school. In *Organised Sport in Industrial America,* John R. Betts writes that nowhere is "the process of Americanisation more in evidence than in sport". To Betts, it is significant that "the greatest fighter of recent decades was a Negro, the most spectacular ball-player a German, the most publicised wrestler a Greek, the most respected football coach a Norwegian, the most successful baseball manager an Irishman, the most highly paid jockey an Italian".[1]

Jews, for instance, have been among those to see the social benefit to be derived from sport. Speaking at a Zionist congress in 1901, Max Nordau, German scientist and publicist, called for the development of "muscular Judaism". The *Universal Jewish Encyclopedia* credits Daniel Mendoza, an eighteenth-century prize ring champion, with having been "a potent psychological influence in the liberation of the Jews of England some years later", and the encyclopaedia goes on to say that the success of Jewish athletes in the twentieth-century United States "did more than any other single factor in convincing Americans that Jewish young men and women were not different from other youths".

In recent years, Negroes have come to occupy an increasingly prominent position in sport. Without doubt, they have achieved their most publicised success in major league baseball. During the 1959 season, fifty-seven of four hundred-odd major league players were Negroes, and they were paid a total salary of a little under a million dollars.[2] Thirteen years before, Jackie Robinson of the Brooklyn Dodgers was the only Negro in major league ball. He was paid five thousand dollars.[3]

The majority of these fifty-seven players showed a strong sense

* This essay is Chapter 3 from Boyle's, *Sport—Mirror of American Life*, Boston, 1963.

of group solidarity. "Negroes aren't supposed to stick together," said Brooks Lawrence, a relief pitcher on the Cincinnati Reds, "but the closest kind of adhesion I've ever known has been among Negro ball-players." The Negro players had their own hangouts, such as the Sportsman Club in Los Angeles. "That's headquarters there," said one. "We won't be in town a half hour before we check in to see what's going on." They also had their own slang, which they guarded closely. "Why should I tell what they mean?" said Bill White of the St. Louis Cardinals when asked the meaning of "mullion" and "hog cutter". "Maybe they're secret words. Maybe we've got a code of our own. Ask someone else, not me. I'm not going to tell you." In addition to all this, the Negro players occupied a special position in Negro society at large. They were, as the late Professor E. Franklin Frazier, chairman of the Department of Sociology at Howard University, phrased it, "an important part of the bourgeois elite".

THE COLOUR LINE

Although it may surprise modern fans, the Negro's participation in baseball goes back to the 1860's when Bud Fowler, the first Negro professional, began playing. Fowler had a remarkably long career by any standards; he lasted well into the 1890's and he would have played longer but for the colour line. The first Negroes to appear in a major league box score were the Walker brothers—Fleet, a catcher, and Welday Wilberforce, an outfielder—who both played briefly with Toledo of the American Association in 1884.[4] They had to quit when the team was threatened with mob violence in Richmond. Fleet Walker went to Newark, where he caught George Stovey, a famous Negro pitcher, but in 1887 he and Stovey, who were known as the "Mulatto Battery", left baseball after Cap Anson of the White Stockings balked at playing against them in an exhibition game. The colour line had been drawn.

In point of fact, a colour bar had existed as early as 1867, when the National Association barred Negro players and clubs from membership, but some players managed to get by. In the eighties and nineties, however, an antipathy towards Negroes, instigated by white politicians in the South, set in throughout the country, and Negroes were driven not only from baseball but from such other fields as horse racing and barbering. Only in the prize ring did Negroes retain a foothold, and then many of them had to agree to lose before they could get a fight. Those were the days when Senator Benjamin Tillman of South Carolina plumped for the killing of thirty thousand Negroes in his home state, and a book called *The Negro a Beast* was a popular seller.

The prevailing attitude towards Negroes in baseball is best summed up by a story which appeared in *Sporting Life* in 1891:

THE DISCOVERY OF THE SLIDE
The Feet-First Slide Due to a Desire to Cripple
Coloured Players

"No," said Ed Williamson, the once great shortstop the other day to a reporter, "ball players do not burn with a desire to have coloured men on the team. It is, in fact, the deep-seated objection that most of them have for an Afro-American professional player that gave rise to the 'feet-first' slide. You may have noticed in a close play that the base-runner will launch himself into the air and take chances on landing on the bag. Some go head first, others with the feet in advance. Those who adopt the latter method are principally old-timers and served in the dark days prior to 1880. They learned the trick in the East. The Buffaloes—I think it was the Buffalo team—had a Negro for second base. He was a few lines blacker than a raven, but he was one of the best players in the old Eastern League. The haughty Caucasians of the association were willing to permit darkies to carry water to them or guard the bat bag, but it made them sore to have the name of one on the batting list. They made a cabal against this man and incidentally introduced a new feature into the game. The players of the opposing teams made it their special business in life to 'spite' this brunette Buffalo. They would tarry at second when they might easily have made third, just to toy with the sensitive shins of the second baseman. The poor man played in two games out of five perhaps; the rest of the time he was on crutches. To give the frequent spiking of the darky an appearance of accident the 'feet first' slide was practised. The Negro got wooden armour for his legs and went into the field with the appearance of a man wearing nail kegs for stockings. The enthusiasm of opposition players would not let them take a bluff. They filed their spikes and the first man at second generally split the wooden half cylinders. The coloured man seldom lasted beyond the fifth inning, as the base-runners became more expert. The practice survived long after the second baseman made his last trip to hospital. 'And that's how Kelly learned to slide,' " concluded the reminiscent Ned.[5]

Barred from organised baseball, Negroes formed their own

teams. Waiters at a smart Long Island hotel formed the first one. To get games, they called themselves the Cuban Giants, and on the field they spoke a gibberish that was supposed to be Spanish. Negro leagues followed shortly. Certainly some players were good enough to star in the majors—Josh Gibson, the home run hitting catcher, to name only one—but the colour line held firm, though now and then it bent slightly. While managing Baltimore at the turn of the century, John McGraw signed Charlie Grant, a Negro second baseman, and claimed he was an Indian named Tokohoma. The ruse worked until Tokohoma went to Chicago for an exhibition game. Jubilant Negro fans jammed the stands, waving a banner: OUR BOY, CHARLIE GRANT.

Although Charlie Grant failed to stay, several light-skinned Negroes undoubtedly did "pass" into organised ball. In his later days, Bud Fowler said he knew of three or four. In the 1920's, Negro players gossiped that Babe Ruth himself was passing. "Look at his nose, his lips," an old-timer said. Told of this, Professor Frazier said that it was not uncommon for Negroes to lay claim to a celebrity who had features that might be Negroid. "The Negroes," said Frazier, "as with any people who have a low status and a negatively valued world, want to go ahead and neutralise that by claiming important people are Negroes."

Life in the Negro leagues was hard. A star might play in as many as three games a day and earn only four or five hundred dollars a month. But after Jackie Robinson broke in, major league clubs began to pick the Negro leagues clean. The Negro National League collapsed. At last report, the Negro American League limps on. In 1956, conditions were so bad that the West team, playing in the annual league all-star game in Chicago, went on strike. The players wound up getting nothing—except a fifty dollar fine. Lonnie Harris of the Memphis Red Sox said: "Man, this is a rough league. In the South, if you're playing in a white town, you don't eat—unless there's a Dairy Queen. You can't get out of the bus. The secretary writes down all the stuff on a list and then hands it in the window, and then brings back the hamburgers and stuff. One night it was raining, and I went in for a cheese bit. You know, a little cheese bit. And the guy says to me, 'You wait outside, boy'. I said god damn to myself. It was raining like hell outside. I just got back in the damn bus. When we ride all night, they're supposed to give us an extra buck for food. But they just give you two dollars. One night we jumped from Greenwood, Mississippi, to Flint, Michigan, for a game. All we got was that two dollars."

Rufus Gibson of Memphis said: "Some of the guys eat steaks

two or three times a week, but a guy can't eat steak like in organised baseball. Most of the guys eat on the run. Like us. Chicago today. Oklahoma City Tuesday. Muskogee, Oklahoma, Wednesday. From there to Little Rock to Memphis to New Orleans by Sunday. We ride all night. A whole lot of nights. If we get into town ten or twelve hours before game time, we usually get a hotel to sleep."

In all fairness, the owners could not be blamed for the meagre salaries and backbreaking schedules. The Negro clubs scarcely made anything from the sale of players to the majors. The most any club got was the twenty thousand dollars the Kansas City Monarchs received for Ernie Banks. Dr. J. B. Martin, president of the Negro American League, took all this philosophically. "When Negro players got into the big leagues, people said it would hurt Negro baseball," he said. "I said, 'Let it hurt it.' When we had an entire Negro outfield—Henry Aaron, Frank Robinson, Willie Mays—on the National League team in the All Star game, well, my chest kind of poked out. I was happy to know it."

NEGROES AND LATINS

In 1959–60, the major league club with the most Negro players was the San Francisco Giants. Ten of the thirty-seven players on the Giants' winter roster were coloured. The man mainly responsible was Alex Pompez, a sixty-seven year old Negro who had owned the New York Cubans in the Negro National League. Pompez, or "Pomp" as he is called, had played a part in the signing of almost every Negro then in the Giant organisation. He got Willie Mays for ten thousand dollars, Willie Kirkland for two thousand and Willie McCovey for only five hundred. His job with the Giants was unique. First of all, he had charge of scouting all Negro and Latin-American players. Secondly, he had charge of all Negro and Latin prospects during spring training. He supervised their food, living quarters (he bunked Dominicans with Dominicans, Cubans with Cubans), manners (no hats on when eating) and dress. He gave them little pep talks.

"When they first start out," Pompez said, "I tell my boys, 'If you want to stay in organised baseball, you got to do things a little bit better. You got to fight, play hard and hustle.' And they do. They're most ambitious, and they're hungry. Every year we got the leading hitter, most valuable player, the big home run hitter." His most delicate task was explaining the colour line to Latin Negroes new to the segregated South. "When they first come here, they don't like it," he said. "Some boys cry and want to go home.

But after they stay and make big money, they accept things as they are. My main thing is to help them .They can't change the laws."

The segregation issue—in fact, the low status of the Negro in the United States—caused friction between the Latin Negro and American Negro players. With the exception of a few—for example, Felix Mantilla and Juan Pizarro of Milwaukee—Latin Negroes did not willingly mix with American Negroes off the field. The reason was simple: to be a Negro in the United States was to be inferior. Therefore Latin Negroes were not Negroes, at least as far as they themselves were concerned. They were Cubans, Dominicans or Puerto Ricans.

For their part, American Negroes did not feel that the Latin Negroes should be compelled to associate with them, but what they often resented was the Latin Negro's attitude. "I don't think I'm any better than they are", said an American Negro, "but I'm not any worse, either. They think they're better than the coloured guy." Another player said, "You could write a book about those guys. We never see them unless we happen to have some choice material or where they're uncertain about things." Told that Latin Negroes sometimes cry when they first encounter segregation, the player said, "I don't cry. We don't cry, and we have it a hell of a lot worse than they do. But we're conditioned, I guess." The player said that while he was in the minor leagues he roomed with a Latin Negro. "I showed him the ropes, how to order eggs and things." The player came back to the room one day and found that the Latin had moved out. The Latin tried to run around with the white players, but, said the American Negro, "they wouldn't tell him where they were having dinner," so he came back. "But I wouldn't take him. He didn't want me, so I didn't want him."

Mal Goode, a Negro advertising man and a member of the Pittsburgh Chapter of the National Association for the Advancement of Coloured People, made it a practice to have Negro players home for dinner. Goode heard about a Latin Negro who was unhappy at not having been invited. "I invited him," Goode said. "After dinner he rubbed his skin and said, almost in tears, 'They say me no want to be coloured, Mal. Look at me, Mal. What else can I be?' He said language was the barrier, but the players say differently, at least about the others."

Besides language, there were other barriers between the Latin and American Negro players. The Latin liked his food highly seasoned. He had his own customs and traditions. He was Roman Catholic while the American Negro was Protestant. Pompez recalled how he used a Cuban witch doctor, a *brujo*, to sign Minnie Minoso for the New York Cubans:

"I was in Havana, and I wanted to sign Minoso. But he wouldn't come. He wouldn't even talk to me. Then I heard about this hoodoo man, this *brujo*. He shined shoes in Havana. I was told to see him. So the first day I went there I say nothing. I have him shine my shoes, then I give him a half-dollar tip and go away. The next day I went back and do the same thing. The third day he says, 'Don't I know you?' I said, 'Maybe. My picture's in the paper. I'm Pompez of the New York Cubans.' He asks me, 'What are you doing in Havana?' I tell him I want to sign Minoso, but he won't sign. I ask the *brujo*, 'Do you know Minoso?' He laughs, ha, ha, ha, like he's going to fall down and says, 'Do I know Minoso!' I ask, 'Can you get Minoso to come to the United States to play ball?' He says, 'Yes.' I ask, 'How do you know that?' And he laughs again, and he says, 'If Minoso no go with you, his leg be broken!' I tell him, 'Okay, you get me Minoso, and I will bring you to the United States the year after next as coach.' He says okay, and I tell him where I will be the next night so Minoso can sign the contract.

"Sure enough, right at six o'clock, there's a knock on the door. It's Minoso. He doesn't say a word. I give him the pen, and he signs to play with the New York Cubans. That's it. Later I sold him to Cleveland for seventy-five hundred dollars.

"The next year" (and here Pomp's voice became hushed) "I bring the *brujo* to the United States as a coach. I give him a uniform. He is now my coach. Now in all my years in the Negro National League I have never won a pennant. The *brujo* comes up to me and he says, 'Hey, Pompez, is it true that you have never won the penant?' I say, 'That's right. In all these years I've never won the pennant.' You know what? The *brujo*, he looks at me and he says, 'Don't worry, Pompez. This year you win the pennant.' And you know what? I won the pennant! I won the pennant!"

Pomp became indignant when it was suggested that he was laying it on a bit. "That's the truth," he said seriously. "You know Mike Gonzalez" (a former St. Louis coach)? "You know why they say Gonzalez's team wins all the time in the Cuban League? Because he got a goat buried under second base!"

By the late 1950's, a few major league clubs were beginning to realise that the Latin and American Negro players come from vastly different worlds. The Giants, for instance, would put an American Negro on a farm team in the South, but they would not do that with a Latin Negro because they were "afraid that segregation might sour a foreign Negro on the United States as a whole". At the time, Latin Negroes were starting to outnumber American Negroes in the minor leagues. Of seventeen Negroes then in the

Giants' farm system, ten were Latin; of thirty-one in the Cincinatti system, seventeen were Latin.

"EVERYBODY HAS PROBLEMS"

In the minors and the majors the American Negro players "hung kind of close". In some clubs there were leaders; in others there were not. There was, for instance, no leader in the Giants. "I think they're all leaders over there," said George Crowe of St. Louis, laughing. "It's like an army with all generals." (Mays, the logical leader, went his own way.) The main leaders were Bill Burton on the Braves, Books Lawrence on the Reds, and Crowe. A budding leader was Bill White of St. Louis. Negro players expected White, a one-time premedical student, to become a "big man" once he got a couple more years' experience in the league.[6]

Crowe was the big man then. He was smart, level headed, responsible and experienced. "Why, he's from the State of New York," said one player in awe. Before going to the Cardinals, Crowe had played for Cincinatti, and he had been the leader there. Vada Pinson, the Cincinatti centre fielder, said that when he joined the Reds, Crowe "took me right under his wing. He came up to me and said, 'If there are any problems, you come to me. I'm your father, your big daddy up here.' He was serious." Later on, Pinson said: "Something would come up about going somewhere, and he would say 'You don't want to do that', or 'We're supposed to be in bed then.' He'd be around eavesdropping while another guy would be talking to me, and after we were through talking, he'd come up to me and say, 'What did you think of what he said?' And I'd say it was good or bad, and he'd tell me what he thought. He was the big daddy. When I see him now I call him dad. We look up to him."

Asked about this, Crowe said, "I like to see everybody keep their nose clean. And when you have fellows who are coming along who are new to this, I'm glad to give guidance. So naturally I introduced myself." Asked what sort of problems a youngster like Pinson would have, Crowe spread his hands, smiled and said, "Everybody has problems. Life itself is a problem."

Crowe was likely to do much the same thing for Negro youngsters on other clubs. "If I knew a kid coming up with the Braves," he said, "I'd say to Bruton, 'Look out for this kid. Show him the places to eat. Don't leave him stand in the hotel. Take him to the movies. Find out what he likes to do.'" Crowe had a sense of responsibility as a "race" man. If, for example, the players were invited to make a public appearance, he always tried to have a Negro player attend. If no one else could, he went himself.

With such a sense of oneness, it was no wonder that the Negro players had what might be called an informal code of behaviour. For example:

A Negro player did not get "the process"—that is, have his hair straightened. Any player who was foolish enough to have this done was ridiculed back into line. "That's for entertainers, not ballplayers."

A Negro player did not criticise another Negro player in front of a white. "Whites talk about each other like dogs," said a Negro player. "We don't. Don't you ever ask me about a coloured ballplayer. I may hate him, but that's none of your business."

Negro players shared with one another. "When you're on the road, you never worry," said a player. "If you need anything, so-and-so will give it to you. And there's no salary jealousy. The best-liked player is Mays. He makes eighty-five thousand a year and every man is happy to see him with it." Many players, the player went on, automatically headed for May's home when they reached San Francisco. They had dinner, then helped themselves to records, shirts or whatever else Mays had received from admirers. Mays said, "A lot of coloured guys don't get that, so I give them to them."

Negro players did not fight each other. "You watch a fight", said one. "All the players will come out, and what we do is pick out one of us and run up and put it on. We're laughing and hugging, and the white guys are just slugging each other. We just hug. We don't try to harm each other. We got to make a living. You hardly ever see two coloured guys fighting. It happens, but you hardly see it. Watch Mays in a fight. He's circling around, circling around, pretending he's looking for someone. Shucks, he's not looking for anyone. Unless it's a guy to pull away." This did not mean that Negroes did not play hard in a game, particularly against each other. "Negroes play harder against Negroes than against whites," said a Negro pitcher. "I'd rather anybody in the world get a hit off me than Mays or Aaron. If they hit, they tease me about it, and that doesn't go down well with me."

The only time Negro players loafed was on barnstorming tours. In the fall of 1959, a group of Negro major leaguers, led by Alex Pompez, toured the South-west and Mexico playing against an all-white major league team. The whites were intent upon winning; the Negroes laughed and joked. "That white team hustles all the time" a Negro pitcher said. "We've laid down a hell of a lot. But not during the season. You know what would happen if we laid down during the season, don't you?" Another Negro player said,

"The whites seem to really want to beat us. They get ahead, they really pour it on. I know that's true because all the guys have talked about it. We know we've got a better team, even though we may take it a little easy, and when we've got a big crowd, we'll beat them."

As a matter of fact, the Negro players took it so easy that they refused to allow Vada Pinson, a youngster who does not know how to stop hustling, to make the trip. Pinson was told, "It's best you don't go. You wouldn't know how to play it. You wouldn't know how to slow down." Pinson did not know how to slow down even when he hit a homer. Once during the 1959 season he sprinted all the way home even though he saw the ball clear the fence as he was rounding second base. When he got back to the bench, Frank Robinson, the Negro first baseman and left fielder, said, "Listen, kid, you'd better just stick to singles and leave those long balls to us cats who can act them out."

HOG CUTTING

As with any intimate group, the Negro major leaguers had their own private nicknames for one another. A few of them were known to white players. Don Newcombe, for example, was Tiger to white and Negro players alike, and Mays was called Buck, not Willie, by Giants of both races. "Anyone who knows me well calls me Buck", said Mays. Among the Negroes themselves, George Crowe was Old Folks; Willie Kirkland, Kingfish; Bennie Daniels, Candyman; Charlie Neal, Snake ("He does things lower than a dog", said a Negro player, laughing); Elston Howard, Steelie; Vada Pinson and Frank Robinson, the T boys (both owned Thunderbirds; Robinson's name for Pinson was Bullet); Jim Pendleton, Road and Li'l James Artha; Gene Baker, the Fugitive; Bob Thurman, Cool Daddy; and Monte Irvin, Muggs. Two other Negro players had names that were so racial in origin that players refused to reveal them.

Charlie White, a catcher with Vancouver in the Pacific Coast League, was called the King of the Mullion Men. White, who was in the majors briefly, was a great favourite among Negro players because of his humour. When Negro players met, they often swapped the latest Charlie White story or began an outlandish phrase by saying, "As Chazz White used to say." Pompez would not think of barnstorming without taking White along. "He's very helpful in keeping the boys contented," Pomp said.

Slang in general was a rich field. The terms mullion, hog cutter, drinker and pimp apparently came from the Negro leagues. Drinker, and pimp barely survived in the majors by 1959. A pimp was a flashy dresser, and a drinker—so Jimmy Banks, a first baseman for the Memphis Red Sox in the Negro National League, once explained—was "a fielder who can pick it clean. He catches everything smooth. He can 'drink' it." Banks also said that a choo-choo papa was a sharp ballplayer, an acrobat was an awkward fielder, a monty was an ugly-looking ballplayer and a foxy girl was a good-looking girl. Mullion and hog cutter were flexible terms. At first, mullion meant an ugly woman, but its range was extended to an ugly man "or even a child". The greeting "What say, mullion?" was standard among Negro major leaguers during the 1959 season. A hog cutter was a player who made a mistake. "Any mistake, that's a hog," said Crowe. "An error. Throwing to the wrong bag. Going into the bag without sliding. That's when you cut a hog." But, as another player explained, it was possible to cut a hog off the field:

"You cut a hog by saying something that you have no business saying. You can cut the hog with anybody, but it's how we feel if you cut the hog or not. For example, forgetting where you are. You'll be with whites, and you'll forget, and you'll sound off about a coloured fellow, 'that black so-and-so'. And they say, 'Oh, he's cut that pig again.' Not much you can do except try to pass over it—the hog's cut then. No one has to say anything. You know you cut it. You can cut the hog at a social gathering when you do something very embarrassing. A big hog is when you have a lot of people, men and women, and everyone stops talking at once, and there you are. You're cussing and saying the nastiest things. Well, you've done it again with a king-sized hog. Hog cutting is filling the most embarrassing moment with the most embarrassing thing."

Asked who the hog cutters were, the player laughed and said, "A hog cutter is everywhere. He's more or less at large. How many of us did you say there were?"

"Fifty-seven."

"Then there are fifty-seven hog cutters," he said, still laughing.

"Are there different kinds of hog cutters?"

"Oh, yeah," he said. "Bruton and Monte Irvin were the quiet hog cutters. We called Monte sneaky. We'd be talking in a group, and you'd look up and he'd be gone. You'd say, 'Well, he's gone to cut one of those pigs'."

"How about Brooks Lawrence?"

"Diplomatic-type hog cutter, the sneaking kind."

"Bill White?"

"Not a hog cutter. Only one who isn't."

"Does Newcombe cut a hog?"

"Elephants!"

"Frank Robinson?"

"King-size!"

"Pinson?"

"Just a little pig cutter, but he's learning."

"Covington?"

"He cuts it—both ways."

"Banks?"

"Not any more. He's quiet. But he can cut the hog before you find out the pig has been sliced."

Hog cutter should not be confused with hot dog, another baseball term. A hot dog was a showboat, a player who called attention to himself, either through his actions or his attitude. It was a white expression, although Negroes used it. Although only Negroes were hog cutters, anyone could be a hot dog, though Latin players had a sort of monopoly in the field. "You automatically assume any Latin is a hot dog until he proves himself otherwise," said a white pitcher. Another white word was flaky; it meant eccentric. Occasionally, Negroes and whites would share in the use of an expression. One expression reflected poorly on mother love, and several years ago, a Cub—a white, by the way— used it so freely that he caused a semantic crisis. Warren Giles, president of the National League, was so distraught that he dispatched a memo to each club forbidding its use, particularly towards umpires, under pain of a five-hundred-dollar fine. In his memo, Giles noted that the expression had been recently introduced into baseball. A Negro player saw this and nudged a buddy, saying proudly, "That means we brought it." The players were faced with the considerable problem of what to use instead.

Negroes and whites alike debated the point. "What are you going to say if the umpire is one?" asked a player plaintively. Finally the Negroes decided upon two substitutes: "You're one of those things!" and "You're five hundred dollars' worth!"

Race itself was responsible for much slang. Among the Negro players, whites were called ofays (generally shortened to fays), grey boys, paddies, them people, those people, the other side, squares, triangles and blow-hair boys. Why triangle? "A triangle is a square in search of a corner," said a Negro player. Why blow-hair boy? "When the wind blows, your hair moves and mine doesn't."

NUMBER TWO

Among themselves, the Negro players referred to one another as scobes (derogatory), skokies (also derogatory), Indians and club members. The last was much in favour. A Negro player said, "We'll get into a town and look around and not see many Negroes, and I might say, 'Mm, this looks like a poor place for club members'."

Asked how St. Louis, a city with a Southern attitude towards racial matters, was for club members, the player said, "A good town for club members. Lot of club members there."

"And Milwaukee?"

"That's a lousy town for club members. But that's a lousy town for anybody."

Other expressions used by Negroes to denote a Negro were Number Two and M Two. The latter was a corruption of the former. Why Number Two? "Well, we're not Number One!" A word used only by Negro players was road. It meant another Negro player, usually, but not necessarily, on the same team. It was supposed to be short for road buddy. "Hey, road, what's doing?" was a common greeting. Road was a new word. "I called a guy road," said a Negro player, "and he thought I said rogue and he got mad." Earl Robinson, a Dodger bonus player with St. Paul in the American Association, said that when the 1959 season began, only Negroes on the Saints used the term road. Then it began to spread. "Once I was standing on second base after a pretty good double," he said, "and the second baseman on the other team said, 'Hey, road, where did you get all that power from?'"

According to Earl Robinson, Negro slang was freely minted in the minors. He and the other Negroes on the Saints began calling one another berries. In short order, one player became young berry, another old berry and so on. Thus, old berry might come into the clubhouse and shout, "Hey, young berry, where's thin berry?" Young berry would reply, "Don't know, old berry. Might be with fat berry." Other slang in use at St. Paul was three bells for .300. To hit the ball "full in the face" or "sit on it" was to hit the ball hard. In night games, a Negro batter going for the long ball would say of the opposing pitcher, "I'm going to hit this guy in the night somewhere", or, "I'm going the night with him." Earl Robinson was of the opinion that "most Caucasian ball-players are not aware that these things are going on".

Negro players joked about race in veiled terms in front of whites. When the Giants fielded seven Negroes for a game, the Negro players on the opposing bench joked, "Look at that big cloud rolling towards us! It's got to rain today!" and, "Look at those mullion men. Be more hog cutting than you can shake a stick at. They can't do right." In a situation like this, a Negro player said,

"All the coloured guys will be laughing, and the whites won't know anything about it. And we feel that's the way it should be."

Negro players seemingly did not care if a white player avoided them. "I'm not up here to make friends," said Harry Simpson of the A's. "I'm here to play baseball. Any team I've been on, I've made friends. But maybe a guy doesn't want to be friends. Well, it's a free country, and that's his privilege." A number of Negro players said that they generally got along better with white Southerners than white Northerners. "The Southern white knows he has to play with you," said Don Newcombe, "and because he is Southern, he is going to try to keep trouble down. He's more cautious of what he has to say." Another pitcher said, "A couple of years ago, the bullpen catcher told me, 'I don't care for coloured players.' I said, 'I don't care for whites.' Then he showed me what I was doing wrong." The pitcher added, "White guys from the South are better. You know where they stand. I don't mind a guy telling me he doesn't like me. I don't want to impose my time on him."

There was little racial abuse from the stands. The same pitcher said, "You get those farmers that come out in St. Louis. That's the only place you expect to hear it. I was warming up one time, and a guy said, 'Hey, snowball, I wish I could pitch like you'. It didn't bother me. I went on pitching, but I had heard it. When I sat down on the bench, the other guys didn't say anything, but they knew I had heard it."

On the other hand, Don Newcombe said, "I can't honestly say that anyone has called me a name. Oh, they've called me a big bum, but that's an honest opinion, and the fan who yelled that may be a hell of a fan."

On occasion, it has been charged that white pitchers have deliberately hit or knocked down Negro batters because of race. Although this may have been true in the early 1950's, the feeling among both white and Negro players was that if more Negro batters were hit, it was because the Negroes were the "hot hitters" on a club. A Cincinnati Negro player said, "When Frank Robinson was knocked down by Cub pitchers, the Reds sent word to the Cubs that they would knock down Banks. Not because Banks is a Negro, but because he was their hot hitter. So Purkey" (Bob Purkey, a white pitcher) "threw four balls around him and under him." A Negro pitcher on another National League club said, "Sure, I'll brush back a coloured player. I've got to make a living. You've got to brush them back. The manager says, 'He's got to go.' You've got to when the guy digs in."

OFF THE FIELD

A peculiar thing about the Negro-white relationship off the field was that if a Negro offered an invitation to a white—and this was not common—it was likely to be accepted. But if the white offered the invitation to the Negro, it was unlikely to be accepted. For example, Jim Brosnan, a white pitcher on Cincinnati, sat in the bull-pen with Brooks Lawrence. They discusssed race, progressive jazz, in which they had a mutual interest, religion—in short, any subject that happened to come up. Yet when Brosnan invited Lawrence to a party at his home in a Chicago suburb, Lawrence refused the invitation. "Brooks said he couldn't make it," Brosnan said. "He said, 'Don't bug me about it'." When Lawrence was asked why he had refused the invitation, he said, "The basic reason goes back long before baseball. It's our environment. If white people come bearing gifts, you're leary. It's probably your subconscious, but you're wondering if the invitation is real. What's his reason? Why? You wonder, 'Why's he doing this? What's he want?' "

There were other factors which kept the Negro player from intimate association with whites. One was women. "You have to ignore them," said a Negro player. "You don't see them. You don't hear them. Boy, you're playing with fire with that, and we all know it." Players who have played with fire have been sent down.

Tension was another factor. "You don't realise the problems we have," said a Negro player. "You can go anywhere, do anything, but we have terrific tensions. We feel good among our own people. What bothers me is when I, well, pay taxes for something like a school, and I can't go there." This player frankly said that he had "a chip on my shoulder about this wide"—and here he held his hands about a foot apart—about the race problem. "What annoys me most is to see a Negro woman with a white man," he said.

At times this player felt the race problem to be such an intolerable burden that he purposely avoided whites, even in his home town, a Northern industrial city. He said: "Sure I've had invitations to speak, but these people didn't know me before. Now that I'm a major league ball player they want me. But I won't go. I stay with my people. I go down to Pine Street and see my friends, my people. Some are poor and some may drink, but they're my people and my friends. It's a funny thing, but in any Negro section I've ever been in, there's a Pine Street. Always a Pine Street. That's where I go when I'm home. You know, I really didn't know I was a Negro until I was in junior high school.

Before, when someone had a birthday party, we'd have it in our home room, and everybody would know. But in junior high school I noticed that I didn't know about the birthday parties any more, and that at the school dances they were on one side of the room and we were on the other."

Another Negro player said that he "found out what it was to be a Negro" when he was eight. "Each class was having a basketball team," he said, "and so I brought in fifty cents for uniform money. But the teacher said, 'Oh, we're not letting coloured play this year.' I'll tell you, I waited. There were two high schools in town, one mostly white and one mostly coloured. I chose the coloured one, and I played every sport I could."

Asked how he did against the white high school, he said, "I wrecked them."

As an adult, this player had what might be called a conciliatory attitude towards whites (he could by no means be called an Uncle Tom), although he was wary on occasion. He said:

"I have the most interesting life in the world. Why? Just being a Negro. I know that when I wake up in the morning and look in the mirror I have a challenge. Where can I find the humour in it? That's what I try to do. It's so ridiculous you have to find the humour in it. If you didn't you'd go crazy.

"My brother-in-law says he has the toughest job in the world being a Negro. But I look at the other side, look for the humour in it, and I think being Negro's quite a job—especially when you can't get out of it."

On occasion, Negro and white players would attempt to bridge the gulf of race by kidding about it in almost bizarre fashion. "We sit around the clubhouse and joke about the Ku Klux Klan, which isn't a joke at all to a Negro," said a Negro player. "Things like that ease tension."

If Negro players had any complaints about the major leagues, they were:

Lack of advertising endorsements. "Negro players shave, too."

Having their lockers all in a row in the clubhouse. "It seems that clubhouse attendants stress 'togetherness' too much. They keep us all together too much."

Training in the segregated South. Many Negro players refused to bring their wives. "The first thing I thought of when I was traded," said one player, "was not the club I was going to, but the fact that they trained in Florida. I don't like Florida." One player said he planned to hold out in the spring so he could "miss three weeks of Florida". Another player said, "Latin Americans are always late. They always try to miss spring training."

They felt that they had to be "better" than white players to stay up in the majors. A Negro pitcher said, "If two players are the same, and one is white and one is coloured and one has to go, nine out of ten times the coloured guy will be the guy." A side to this that the Negro players did not always see was the outright discrimination against them. American League clubs were far slower to take Negroes than were National League teams. Of the fifty-seven Negroes in the majors a few years ago, forty-one were in the National League. "I haven't been told not to take Negroes," a scout for an American League club said. "The only thing is, you want a good one. Know what I mean? There's still a little taint. Know what I mean?"

Lower, much lower, bonuses. Earl Robinson got "in excess of $50,000" from the Dodgers to sign, but he was a rarity. "I signed for four thousand dollars," said a Negro player, "and if I'd been white I could have signed for thirty or maybe forty thousand. A lot of white ball-players I played with in high school got far more than I did, and I was twice the ballplayer they were."

Even the fairest major league front offices admitted that the Negroes did not get the big bonus. "If the kid were another Willie Mays, yes," said one farm system supervisor, "but generally we would have to think twice about a big bonus. There's a limited number of places he can play, and so it's harder to develop him. Negroes can't play in the Southern Association or the Alabama-Florida League. If I went to make a working agreement with a club in either league, I would be told they can't take Negro players."

The farm supervisor went on to say that minor league clubs that did take Negroes did not set a strict quota as such, but "You'll be told by a certain town, 'Don't bring in more than four. That's about all we can handle'. Or, 'Two is about the saturation point here'. Of course that's sometimes due to the fact that there may be only one Negro family in town that could board them. Also, the bulk of the fans are white, and you have to consider their reactions."

SYMBOLS OF ACHIEVEMENT

Away from baseball, the Negro major leaguers had a higher status in their own communities than white players did in theirs. The minimum major league salary was seventy-five hundred a year, and only one half of one per cent of the seventeen million Negroes in the United States then made more than five thousand a year. "The Negro ballplayers have become symbols of achievement, symbols of Negro participation in a white world," Professor Frazier said, "and with their high incomes and conspicuous consumption they are an important part of the bourgeois elite."

Negro ballplayers were much in the mind of the Negro in general, and at times they were regarded with awe, although a big name would no longer "sell" a business. When Don Newcombe walked into a faculty cafeteria at Howard, everyone arose except for a professor of anthropolgy who did not know who Newcombe was. After he found out, he still refused to stand up. Later he complained to Frazier, "Imagine professors standing up for a ballplayer!"

Frazier placed sports, with baseball in the lead, as the number one topic of conversation among Negroes, and in *Black Bourgeoisie*, he wrote:

> Once the writer heard a Negro doctor who was prominent "socially" say that he would rather lose a patient than have his favourite baseball team lose a game. This was an extreme expression of the relative value of professional work and recreation among the black bourgeoisie. At the same time, it is indicative of the value which many Negro professional men and women, including college professors, place upon sports. Except when they are talking within the narrow field of their professions, their conversations are generally limited to sports—baseball and football. They follow religiously the scores of the various teams and the achievements of all the players. For hours they listen to the radio accounts of sports and watch baseball and football games on television.

Wilson Record, a sociologist at Sacramento State College, said that when he was doing field research in Chicago, Negroes who played the numbers game, an illegal lottery usually based on pari-mutuel returns at race tracks, would keep tabs on a special box the *Chicago Daily Defender* carried listing the batting averages of all Negro hitters. "From this," said Record, "they would get a number to play."

A curious, but perhaps valid, insight into the Negro regard for baseball might be obtained by consulting the various dream books sold to numbers players in Harlem and other Negro communities. These books interpret the subject matter of a dream and give the reader a number to play. Some subjects are good luck, others bad.

The Lucky Star Dream Book, by a Professor Konje, carried this entry on baseball: "To dream that you play this game denotes safety of your affairs and a happy re-union among your neighbours. 100." In *The Success Dream Book*, by a Professor De

Herbert, was this entry: "To dream of playing base-ball is a sign that you will live to a good old age, and then die happily. 945. To see others play this game is a sign of peace and satisfaction. 567." The symbolism is obvious.

Generally speaking the Negro ballplayers, unlike some Negro entertainers who were quick to express hostility to the Negro world below them, were "race" men. Mal Goode said: "The Negro players do accept responsibility as race men. Fifteen of them are buying or already have bought life memberships in the NAACP. That's five hundred dollars. Also, many of them have made special contributions to the NAACP. When the NAACP was fighting in the Supreme Court, the NAACP would send telegrams asking players for money. I've only heard one" (Negro) "ballplayer make a derogatory remark. He said, 'Don't you think the NAACP stirs up trouble?' I said, 'Do me a favour. Never say anything like that again.'"

Professor Frazier was not surprised at the ballplayers' being race men. "A baseball player is attached to conventional worlds," he said. "An entertainer isn't." As he saw it, the entertainer dwelt in "the House of Satan", so to speak, where anything went and ties were broken in the process. But the ballplayer did not. After all, said Frazier, "Baseball is an American sport with American respectability."

NOTES

1 Joe Louis, Babe Ruth, Jim Londos, Knute Rockne, Joe McCarthy and Eddie Arcaro.

2 This essay is based on a study made by the author at the end of the 1959 season.

3 At this writing, eighty-five of five hundred major leaguers are Negroes. They earn a total salary of almost two million. See "The Negro in Baseball: 1962: Year of the Big Money", *Ebony*, June, 1962.

4 Between 1882 and 1891, the American Association ranked as a major league.

5 Williamson was no bully and his account is undoubtedly exaggerated, but he reflected the attitude of his times. The Negro player referred to was Frank Grant. He was known as the "Black Dunlap", an enormous compliment comparing him to Fred Dunlap, king of the second basemen. Joseph M. Overfield, authority on Buffalo baseball, says Grant seldom missed a game or retired in the middle of one.

6 Crowe has since left the Cardinals, and White, as expected, has become the big man on the Cardinals, if not in the league, on matters of race. He and Bruton, now on the Tigers, have been the spokesmen for Negro players' complaints about spring training conditions in Florida.

7 See "On the Supremacy of the Negro Athlete in White Athletic Competition," *Psychoanalytic Review*, Vol. 30, 1943, in which Laynard L.

Holloman, M.D., of Provident Hospital, Chicago, cites revenge, compensation and a desire to identify with the white race as the motivating factors behind the Negro's success in athletics. It is nonsense to attribute this success to anything physical. American Negroes are largely a mixture of Negro, Indian and white stock, principally British, and although they differ from whites in some respects—for instance, they are less heavily bearded—they have no physical characteristics that would give them an advantage over white athletic competitors. For examinations of this, see M. F. Ashley Montagu, "The Physical Anthropology of the American Negro", *Psychiatry*, February, 1944; "Physical Characteristics of the American Negro", *Scientific Monthly*, July, 1944; and Montague Cobb, "Race and Runners", *Journal of Health and Physical Education*, Vol. 7, 1936.

8 An official of one of the new major league clubs set up in the recent expansion said that his club wanted no more than five or six Negroes on the squad. The feeling was that "too many" Negroes might hurt the gate, particularly if the team was a losing one, as a new one was bound to be.

PART III (C)

SPORT AS AN OCCUPATION

Introduction

The rise of spectator sports as part of the entertainments industry"
is one of the most striking features in the recent development of
Britain and many other societies. Clubs run as commercial enterprises; men who earn their living solely or mainly by playing
sports; full-time administrators, managers and trainers; national,
even international controlling bodies; paying spectators in their
thousands: all of these are firmly established parts of the modern
social scene. They pose innumerable questions for the sociologist.
As yet researchers have hardly begun to scratch the surface of
them. A number of studies have, however, been made of careers
in professional sport and two of the best of them have been
selected for inclusion in this section. They are, "The Occupational
Culture of the Boxer" by Kirson S. Weinberg and Henry Arond
and "Wrestling: The Great American Passion Play" by Gregory
P. Stone. Each of them can serve as a model for studies of careers
in other sports. They illustrate the type of questions to be asked,
suggest some of the concepts likely to be useful in this connection
and are rich as sources of hypotheses for further research.

Weinberg and Arond's study is an analysis of the recruitment
patterns of boxers, their practices and beliefs and the overall social
organisation of professional boxing in the United States. Boxing,
they found, is firmly rooted in the culture of the slum. The adolescent culture there emphasises fighting and boys are able to learn
the skills of boxing at a very eary age. Because they can fight,
boxers are accorded high status and, in addition, the career in
boxing is believed to offer an easy and attractive route to fame and
fortune. Weinberg and Arond show, however, that only very few
boxers experience permanent upward social mobility. Most of them
never pass beyond the lowest reaches of the sport. Even many of
those who gain national or international recognition experience a
sharp status-decline once their active careers are over. That this should
happen is firmly built into the social structure of the boxing world.

Boxers are subjected to a kind of "multiple subordination".
Above them stand their trainers, the managers and the promoters.
Of these, the managers and promoters are by far the most power-

ful but they care little for the welfare of the boxers. Their primary
interest is financial gain. The managers are organised into a guild
and use this organisation in order to limit the independence of the
boxers. They firmly resist any attempts on the boxer's part to form
a union among themselves. They try to keep them in a permanent
state of financial and emotional dependency, for example by encouraging them to squander their winnings and lending them
money, thus keeping them more or less permanently in debt and
in a situation where they need to fight more often than is good for
them. They "overexpose" their fighters, force them to fight when
they are unfit and match them with superior opponents, all in the
interests of personal financial gain. Given the weakness of boxers
in relation to managers and promoters, it is hardly surprising that
so few of them do well economically out of the sport. As Weinberg
and Arond show, the most permanent result for the majority of
them is some kind of injury or disfigurement. Broken noses and
"cauliflower ears" are normal occupational hazards. According to
one estimate which the authors cite, fully 60% of boxers become
mildly "punch-drunk" and 5% severely so. It seems that the cards
are stacked against the slum-dweller even when he tries to escape
from his environment through a socially acceptable channel.

It would be interesting to discover whether the career in boxing
follows a similar pattern in this country. On *a priori* grounds, it
seems likely to be similar in certain respects and different in others.
It is probably similar in that the majority of boxers are recruited
from the poorer social classes and that the sport serves as a
channel of permanent upward mobility for only a very small proportion of boxers, but different in that it may not be so tightly
controlled by petty racketeers as it is in the U.S.A. This, coupled
with the fact that state control is probably firmer here, may mean
that British boxers are somewhat more autonomous in relation to
managers and promoters than their American counterparts. But
whatever turns out to be the case in this respect, there can be no
doubt that Weinberg and Arond's study provides an excellent
model on which to base a research project into professional boxing
in this country.

"Wrestling: The Great American Passion Play", by Gregory P.
Stone, also represents an excellent model for further research. It is
a highly original study in which the author analyses the transformation of wrestling from a sport into a form of drama, the organisation of the wrestling enterprise, the career in wrestling and the
social and social psychological character of the wrestling audience.

After reviewing the early history of the sport, Stone notes that
it probably became professionalised in the United States around

the middle of the nineteenth century. At the beginning of the twentieth, however, it ceased to be a "pure" sport and began to be transformed into a type of commercial drama. Matches ceased to be genuine contests of strength and skill and began to become a complex form of pre-arranged "tumbling act". Like forms of drama generally they represented conflicts and tensions in the wider society such as the class and status struggles, the battle of the sexes and the conflict between ugliness and beauty. Underlying all of these, however, Stone detects a common unifying theme: the struggle between good and evil. He argues that, accordingly, modern professional wrestling is best conceived not as a form of sport but as a twentieth century equivalent of the medieval "passion play".

Several factors played a part in this transformation. Among them were the fact that a wave of disgust at violence in sports swept through the United States in the early 1900's. Professional wrestling at that time was violent and highly dangerous. It ran the risk of being abolished unless it considerably reduced its level of violence. More important, however, was the fact that, from the very outset, professional wrestling in America fixed on submission as the test of victory. This had two important consequences. First, if the sport was to involve seriously trying to wrestle an opponent into submission, it mean that the risk of injury would be great and that the career in wrestling was likely to be very short indeed. Secondly, since submission holds are relatively easy to establish and *impossible* to break, it would mean that the sport would involve long periods of inactivity and this would spell boredom for spectators. Therefore, Stone argues, it was in the interests of wrestlers and wrestling promoters to transform it from a sport into a type of farce. This would reduce the risk of injury, lengthen the active career of the wrestler and provide a means of evoking spectator interest and excitement.

The transformation of wrestling from sport into drama had important consequences for the career as a wrestler. The professional began to become less a type of sportsman and more a type of actor. He had to pay attention not only to physical fitness and learning the physical skills required by wrestling, but also to the development of an identity which would enthrall the audience. Thus, wrestlers began to cultivate images as heroes or villains, to create an aura of mystery by appearing in masks and to dress themselves up as ghouls and monsters. The lesser chance of physical injury meant that they could wrestle as much as five or six nights a week and remain in the "sport" until their forties or early fifties. Wrestling soon became the most lucrative professional "sport" in the United States. Stone estimates that there are currently between two and four thousand professional wrestlers in that country. Many of them are recruited from the ranks of college footballers. A typical career pattern consists in working six months of the year in professional football and six in professional wrestling. Thus, not only are many professional wrestlers in the United States more highly educated than is usually the case with professional sportsmen, but they are also able to gain a level of income and financial security which few professionals in other sports can match.

By the early 1960's, wrestling in the United States had come to attract more than twenty-five million paying spectators annually. It thus exceeded paid attendance at other major American sports such as baseball, basketball and horse-racing. A survey conducted by Stone in the Minneapolis–St. Paul metropolitan area showed that the majority of wrestling spectators and wrestling "fans" tend to be low status members of the older generation and that women outnumber men by a ratio of two to one. Stone hypothesises that the social characteristics of these groups can help to account for their fascination with the "sport". The social environment of the lower working classes, he argues, is conducive to the formation of an "authoritarian personality". People with this type of personality tend to be unsophisticated and to see the world in black and white terms. They seldom question their surroundings. It is not surprising, therefore, that they take pleasure in watching a simple dramatic representation of the struggle between good and evil. It is more difficult to account for the fact that so many women are fascinated by wrestling but Stone hypothesises that it may have something to do with the fact that they are the traditional guardians of morality.

All in all, Stone's essay represents a remarkable piece of sociological research. It throws considerable light on to professional wrestling not only in the United States but also in this country, since the American form of the "sport" has now become highly popular here as well. It also has more general implications; Stone shows that in order to understand the career in sport all sorts of factors must be taken into account such as the development of the sport itself, its overall organisation, the nature of the satisfactions derived by spectators and their relations with the "players". It cannot be understood by extracting it from its wider setting. Above all, Stone sheds light on the pressures which arise when a sport becomes a form of entertainment. Not all professional sports have become more or less totally transformed into a type of drama as has happened with professional wrestling, but there are strong pressures in that direction. It is probably the fear of this, as much as anything else, which lies at the heart of the controversy over amateurism and professionalism.

CHAPTER 14

The Occupational Culture of the Boxer*

S. Kirson Weinberg and Henry Arond

Herein is described the culture of the professional boxer as discovered by personal experience, by reading of firsthand literature,
and by interview with sixty-eight boxers and former boxers, seven
trainers, and five managers.[1] The aspects covered are recruitment,
practices and beliefs, and the social structure of the boxing world.

RECRUITMENT

Professional boxers are adolescents and young men. Nearly all
are of low socioeconomic background. Only two of our fighters
might possibly have been of middle-class family. Most are immigrants to the city and are children of such. Their residences at the
time of becoming boxers are distributed like the commoner forms
of social disorganisation, being almost all near the centre of the
city. Nearly all Chicago boxers lived on the Near South and Near
West sides. There is an ethnic succession of boxers which corresponds to that of the ethnic groups in these areas. First Irish, then
Jewish, then Italians, were most numerous among prominent
boxers, now, Negroes (Table 1).

The traditions of an ethnic group, as well as its temporary location at the bottom of the scale, may affect the proportion of its
boys who become boxers. Many Irish, but few Scandinavians, have
become boxers in this country; many Filipinos, but very few
Japanese and Chinese.

The juvenile and adolescent culture of the lower socioeconomic
levels provides a base for the boxing culture. Individual and gang
fights are encouraged. The best fighter is often the most admired,
as well as the most feared, member of a gang. A boy who lacks
status tries to get it and to restore his self-esteem by fighting.[2]
Successful amateur and professional boxers furnish highly visible
role-models to the boys of the slum; this is especially so among

* Reprinted from *The American Journal of Sociology*, 57, Vol. 5, March,
1952, pp. 460–9.

urban Negroes. Since he has otherwise little hope of any but un-skilled, disagreeable work, the boxing way to money and prestige may appear very attractive. As an old-time manager put it, "Where else can a poor kid get a stake as fast as he can in boxing?"

Since the ability to fight is a matter of status among one's peers, is learned in play, and is the accepted means of expressing hostility and settling disputes, boy's learn to fight early.

One fighter thought of becoming a boxer at the age of ten, be-cause he could not participate in team games as a child; his mother insisted that he had a "bad heart". He stated: "I tried to fight as soon as I got old enough, to be the roughest, toughest kid on the block". He fought so frequently and was arrested so often for fighting that one policeman told him that he might as well get paid for it. At the age of fourteen he participated in fights in vacant lots in the neighbourhood. Because of his prowess as a fighter, the other boys in the neighbourhood began to respect him more, and he began to associate status with fighting. When he was about seventeen, an amateur fighter told him about a gymnasium where he could learn to become a "ring fighter" instead of a "street fighter". He claimed: "I love fighting. I would rather fight than eat."

TABLE 1.

Rank Order of Number of Prominent Boxers of
Various Ethnic Groups for Certain Years*

Year	Rank		
	1	2	3
1909	Irish	German	English
1916	Irish	German	Italian
1928	Jewish	Italian	Irish
1936	Italian	Irish	Jewish
1948	Negro	Italian	Mexican

* Data tabulated from *World's Annual Sporting Record* (1910 and 1917); *Everlast Boxing* (1929); *Boxing News Record* (1938); and *Ring* (1948 and 1949). The numbers in the succeeding years are: 103, 118, 300, 201, and 149. There may be biases in the listings, but the predominance of two or three ethnic groups is marked in all the years. The Irish were very much above others in 1909 and 1916 (about 40% of all boxers listed); in 1948 nearly half of all boxers listed were Negro. The Jews and Italians did not have so marked a predominance.

Most boxers seem to have been influenced to become "ring fighters" by a boxer in the neighbourhood or by a member of the family.[3] One middleweight champion claimed that he "took after" his brother, followed him to the gymnasium, imitated him, and thus decided to be a boxer before he was fifteen years old. Another fighter was inspired by a neighbour and became his protegé. He continually followed his hero to the gymnasium and learned to fight himself. Eventually the neighbour induced his manager to take his protegé into the stable. A third fighter has stated:

I was twelve when I went to the gym first. If there's a fighter in the neighbourhood, the kids always look up to him because they think he's tough. There was an amateur in my neighbourhood and he was a kind of hero to all us kids. It was him that took me to the gym the first time.

A former welterweight and middleweight champion who has been boxing since he was eleven years old has written in a similar vein:

I didn't do any boxing before I left Detroit. I was too little. But I was already interested in it, partly because I idolised a big Golden Gloves heavyweight who lived on the same block with us. I used to hang around the Brewster Centre Gym all the time watching him train. His name was Joe Louis. Whenever Joe was in the gym so was I. He was my idol then just like he is today. I've always wanted to be like him.[4]

Some managers and trainers of local gymnasiums directly seek out boys who like to fight and who take fighters as their models. One such manager says that he sought boys who were considered the "toughest in the block" or "'natural fighters'". He would get them to come to the gym and to become amateur boxers. He entered some in tournaments, from which he received some "cut", then sifted out the most promising for professional work.

It is believed by many in boxing circles that those in the lower socioeconomic levels make the "best fighters":

They say that too much education softens a man and that is why the college graduates are not good fighters. They fight emotionally on the gridiron and they fight bravely and well in our wars, but their contributions in our rings have been insignificant. The ring has been described as the refuge of the under-privileged. Out of the downtrodden have come our greatest fighters. . . . An education is an escape, and that is what they are saying when they shake their heads—those who know the fight game—as you mention the name of a college fighter. Once the bell rings, they want their fighters to have no retreat, and a fighter with an education is a fighter who does not have to fight to live and he knows it .. Only for the hungry fighter is it a decent gamble.[5]

It can be inferred tentatively that the social processes among juveniles and adolescents in the lower socioeconomic levels, such as individual and gang fights, the fantasies of "easy money", the lack of accessible vocational opportunities, and the general isola- tion from the middle-class culture, are similar for those who be- come professional boxers as for those who become delinquents. The difference resides in the role-model the boy picks, whether criminal or boxer. The presence of one or several successful boxers in an area stimulates boys of the same ethnic groups to follow in their footsteps. Boxing, as well as other sports and certain kinds of entertainment, offers slum boys the hope of quick success with- out deviant behaviour (although, of course, some boxers have been juvenile delinquents).[6]

Within the neighbourhood the professional boxer orients his be- haviour and routine around the role of boxer. Usually acquiring some measure of prestige in the neighbourhood, he is no longer a factory hand or an unskilled labourer. He is admired, often has a small coterie of followers, and begins to dress smartly and loudly and to conceive of himself as a neighbourhood celebrity, whether or not he has money at the time. Nurtured by the praise of the trainer or manager, he has hopes that eventually he will ascend to "big-time fights" and to "big money". The money that he does make in his amateur and early professional fights by comparison with his former earnings seems a lot of him.

OCCUPATIONAL CULTURE OF THE BOXER

The intrinsic occupational culture of the boxer is composed of techniques, illusions, aspirations, and structured roles which every boxer internalises in some measure and which motivate him both inside and outside the ring. At the outset of his career the boxer becomes impressed with the need for training to improve his physical condition and to acquire the skills necessary to win fights and to avoid needless injury. When he has such status as to be sought out by promoters, he assigns a specified interval for train- ing before the bout. But in the preliminary ranks he must keep himself in excellent physical shape most of the time, because he does not know when he will be summoned to fight. He may be booked as a substitute and cannot easily refuse the match. If he does, he may find it difficult to get another bout. The particular bout may be the chance he has been hoping for. The fighter is warned persistently by tales of the ritualistic necessity of "getting in shape" and of the dire consequences if he does not. "There is no more pitiable sight," stated one boxer, "than to see a fighter get into the ring out of condition."

The boxer comes to regard his body, especially his hands, as his stock-in-trade. Boxers have varied formulas for preventing their hands from excess swelling, from excessive pain, or from being broken. This does not mean a hypochrondriachal interest, because they emphasise virility and learn to slough off and to disdain punishment. But fighters continually seek nostrums and exercises for improving their bodies. One practised Yogi, another became a physical cultist, a third went on periodic fasts; others seek out lotions, vitamins, and other means of improving their endurance, alertness, and punching power.

"You have to live up to being a fighter." This phrase justifies their deprivations and regulated living. There is also a cult of a kind of persevering courage, called a "fighting heart", which means "never admitting defeat". The fighter learns early that his exhibited courage—his ability, if necessary, to go down fighting—characterises the respected, audience-pleasing boxer. He must cherish the lingering hope that he can win by a few more punches. One fighter was so severely beaten by another that the referee stopped the bout. The brother of the beaten fighter, a former fighter himself, became so outraged that he climbed into the ring and started to brawl with the referee. In another instance a boxer incurred a very severe eye injury, which would have meant the loss of his sight. But he insisted on continuing to fight, despite the warnings of his seconds. When the fight was stopped, he protested. This common attitude among boxers is reinforced by the demands of the spectators, who generally cheer a "game fighter". Thus the beaten fighter may become a "crowd-pleaser" and may get matches despite his defeat. On the other hand, some fighters who are influenced by friends, by wives, or by sheer experience recognise that sustained beatings may leave permanent injuries and voluntarily quit when they are beaten. But the spirit of the code is that the boxer continue to fight regardless of injuries. "If a man quits a fight, an honest fight," claimed one fighter, "he has no business there in the first place."

Fighters who remain in the sport are always hopeful of occupational climbing. This attitude may initially be due to a definite self-centredness, but it is intensified by the character of boxing. Boxing is done by single contestants, not by teams. Emphasis is on the boxer as a distinct individual. The mores among boxers are such that fighters seldom admit to others that they are "punchy" or "washed-up".[7] One fighter said: "You can tell another fighter to quit, but you can't call him punchy. If you do, he'll punch you to show you he still has a punch." He has to keep up his front.

Further, the boxer is involved in a scheme of relationships and traditions which focus upon building confidence. The boxing tradition is full of legends of feats of exceptional fighters. Most gymnasiums have pictures of past and present outstanding boxers on the wall, and identification with them comes easy for the incoming fighters. Past fights are revived in tales. Exceptional fighters of the past and present are compared and appraised. Second, the individual boxer is continually assured and reassured that he is "great" and that he is "coming up". As a result, many fighters seem to overrate their ability and to feel that all they need are "lucky breaks" to become champions or leading contenders. Many get self-important and carry scrapbooks of their newspaper write-ups and pictures.

The process of stimulating morale among fighters is an integral accompaniment of the acquisition of boxing skills and body conditioning. The exceptions are the part-time fighters who hold outside jobs and who are in the preliminary ranks. They tend to remain on the periphery of the boxing culture and thus have a somewhat different perspective on the mobility aspects of the sport.[8]

Since most bouts are unpredictable, boxers usually have superstitions which serve to create confidence and emotional security among them. Sometimes the manager or trainer uses these superstitions to control the fighter. One fighter believed that, if he ate certain foods, he was sure to win, because these foods gave him strength.[9] Others insist on wearing the same robe in which they won their first fight: one wore an Indian blanket when he entered the ring. Many have charm pieces or attribute added importance to entering the ring after the opponent. Jou Louis insisted on using a certain dressing-room at Madison Square Garden. Some insist that, if a woman watches them train, it is bad luck. One fighter, to show he was not superstitious, would walk under a ladder before every fight, until this became a magical rite itself. Consistent with this attitude, many intensify their religious attitudes and keep Bibles in their lockers. One fighter kept a rosary in his glove. If he lost the rosary, he would spend the morning before the fight in church. Although this superstitious attitude may be imported from local or ethnic culture, it is intensified among the boxers themselves, whether they are white or Negro, preliminary fighters or champions.

When a fighter likes the style, punch, or movement of another fighter, he may wear the latter's trunks or one of his socks or rub him on the back. In training camps some fighters make a point of sleeping in the bed that a champion once occupied. For this reason, in part, some take the names of former fighters. All these practices focus towards the perspective of "filling the place" or taking the role of the other esteemed fighter. Moreover, many fighters deliberately copy the modes of training, the style, and the general movements of role-models.

Since fighters, in the process of training, become keyed to a finely balanced physical and emotional condition and frequently are irritable, restless, and anxious, they also grow dependent and suggestible. The superstitutions and the reassuring statements of the trainer and manager both unwittingly and wittingly serve to bolster their confidence.

Before and during the bout, self-confidence is essential. Fighters or their seconds try to unnerve the opponent. They may try to outstare him or make some irritating or deflating remarks or gestures. In the ring, tactical self-confidence is expressed in the boxer's general physical condition and movements. His ability to outslug, to outspar, or to absorb punishment is part of his morale. The ability not to go down, to out-manoeuvre the other contestant, to change his style in whole or in part, to retrieve his strength quickly, or to place the opponent off-balance inevitably affect the latter's confidence. A fighter can feel whether he will win a bout during the early rounds, but he is always wary of the dreaded single punch or the unexpected rally.

Boxers become typed by their style and manner in the ring. A "puncher" or "mauler" differs from a boxer" and certainly from a "cream puff", who is unable to hit hard. A "miller", or continual swinger, differs from one who saves his energy by fewer movements. A "butcher" is recognised by his tendency to hit hard and ruthlessly when another boxer is helpless, inflicting needless damage. A "tanker" is one who goes down easily, sometimes in a fixed fight or "set-up". The "mechanical" fighter differs from the "smart" fighter, for among the "smart" fighters are really the esteemed fighters, those who are capable of improvising and reformulating their styles, or devising original punches and leg movements, of cunningly outmanoeuvering their opponents, and of possessing the compensatory hostility, deadly impulsiveness, and quick reflexes to finish off their opponents in the vital split second.

Boxers have to contend with fouls and quasi-fouls in the ring. At present, these tactics seemingly are becoming more frequent. They may have to contend with "heeling', the manoeuvre by which the fighter, during clinches, shoves the laced part of his glove over the opponent's wound, particularly an "eye" wound, to open or exacerbate it, with "thumbing" in the eye, with "butting" by the head, with having their insteps stepped on hard during clinches, with punches in back of the head or in the kidneys, or with being tripped. These tactics, which technically are fouls, may be executed so quickly and so cleverly that the referee does not detect them. When detected, the fighter may be warned or, at worst, may lose the round. The boxers are thus placed in a situation fraught with tension, physical punishment, and eventual fatigue. They may be harassed by the spectators. Their protection consists of their physical condition and their acquired confidence. Moreover, the outcome of the fight is decisive for their status and self-esteem.[10]

The boxer's persistent display of aggression is an aspect of status. Thus his aggression becomes impersonal, although competition is intense. Thus two boxers may be friends outside the ring, but each will try to knock the other out in a bout, and after the bout they may be as friendly as competition permits. Furthermore, the injury done to an opponent, such as maiming or killing, is quickly rationalised away by an effective trainer or manager in order to prevent an access of intense guilt, which can ruin a fighter. The general reaction is that the opponent is out to do the same thing to him and that this is the purpose of boxing: namely, to beat the opponent into submission. The exception is the "grudge fight", in which personal hostility is clearly manifest.

In a succession of bouts, if the fighter is at all successful, he goes through a fluctuating routine, in which tension mounts during training, is concentrated during the fight, and is discharged in the usual celebration, which most victorious fighters regard as their inevitable reward. Hence many boxers pursue a fast tempo of living and spend lavishly on clothes, women, gambling, and drink, practices seemingly tolerated by the manager and encouraged by the persons who are attracted to boxers. Many boxers experience intense conflict between the ordeals of training and the pursuits of pleasure.

SOCIAL STRUCTURE AND SOCIAL MOBILITY

Boxers comprise a highly stratified occupation. Rank is determined by their rating in a weight division, by their position in a match, and by their status with stablemates who have the same manager. Annually, for each weight division, fighters are ranked. The champion and about twenty leading contenders are listed on top.[11] The other fighters are listed into "A", "B", and "C" categories. Many local preliminary fighters are not listed. Only the first twenty contenders and the "A" category seem to have any importance. Of 1,831 fighters listed for 1950, 8.8% comprised the champion and leading contenders; 16.9% were in the "A" category; 74.3% were in the "B" and "C" categories.

To determine the vertical mobility of fighters, the careers of 127 fighters were traced from 1938 onwards.[12] Of these, 107, or 84.2%, remained in the local preliminary or semiwindup category. Eleven boxers, or 8.7%, became local headliners, which may be in the "A" category. They had been professional boxers for an average of almost eight years. Eight boxers, or 7.1%, achieved national recognition, that is, among the first ten leading contenders. They also had been professionals for an average of almost eight years. One fighter became champion after twelve years in the ring.

The boxers who remain in the sport believe that they can ascend to the top because of the character of the boxing culture, in which the exceptional boxer is emphasised and with whom the aspiring boxer identifies. When the boxer ceases to aspire, he quits or becomes a part-time boxer. Yet the aspiring hopes of many boxers are not unfounded, because climbing in the sport does not depend upon ability only and also can be a result of a "lucky break".

RELATIONSHIPS OF THE BOXER

Boxers live in a wide social milieu of trainers, managers, and promoters. The boxer and trainer usually form the closest relationships in the boxing milieu. At one time, many managers were trainers, too; and a few owners of local gymnasiums still combine these roles, but their number has declined. Furthermore, the relationships between boxer and trainer are becoming increasingly impersonal. Consequently, the careful training and social intimacy which characterised the conditioning of many boxers by trainers in the past has also declined.[13]

Generally, the specialised trainer or trainer-manager represents the authority-figure to the boxer, transmits boxing skills to him, and becomes his anchor point of emotional security. The trainer's relationship with the boxer becomes crucial to his development. The effective trainer polishes his skill, compels him to train regularly, and distracts him from worrying about the fight, and he can control him by withdrawing praise or can restore his morale when he has lost. For example, a trainer reviewed a lost fight to his charge so skilfully that the boxer began to believe that his opponent had won by a few lucky punches. Had he averted these "lucky" punches, the fighter felt that he would have won. His confidence restored, he renewed his training with added vigour and determination.

The trainer may be of distinct help to the boxer during the bout. Frequently his "second", he may advise him of his opponent's weakness and of his own faults. In addition, he can be a continuing source of confidence to the fighter. A fighter recalled that before a bout his trainer became ill. He felt alone and somewhat diffident when the fight began. He regained his confidence in the third round, when he felt that his opponent could not hurt him. Since the trainer can become so emotionally close to the fighter, he can help or hinder him, depending upon his insight and knowledge of boxing. Though very important to the fighter, the trainer is not a powerful figure in the boxing hierarchy, and some trainers are as exploited as are fighters by the managers.

One boxer has characterised managers as follows: "Some managers are interested in the money first and in the man second; other managers are interested in the man first." Our observations lead us to infer that the vast majority of managers at the present time are in the first category. They regard boxing as a business and the fighter as a commodity and are concerned mainly with making money. To do so, they are compelled to please the promoters and to sell their fighters' abilities to the promoters. Unless the manager is also a trainer, he is not concerned with the technniques of boxing, except to publicise his charge and to arrange matches which will bring the most revenue.

While the boxer devotes his aggressions to training and fighting, the manager slants his aggressions to machinations for better matches and for more money. Having few illusions about the fight business, acquainted with and often accepting its seamier side, he conforms to the standard managerial pattern of having the advantage over "his" boxers in every way. First, managers are organised into a guild, and, though some managers will try to steal boxers from one another, they usually bar fighters who run out on managers.[14] (One boxer, on the other hand, tried to organise fighters into a union. His efforts were squelched quickly, and he was informally blackballed from fighting in New York City.) Second, many managers try to keep their fighters financially and, if possible, emotionally tied to them. Some managers will encourage fighters to borrow money from them and usually will not discourage them from squandering their earnings. One manager stated characteristically: "It's good to have a fighter 'in you' for a couple of bucks." By having fighters financially indebted to them, they have an easy expedient for controlling individuals who are unusually headstrong. Some fighters are in the continual process of regarding every fight as an essential means for clearing their debts.

Legally, managers cannot receive more than one-third of the

fighters' purses, but many do not conform to this rule. Frequently, they take one-half the purse, or they may put their fighters on a flat salary and get the rest. Some managers tell their preliminary fighters that the purse was less than it was actually and thus keep the rest for themselves.

Furthermore, many managers abuse their fighters so as to make money quickly. They may overmatch them with superior fighters, "rush" them into too many fights, force them to fight when they are out of condition, and hint that the fight is "fixed" and instruct them indirectly to lose. A few managers will match their fighters in another state when they are barred in one state because of injuries; they will obtain matches before the required sixty days have elapsed after their fighters have been knocked out. Fighters may be severely hurt, even ruined, by these tactics.

Some managers, however, are concerned mainly with building up their fighters and doing everything possible to develop their maximum ability; but these managers are in the minority. In short, managers have no informal standards to protect their boxers and are guided chiefly by their own personal considerations in these activities.

Since many ruthless individuals and petty racketeers who know little about boxing are increasingly drawn into this sport with the prime purpose of making money quickly, boxers tend to have little, if any, protection from managers except that provided by boxing commissions, whose rules can be evaded without difficulty. Moreover, it is extremely difficult for a boxer to climb or get important matches unless he has an effective manager.

THE BOXER AND THE PROMOTER

The boxer's relationship with the promoter is usually indirect. Yet the promoter is the most influential person in the boxing hierarchy. He is primarily a showman and businessman, emotionally removed from the fighter, and regards him chiefly as a commodity. His aim is to get the most from his investment. Thus the "show" comes first, regardless of the boxer's welfare. To ensure his direct control over many boxers, the promoter, who legally cannot be a manager, may appoint one or a series of "managers" as "fronts" and thus get shares of many boxers' earnings, as well as controlling them. Furthermore, he can reduce the amount of the fighter's share because the nominal manager will not bargain for a larger share. In effect, most boxers are relatively helpless in dealing with promoters, especially at the present time, because of the monopolistic character of boxing.

When a potentially good fighter wants to meet leading contenders, the manager may have to "cut in" the promoter or "cut in" some other manager who has connections with the promoter. Thus the mobility of the fighter depends in large part upon the manager's relationship to the promoter. When the manager does not have this acceptable relationship and is unwilling to "cut in" a third party, he will not get the desired matches.[15]

Since the promoter is concerned primarily with attracting a large audience, he tries to select and develop fighters who will draw customers.[16] Thus the fighter must have "crowd-pleasing" qualifications in addition to ability. In this connection, the race and ethnic group play a part. A good white fighter is preferred to a good Negro fighter; and in large cities, such as New York and Chicago, a Jewish fighter is considered highly desirable because the majority of fight fans are Jewish and Italian. Despite the efforts of promoters to attract white fighters, especially Jewish fighters, few Jewish fighters have emerged because the role-models and practices in the local Jewish communities have changed. Even Negro fighters, despite their dominance of the sport in quality and quantity of fighters, are increasingly turning to other sports because the role-models are slowly shifting.[17]

The fighter whom a promoter does select for grooming can easily be made mobile once he has shown crowd-pleasing tendencies. He can be, as it were, "nursed" to the top by being matched with opponents who are easy to beat or by meeting "set-ups" who are instructed to lose. Thus he builds up an impressive record and is ready for big-time fights. Hence, it is difficult to tell how competent a fighter is on his early record alone, for his record may be designed for publicity purposes. When a fighter has won all or nearly all of his early matches and then loses repeatedly to leading contenders, he has been "nursed" to the top by the promoter, unless the fighter has incurred an injury in one of his later fights. In these ways the promoter can influence decisively the occupational career of the boxer.

EFFECT UPON THE BOXER

The punitive character of boxing, as well as the social relationships in the boxing milieu, affects the boxer-participants during and after their careers in the ring.

First, the physical effects of boxing, which are intrinsic to the sport, operate to the boxer's detriment. Although boxers may cultivate strong bodies, the direct and indirect injuries from this sport are very high. In addition to the deaths in the ring, one estimate is that 60% of the boxers become mildly punch-drunk and 5% become severely punch-drunk.[18] The severely punch-drunk fighter can be detected by an ambling gait, thickened or retarded speech, mental stereotypy, and a general decline in efficiency. In addition, blindness and visual deficiency are so pervasive that eye injuries are considered virtually as occupational casualties, while misshaped noses and cauliflower ears are afflictions of most boxers who are in the sport for five or more years. Despite these injuries, attempts to provide safeguards, such as headguards, have been opposed by the fans and by many boxers because such devices presumably did not "protect" and did not fit into their conceptions of virility and presumed contempt for punishment.[19]

Second, the boxing culture tends to work to the eventual detriment of the boxer. Many boxers tend to continue a particular fight when they are hopelessly beaten and when they can become severely injured. Many boxers persist in fighting when they have passed their prime and even when they have been injured. For example, one boxer, blind in one eye and barred from fighting in one state, was grateful to his manager for getting him matches in other states. Another old-time boxer has admitted characteristically: "It's hard to quit. Fighting gets into your blood, and you can't get it out." Many fighters try to make one comeback, at least, and some fight until they are definitely punch-drunk.

Boxers find further that, despite their success in the sport, their careers terminate at a relatively early age.[20] Since their physical condition is so decisive to their role, when they feel a decline in their physical prowess, they tend also to acquire the premature feeling of "being old". This attitude is reinforced by others in the sport who refer to them as "old men", meaning old in the occupation. Since boxing has been the vocational medium of status attainment and since they have no other skills to retain that status, many boxers experience a sharp decline in status in their postboxing careers. As an illustration, of ninety-five leading former boxers (i.e. champions and leading contenders), each of whom earned more than $100,000 during his ring career, eighteen were found to have remained in the sport as trainers or trainer-managers; two became wrestlers; twenty-six worked in, "fronted for", or owned taverns;[21] two were liquor salesmen; eighteen had unskilled jobs, most commonly in the steelmills; six worked in the movies; five were entertainers; two owned or worked in gas stations; three were cab-drivers; three had news-stands; two were janitors; three were bookies; three were associated with the race tracks (two in collecting bets and one as a starter); and two were in business, one of them as a custom tailor. In short, the successful boxers have a relatively quick economic ascent at a relatively young age in terms of earning power. But the punitive character of the sport, the boxers' dependence upon their managers, and their carefree spending during their boxing careers contribute to a quicker economic descent for many boxers. Their economic descent is accompanied by a drop in status and frequently by temporary or prolonged emotional difficulties in readjusting to their new occupational roles.[22]

NOTES

1 One of us (Arond) has been a boxer, trainer, and manager. We first determined some common values, beliefs, and practices by a few unstructured interviews. We used the material thus gained to plan guided interviews which would help us sift out what is ethnic from what belongs properly to boxing culture. Mr. Leland White helped in the interviewing.

2 Some juveniles who fought continually to retrieve their self-esteem and also in sheer self-defence later became boxers. One adolescent who was half-Negro and half-Indian was induced to become a boxer by a trainer who saw him beat two white opponents in a street fight. Another boxer admitted that he fought continually because other boys called him a "sissy". A third boxer fought continually because he was small and the other boys picked on him. This compensatory drive among boxers is not unusual.

3 For the last twenty-five years of boxers, we found the following brother combinations among boxers: 3 sets of five brothers, 5 sets of four brothers, 24 sets of three brothers, and 41 sets of two brothers. We also found sets of father-son combinations. This number, very likely, is less than the actual figures, because some brothers fight as amateurs only and not as professionals, and thus their records cannot be traced.

4 "Sugar Ray" Robinson, "Fighting Is My Business", *Sport*, June, 1951, p. 18.

5 *Ring*, July, 1950, p. 45.

6 Merton has noted that, while our culture encourages the people of lower standing to orient their conduct towards wealth, it denies them opportunities to get money in the framework of accepted institutions. This inconsistency results in a high rate of deviant behaviour (Robert K. Merton, *Social Theory and Social Structure*, [Glencoe, Ill.: Free Press, 1949], p. 137).

7 Because of the changing character of boxing, promoters or managers may sometimes tell fighters that they are "through"; but fighters, as we have indicated, seldom make these appraisals of other fighters.

8 Since the number of local bouts have declined with the advent of television, many preliminary fighters and local club fighters are compelled to work at outside jobs in order to meet their daily expenses.

9 According to boxing folklore, a former heavyweight champion, Max Baer, was stimulated into action by his trainer who gave him a mixture called "Go Fast", which presumably had the properties of making a "tiger" out of the one who drank it. The suggestive effects of this drink were so great that Baer knocked out his opponent. Thereafter, he de-

manded it in subsequent fights. This suggestive play also proved effective with a former middleweight champion, Ken Overlin. The drink itself was composed of distilled water and a little sugar.

10 Some defeated boxers, as a result of physical fatigue and self-recrimination, lapse into a condition resembling combat exhaustion or anxiety. They react by uncontrollable crying spells, tantrums, and random belligerency. The restoration of their confidence is crucial for subsequent fights. Some trainers and managers are quite skilled in accomplishing it.

11 Data taken from *Ring*, February, 1951.

12 These computations were made by following the fighters in every issue of *Ring* from 1938 on. This magazine lists all the fights for every month.

13 "One of the troubles with boxing is what I call assembly line training. There are too few competent trainers and most of them have too many fighters to train. For the most part the boxers look upon training as a necessary evil ... [In the past], hours were spent on perfecting a movement—a feint, the proper tossing of a punch, the art of slipping a blow successfully. [This] marked the difference between a skilled craftsman and a lumbering wild-swinging tyro" (Al Buck, "Incompetency the Cause", *Ring*, September, 1950, p. 22).

14 The managers' guild also serves in part as a kind of collective protection against promoters.

15 e.g., an outstanding light-heavyweight contender is unable to get a title match, although one whom he has defeated will get the match. He was slighted because his manager had not signed with the International Boxing Club. His manager has stated: "The I.B.C. dictates who fights who and when and where. They're big business. But I'll fight; I'm trying to keep the independents [boxers and managers] in business" (*Time*, 9 July, 1951, pp. 58–9).

16 The tastes of contemporary fight fans is directed mainly towards punchers rather than boxers. In the past, clever boxers were highly appreciated.

17 "In 1937 when [Joe] Louis won the crown from Jimmy Braddock, every Negro boy in all corners of the country worshipped him. Their thoughts centred on boxing and boxing gloves ... The boys who once worshipped Louis as boxer have gone daffy about a baseball hero, Jackie Robinson ... The eyes of the boys who once looked upon Joe Louis with pride and envy and wanted to emulate him, now are focused on Jackie Robinson and other top-notch ballplayers" (Nat Loubet, "Jackie Robinson's Rise, Blow to Boxing", *Ring*, September, 1950, p. 5).

18 Arthur H. Steinhaus, "Boxing—Legalised Murder", *Look Magazine*, 3 January, 1950, p. 36.

19 Some precautions have been innovated recently for the boxer's protection, such as the thickness of the padding on the floor of the ring or the absence of protrusions or sharp corners in the ring.

20 Although the boxing myths emphasise the exceptions who fought past the age of forty—e.g. Bob Fitzsimmons fought until he was about fifty-two—the average fighter is considered "old" after he is thirty years of age. At present, some "old" fighters are still successfully active— e.g. Joe Louis and "Jersey Joe" Walcott, who are thirty-seven years old. In addition to being exceptions, their successful participation in the ring is also a result of the fact that few new heavyweights are entering boxing.

21 Since successful boxers retain a reputation in their respective neighbour-

hoods after they have quit the sport, some businessmen use their names as "fronts" for taverns or lounges. Hence it was difficult to find out whether the boxers themselves owned the taverns. In five cases they did not, although the taverns were in their names.

22 One former champion said: "I like to hear of a boxer doing well after he leaves the ring. People think all boxers are punchy. We have a bad press. After I left the ring, I had a devil of a time telling people I wasn't punchy." The Veterans Boxing Association, an organisation of former boxers, have protested occasionally against radio programmes which present what they consider a false stereotype of the former boxer.

CHAPTER 15

Wrestling—The Great American Passion Play*

Gregory P. Stone

Several years ago I took a friend to the railroad station. We arrived early and went to a nearby tavern to kill time. Those were the days when wrestling was a tavern TV fixture, and the set at the bar was presenting the then current struggle—the Russians (Kalmikoff brothers, one since deceased) *versus* the local heroes (good, clean-cut Americans). We chose to ignore the spectacle in favour of conversation, but were suddenly interrupted as a lone beer-drinker slammed his fist on the bar and shouted: "I don't give a damn if it is a fake! Kill the son-of-a-bitch!" I have pondered those lines ever since: how can the wrestling fan who seemingly has penetrated the facade of the match still be caught up in the "heat" of the performance? This is the primary question that orients this essay. The question seems simple, and perhaps it is. But the answer is highly involved and complex. It requires a consideration of the historical transformations of wrestling, the social organisation of the enterprise, wrestling careers, and, of course, the social and social psychological character of the audience and the wrestling fan.

HISTORICAL TRANSFORMATIONS OF WRESTLING

Wrestling as work and play—There is archaeological evidence that wrestling existed in human society 5,000 years ago,[1] but by that ancient time it was carried on almost exclusively as sport or play. Wrestling is certainly as old as the appearance of man or quasi-man on earth and probably older. If we indulge in a bit of anthropomorphism, it becomes easy to imagine that beasts

* This article is a slightly revised version of a chapter (co-authored by Ramon Oldenburg) in Ralph Slovenko and James A. Knight (eds.), *Play, Games and Motivations in Sports*, Springfield, Ill., 1967, pp. 503–32. Although Mr. Oldenburg co-authored the original version, responsibility for revisions is entirely my own. I am indebted to my colleague, Scott McNall, for his suggestions concerning these revisions.

"wrestle" their prey to the ground, or that kittens and cubs "play" at "wrestling". We can speculate, then, that wrestling in human society began at once as work and play. Wrestling is the most primitive mode of human combat and, at its inception, was probably a type of work carried on in the struggle man waged with beasts and other men. Wrestling play could undoubtedly be found at the same time in what we think of today as childish pranks. Body control is an essential dimension of poise (one way we signal to others our readiness for interaction) and is unknowingly cultivated in young people, as they push, trip, tickle, tackle, and otherwise grapple with one another. With the development of a more efficient combat technology, the *work* of wrestling ceased, and wrestling persisted in society as a play form, except, of course, in emergencies and other uncontrolled situations. An important function of play is the *re*creation and maintenance of obsolete work forms, making history a viable reality for mankind. Thus, canoeing, archery, and horseback riding persist in society today as play. Wrestling is no exception.

Before the twelfth century and after the demise of the Roman Empire, wrestling was a universal play form in Europe, engaged in by all strata of the male population without reference to social rank. After the twelfth century, with the crystallisation of an aristocracy, the character of play underwent a change:

> This marked the beginning of the idea that noblemen should avoid mixing with villeins and taking their sport among them: an idea which did not succeed in imposing itself everywhere, at least until the eighteenth century, when the nobility disappeared as a class with a social function and was replaced by the bourgeoisie.[2]

Wrestling was one of the earliest sports set apart and marked off by the aristocratic stratification of European society. It became a common sport and not a knightly game in the twelfth century. Of course, there are many exceptions—Henry VIII was a skilled wrestler—but, by and large, wrestling has been a lower status sport in Western civilisation for eight hundred years.

There was probably an element of snobbery in all this. Ariès cites a sixteenth century account which reports some protest at the continuing mixing of nobles and peasants in festival games: "If there is anything which is too ugly and shameful for words, it is the sight of a nobleman being defeated by a peasant, especially in wrestling."[3] Yet, an additional reason for the relegation of wrestling to the lower strata is to be found in precisely its "primitive" character. It is the least elaborated of all sports with the possible exception of walking and running. Even in these instances, a comparison of, let us say, the equipment of the Japanese *sumo* wrestler with that of the track athlete suggests that the technology of wrestling is impressively less complex. In general, the more elaborate the technological paraphernalia of a sport, the higher its social status. There have been elaborations of wrestling equipment, as with the *Schwingenhosen* of the Swiss and Tyrolese or the canvas jackets used in Cornish wrestling, but these have not caught on widely at all. In contrast to *sumo* wrestlers, *judo* wrestlers do have a uniform, and, perhaps more than anything else, this betrays the fact that *jiu-jutsu* developed among the *samurai* in Japan, while *sumo* was the national or common sport.

In its early history, then, wrestling was abandoned early as a form of work in society, but persisted as a play form. In Europe it was established as a lower status adult recreation long ago, and, with the exception of wrestling play, it continues as a lower status spectator sport today.

Wrestling as sport and drama in the United States—Sport, as we have said, is a transformation of work and play forms. Amateur sport is usually a transformation of work into play; professional sport, a transformation of play into work. Precisely when wrestling became a professional sport in America is not known. Quite likely it emerged along with other professional sports, in the last half of the nineteenth century. If we do not know when professional wrestling originated in America, we do know that the last sporting wrestler was Frank Gotch.[4] Gotch wrestled for thirteen years, winning 156 out of 160 matches (about one match per month—compare the schedules of present day wrestlers, often five or six matches a week). He retired in 1912.

After Gotch, the character of the sport changed dramatically, for it became a drama. It is very difficult to arrive at any definitive explanation of the transformation of wrestling into commercial drama,[5] but at least four factors contributed to the change: (1) the nature of the sport, itself; (2) the urbanisataion of the United States; (3) a general revulsion against violence in sport which arose shortly before Gotch's retirement; and (4) the development of wrestling "trusts".

1. *The nature of wrestling.* The risk of severe injury to the participants is high. As a consequence, with the evolution of wrestling as playful work, rules were devised to mitigate the physical risk. Amateur wrestling became focused on matters of poise. Points were scored by completely destroying the poise of one's opponent, as in the "pin"; by disturbing it momentarily by tripping, upsetting, or forcing the opponent out of a sharply demarcated play

area; or by regaining one's own poise as in "escapes" and "reverses". This focus persists today, not only in amateur wrestling, but in wrestling play—"Indian wrestling" and "arm wrestling". However, this kind of match does not command great audience enthusiasm, though it might well enthuse the participants. The alternative mode of victory is submission of the opponent, and this is the mode professional wrestling has adopted. Although it *may* command great and extensive enthusiasm among spectators for reasons we shall discuss later, earnest attempts at submission can be very boring indeed for the onlooker. It can hardly command the enthusiasm of the participants over the long run. Gotch left an incredible string of broken legs in the wake of his 156 victories, and a broken leg forced his own retirement. This is just the point: wrestlers cannot anticipate *any* extensive career if submission of the opponent is the test of victory, and the match proceeds on the basis of catch-as-catch-can.

Submission holds are easily established and *impossible* to break. This fact has a dual consequence. First, spectators must resign themselves to long periods of inactivity, and this must inevitably depress their interest. Specifically, when Gotch met Hackenschmidt for the world title in 1904:

> Gotch followed his strategy rigidly with the result the match developed into a dull pull-and-haul affair with the champion and the challenger on their feet for two hours. The crowd of 18,000 who paid approximately $70,000 to see the match . . . booed the contestants for lack of action.
>
> After two hours and three minutes of tussling, Gotch finally manoeuvred to get behind Hackenschmidt to whip a waistlock on him. The Iowan then lifted the Russian off his feet and banged him down on the mat. "Hack" immediately informed the referee . . . he would forfeit the fall to Gotch.[6]

The tedious achievement of submission bores the audience and undoubtedly depresses the market. Second, the consequence of early severe bodily injury to the wrestlers is highly probable. We have already mentioned the frequency of fractures that attended early professional wrestling in the United States, but, in this respect, the superiority of wrestling over boxing as a combative technique has been unambiguously established. William Muldoon, the "greatest Roman of them all", defeated the great John L. Sullivan in 1887, and, in 1935, it took Ray Steel, a heavyweight wrestler of no great merit, thirty-five seconds to subdue King Levinsky, a heavyweight boxer subsequently knocked out by Joe Louis. By 1937, "Strangler" Lewis, Jack Dempsey, Benny Leonard, and Dean

Detton all agreed that wrestlers could defeat boxers, each fighting his own style.[7]

My point is that, when professional wrestling opted for the alternative of submission to adjudicate victory, it sharply curtailed the "life expectancy" of the business. No economic enterprise in American is established with the prospect of going out of business, and the continuity of business presupposes the continuity of the clientele and the *gradual* replacement of key personnel. Consequently, wrestling as a professional sport, i.e. play transformed into work, was primed for some kind of transformation when it seized upon submission as the test of victory.

Since professional sports must build up followings, fans must identify with the symbols or representations of the sports. The representations of combative sports are the individual combatants, and identifications with combatants (unless the fan is caught up in the snares of nostalgia, or, as we shall see below, the relationship between fan and combatant is relatively intimate or bolstered by other bonds) can only persist as long as the combatant is active. In team sports, on the other hand, the name of the team with which the fan identifies typically persists beyond the career of any given individual player. The players represent the collectivity. In the case of wrestling, then, a way had to be found to extend the careers of the wrestlers or to cloak the sport in representations that transcended individual wrestling careers.

2. *Urbanisation.* This exigency was made all the more urgent by the rapid urbanisation of the United States in the early twentieth century. When wrestling was a young sport, wrestlers followed a circuit of small towns where almost every resident knew almost every other. Local heroes were pitted against alien villains, and identifications with local representatives were strong and long established. Interest ran high in such matches, as manifested in extensive gambling, so that fairly large turn-outs could be anticipated, despite the fact that the outcome of matches was usually decided by upsetting rather than overwhelming the opponent. Beginning in 1828, Abraham Lincoln wrestled throughout the Mississippi and Ohio river country, and it has been estimated that he engaged in some three hundred matches before his political career precluded further participation. The mark of his extensive wrestling remained as a life-long imprint—the huge cauliflowered left ear. He was a kind of representative of the wrestling of his time, and it is significant that his outstanding championship match took place at Coles County, Illinois, two counties south of what is now Champaign-Urbana, hardly an urban centre.[8] With the rise of cities and relocation of the wrestling "market", wrestlers could no

longer appear as representatives of local small towns, but were forced to establish themselves as representatives of larger, nation-wide, or world-wide social units which could cut across and mobi-lise the identifications of socially heterogeneous and anonymous spectators.

3. *Disgust with violence*. Shortly before Gotch's retirement, a wave of revulsion against violence in athletics swept the nation. In 1905, Teddy Roosevelt was so enraged by the bloody brutality of a Swarthmore-Pennsylvania football game that he threatened to abolish that sport by executive edict, unless extreme measures were taken to reduce the violence.[9] Boxing had not been legalised at that time in most of the states, in part because of the attendant vehemence. This public temper may well have contributed towards reducing the probability of grave bodily injury in professional wrestling by making wrestlers even more keenly aware of the very real physical risks that their profession entailed.

4. *The "wrestling trusts"*. Finally, to explain the transformation, we must consider the whole network of events touched off by the problem of effecting a transfer of power after Gotch's retirement, for the way in which this was done culminated in the formation of the great wrestling "trusts".

When Gotch retired, he designated two wrestlers to engage in an elimination bout for his title. The winner was defeated in 1914 by Charles Cutler, who proceeded to subdue all significant opposi-tion.[10] In a desperate search for a worthwhile opponent, Cutler located a young Nebraskan, Joe Stecher, who was a good wrestler, but, because of his inexperience, hardly of championship calibre. In 1915, Stecher defeated Cutler in straight falls, and wrestling fans lost thousands of dollars in wagers. This initiated a steep decline of public confidence in the sport. The fate of wrestling as a sport was undoubtedly sealed in 1917, when, for as yet unstated reasons, Stecher refused to appear for a third and deciding fall and lost his title to Earl Caddock. Again the betting public took a severe beating.

Clearly, the "fix" was on. Wrestling could no longer be con-ceptualised in the public mind as a sport with genuinely uncertain outcomes, and, today, the absence of any large scale betting on matches is one clear sign that wrestling has been transformed from sport into a drama. To revive and sustain a wrestling fol-lowing—to make money—wrestlers joined with promoters and managers to form "trusts". These trusts sought to bring as many wrestlers as possible under their control and arranged dramatic, colourful encounters, called "working matches" in the trade, on extensive circuits across the nation. An outstanding trust was known as the "Gold Dust Trio", comprised of Ed "Strangler" Lewis, Joe "Toots" Mondt, both top flight wrestlers, and Billy Sandow, one of the shrewdest promoters and managers in the history of American professional wrestling. At one time, this trust had five hundred wrestlers under contract.[11]

This *joint* participation of wrestlers, themselves, with promoters and managers in promotional and match-making operations is extremely important. Not only did it consolidate the transformation of wrestling into drama, it also marked off the history of professional wrestling from that of professional boxing in the United States. The career of the dramatic actor is notoriously longer than that of the professional athlete, and it is in the *interest* of the professional wrestler to prolong his career. Moreover, with few exceptions and until recently boxers have typically had no control over their own professional destinies. Indeed, boxing managers are said, in the trade, to run "stables". This lack of participation by most boxers in management, promotion, and match-making accounts in no small measure for the much greater occupational and economic success of professional wrestlers as contrasted with that of professional boxers.[12] Nevertheless, there are great pressures towards the dramatic transformation of boxing as some boxing champions do undertake management functions or, at least, participate in them. Evidence for the trend can be seen in the shenanigans of Cassius Clay or Mohammed Ali.[13]

Although wrestling had been firmly established as drama with the rise of trusts, it is not as though there were no real or "shooting" matches. Where there are trusts, there are "trust-busters", and wrestlers would often sign to "work" a card, but would "shoot" instead. To lessen the likelihood of this kind of double cross, "policemen" were used to test the ability of wrestlers whose motives were suspect, prior to matching them with a champion. It is said that Mondt was "Strangler" Lewis's policeman.[14] Moreover, wrestlers would at times become discontent with their status in the trust, and shooting matches would be arranged. Even today, there is a chance of an occasional double cross, an indefensible complaint, or an indeterminate ranking so that shooting matches still occur.[15]

No better documentation of the fact that wrestling had become drama is to be found than a reference to the career of Jim Londos, who belonged to one of the most lucrative trusts in wrestling. Londos, born Christopher Teophelus, was a mediocre wrestler whose career began before World War I and lasted until the mid-thirties. He had been defeated countless times by countless wrestlers until 1930, when he became *a* world champion in a Philadelphia match. Belatedly, *Ring* magazine marked October, 1934 as the end of wrestling as a professional sport in the United States.[16] That was the year Londos shared the "title" with Ed Don George. Londos was most significant for the transformation of wrestling into drama. First, he was "box-office":

> Londos met his hand-picked opponents in bouts night after night, sometimes locking grips with the same wrestler four times in one week, in different cities, of course.
>
> The number of times he "wrestled" Ray Steele, Rudy Dusek, Gino Garibaldi, Sammy Stein, Karl Pjello, Jim McMillan in "matches" advertised for the title runs into the hundreds.
>
> The gates for these bouts totalled thousands of dollars. In fact, after meeting Steele in some sixty-eight "contests" Londos "wrestled" the latter in an open air "match" at the Yankee Stadium, New York. The bout drew close to seventy thousand dollars, a new high for the wrestling gates in New York, a record never since equalled in the New York metropolitan area in money or gullibility on the part of meat tossing enthusiasts.[17]

Second, Londos introduced the "freak" into the drama—the contest between "beauty and the beast" remains in the wrestling repertoire at the present day. Third, the "Golden Greek" lured women into wrestling fandom.

Londos was *a* champion and a significant catalyst in the transformation of wrestling, but the trusts promoted different personalities in different parts of the country, and there were regional as well as national trusts. In 1933, there were six "world champions"; in 1934, two; but, by 1943, the list had swelled to fifteen; and today there are at least five world champions and probably as many regional "world" champions as there are TV viewing areas. Verne Gagne, one-time American Wrestling Alliance champion, has been dubbed affectionately by at least one sport columnist in the Twin City area "world champion of the five county mosquito control district". In addition, there are "tag team champions", "women champions", "midget champions", etc. This multiplication of champions has been enabled precisely by the removal of wrestling from the world of professional sports. It meant that sportswriters lost interest, with the result that the national wire services ceased to report wrestling results.[18]

Wrestling is played down in the local press as well. In the Minneapolis *Tribune* sports section for Sunday, February 7, 1965, the first page was given over to accounts (continued on the inside) of University of Minnesota hockey and basketball games. Attendance at those matches was 5,093 and 6,273, respectively. The "world championship" wrestling match between Verne Gagne and "Mad Dog" Vachon received $2\frac{1}{2}$ column inches on page four. Attendance was 6,389! Almost two and a half months later, the situation had changed very little. On 18 April, 1965, the front page was mostly concerned with the Minnesota Twins' 3-0 victory over the Cleveland Indians. That game attracted 4,492 spectators. The rematch between Gagne and Vachon was reported on the third page this time and given $3\frac{3}{4}$ column inches. The rematch attracted 8,900 spectators, about twice the attendance of the major league ball game! By 7 August, 1965, the Twins were clearly in contention for the American League Championship and, in a contest with the Boston Red Sox, drew 16,220. The tag-team match, Harry Hennig and Harley Race *vs.* Verne Gagne and "The Crusher", attracted 9,652. On the same day, Pittsburgh *vs.* Philadelphia drew 8,204; Houston *vs.* Kansas City, 8,123. Even during the World Series a Twin City wrestling match was attended by more than 9,000 spectators.

This, of course, rankles the wrestling audience, and sportswriters are also disturbed. Sportswriters feel a strong obligation to all sports fans, but they also have a great pride in their craft. They are critics. Long ago they concluded that there was nothing left to criticise in professional wrestling, so perhaps two or three inches on page three or four of the sports pages is the best compromise they can make. They're damned if they do report wrestling and damned if they don't. At any rate, the lack of any national or interstate press coverage facilitates the drama. Drama permits a single actor to play many roles, and wrestlers use different names in different places. Thus, the dedicated fan cannot discover, except fortuitously or by an unlikely search, that the world champion of his own local area is not, in fact, *the* world champion.[19]

This overview of the transformation of wrestling from work and play to play to professional sport to drama has touched upon some of the facets of the social organisation of professional wrestling in the United States, but important details have been omitted.

SOCIAL ORGANISATION OF WRESTLING

When the sociologist first attempts to probe the present-day social organisation of wrestling, his reaction is one of wonder at the fantastic extent of a marvellously controlled "conspiracy of silence". As he continues his study, the wonder gives way to consternation at the impenetrability of the conspiracy. Finally, his attitude becomes one of dull resignation and reluctant acceptance of the fact that many of his conclusions will be more often inferences than demonstrations. In a letter to Scott McNall, a colleague at the University of Minnesota, an anonymous wrestler writes:

> I am not sure if you plan to write about [professional wrestling] or engage in it. If you plan to write about Pro. Wrestling, and want to be absolutely correct, my advice is to forget it. You will never get all the actual facts you would require ... As an industry, Pro. Wrestling is sort of a closed corporation. If you become part of it you will learn all the little tricks of the trade, but don't expect anyone to tell them to you to write about. There is too much money at stake. Wrestling is show business and very well run. They intend to keep it that way.[20]

The point is underscored by the reaction of a Twin City editor to an interview with myself and Ramon Oldenburg. The editor had been in the "trade" for thirty-five years, and his career included a stint in New York, as well as the West Coast and other midwestern cities. In a Sunday column, he admitted publicly that he had no answers for most of our queries. Apparently the deepest "penetration" he had made of the conspiracy was securing an admission from a local promoter that he had "never told a wrestler to lose a match"—scarcely more than a knock on the door of the inner sanctum.

Moreover, sportswriters often make friends of professional athletes and, in the give and take of friendship, become party to trade secrets. This may not be the case with wrestling. One of the reporters on the editor's staff established a close relationship with a wrestling tag team, accompanying them on fishing trips and participating with them in other leisure activities, but he never became privy to the secrets of the sport. This analysis of the inside organisation of wrestling, then, is necessarily deductive. For the outside organisation, it is, of course, a simpler, more direct matter.

Size of the industry—In 1952, there were approximately fifteen million paying spectators of professional wrestling. By 1959, the number had risen to 24,000,000 and had exceeded 25,000,000 by the early sixties.[21] Not only does this latter figure exceed the paid attendance for such other professional sports as major league baseball, professional basketball, and horse-racing, but the number of wrestling spectators (excluding the TV viewers) has risen at a rate greater than our overall population increase. The number of active professional wrestlers has been variously estimated at between two and four thousand. There are more than five hundred regularly used wrestling arenas in the nation. Gross gate receipts in the early fifties exceeded $20,000,000 and, today, they probably come close to doubling that figure. Moreover, wrestling in the

American fashion has spread to other countries, notably Australia, Great Britain, and Japan, and there are currently signs of the development of an international circuit which attracts the top wrestlers. In short, professional wrestling is big business.

Regional organisation in the United States—Although the *Encyclopaedia of Associations* does not list a single professional wrestling organisation, there are certainly four and probably more which organise wrestling on a regional basis in the United States: the World Wide Wrestling Federation, centred in New York; the National Wrestling Alliance, located in St. Louis; the American Wrestling Alliance, headquartered in Amarillo, Texas; and the World Wrestling Alliance, located in Los Angeles. A fifth organisation quite probably organises the southeast, perhaps centred in Miami, Florida, and there may be a second northeastern organisation, the International Wrestling Alliance. The Minneapolis Club, from which most of our observations have been drawn, is in the AWA.

How these organisations function is not completely clear. They *may* exert sanctions on participating wrestlers. As an example, Larry Hennig and Harley Race were recently declared southwest tag-team champions by Sidney Blackburn, president of the American Wrestling Alliance. Following a conversation with Blackburn, Hennig asserted that he had been assured that top tag-team combinations would be dropped from title contention, if they declined to meet the southwest champions.[22] How much of such talk is ballyhoo and how much is factual reporting is impossible to determine. My guess favours the ballyhoo. Yet, reports do appear, from time to time, of fines and suspensions exacted by wrestling alliances or commissioners against recalcitrant and "berserk" wrestlers. There is also probably some control exerted over "champions" by underwriting their appearances on the organisation circuit.

Certainly, the alliances do see to it that matches promoted by affiliated clubs remain within the letter of state legislation. For example, a Texas statute declares that it is a criminal offence

> knowingly to conduct or give or participate in any sham or fake fistic combat match, boxing, sparring, or wrestling contest or exhibition except it be as burlesque.

Legally, therefore, wrestling is defined as burlesque in Texas, although, of course, the definition is not publicised. There is no statutory regulation of professional wrestling in Minnesota. Indeed, at least in Minnesota, wrestling is not only big business, but must command considerable power. Wrestling became a major sport in the state in the early '30's, and the athletic commission has tried for twenty years to bring professional wrestling under its control. In this attempt, the commission has had the overwhelming support of the State House of Representatives, but to no avail.

In 1961, the house passed the amendment by a majority of 116 to 3. At that session the wrestling amendment did not get out of the senate committee. In 1963, the house passed the amendment by a margin of 122 to 4, but the amendment died in the senate committee. At the 1965 session, the wrestling bill was by-passed by both house and senate.[23]

In a general way, the territory staked out by each regional association sets boundaries marking off contiguous TV viewing areas within which canned performances of regional heroes and villains are circulated. Today, the area in which any given wrestling league is popular is determined almost wholly by the exposure of the area to televised wrestling. Promoters have found that interest in the sport cannot be maintained without televising wrestling matches regularly.[24] One of the major decisions to be made in any region is the allocation of time to the televising of wrestling matches. In one region it was decided that a minimum of two hours per week is essential, but that it would not be judicious to exceed two and a half or three hours.

All major professional wrestlers follow their canned performances around the country. From the Twin City area, for example, canned shows are sent regularly to Illinois, Nebraska, and Colorado. When fan appetite has been sufficiently whetted, the wrestlers who have been viewed on TV in those areas make live appearances. Fan interest can also be diverted by the sponsorship of canned matches originating in rival regions, though this rarely occurs. When it did happen in one area, the local promoter remarked, "Well, of course, he (the rival promoter) doesn't give a damn what happens to us here." Probably alliances establish treaties about the distribution of canned performances, and this may be a major function. If wrestling were more popular as a national TV attraction, and advertisers sought to sponsor it, a "battle of the leagues" could develop. Instead of engaging their respective "world champions" in frequent decisive combat, the war would be waged by sending canned matches into rival territories. Again, we can see how the "conspiracy of silence" operates to maintain the status quo. The lack of national press coverage makes the battle of the leagues an extremely unlikely eventuality. Moreover, a nationwide battle of the leagues would militate against the easy mobility of wrestlers by ruling out the strategy of most "identity switches" (the exception, of course, is masking).

Whether or not the above functions characterise the operation of the alliances, one function is certain. The existence of diverse alliances reduces the probability of embarrassment for the champions. When Verne Gagne was asked to explain the multiplicity of wrestling champions on the national scene, he scarcely raised an eyebrow. "Is that so unusual?" he asked. "The AFL and the NFL each has its own champion. Why shouldn't that be the case for each wrestling league?"

Local organisation—Regional wrestling alliances seem to be loose, wispy federations of local clubs. Indeed, in a description of the organisation of wrestling, one professional wrestler did not refer to "alliances" at all, but put it this way: "The U.S. is divided into districts, called circuits. Each has a man who oversees it."[25] Perhaps, at best, they demarcate audiences for whom passionate dramas between good and evil are enacted. However, when one takes a hard look at local organisation, the structure seems to come alive. The metropolitan club is the core organisation of professional wrestling. Probably the alliances provide a kind of clearing house for wrestlers somewhat on the order of a union hall, but local promoters do the hiring and firing in cities, or sometimes in several cities.[26]

Viewed from the outside, the club tightly organises the relationships among the promoter, the matchmaker, the wrestlers, an announcer, referees, and lesser figures, such as seconds, (off-duty) policemen, and badge-wearing arena ushers. In local TV presentations, most of the personnel play a part in the ongoing drama. Will the promoter bring in some new and rugged hero to threaten the reign of a devilish villain? Will the matchmaker arrange a meet between the two bad guys? Will the commissioner of the alliance act on the referee's request to suspend the villain who has hospitalised two fine young wrestlers? Such questions are planted in the fan mind by the announcer and those he interviews between bouts. The announcer stresses two themes: (1) he is instructed by the local promoter to "boost" each wrestler who appears in the ring; and (2) he continually echoes and inspires the sentiments appropriate for developing identifications among the fans: "My goodness, Ladies and Gentlemen," he will say, "this is the most barbaric thing I have ever seen in the ring! I don't know why they allow him to get away with that." Of course, it is the referee that permits the barbarism. Referees are often as important a part of the drama as the wrestlers, themselves, and they assume as many different identities. These range from local sports heroes, through national sports heroes who are "over the hill", to figures like "Blind Anthony", who is led into the Chicago ring by a seeing-eye dog.

Obviously referees are not those who oversee what goes on; they overlook it.

Promotion—At the heart of the local organisation of professional wrestling is the promoter of the metropolitan club. Most of the money is made in the metropolitan arenas, and all of the top flight wrestlers regularly appear in those rings and on the metropolitan TV station. Wrestling no longer depends to any great degree upon the small town carnival or the fair to attract its paying audiences. Indeed, as we have shown, it cannot. Nevertheless, an important function of the metropolitan promoter is to maintain a liaison with small town promoters and fans. Small towns often act as feeders for metropolitan clubs, and, consequently, wrestling is cultivated there. They also form the "fringe sectors" of TV viewing areas. Fan loyalty in the fringes is typically high and must be sustained, for fans in remote places add to TV ratings.

Therefore, some wrestlers still make appearances on the carnival scene. Usually they appear in what has come to be called the "at show" (from "athletic show"). Besides touring "pros", two kinds of wrestlers are likely to be found in the at shows. There are the younger and non-college-educated wrestlers who use this opportunity to establish professional wrestling careers. By appearing in these shows, they come under the watchful eyes of club promoters who keep a constant vigil for new box office attractions. Then, there are those who have retired from the more strenuous activities of the metropolitan arenas. Wrestling matches at carnivals are usually short in duration, often carried on under a five minute time limit (cf. the Gotch-Hackenschmidt match discussed earlier, p. 304).

Carnival wrestlers frequently issue challenges to club wrestlers who may be in the area, and, if scheduling permits, club wrestlers usually accept them. Of course, it's an "extra buck", but also, as one club promoter told us, "They never know what they're going to meet in that kind of ring." Thus, for the club wrestler, the occasional carnival or at show can serve as one guarantee against "going stale".[27] Moreover, as we shall see, the appearance of the club wrestler in the small town is a vital part of the promotion process.

A far more lucrative carry-over from the old days of carnival wrestling is the "fair date". Fair dates are regarded as "sure things", since such celebrations are always insured against non-attendance. Usually, the participating club is given the lion's share (60% is common) of a guaranteed $1,500 gate.

Other than club promoters, the promoter of a wrestling event may be a person, a corporation, an established religious group, a city council, or a local chamber of commerce. Any duly recognised person or group may be the occasional promoter of a wrestling match. In almost all cases, the occasional promoter will work with the metropolitan club in the promotion of wrestling and *vice versa*. The established metropolitan club will usually have at least two small trucks or "panel jobs" which carry collapsible rings and whatever other paraphernalia is necessary. This "set-up" is always ready to go. Should inclement weather make travelling difficult, or mechanical trouble cause a late arrival, there is seldom any real problem. Though the panel truck may be an hour late in arriving before a frustrated audience, once there, it is possible to set up for the event in fifteen minutes' time.

While the metropolitan club rarely refuses to co-operate in the promotion of a small town event, there are often difficulties. At times, the total gate may be as little as $600 or less, and this hardly compares to the $900 guarantee at a fair date. Moreover, compared to the routine $10,000 arena gates, the small town "take" is ridiculously small. Small town engagements, then, are construed as profitable in a long-run promotional sense, and the main problem is that of providing a suitable card of wrestlers for the small audiences. It is seldom that a "world champion" will undertake an engagement for less than a guaranteed $100, and the occasional world champion of the AWA, "Mad Dog" Vachon, demands $750 for each appearance. Understandably, every occasional promoter would like to have the "champ" on his card, and wrestling alliances often make this possible. The "champion" is the one wrestler over whom the alliance does exert control in the scheduling of appearances. Champions have always been reasonably willing to comply with the schedules set for them by the association which has awarded them the crown.

Be these things as they may, the journey of the club wrestler to the small town is a powerful technique for solidifying the market. Whether the "champion" appears or not, it is certain that some notorious hero or villain will put in a personal appearance in the small town. The sport figure who appears on TV can, at any moment, become a living reality for the small town viewer. In only one other professional sport is this the case, and the consequent loyalty of the fans is brute testimony to the efficacy of the device as a rhetoric of identification.[28] Probably no other sport organisation commands the pervasive support of the fans than that of the Green Bay Packers! Their stadium is always filled.

Club promoters and matchmakers sit at the seat of power in professional wrestling. Matches in adjoining metropolitan centres, e.g. Minneapolis and St. Paul, run the risk of box office competition, but a "gentleman's agreement" usually obviates this possibility. As Riesman has observed of the nation, so it is with professional wrestling: "free trade" has given way to "fair trade".[29] When a neighbouring promoter offers a competing card at the same time another promoter has scheduled a "big" match, fireworks may ensue. Ordinarily, there are threats to build up the competing match with "championship blood" from rival TV viewing areas. In the "give and take" of threat and counterthreat, compromises are formed, and the market remains undisturbed by the existence of spectator choice about which of the competing matches to attend.

WRESTLERS' CAREERS

Like all occupations, wrestling is characterised by careers demarcated by the stages of recruitment, establishment of position, mobility, and termination. Moreover, wrestling, like other occupations, has its sidelines and is, on occasion, a sideline itself.

Recruitment—The recruitment of new blood into the profession is accomplished, in the main, by the watchful eye which established promoters and wrestlers keep over college and university athletic departments. The majority of professional wrestlers have had careers as college wrestlers, college football players, or quite often, both. Any lineman or back on a college football team, if he is both big and agile, comes under close scrutiny as a potential professional wrestler. The proposition put to him is usually directly to the point: "Do you realise", the promoter may ask, "just how much money you can make in this game?" And, indeed, the inducement is formidable.

While many promoters insist that wrestling gates are lessened during the height of football enthusiasm, football and professional wrestling are complementary in many respects. *Via* football, many local wrestling heroes win that fame with which so many wrestling fans will come to identify and pay to watch. Further, we have already cited the problem which the active wrestler faces—that of "going stale". Many professional athletes work six months at professional football and the remaining six at professional wrestling. One activity keeps the body in shape for the other.

The great majority of professional wrestlers are fine athletes, and, as we are suggesting, most recruiting is from communities of trained, well-educated, amateur athletes. There are two notable exceptions to this convention: the "freak" and the "physique". In recent years, however, professional wrestling has moved away from the freakish, the "physical", and the feminine in terms of the identities it presents to its fans. One still sees a liberal enough sprinkling of atavistic monstrosities, awesome behemoths, golden tresses, and smooth bodies among the matmen, but the recent emphasis is on the masculine, clean-cut, Frank Merriwell type. Yet, as we have said, the incipience of feminine mockery can be detected.

A few men find their places among the ranks of professional wrestlers because of their physiques alone. Thus, an occasional weightlifter may appear in a series of (to us) unconvincing bouts which consist mainly of muscle-flexing and the use of "naked power" in breaking holds. In contrast to some of the great men of the game, who become "Masters" of a Thousand Holds," those fellows may manage but three or four. Also enjoying some popularity is the three-hundred-pound-plus pachyderm whose simple gimmick may be that of falling upon his hapless victims, repeatedly "crushing" them amid all the blubber. Yet, these "wrestlers" are the exception rather than the rule, and the fan seems now to bestow most favour upon the accomplished wrestler and imaginative performer. Organised wrestling recruits mostly ability and intelligence and recruits the body only for occasional colour.

Establishment of position—There are, then, two essential qualifications for professional wrestling, skill and audience appeal, and the two compromise antinomial principles. "Shooting matches" or tests of skill are unappealing, and emphasis upon audience appeal —the display—may destroy the illusion of reality. For the most part and with the exception of the freaks, skill must be established first. This is crucial, for one of the risks that professional wrestlers face is confronted when they are matched against unskilled opponents. Today wrestling is a complex tumbling act. Timing and the correct interpretation of cues are vital, for mistakes in either can mean serious injury. For this reason, the "old pro's" are often reluctant to encounter "new blood". The recruit, then, must somehow establish his competence before his acceptance on the circuit. Consequently, young wrestlers, the new blood, ordinarily appear precisely as wrestlers with minimal improvisation on identity.

Once skill has been established and he has been accepted on the circuit (by the alliance?), the recruit becomes a wrestler in fact. Ordinarily he signs with a metropolitan promoter for "a period of time, usually three months".[30] Thence, his "work" really begins:

An ordinary wrestler works 5 nights one week and 6 nights the next. Main event men will sometimes work only 3 nights per week. Some work for a flat salary, some for so much per match, some for a percentage of the gate, or a combination of % and flat rate. Their price depends on reputation, experience, and showmanship.

In the trade a match is discussed in terms of so many changes, or exchanges of holds. A promoter asks the wrestlers for so many "changes" for a given time. As to who wins—that depends on the local conditions. Whatever will draw the best crowd for next week will be the deciding factor. The *wrestlers* normally would *not* decide such matters. They are hired help.[31]

I think we can assume that the young wrestler aspires to most money at least expense of effort, and, once he is established on the circuit, the prime route to these ends is identity-work. Once his skill has been established, he can concentrate his efforts on audience appeal.

Identity-work—The major task of the established professional wrestler is identity-work—building and husbanding an identity that can mobilise the appreciations of the audience and maintain them over time. Identity-work is the most crucial activity of the professional wrestler. The very mention of the task to Verne Gagne in an interview enthused that occasional world champion. He stated that decisions about identity—whether to be a hero or a villain, a "wrestling dentist" or a "mad dog"—are all up to the wrestler himself, as is his choice of other marks of identity—distinctive holds and techniques of "hooking" (manoeuvring an opponent into an inescapable position). Wrestlers often lose sleep perfecting their remarks and styles of delivery for television interviews. Gagne waxed poetic about the high points of creativity required for working up an identity that permits the wrestler's "real self" to emerge in the contest or the appearance.

While the concept of the "real self" poses many problems,[32] I wish to invoke the dictum of W. I. Thomas: "If men define situations as real, they are real in their consequences". For selves are very much a part of social situations, and identity is a major dimension—in fact, the substance—of the self.[33] Consequently, if identities are defined as real, they are real in their consequences, and *becoming* a worked-up identity may carry serious risks for the wrestler. The "cover story" can become an efficient trap, once it is accepted by those to whom it is presented, for there is a reverberating influence upon the one who presents the cover. Fans *place* the wrestler in his *announced* identity, and there is no more powerful identity cement than consensual validation.[34] Harley Race, after he was designated southwest tag team champion, believed he was a champion and championed the cause of an underdog in an argument at a Minneapolis bar early in 1965. Race was shot and seriously wounded for his heroic effort. Becoming the worked-up identity may even mean death. Rikidozan, the highly popular

Japanese champion, was convinced of his professed invincibility and walked six blocks to a hospital, after an assassin had completely transfixed his torso with a sword in December, 1963. He left his hospital bed against medical advice, aggravating his wound, and that was the end of that invincible champion.

One reason that the intelligent and educated wrestler is organisationally superior to the "meathead" is that he will be able to exercise imagination in working up an identity which fans will find attractive, or, at least, attracting. A case in point is that of Bill Miller,[35] a licensed veterinarian and ex-Ohio State Rose Bowl football player. Miller, an excellent wrestler, consistently failed to draw. Conceiving that the failure indicated an identity problem, he proceeded to make his identity problematic and became the masked "Mr. M.". The result was a rapturous fascination on the part of fans and a novel business success for Bill Miller. Indeed, a fan became so mesmerised by the villainous identity of Mr. M. that, when the spell was broken by the inevitable unmasking, he smashed Miller on the head using a two by six-inch plank with a one inch cleat fastened on the end. Miller was knocked unconscious, rushed to the hospital, found suffering from a brain concussion, and transferred to the Mayo Clinic. Luckily, Miller was able to return to the ring after an extended convalescence. Besides eliciting mayhem, the unmasking of "Mr. M." mobilised revised appreciations of "Bill Miller".

Identities, then, can be established by revelation, and this may also serve to resurrect identities that have died. As Ernest puts it:

> Don't be surprised if Big Bill does go back to a mask someday if his pursuit of the title flags down a bit. Only this time he'd probably assume a dual personality—and wrestle as a masked man in the same territory as the real Bill Miller.[36]

The observation permits an additional inference, *viz.* identity-work can also serve to offset the omnipresent risk of "going stale".

Identities have been worked up so well and appropriated so completely that they persist beyond the active career of the wrestler. Lou Thesz was a hero during his career,[37] and this identity persisted beyond his retirement. When a villain, Buddy Rogers, became "world champion", Thesz felt it was necessary to come out of retirement: ". . . Buddy Rogers' wearing the World's Heavyweight Championship belt was just too much!"[38] In 1962, Thesz did come out of retirement, "defeated" Rogers for the NWA crown, and had this to say:

> With Rogers out of the way, I feel that wrestling has taken a

big step towards eliminating a character with which wrestling has, to a degree, become identified in recent years. I am as proud of having helped to bring this about as I am of having won the title for an unprecedented sixth time.[39]

Terminations—There are two terminal points in the wrestling career: one, temporary and local; the other, permanent and total. Temporary local terminations have to do with movements away from metropolitan clubs, generally to other TV viewing areas. Taken together, such terminations, demarcating appearances of varying lengths, constitute the wrestler's itinerary. Wrestlers may stay with any given club for as short a time as two or, more usually, three months. Thus, Sailor Art Thomas, "a nice enough guy, but not very bright", in the words of a highly successful wrestler, will probably never learn to wrestle. Unskilled in identity-work, the "meathead" can never command audience appreciations for any extensive length of time. Art Thomas remained on Minneapolis cards somewhat more than two months. In contrast, the "Crusher" remained on the Twin City scene for two years, "cooled it" for a short time in Milwaukee, and recently returned to the Twin Cities, where his identity has been reworked from simple villain to the "good-bad guy"[40] A local teenager pressed a national best-selling rock-and-roll record, "The Crusher", featuring that erstwhile wrestler's current identity mark—the gravelly voice. This may well have contributed to his tremendous local appeal, since a large proportion of the wrestling audience is made up of teenagers.

Probably the success or failure of identity-work is the crucial variable determining temporary local terminations, but there are others. There is the matter of the overall strength of the card. Too many mediocrities—*not* failures—mean that the card must literally be "beefed up" and that some mediocrities must go. Wrestlers may, for various reasons, lose rapport with the local organisation. Won-lost records may become monotonic with a consequent loss of audience heat. Better offers from other clubs may lure the wrestler away. Finally, career contingencies[41]—the opening of the football season—may bring the wrestler's local appearances to a temporary halt.

Except for the wrestler who simply fails to become a draw, permanent and total terminations seem to be exclusively physical. By the mid-fifties, the bones become brittle, the spring is gone from the muscles, and it is better that the wrestler take his business elsewhere. This is precisely what he does. Wrestlers whose careers have persisted until this age are generally quite well off and have accumulated considerable business experience which they generally invest into proprietorships. However, there are more abrupt permanent and total terminations—compound bone fractures and fatal heart attacks. There are no data on the frequency or fate of wrestlers whose careers are ended by extensive physical damage, but Verne Gagne estimated that two or three of his associates, usually in their forties, die of heart attacks each year (the fate of "Georgeous George" Wagner, who died in December, 1963 at the age of forty-eight).

Side-lines—Wrestling, as we have said, is a side-line for some football players, though, when the shorter football career ends, wrestling may well become the central vocation. Yet, wrestling has its own side-lines. The successful wrestler often markets health products, such as vitamin preparations, on the side, and can use his TV appearances to promote those products. Indeed, in at least one case, the side-line became the sponsoring agency for the televising of local live wrestling bouts. Health clubs and hair salons are other examples of side-lines carried on profitably by successful wrestlers. And highly successful wrestlers have extended their promotional activities to boxing and horse-racing.

All wrestlers, however, receive some additional income from the sale of photographs. Consider this excerpt from a field report:

I had waited for about twenty minutes in the front office of the Minneapolis Club, when a smallish man in a neat summer suit came in and energetically began examining all the pictures of wrestlers covering three of the four walls of the outer office. Of approximately one hundred photos, he seemed to recognise all but three. When he didn't recognise a wrestler, he would call the secretary over to get the name. In all, he made her leave her work five times in the ten minutes he was there. He purchased two 8 in. x 10 in. glossy prints which the club stocks for the more avid fans. "What I do is put them in real nice albums," he explained. He asked the secretary for directions to a local pornography shop and left. When he was out of earshot, the secretary took off her glasses, put her head down on the desk, and laughed almost hysterically. We had both placed him as a homosexual, and she said that this sort of photo-collector is not rare, but that women purchase most of the photos, with high-school-age boys who have taken up wrestling running a close second.

All in all, for the players, wrestling is probably the most lucrative of American professional sports,[42] and certainly it is the one sport in which the athlete exercises greatest control over his own destiny. As Verne Gagne put it:

It's the only free enterprise left in America. You wrestle when you want to, whom you want to, and you take a vacation whenever you want to. You come to the match, and you bring your own soap and towel.

Our wrestling letter writer put it this way: "A 'Pro.' Wrestler or Boxer fights anybody, any time, any place, *if* the price is *right*."[43] And it usually is!

THE FASCINATION OF THE FANS

In the trade it is generally recognised that wrestling is entertainment or "show business". It is defended on that ground and rightly so. Catch-as-catch-can wrestling, as it was fought prior to World War I, could not hold the attention of large numbers of spectators, nor did that style of wrestling-in-dead-earnest permit the economic growth of the professional sport. Defenders of professional wrestling, however, draw a sharp line between entertainment and fakery. That wrestling is artfully contrived has, as we have shown, been established for a long time. And, if doubting Thomases persist, let them note that there are no acknowledged critics of the sport; there is little speculation about outcomes; there is no large scale betting; and there is no superstition among wrestlers.[44] Yet, there is a certain honesty about the deception, for the fan may anticipate, at least, that wrestlers will remain in character during their performances. If they do not, the show has not come off, and the fan is quick to register his protest.

Consequently, we can dispense with the distinction between fakery and entertainment. *Wrestling is drama*, and no member of the dramatic audience accuses the actors of misrepresentation. James Arness is not accused of fakery, when he appears week after week as Marshall Dillon, nor is Laurence Olivier disesteemed because he presents himself as a long departed Shakespearean hero. On the other hand, the response of the wrestling fan to the drama is rather more like that of the child at the Saturday matinee —audibly warning the cowboy hero that the villain lurks ahead in ambush—than the response of the critical viewer of the legitimate theatre. The fan is fascinated.

Many forces combine to establish this fascination. Matches are brilliantly staged,[45] but, as we shall see, the effectiveness of the staging is underwritten by the attitude of the audience. The audience comes to the arena primed for violence, or, more mildly, to see justice done. The entire drama emerges as a magnificent fugue. The theme is set by the match; the audience provides the contrapuntal impetus—a rule is violated; the referee doesn't notice; the crowd roars; the referee looks; the villain "covers up". I have also suggested that another contrapuntal passage may be established by the mockery of the fans by the wrestler,[46] and this is a powerful weld, for wrestling is one of the very few sports where the mutual recognition of the fan and athlete seemingly catches each up in an ascending spiral of affect. Indeed, in some sports, e.g. professional baseball, rather severe penalties are incurred by such recognition. At any rate, the fugue generally culminates in an awesome chorale—the main event. The fugue has run its course in a climactic, exhaustive, and probably exhausting[47] *denouement*.

It is not as though there is no expertise on the part of wrestling fans. Fans claim they can distinguish the "real" from the "fixed".[48] However, the very distinction coerces the fan into a defence of his fandom and tightens his attachment to the sport. As in any sport, the fan can distinguish play from display, or over-stepping the "practical norms" from over-stepping the "formal rules".[49] This makes him something of a critic. The audience can discern the "bad actor", but this is different from the villain. In wrestling, the villain must be a very good actor. As an example, in a "championship" bout witnessed by Ramon Oldenburg, the challenger—a villain —constantly failed to press obvious advantages and was greeted by cries of "chicken" from the audience. In the vernacular of hot-rodding teenagers, the challenger had veered off the course of confrontation—had "hit the shoulder"—too long before the collision was imminent. Villains, in the view of the audience, are not very convincing if they abandon their role too soon—before the climactic phase of the drama. In all this, the fan is not concerned, as Denney has so cogently observed,[50] with the story structure. He is rapt in identities.

Much drama *re*presents the activity of the larger society, and this is the case with wrestling. At the wrestling match, one can view and become caught up in *re*presentations of the class or status struggle, the eternal conflict between beauty and ugliness, the battle between the sexes (including the third and fourth sexes), the "cold war", or the bitter antagonism between local provincialism and cosmopolitan sophistication. Such struggles cut across the hostilities and loyalties of the nation and operate as powerful attractions for a heterogeneous anonymous mass audience, because all these struggles feature one common denominator—the universal agony of morality, the passionate tension between good and evil. For this reason, the drama of wrestling is best conceived as a passion play.

Nevertheless, the drama of wrestling does not catch up all the members of society. The spectators of wrestling are drawn from clearly definable segments of the population. There are, first of all, the deviants, but our estimate is that these represent a relatively small proportion of the wrestling audience. They include homosexuals, voyeurs, women with a perduring hostility towards men, and the "touchers". The latter came to our attention in an observant conversation with a knowledgeable fan:

I talk "homesy-folksy" about imaginary problems, and we become good friends, because I listen well. She tells many incidents about her hated high school book-keeping teacher whom she disliked intensely "because he was too free with his hands". This business of touching bodies was brought out again, when she talked about other female wrestling fans who like to touch the wrestlers as they walk by. They seem, she insisted, to like to touch sweaty bodies after the matches, more so than dry bodies before the matches.

A larger block of fans is made up of teenagers, and, while there are no first hand data on them, as many as one-eighth of those attending wrestling matches may be teenagers. For the bulk of the audience we have more precise data.

Characteristics of the adult audience—Several years ago, in 1958, a survey of 566 adult married residents of the Twin City metropolitan area was completed.[51] The sample was not a random sample of the population, but an analytic purposive quota sample which selected approximately equal numbers of respondents in each of twenty-four cells generated by the cross-tabulation of four variables: sex, age (over and under forty), residence (urban-suburban), and socio-economic status (upper, middle, and lower). Among the questions asked was: "When you hear the word 'sport', what activities do you think of?" Fifty respondents— almost one-tenth of the sample—mentioned wrestling.

Unlike mentions of most sports, sex proportions were about the same—9.5% of the men mentioned wrestling, as did 8.2% of the women. Residence showed a somewhat greater discrepancy with 10.6% of the suburban residents mentioning wrestling, compared to 6.9% of the urban residents, but that difference is not statistically significant. It is a different matter for age and socio-economic status. The proportion of older respondents mentioning wrestling (11.7%) was almost twice the proportion of younger people (6.1%), and the largest proportion of mentions was found in the lower socio-economic stratum, as Table 3–1 shows.

TABLE 3–1.

Proportion of Respondents in Three Socio-Economic Strata
Making Spontaneous Mention of Wrestling as a Sport

Stratum	Per cent	Total in Stratum
Upper	6.8	192
Middle	6.0	183
Lower	13.6	191
Totals	9.0	566

These data indicate that wrestling is a salient sport for older, lower-status people and that women, although not significantly differentiated from men in this respect, are probably over-represented in comparison to the attraction that other spectator sports ordinarily hold for them. That this latter contention is likely is confirmed by Vance Packard, who has reported that "a Nielsen check of TV fans watching wrestling matches revealed that ladies outnumbered men two to one".[52] Moreover, the sports editor of the *St. Paul Dispatch*, commenting on the avidity of wrestling fans, surmised that fewer complaints would follow the failure of the sport page to report major league baseball results than the failure to report wrestling results. When his paper did occasionally fail to report wrestling matches, about seven of every ten complainants, in his estimate, were women. Recently, local TV sportscasts have also reported wrestling results as an acknowledged result of fan pressure.

In combination, age, sex, and status generate the largest proportion of respondents mentioning wrestling as a sport. Almost a fifth (19.6%) of forty-six older lower-status women mentioned wrestling as a sport. This proportion was followed by older, lower-status men (16.0%); then, by younger, lower-status men (12.8%). One other category of respondents contributed more than 10% of its numbers to those who mentioned wrestling as a sport: 10.6% of the older, upper-status women. However, there is a possibility that the women in that category included amateur college and high school wrestling in their ken, and this is most unlikely for the lower-status respondents. Whether or not this is the case, lower-status is the definitive characteristic of those for whom wrestling has saliency as a sport. This has also been confirmed by an interview conducted with the matchmaker of a local club. He expressed some guilt about the considerable sacrifice made by most people who attend wrestling matches, and spectators in the most expensive seats appear to be those who can least afford it. Status is followed by age and sex, respectively, as differentiating variables, but the three variables operating conjointly generate the greatest relative frequency of those who include wrestling in their conception of sport.

Fans—Among the fifty respondents who mentioned wrestling as a sport in our Twin City survey, thirteen were classified as fans. These people either mentioned wrestling as a sport activity first, claimed wrestling as their favourite spectator sport, or explicitly identified themselves as wrestling fans.[53] The social characteristics of these fans did not differ markedly from those of the larger wrestling audience. Again, the convergence of sex, age, and status placed the largest number (five) in the category of older, lower-status women. Only two other categories—older, lower-status men (two) and younger, lower-status women (three)—included more than one fan. The remaining three fans were scattered. One was a younger, lower-status man; another, an older, middle-status man; and the last a younger, middle-status man. There were no upper-status fans.

Intensive analysis was made of the interviews taken with these fans. This established the relatively low education of the fans compared to the larger audience. Specifically, no middle-status member of the larger audience had acquired less than a high school education, while one of the two middle-status fans had not completed high school. In the lower stratum, the difference was not as striking, but was, nevertheless, in the same direction. The average years of school completed for the lower status audience was 9.1 years; for the fans, 8.5.

Fans relied mostly on TV for their information about wrestling. For seven of them, TV was their most important source of information; for four, attendance at the matches; and for the remaining two, the newspaper. This finding, of course, is hardly startling and is quite logically congruent with the other characteristics of the fans, the sparse reportage given professional wrestling by the press, and, of course, the way in which the drama is promoted.

An additional finding disclosed by the interview analysis is of particular significance. Fans are people who rely more than others on appearances in their assessment of people. They seldom seek to penetrate the facades and masks that the members of our society conventionally offer to others in their day-to-day encounters.

Besides raising questions about sport, the interviews taken with the residents of the Twin City area focused on the variety and use of status symbolism in the anonymous situations of urban life. Respondents were asked:

If you met a stranger downtown and took a strong personal liking to him (her), what kinds of things would you want to know about him (her) before you would invite him (her) to your home?

Afterwards, they were asked how they would secure such information. It is this latter question that is pertinent here. People can either be subtle about such matters, e.g. by engaging the stranger in seemingly unrelated conversation; they can be blunt, i.e. by employing direct questions; or they can rely on appearances. Of course, any or all of these approaches may be used in combination. None of the wrestling fans relied exclusively on the blunt approach; four were primarily subtle and indirect; but nine depended primarily on appearances to provide the information they desired about the stranger. In short, there was a pronounced tendency for the fans to accept appearances at face value. Moreover, this seems to be generally characteristic of lower-status people. The same questions were asked of 125 adult respondents in Lansing, Michigan. In that study, more than a third of the lower-status respondents (38.1%) used observation to validate their inferences about the hypothetical stranger, compared to 11.8% of the middle-status and 21.9% of the upper-status respondents. Lower-status respondents resorted least often to subtle probing—23.8%, compared to 60.8% of the middle-status and 62.4% of the upper-status respondents.[54]

The "mentality" of the wrestling audience—Pulling together all the information we have assembled on the wrestling audience and fans permits considerable insight into the attitude of the wrestling spectator, into just what it is that is interpreted at the match or on the TV set.

As we have shown, those who make up the wrestling audience are predominantly lower-status, and, as such, their stance is probably pervaded by what Lipset has termed "working-class authoritarianism". He points out that:

The social situation of the lower strata ... predisposes them to view politics in simplistic and chiliastic terms of black and white, good and evil.[55]

Later:

All of these characteristics combine to produce a tendency to view politics, *as well as personal relationships*, in black and-white terms, a desire for immediate action without critical reflection, [and] impatience with talk and discussion . . .[56]

To the extent that this is the "set" of the wrestling spectator, then, he (she) comes to the match primed for the active immediate struggle between good and evil. Nor is he concerned with the development of the plot:

> This concern with the immediately perceivable, with the personal and concrete, is part and parcel of the short time-perspective and inability to perceive the complex possibilities and consequences of actions which is referred to ... as a lack of social sophistication.[57]

The wrestling spectator is *rapt by the identity* of the wrestler *at that moment* and *in that place*. Moreover, in the counterpoint of the match and audience response, the relationship is personalised and further concretised, thereby heightening the rapture. That the lower-status person sees the world in black-and-white terms also helps explain why the greatest audience "heat" is generated "not so much [in] the indeterminate moments of the contest ... as the moments in which one contestant is very much ahead",[58] and why the long hours of indecision in many of the bouts carried on before World War I failed to hold the audience.

Recently, Lipset's observations of working-class authoritarianism have been criticised on the grounds that the authoritarian perspective is more a function of inadequate education than working-class membership, although the two variables are highly correlated.[59] How this constitutes a critique somewhat escapes us, since Lipset explicitly stated the priority of education over occupation as a determinant of authoritarian attitudes.[60] Nevertheless, low education does seem to play a more influential role in establishing the authoritarian perspective than does occupational status, and this permits the inference that our remarks about the wrestling spectator are all the more true of the fan. His lower education increases the probability that he has come to the match in the authoritarian attitude.

Lower-status persons seldom question the concrete world about them. Consequently, they are more susceptible to staging than persons on higher status levels. Indeed, among the middle-classes, individuals often see staging where there is none. "Why do they have these things at this time of day?" queried the middle-class lady, inconvenienced by the time of a solar eclipse. We suspect, too, that Candid Camera is most successful with working-class people and children. Lower-class people have less control over staging and are less familiar with it.[61]

There is evidence for this. As a part of a study of dress, 172 married men and women were shown a picture of a woman with an emphatic bust-line clad in masculine-appearing dress and pre-senting a masculinised hair-do. Twelve per cent of the respondents misplaced the woman as a man, but this proportion included 16.8% of the lower-class, 9.8% of the middle, and no upper-class persons.[62] In other words, more than people in other strata, lower-status persons seem inclined to believe that people are what they appear to be. This being the case, we can deduce that wrestling spectators and, especially, wrestling fans believe that the wrestling hero is *really* good and that the villain is *really* bad, particularly if the identity-work has been well done.

This reliance on appearances also increases with increasing age. With reference to the picture discussed above, 6.6% of the younger respondents misplaced the woman as a man, 11.5% of those between thirty-five and forty-seven years of age, and 20.0% of those forty-eight years of age and older.[63] Although a second portrayal depicting a man clad in the jacket and skirt that is common male attire in southeast Asia, but feminine appearing to unsophisticated Western eyes, elicited no marked status differences in sex misplacement, age differences persisted. Almost a third (31.8%) of the respondents misplaced the man as a woman, and this propor-tion included exactly half of those forty-eight years of age and older, but only 26.2% of those in the middle age range and 23.0% of the young respondents.[64]

There were no significant sex differences in these misplacements of sex (as we would expect, men were more often "taken in" by clothes than women, themselves skilled in the arts of deceptive dress), but there is some reason to suspect that women are more easily deceived in other areas of life than men. Specifically, Bloch, in his discussion of the "con-game", mentions that about 10% of the victims of the "long con" (where the "mark" must leave the scene, collect his money, and bring it back to the scene) are "repeats", and most of these are elderly women.[65] Geis has also noted that middle-aged women are frequent marks.[66] Despite the fact, then, that women see through clothes more easily than men, they are not unsusceptible to apparent misrepresentations. On the other hand, we suspect that much more research must be done to develop a convincing explanation of the appeal that wrestling has for the female spectator.

Lower-status and older age, therefore, generate a whole complex of social and social psychological conditions which both ready most spectators for the harsh violence of the match and lend a credibility to the performance which is difficult to comprehend in other social circles. Most spectators are prepared for a bloody clear-cut struggle between good and evil (in whatever form) in which an overwhelming victory will be won from whatever quarter, for the victory of either good or evil serves, in the final analysis, to reinforce the sentiments that are expressed by the audience. Unaccustomed to questioning appearances and extremely susceptible to staging techniques, the great majority of the audience is caught up by the rhetoric of the match and establishes strong identifications with the performers. This is all the more the case with the fans whose social characteristics render them even more prone to the fascinations of the drama.

The rapturous devotion of women to the sport is more difficult to explain. Though they can be conned, there are other features of staging with respect to which they display more sophistication than do men. On the other hand, in our society, women are the traditional custodians of morality, and this may account, at least in part, for their captivation by the blatant struggles between good and evil in the wrestling ring. There is some probative support for

TABLE 3–2.

Sex Differences in the Degree of Importance Attached to
"Morality" In the Appraisal of Social Standing

Importance	Males		Females		Totals*	
	Number	Per cent	Number	Per cent	Number	Per cent
Very Important	131	48.1	175	60.3	306	54.4
Important	113	41.5	96	33.1	209	37.2
Unimportant	28	10.3	19	6.6	47	8.4
Totals*	272	99.9	290	100.0	562	100.0

$^2 = 8.89$ .05 $p < .02$

* Two men and two women did not respond to the question. They are not included in these computations.

this contention in our interview materials. When we asked our Twin City respondents how important "morality" was in their assessment of other people's social standing, we found that women attached significantly greater importance to morality than did men. The findings are presented in Table 3–. However, even these data may be misleading. When we examined social class differences in the importance attached to morality, differences approached, but did not meet our criterion of statistical significance. In this case, the greatest differences were provided by lower-status respondents who played down the importance of morality in greater proportions than could be expected by chance. Moreover, sex differences in these respects were not characteristic of lower-status respondents. Finally, we found that, of our thirteen wrestling fans, only three felt that morality was "very important" in appraising the status of others. When we compare that proportion (23.1%) with that for the sample as a whole (54.4%), we see immediately that we are treading on dangerous ground if we employ these data to explain the fascination that the sport holds for its followers. The mystery of lower-status *feminine* rapture continues to elude us.

CONCLUSIONS

Yet, wrestling cannot be construed as a con-game. At least there is no larceny in the heart of the fan, though there may well be mayhem. Wrestling is a drama, and, concerned as it is with morality—the breaching and upholding of moral codes—it is perhaps best conceived as a passion play. It is a passion play, however, in which the plot is irrelevant, and only the character of the cast of characters matters, together with the "passion" that the characters must undergo. For the audience has little concern with the sequence of events, but is very much concerned with the concrete persons who enact them and the agony that they suffer for the punishment of their sins or the vindication of the good life. Moreover, the audience *believes* in the performers, and the belief is passionate, mobilised by simple and powerful sentiments. In short, they *don't* give a damn if it (the match) is a fake! Kill the (*really* evil) son-of-a-bitch!

NOTES

1 Except as noted otherwise, I have relied on various encyclopaedia accounts for my discussion of ancient, pre-industrial, European, and Asiatic wrestling. The sources are standard, and I have not included them in my list of references.

2 Phillipe Ariès, *Centuries of Childhood*, translated by Robert Baldick, New York: Alfred A. Knopf, Inc., 1962, p. 93.

3 *Ibid.*, p. 93.

4 With the exception of a few encyclopaedia references, I am almost totally dependent upon Marcus Griffin, *Fall Guys*, Chicago: The Reilly and Lee Co., 1937, for the early history of wrestling in the United States. On general matters and with reference to incontestable events, I have not cited page references. Quotations and references to materials which might be disputed do provide page references. Of course, responsibility for the interpretation of Griffin's materials is my own.

5 Drama, like work and play, is found in all sport, as in the dramatisation

of fouls in basketball. It is a question of which predominates, and, of course, why.

6 George A. Barton, *My Lifetime in Sports*, Minneapolis: The Olympic Press, 1957, p. 304.

7 Marcus Griffin, *op. cit.*, pp. 27-8.

8 *Ibid.*, pp. 24-5.

9 Reuel Denney, *The Astonished Muse, Chicago*: University of Chicago Press, 1957, p. 112.

10 Possibly World War I contributed in a minor way to the shortage of suitable contenders.

11 Marcus Griffin, *op. cit.*, p. 50.

12 See the excellent account by Kirson Weinberg and Henry Arond, "The Occupational Culture of the Boxer", *American Journal of Sociology*, LVII (March, 1952), pp. 460-9, which is also included in this section of the Reader.

13 In discussing his weigh-in tantrums and "I am the greatest" front, Clay noted it all started while watching a wrestling programme on television. "There was this wrestler. I think his name was Gorgeous George. He was shouting, 'I'm going to annihilate the bum, kill him, pull his hair. He better not show up'." AP dispatch, Minneapolis *Tribune*, Sunday, 30 January, 1966, p. 35. After the Clay-Liston fiasco, the professional wrestler, Verne Gagne, observed, "Now, *we're* legitimate".

14 Marcus Griffin, *op. cit.*, p. 56.

15 In a letter to my colleague, Scott McNall, dated December 22, 1965, a professional wrestler, whose name shall remain anonymous, writes: "In order to see if one is really good sometimes it is necessary to 'shoot' a match. *That is when the best man really wins and these are hard nights for a wrestler to work. He must win and still look good, not an easy thing to do. The crowd must be pleased at all costs so a 'shoot' is used only when necessary.* Much more than most people think however." (Italics mine.) Such shooting matches are overwhelmingly *arranged*, and my guess is that the double-cross is extremely rare. The wrestler has too much to lose. This is a commentary on the business enterprise, not on the ability of wrestlers. There are many cases of sceptical observers whose challenges were quite effectively met by professional wrestlers. A local sports editor has told me about one of his staff, a two hundred pound ex-marine, who challenged a local wrestling mediocrity. The challenge was met, and the ex-marine was pinned in a matter of seconds.

16 Marcus Griffin, *op. cit.*, p. 170.

17 *Ibid.*, p. 107. Griffin was writing in the depression years, so the seventy thousand dollar gate is doubly impressive, and he was writing about New York, where wrestling has never enjoyed the success it has enjoyed in other parts of the United States. As early as 1911, some 25,000 fans paid $87,00 to watch Gotch defeat Hackenschmidt in Comiskey Park. (cf. George A. Barton, *op. cit.*, p. 305). Probably the largest gate that professional wrestling has enjoyed occurred in 1961, also at Comiskey Park, where 34,995 fans paid $127,000 to view the Buddy Rogers-Pat O'Connor match.

18 *Ibid.*, p. 89.

19 However, gossip columns in wrestling magazines devote considerable space to establishing the "real" identities of popular wrestlers. This game of "Guess Who?" is interminable and probably contributes in some indeterminable way to the rapture of the fan.

20 Letter to McNall, *op. cit.*

21 These figures and the figures below are taken from popular accounts in *Readers' Digest* and *Look* magazine.

22 *Wrestling Facts*, Volume 1 (10 October, 1964), St. Paul, Minnesota, p. 4.

23 George A. Barton, Minnesota Athletic Commissioner, "Letter to the Editor", *Minneapolis Tribune*, 8 January, 1966.

24 It will become evident later on that interest in the televised matches, particularly in fringe areas, cannot be maintained without the promotion of live matches. Actually, the live match and the canned performance mutually enhance one another in the eyes of spectators.

25 Letter to McNall, *op. cit.*

26 *Ibid.*

27 The danger of "going stale" is one of the distinct career hazards of the popular wrestler, i.e. one who may wrestle on an average of five to six times a week for as many as forty-eight weeks of the year.

28 Kenneth Burke, *A Rhetoric of Motives*, New York: Prentice-Hall Inc., 1950.

29 Davied Riesman, Nathan Glazer, and Reuel Denney, *The Lonely Crowd*, New York: Doubleday Anchor Books, 1953, pp. 157–61. In the Twin Cities there is a regular alternation between Minneapolis and St. Paul sites.

30 Letter to McNall, *op. cit.*

31 *Ibid.* Note well that they are often hired by other wrestlers.

32 The nuances of these problems have been best portrayed in the plays of Pirandello and the novels of Malcolm Purdy, but see especially Nigel Denis, *Cards of Identity*, New York: Meridian Books, Inc., 1960.

33 Gregory P. Stone, "Appearance and the Self", in Arnold Rose (ed.), *Human Behaviour and Social Process*, Boston: Houghton Mifflin Co., 1962, p. 93.

34 *Ibid.* pp. 93–6 and p. 104.

35 Max Ernest, "Why Big Bill Miller Wore a Mask", *Wrestling Confidential*, I (July, 1964), pp. 15–17 and 62–3.

36 *Ibid.*, p. 64.

37 Indeed, a local sportswriter fantasised nostalgically that Thesz was the last of the "real" wrestlers.

38 J. R. Hogan, "The Real Reason Why Lou Thesz Returned to Wrestling", *ibid.*, p. 53.

39 *Ibid.*, p. 55. Ed "Strangler" Lewis held the previous record of five championships. I have placed "defeated" in quotes to indicate some scepticism about all this. Since his retirement, Thesz has never wrestled in California, which forbids wrestling competition after the age of fifty. Moreover, Thesz's purge of the wrestling ring has not been extensive. At this writing, "Mad Dog" Vachon still rules as world champion of the AWA.

40 A depiction taken from Martha Wolfenstein and Nathan Leites, "The Good-Bad Girl", in Bernard Rosenberg and David M. White (eds.), *Mass Culture*, Glencoe, Illinois: The Free Press, 1960, pp. 294–307.

41 Howard S. Becker, "Some Contingencies of the Professional Dance Musician's Career", *Human Organisation*, XII (Summer, 1953), pp. 22–6.

42 As an example, a confidential report on one top U.S. wrestler, estimates his annual *salary* (as opposed to income) at $35-40,000. In addition, he maintains an incorporated foundation for physical fitness, a health product company, and has other enterprises. His home is estimated at $60,000 and his net worth at $150,000 to $200,000. My guess is that

these are gross underestimates, but the reader should compare this economic position *and* length of career with that of any other professional athlete. Mickey Mantle comes to mind. His salary for the 1966 season has been reported at $100,000. He broke into the minor leagues in 1949 and joined the Yankees in 1951. Older than Mantle, the wrestler referred to here has wrestled for fifteen years, but, in contrast to Mantle, he is still going strong.

43 Letter to McNall, *op. cit.*

44 Kirson Weinberg and Henry Arond, *op. cit.*

45 On staging see Erving Goffman, *The Presentation of Self in Everyday Life*, New York: Doubleday Anchor Books, 1959; and Edward Gross and Gregory P. Stone, "Embarrassment and the Analysis of Role Requirements", *American Journal of Sociology*, LXX (July, 1964), pp. 1–15.

46 Gregory P. Stone: "American Sport: Play and Dis-Play", *Chicago Review*, Vol. 9, No. 3 (Fall 1955), pp. 83–100. See also Part I of this Reader.

47 I use the word "exhausting" advisedly. Considerable empathy is established among fans. At one match I attended, my observations were perpetually interrupted by the grunts, groans, and elbow smashes of a young man in an adjoining seat. These empathic responses reached their peak during the main match.

48 Reuel Denney, *op. cit.*, p. 133.

49 *Ibid.*, p. 134.

50 *Ibid.*

51 For making possible the analyses of these data, I am indebted to a grant provided by the Graduate School of the University of Minnesota.

52 Vance Packard, *The Hidden Persuaders*, New York: Pocket Books, Inc., 1957, p. 73.

53 Only three respondents explicitly identified themselves as fans, and I suspect a status block here: To acknowledge wrestling fandom is to acknowledge lower status. Consequently, I have extended the definition of wrestling fandom to include first mentions and acknowledgment of wrestling as a favourite sport.

54 William H. Form and Gregory P. Stone, "Urbanism, Anonymity, and Status Symbolism", *American Journal of Sociology*, LXII (March, 1957), pp. 512–13.

55 Seymour M. Lipset, "Democracy and Working Class Authoritarianism", *American Sociological Review*, XXIV (August, 1959), p. 483.

56 *Ibid.*, p. 495.

57 *Ibid.*, p. 494.

58 Reuel Denney, *op. cit.*, p. 133.

59 Lewis Lipsitz, "Working-Class Authoritarianism: a Re-evaluation", *American Sociological Review*, XXX (February, 1965), pp. 103–9.

60 Seymour M. Lipset, *op. cit.*, p. 489.

61 One reason, of course, is simply that the symbols used in staging cost money. Clothing and furniture serve as examples, and these are ordinarily purchased. If we think of such items as constituting a kind of vocabulary of apparent symbolism that is implemented in the staging process, we can see that the vocabulary of the lower-status levels is limited indeed. That they often must wear hand-me-downs underscores the paucity of their staging vocabulary.

62 Gregory P. Stone, "Clothing and Social Relations", unpublished Ph.D.

dissertation, Department of Sociology, University of Chicago, 1959, p. 36.
63 *Ibid.*, p. 35.
64 *Ibid.*, p. 34.
65 Herbert A. Bloch, *Man, Crime, and Society*, New York: Random House, 1962, pp. 578–9.
66 Gilbert L. Geis, *The Big Con*, New York: Signet Books, 1962, p. 116.

PART III (D)

CONFLICT AND SOCIAL CONTROL IN SPORT

Introduction

Competition, conflict and the outbreak of violence are common features of social life. They, or at least the potential for them, are built into its very fabric. The field of sports is no exception. Fights among players and riotous behaviour on the part of spectators are almost everyday occurrences. On this account, they pose important problems for the sociology of sport. The two articles in this section are concerned with this type of issue. They are essentially exploratory in character and do not pretend to present final or definitive solutions to the problems which they tackle. In their own way, however, each of them advances our understanding and provides a number of useful leads for further research in the field.

In "Notes on Inter-Group Conflicts in International Sports", Kalevi Heinila discusses the contrast between ideology and actuality in the field of international sports. Sports, he notes, have been proclaimed as one of the most influential peace-producing agencies of our time, yet conflict and controversy are as much the norm in international sports as peace and harmony. It is therefore important, he argues, for us to gain more knowledge of the causes of such inter-group conflicts if we are to secure a position where international sport can begin to perform the functions stressed in the sports ideology. His paper makes a start in that direction by discussing some of the conceptual and theoretical issues which the subject raises. He bases his discussion on insights derived from small-group theory in social psychology, the work of Muzafer and Carolyn Sherif on problems of group harmony and tension and George Caspar Homans' studies of the elementary forms of social behaviour.

According to Heinila, it is not really surprising that sports are frequently accompanied by conflict and tension. They are competitive in character, and competition, by its very nature, is susceptible to controversy and the arousal of conflict. There must be losers, and losing in a sports event can lead to severe frustration if the losers have a high investment in victory, possibly of an emotional and not necessarily of a material kind. However, by itself, he argues, competition is not always a sufficient cause for conflict. Sports have the capacity to evoke strong feelings of group identification among players and spectators. Where this happens, processes of "in-group" and "out-group" formation occur in which groups glorify themselves and denigrate their rivals. Heinila maintains that such processes are especially conducive to conflict in situations where the groups involved are already strongly prejudiced against each other and where the flames of prejudice are fanned by ethnocentric reporting in the press and other mass media. He suggests, however, that not all sports and types of sporting competition are equally prone to the arousal of conflict. Conflict is most likely in connection with team sports and dual international competitions, i.e. those in which only two countries are involved. It is far less likely in connection with sports such as tennis which only involve competition between single individuals, because sports of this type do not appear to lend themselves so readily to strong feelings of group identification. It is also less likely in "multipolar" international contests such as the Olympic Games. In such cases, group identifications tend to be diffused and "defused", thereby losing some of their "sting". Contests of this type are not a question simply of "my country" *versus* a "hated rival" but of "my country" *versus* many rivals. One's own country may well lose but so may its most hated rival. The chances are that in many cases, the winners will be drawn from countries towards which one is neutral.

"Football Mad": A Speculative Sociology of Football Hooliganism" by Ian Taylor is also concerned with conflict and problems of social control. It is an analysis of the part played by football in the subculture of the British working classes. Taylor's central concern is to explain why football "hooliganism" first became viewed as a serious "social problem" during the 1960's. Similar types of crowd behaviour, he notes, had occurred previously, but had not evoked such widespread concern. The reason, Taylor suggests, is to be found in contemporary changes in the game which threaten the interests of traditional football supporters. These changes are leading specific groups among them to react in ways which are viewed as threatening by the powers that be inside and outside the football world.

Professional football was first developed by and for the working classes. Clubs, Taylor argues, were originally representative of working class groups and players and fans were characterised by common class membership. There was a close relationship between them and it was not threatened by the small wages received by early professional players. They had no reason to reject the working-class culture which had nurtured them, but served as representatives of its core values. Players, managers, directors and fans were all engaged in a kind of working-class "participatory democracy" in which the supporters' club played an important role. The central objective of this "democracy" was to ensure victory for the team and thus to vindicate the subculture and its values.

According to Taylor, it has been seriously threatened by post-war changes in the game. Faced with falling gates, the clubs and the Football League have begun to inject new elements of competition into football in order to increase its excitement and crowd-pulling power. They have entered international competitions and introduced new domestic competitions such as the Football League Cup. They have also begun to "bourgeoisify" the game in the sense that they have become more concerned with making a profit, than with simply representing the working-class groups which originally nurtured them. At the same time, they have abolished the former wage system in terms of which players were not entitled to more than a specified maximum wage and have devised means for making the game appeal to a wider cross-section of the public. In this connection, they have introduced glossy magazines, marketable mascots, clothed their teams in more "with it" playing strips, and begun to emphasise spectacle, skill and efficient performance in the game rather than mere victory.

These changes, Taylor argues, have been traumatic for members of the working-class football "subculture", especially for those who have been left out of the increasing affluence of our time by virtue of the fact that they are unemployed, unemployable or downwardly socially mobile. Such people constitute what he calls a kind of "subcultural rump". It is they, he argues, who principally engage in behaviour which the authorities designate as "hooliganism". Their response to current changes is ambivalent. They welcome competition with foreign teams because it offers the chance to vindicate the values of their subculture in a wider field of competition. But they resent the highly paid, sports-car driving, "jet-setting" modern player, because he appears to have severed his links with the working classes. Above all, they resent the fact that the game is changing in ways beyond their control. The decision to internationalise and "bourgeoisify" football was taken without their consent. Much of their so-called "hooliganism", Taylor suggests, is a more or less rational attempt on their part to reassert the control which they believed they could formerly assert in helping their side to achieve victory. Shouting, chanting, singing, throwing stones, bottles and beer cans at opposing players are more or less rational ways, he argues, of attempting to put them off their game and to increase their own side's chance of winning. Running on to the pitch when a goal has been disallowed, may be a way, he suggests, not only of expressing disapproval but of magically attempting to persuade the referee to reverse his decision. Being caught and escorted from the ground by the police is a way of telling players and managers who the *really genuine* supporters are and that they have abandoned them by introducing undesirable changes into the game. For their part, however, the authorities interpret such behaviour as a threat to changes which, on the one hand, they have been forced to make by economic circumstances and which, on the other, they regard as desirable since they believe they make for a better game. Thus, the fact that football "hooliganism" was identified as a significant "social problem" for the first time during the 1960's does not present any insuperable problems for sociological analysis. It is, Taylor suggests, the inevitable result of a clash of values which has come about because of the ways in which the game is currently being changed.

CHAPTER 16

Notes on Inter-Group Conflicts in International Sport*

Kalevi Heinila

According to the ideology of sport and especially that of the Olympic movement, one of the fundamental functions of international sport is to promote international understanding and goodwill among the youth of the world. Sport has even been referred to as one of the most influential movements for peace. No doubt the history of international sport and that of the Olympic Games provide numerous examples of the functions of sport for building ties of friendship between the different countries, but evidence to the contrary, though not perhaps as much, can also be provided. International sport has often played its part in producing controversies, conflicts and even the interruption of relations between nations. In the peace-loving and cool-tempered North, for example, the history of track and field contests between Sweden and Finland has long been characterised by a "cold war" atmosphere. In the 1930's, this erupted into open conflict, resulting in the interruption of athletic competition between the two countries for several years. More recently, this kind of "ultimate resolution" of competitive sport has been widely discussed in the newspapers. The potential threat of conflict and disharmony in international sport hardly needs any further indication.

It is important for the development of international sport and for the realisation of the goodwill function contained in the sports ideology that we secure more knowledge about those situational factors which (i) contribute to the promotion of international understanding and (ii) appear to lead to inter-group conflict. The study of these opposing situations is surely advisable since the best practical policy for promoting international understanding would be to aim at optimising the favourable conditions and at minimising those conducive to conflict. As far as is known, there is a lag

* Reprinted from *The International Review of Sport Sociology*, Vol. 1, Warsaw, 1967.

in scientific exploration in this area. Nevertheless, inter-group conflict in international sport has been the focus of a considerable amount of discussion and thinking by intellectuals and by international bodies.[1]

It is important to document the literature on this subject for the possible stimulus it may have on much needed research. Further, fruitful theoretical approaches and working hypotheses may be found in the area of small group studies, especially those of the group dynamics school and of social psychologists such as Muzafer Sherif.[2] The theories and studies of collective behaviour are also worth mentioning as sources of reference.[3]

By its nature, competition as a social process is susceptible to controversies and conflicts. Competition tends to reward exclusively but to frustrate inclusively or, putting it another way: in competition there is only one winner but many losers. In a series of well-known small group experiments, Deutsch observed that unfriendly inter-individual relations were more typical of competitive than of co-operative groups. Competition, by its very nature, may sometimes be a sufficient cause for conflict but this is not invariably so. We must also look for other factors.

In the view of this writer, one of the more favourable conditions for potential conflict in international sport is a situation of strong group-identification on the part of the two adverse parties. In sociology, this process is referred to as "in-group" and "out-group" formation. According to Sherif, "when groups engage in reciprocally competitive and frustrating activities ... unfavourable stereotypes come into use in relation to the out-group and its members. In time, these unfavourable stereotypes are standardised in a group, placing the out-group at the prejudicial distance. ... Concomitant with the rise of mutually prejudicial attitudes between groups, self-glorifying or self-justifying attitudes towards the in-group are strengthened. The performance of the out-group is deprecated and the moves of the out-group and its members are perceived in a suspicious light."[4]

By definition, in-group attitudes are based on strong feelings of belongingness and on strong identification with the group. In certain situations, however, this we-feeling gets exaggerated and becomes ethnocentrism (i.e. chauvinism, to use a more familiar term). Open conflicts are more or less certain in situations of in-group and out-group cleavage, especially in the more distinct phases of such a process.[5] Jones gives a striking description of in-group and out-group formation in the sphere of international sport. He writes, "... the thousands of spectators and sometimes the players as well, seem to behold a mighty contest between their 'country' and the 'enemy'. The national prestige is at stake; a victory is no longer the success of the team that could play better but becomes a national victory and is an occasion for national rejoicings out of all proportion to reality. Such an attitude is *not* favourable to international understanding."[6]

As Sherif states, the competitive system as such is vulnerable to the arousal of in- and out-group attitudes. Operating in the same direction and reinforcing ethnocentrism are certain other situational determinants such as the national stereotypes held by the opposing parties which may involve distinctive differences regarding, for example, the historical, cultural, political and social conditions of life. In spite of sports ideologies, players and spectators often act, more or less consciously, in terms of their citizenship roles. They often comply with these roles in a manner completely alien to their sports ideologies and frequently loaded with national prejudices and stereotypes which are often intentionally activated by manifest symbols such as flags and anthems or by cheer-leaders. It is probable that prejudice and antagonistic attitudes dictated by compliance to the role of citizen feed back into group solidarity and identification or, to state this in terms of an hypothesis: the greater the strength of attitudes towards the out-group, the greater the strength of in-group solidarity, the more probable ethnocentrism and chauvinism and likewise inter-group conflicts. It is also reasonable to expect that in- and out-group attitudes will reinforce each other in a circular fashion, i.e. group solidarity strengthens attitudes towards the out-group and again, attitudes towards the out-group have a feed-back effect, reinforcing in-group attitudes.

It is a matter of common observation that team sports are more attractive for spectators than individual sports. Kleinman's study points this out and indicates further that in team sports conflicts are more probable than in individual sports.[7] It seems to be psychologically easier for the public and spectators to identify with a team than with an individual participant just as it is more conventional to say "our team won" rather than to say "our Paavo Nurmi" won. It seems likely that the most favourable conditions for strong group identification and for the formation of distinct in- and out-group attitudes—and thus for inter-group conflicts also—are offered in an international dual contest. Because the universality of participation and of spectatorship in the Olympic Games does not provide such a positive basis for national identification the potential for conflicts in these games is rather insignificant.

The great expansion of spectator sports in the more urban and industrial countries probably reflects the acute identification problems which detached, "lonely-crowd" people have. It probably reflects as well their urgent need to look for and to define their individual identities in terms of a group affiliation, however superficial or imaginary it may be. Spectators are looking for some way of obtaining vicarious success and for some form of positive identity. They often secure this identity by identifying with a team or with individual athletes with whom they have something at least in common and by generalising their victories into victories for all. Caillois' theory runs in the same direction when he writes: "The majority fail in competition or are ineligible to compete, have no chance to enter or succeed.... The majority remain frustrated. Everyone wants to be first and in law and justice has a right to be. However, each knows or suspects that he will not be, for the simple reason that by definition only one may be first. He may therefore choose to win indirectly, through identification with someone else, which is the only way in which all can triumph simultaneously without effort or chance of failure."[8]

It is not only the athletes and the teams that win or lose but also at the same time the public and the spectators, or all those who share a common identity. "Well, aren't we Finns really good," boasted an old man long ago when hearing about Paavo Nurmi's superiority in the Olympic Games.

The higher the expectations of teams and of the public with respect to success, the more frustrated will the "in-group" be in case of failure—and the higher the probability of unfair behaviour and inter-group conflict of some kind or another. Newspapers and other media of mass communication are often loaded with ethnocentrism and are inclined to awaken unrealistic expectations among their sports publics. Created beliefs in national success and superiority are conducive to strengthening group identification and to furthering in- and out-group cleavages among the spectators and teams—and this, once again, increases the probability of intergroup conflict. The development of this kind of atmosphere can often be clearly observed in a dual competition on the national level when the teams have an equal chance of victory and when each one represents its country as a reference group with respect to social life as a whole, including the sport itself. For instance, Sweden is related to Finland in the following way: these countries are roughly equal in strength in many fields of competitive sport and, from the point of view of Finland, Sweden functions as a "reference group", i.e. as a basis for comparison and evaluation in the cultural, economic, and educational spheres of life. As far as contests between the teams of these two countries are concerned there has been, and surely will continue to be, a characteristic heightening of emotionality and involvement, strong in- and out-group formation, and consequently, a susceptibility to controversies and conflicts of all kinds. It is also worth mentioning the effect of a large number of new national records in this connection. On the other hand, in the contests in various branches of sport between the Soviet Union and Finland, the distinct formation of in- and out-group attitudes has been quite foreign, mainly due, perhaps, to the great differences between the two countries, e.g. in social structure and in size, which makes comparisons, evaluations, and any other functions of the Soviet Union as a reference group irrelevant. For that reason, it is not "degrading" to lose to a team from the Soviet Union, but it is quite frustrating and, to use Rene Maheu's words, almost like a "national defeat" to be beaten by a Swedish team. Contrariwise, it is a greater cause for satisfaction and joy to beat Sweden than it is to beat the Soviet Union—at least if this writer's interpretation of national feelings is right.[9]

There are, of course, other situational determinants independent of group identification which are also frequently connected with the conflict potentiality of international sport in modern times. The professionalisation of sport, mainly due to the heightened level of demands to which participants in championship sport are exposed, results in an upgrading and overevaluation of victory and success. This tendency is further reinforced by the extensive publicity given to championship sport. Interpreted in terms of Homan's "exchange theory", professionalisation means increased "investments" and "costs" for participants and likewise, increased reward expectations proportional to the greater investments and costs. From his proposition on "distributive justice", the potentiality of a conflct situation can be deduced. Homans states this in the following terms: "The more to a man's disadvantage the rule of distributive justice fails of realisation, the more likely he is to display the emotional behaviour we call anger."[10]

This tendency towards upgrading victory along with changes in the intrinsic and extrinsic nature of rewards as a result of the professionalisation of championship sport contributes to unfair behaviour and disloyalty to rules. It also leads in similar fashion to the development of inter-group conflicts. This is more likely now than it was in the days of real amateurism in the past.

The potential for inter-group conflicts—which is inherent in competition as such but especially in international sport—is worthy of serious attention by the authorities in international sport. But first of all, it requires serious study and this underlines the very purpose of this paper.

It has been proposed that some trends in international sport have been conducive to an increase in conflict potential. As a situational determinant, the extensive involvement and exposure of the public to international sports events seems to be one of the main conditions for group-identification and ethnocentrism, thus rendering the situation vulnerable to inter-group conflict. Further, the heightening level of demands as a necessary condition for success and the concomitant "totalitarianisation" of each national sports system as it strives for international glory tend to upgrade victory to the extent that the temptation to behave unfairly and be disloyal to the rules, and hence also conflict, is likely. The concept of the totalitarianisation of a national sports system refers to the fact that success in international competition is no longer, as it was in the past—in the era, for example, of Paavo Nurmi—a matter of individual effort and the resources of the participant but instead a matter of the effectiveness and total resources of the whole national sports system: this can be taken to include human reserves in sport, the level of sports sciences, the efficiency of organisations and of training systems etc. In other words, the success and effectiveness of the individual athlete or the single team depend more and more on the resources and effectiveness of the total systems of national sport and less on individual effort independent of the system as a whole.[11] Little attention has been paid so far to this trend and its consequences but surely they are worthy of serious consideration and study.

The expansion of spectator sports all over the world indicates that, today, even those sections of populations who have not themselves taken an active part in sport and who, for that reason, have not had the ideology of sport and the norms of "fair play" impressed upon them, are now interested and involved in sport as enthusiasts and "identifiers". However, the extension of active participation in sport noticed in many countries probably mitigates the trend mentioned above: one of the most effective ways to learn and internalise the ideals and conduct proper in sport is surely active personal participation. These ideals can still be found by anybody who participates as they were by Roger Bannister who said: "Sport has an individual basis and an individual meaning, and is not a national or moral affair."

One basic and generally recognised condition for the actualisation of the goodwill and friendship function of international sport is absolute loyalty to the written and unwritten rules. The recent action of the International Council of Sport and Physical Education in creating the Pierre de Coubertin Trophies for promoting fair play in competitive sport certainly exemplifies the type of policy needed from the international authorities in sport and physical education. However, some empirical data indicate that there hardly exists sufficient consensus concerning norms of fair play and on the conceptions of behaviour proper in various competitive situations, not even among the athletes themselves.[12] If this is true among the athletes, it can probably be expected that even greater variations in these conceptions are held by spectators and sports authorities. In this light, the action of the ICPSE would seem to be somehow premature. An identification and a clarification of the very concept of fair play is first needed and then this must be followed by a common recognition of and commitment to the clarified principles and norms by the international authorities. Until these steps are taken, rewarding and promoting actions hardly seem appropriate. Disagreement about rules and different interpretations of "fair behaviour", provide situations in which potentially open conflict is inherent. It can only be eliminated by means of a statement of specific common rules and proper conduct.[13]

There is some evidence that too great a deviation from the norm of "equal terms" tends to mitigate proper competition and may lead to an increase of conflict as well. On this point, the author disagrees with Jones when he says: "In sport, it is quality that counts and not the quantity. This is probably the most important factor behind the great development of international sport. A small country has an even chance when competing against large countries."[14]

The author's proposition is that it is the total efficiency and the total resources of a national sports system which count most and this surely is a factor which favours the larger countries.[15] In the near future, this trend in international sport might become even more apparent: as a deviation from equal terms it might result in an unexpected realignment and reorganisation of international sport. It might even threaten the current organisation and status of the Olympic Games. In any case, changes in the social system of international competitive sport are probably tending towards a situation in which the vital norm of "equal terms" will be appropriately realised. A study of recent changes in the competitive contacts between different countries, regarding size of country as an independent variable, could test and would probably disprove the author's proposition concerning the primary importance of "equal terms" as a determinant of competition. Such a trend study might well be carried out by some research institute with adequate resources.

This kind of prediction must only be regarded as a conjecture given the present level of knowledge in the sociology of sport; it may, however, be worth consideration. In spite of the increasing potential for inter-group conflict in international sport, Jones' statement is still as valid as ever when he says: "Sports may, indeed, become a tremendously positive factor for improving international understanding. All those engaged in sports may become agents of goodwill between the peoples of the world. Theirs is a great opportunity. It is the sacred responsibility of all sportsmen that this opportunity shall not be missed."[16]

NOTES

1 For useful contributions on this subject, see e.g. R. W. Jones, *Sport and International Understanding*, report of the Unesco Congress "Sport —Work—Culture", Helsinki 1959, pp. 159–70; and G. D. Sandhi, *New Forms of International Cooperation*, report of the I.C.S.P.E. Conference, Paris, 1963, pp. 31–7.

2 M. and C. W. Sherif, *Groups in Harmony and Tension*, New York, 1953; M. Sherif (ed.), *Intergroup Relations and Leadership*, New York, 1962.

3 N. J. Smelser, *Theory of Collective Behaviour*, London, 1962; M. Deutsch, *The Effects of Cooperation and Competition Upon Group Processes*; D. Cartwright and A. Zander (eds.), *Group Dynamics*, Evanston, 1953.

4 Sherif, *op. cit.*, p. 10.

5 According to Catton's theory, ethnocentrism is conditioned by group solidarity, the conformity of members, and by group effectiveness. In this connection, it is relevant to note that, in line with Catton's theory, ethnocentrism increases the probability of conflict with the out-group or results in the withdrawal of the in-group from interaction with out-groups. This hypothesis is supported by many instances in the history of international sport. See R. W. Catton Jr., "The Functions and Disfunctions of Ethnocentrism: A Theory", in *Social Problems*, Vol. 8, No. 3, 1960–61, pp. 201–11.

6 R. W. Jones, *op. cit.*, p. 163.

7 S. Kleinman, *A Study to Determine the Factors that Influence the Behaviour of Sports Crowds*, mimeo. dissertation, Ohio State University, 1960, p. 45.

8 R. Caillois, *Man, Play, and Games*, Glencoe, Ill., 1961, p. 120.

9 The hypothesis of the significance of reference-group countries as a condition for ethnocentrism might be elaborated in line with Galtung's very interesting "structural theory of aggression" based on the concept of rank disequilibrium with reference to the various dimensions of national resources. See J. Galtung, "A Structural Theory of Aggression", *Information*, 1, 1964–65, pp. 15–38.

10 G. C. Homans, *Social Behaviour—Its Elementary Forms*, New York, 1961, pp. 72–8.

11 One can become convinced of the role played by the national training system on the success and effectiveness of an individual sports unit by becoming acquainted, for instance, with the system prevailing in the Soviet Union and in other leading countries. See, e.g. N. Ozolin, "The Soviet System of Athletic Training", in E. Jokl and E. Simon (eds.),

International Research in Sport and Physical Education, ICPSE, Springfield, Ill., 1964, pp. 468–78.

12 The author is conducting some explorative factor analyses on the various conceptions held by young athletes and students of physical education on fair play in competitive sports.

13 The specification of fair play norms calls for international co-operation. Efforts in this direction have, of course, already been made but much more needs to be done. See e.g. P. Martin, "Introduction to the Charter of Sportsmanship", Report of the UNESCO Congress, *Sport—Work—Culture*, Helsinki, 1959, pp. 122–4.

14 R. W. Jones, *op. cit.*, p. 160.

15 This trend can be clearly seen in the track and field finals of the 1965 European Cup. The six countries qualifying for the finals were the Soviet Union, England, France, Poland, East- and West-Germany.

16 R. W. Jones, *op. cit.*, p. 170.

CHAPTER 17

"Football Mad": A Speculative Sociology of Football Hooliganism*

Ian Taylor

Inter-personal and property vandalism in and around professional football grounds is currently running a close second to political deviance in Grosvenor Square in the "Top Twenty" of society's social problems. These, at least, are the placings reflected in the mass media and in the murmurings of society's appointed social commentators. The sociologist's suspicions would already be aroused were it not for the fact that Howard S. Becker has already articulated for us the lack of symmetry between the subjectively-defined and the *real* social problem.[1]

As sociologists, we cannot assume that any objective increase in the amount of physical and property violence in soccer has, in fact, occurred during the 1960's. Most histories of football are quite explicit both about the violent origins of the game and about its association with social conflict throughout the course of its development.[2] Bearing this in mind, the discussion of "soccer violence" which follows can usefully be opened by making two substantive points—one methodological, the other empirical;

(i) Consistent with Becker's concern to develop a "natural history" approach to social problems,[3] we might attempt to explain the ways in which football has achieved its current status as a subjectively-defined social problem.[4] The importance of such an approach would lie in its capability of enabling us to understand that the social problem is here to stay. That is, the widespread subjective awareness of "the problem on the terraces" among the members of social and penal agencies will continue to produce

* This essay is an expanded version of a paper read under the same title to a national symposium on the sociology of deviance held at the University of York on 2 November, 1968. Many of the examples used here derive from the recent history of Sheffield Wednesday, a part of the author's social world. Hopefully this is forgivable in a paper that calls itself, "speculative": I am assured that the examples used could be replicated with examples from other clubs.

increasing numbers of football "hooligans" in the criminal statistics; and this will produce "objective" evidence of the continuing "social problem". Government reports and psychological investigations will be important in confirming the "objectivity" of the problem. In other words, we might, in adopting such an approach, want to claim that society, through its agencies of social control, is creating its problem of "football hooliganism" in precisely the same way that it created its problem of "mods" and "rockers".[5]

(ii) In our desire to emphasise the ways in which social problems develop, we might be led to ignore the fact that there are empirical differences between the violence in football in the 1960's and the violence which characterised earlier stages in the game's development. However, an adequate theory of violence in football cannot afford to ignore these differences. Most obviously of all, the invasion of the playing pitch by the spectator is quite clearly a new development.[6] As John Arlott, an experienced sports commentator, has written:

Collective memory suggests that this practice began about eight years ago. When McPheat equalised for Sunderland in their Sixth-round F.A. Cup-tie against Tottenham Hotspur in the 1960–61 season, a mob of boys rushed across the ground. They were seen on television, which provides an unwitting but powerful encouragement to others.[7]

Moreover, it has been suggested that the techniques adopted by the spectators in willing their teams to victory are substantially different from those of the early fifties and, even more markedly, from those of the inter-war years. The use of songs and catch-phrases derived from contemporary mass-culture is widespread and, more directly, the use of noise in an attempt to distract a goalkeeper's attention, especially when he is taking goal-kicks.

It may well be that these techniques are in themselves responsible for the reactions from clubs and from society at large to terrace behaviour and that, as such, they represent the beginnings of the social problem. That is, attempts by the crowd to influence the results of matches (by invading the pitch, influencing goal-kicks) may be seen as illegitimate normatively in a spectator sport. It may be that the clubs (and responsible agencies) in response to the techniques adopted on the terraces, are asserting that football is, always has been, and always must be, a *spectator* sport. To this, of course, it might be objected that football clubs characteristically do not reject the vocal and financial support of their supporters on the terraces or the ongoing cultural identification in the clubs and pubs. It might also be objected that the identification of the football supporter with his club is recognised widely as qualitatively different from the expectations we have of spectators in other sports. In other words, it might be objected that "everybody knows" that football is *more* than a spectator sport.

Nevertheless it is clear that it is precisely at the point of attempted intervention by supporters in the focal concern of the club—the match and its result—that the cultural manifestation of support is rejected. Statements from clubs are currently differentiating between the "hooligan"—the supporter who attempts to intervene— and the "real" or "genuine" supporter who doesn't. Our empirical concern suggests immediately that the function of these new techniques of vociferous support and intervention is not simply to enhance the enjoyment of a Saturday afternoon's entertainment but is rather to influence the actual result of the game. It is an attempt to assert *control*. We shall go on to argue that the general welfare of a club—particularly its success in League and Cup—and, often, too, the results of particular games are important in the social world of the subcultures associated with football teams, particularly of those teams which draw their support from urban working class areas. Apart from the commonplace that the failure of teams in important matches can result in drops in industrial productivity in the area during the following week, it may well be that these results will define the social experiences of supporters for long periods of time, until, for example, the opportunity to recover esteem arises in another important game. It may also be the case that traditional sociologies are inadequate for examining these processes.[8] But it is certainly true that a major theme in industrial sociology—that of occupational choices defining leisure pursuits— will have to be turned on its head to encompass the football supporter whose choice of occupation follows from, and does not precede, the examination of a season's fixture list.

In general, the concern of this paper is to argue that it is useful to use the notion of *control* in order to understand the nature of the violence and the changing techniques of support manifested on the terraces. It is even more illuminating to see this attempt at control as connected with the changing functions of football matches—and football supporting—for urban working-class communities. Such an approach offers some possibility of explaining both how "football hooliganism" has come to be subjectively defined as a social problem and also why any real or objective increase in "hooliganism" that may be found has occurred. As an approach, it is quite different from contemporary attempts to develop typologies of "hooligans". Our concern is to understand why society should have this social problem *now*, why society finances this kind of investigation *now*—and did not previously—and why the problem *has* to be seen as linked with processes in the wider society. Easy generalisation about "violence in society at large" is not involved in our approach. John Harrington, however, the Research Director of a team of psychologists recently appointed by the Minister of Sport to examine soccer "hooliganism", sees evidence of an increasingly violent society in a set of psychological characteristics exhibited jointly by "Vietnam Solidarity Campaign" demonstrators and arrested football "hooligans". He warns:

> The most interesting thing from our point of view is that even stable people with good backgrounds can get carried into a situation of violence, and it's a situation of no return.[9]

The type of approach adopted by Harrington offers little hope of explaining the development of football as a social problem. Presumably there have always been people of high emotional instability going to football matches, in conditions of overcrowding and in situations of potential "mass hysteria". In fact, during the inter-war years, the immediate post-war years and the early fifties, attendances at matches were higher and conditions of accommodation worse than they are now. But it was always thought safe and sensible to send young children to matches—with sixpence for entry and threepence for pocket money—in those periods.[10] It was felt to be the solution to the social problem of what the working classes should do with their offspring on a Saturday afternoon rather than a source of socially problematic violence and hooliganism. But now we are informed that the presence of emotionally unstable hooligans makes some grounds—or, more cautiously, some parts of some grounds—unsafe for the "genuine" young (or old) supporter. However, this kind of explanation requires further elaboration before it can be taken seriously.

There is just one more different approach which merits consideration before proceeding further, since it currently attracts both the egghead journalist and the gutter pressman. It may receive some academic attention in time, if only because it does purport to explain soccer violence in terms of the *changing* social context in which professional soccer is played. This is the "racial" diagnosis, the notion, for example, that Southern American football players are "neo-Lombrosian throwbacks"—"animals", in the words of Sir Alf Ramsey. Such a diagnosis has been purveyed, for example, by Brian Glanville, an egghead journalist for one of the "posh" Sundays:

The present, cynical Argentinian violence is something quite novel, something quite coldly applied, rather than something which erupts in the heat of the moment. If you automatically fell a man as soon as he goes past you, as Argentina's defenders did in that World Cup match against England at Wembley, if you spit in the face of an opponent as Racing's players did, from the first, against Celtic last year, you are acting from calculation rather than passion.[11]

Usually, articles of this kind—and there has been a spate of them in 1968—qualify their social anthropologies with observations about the ambiguous behaviour of Nobby Stiles, Billy Bremner or Jimmy Johnstone in such-and-such a match abroad, or about the confusion over interpretation of the rules among the governing bodies of the game. But these qualifications rarely extend to comparative analysis of the game's functions in different cultures and sometimes alterations to the British game derived from abroad, like the introduction of the substitute rule, are systematically interpreted as essential to British conditions.[12]

The important point for present purposes, however, is that the *contamination* thesis—the notion that violence, along with "unfair play", was imported from abroad—is entirely confused with the useful thesis of professionalisation and internationalisation, a thesis which attempts to describe the structural changes in the game since the war. We shall want to argue that these structural changes reflect changes in the wider society and that they impinge on the social world of the football supporter, both in his activity within the game and in his activity outside it.

We can state briefly what is meant by the notions of professionalisation and internationalisation. They are used very schematically and cautiously in this paper. They are derived from the sociologies of "mass society" where they have often been used very incautiously. Just as in the 1950's the cinema industry attempted to preempt its falling popularity as mass entertainment by introducing "3-D", "Cinemascope" and then "Spectaculars", at around the same time, professional football introduced floodlit games, glossy magazines, marketable mascots and international competition. The intentions of the innovators were unambiguous: to introduce into the industry new elements of competition and thereby excitement —ideologically equated with crowd-holding power. That is, the ideological concern was to give diversity and interest to the season in a way which "bread-and-butter" League games were unable to do.

Now the success of commercial ventures in entertainment is

dependent on publicity and, where the entertainment is available only locally, it is very much dependent on the local press. The prospect of international football at the local stadium was one which attracted much support in the press offices. The cosmopolitan spice—and the chauvinistic possibilities—held out more hope of "a story" than the unending succession of League games and the associated "minor injury" traumas. Informally, then, in areas where international competition was introduced, the press participated in the redefinition of local football as "professional" and "international". The press and the "genuine" supporter were to be at one in defining as focal interests: conflicts over the rules of the game, the merits of the "4-2-4" formation, and the styles and tactics of teams playing their football some thousands of miles away. The concerns of club management were bound up with these interests, too, but were unambiguously economic concerns in origin.

It is against the background of this process of professionalisation and internationalisation that a dynamic theory of football "hooliganism" is possible. Not only does international professional football provide spectacle and colour,[13] but it also provides an arena in which the football supporter can demonstrate the merits of his subculture and fight it out with the world in full view of the back pages of the press and with Kenneth Wolstenholme evaluating his performance.[14] That is, the professionalisation of football meets a democratic response from its "electorate" and this response is a demand for control and for participation in the struggles which the club is waging.

Let us now proceed to specify the elements of this theory. Historically, while it is true that the regulation of football was initially achieved in the public schools,[15] the establishment of professional football and the moves which led to it were carried out within the working classes. The great majority of the League Clubs of today grew out of the concern of groups of working men to develop their primary-group relationships in what leisure-time they had. Many of these clubs grew directly out of autonomous occupational groups. For example, Sheffield United was started by a group of "little mesters", cutlers in the small workshops of Sheffield[16]—a derivation reflected in their nickname, "the Blades"; West Ham United was started by a group of workers at the Thames Iron Works and Manchester United by workers on the Lancashire and Yorkshire railway.

Other clubs grew out of corporate, rather than autonomous working-class groups. From the institutions created by Victorian society for the moral and educational betterment of the "dangerous classes" came Everton (St. Domingo's Sunday School), Queen's Park Rangers (Droop Street Board School), Wolverhamption Wanderers (St. Luke's Church School) and Sunderland (the District Teachers' Association). From the military section of Victorian society came Arsenal (a team of workers from the old gunnery), and Third Lanark (from the regiment of the same name). And from corporate neighbourhood groups came Tottenham Hotspur (originally a village team which played on the Tottenham marshes) and Chelsea (formed from a group of drinkers in a Fulham pub). These illustrations of the working-class subcultural origins of the clubs could be augmented considerably with data on the numerous clubs, particularly from small northern communities, which could not withstand the developing competition from larger conurbations and were either amalgamated or dropped from the League. Recent examples of drop-outs from the League suffering from these characteristic problems include Accrington Stanley (proximity to Burnley and Blackburn) and Gateshead (proximity to Newcastle United and Sunderland).

The relationship which developed between player and supporter within the professional football club has been ignored by sociologists but widely written up in journalism and in fiction.[17] These accounts are usually nostalgic and impressionistic and need systematisation. We can specify, however, that the relationship was initially characterised by common class membership and that this was not threatened by the small wages the early part-time professionals received in addition to their wages from work. Even with the introduction of full-time professionalism—it was legalised in 1885—the income of professional football players did not deviate markedly from that of the successful working man. The "ideal—typical" footballer was the local boy who made good. Fame was the reward; the fortunes few. In the soccer subcultures of the working class, it was expected that the local lad would not reject the subculture which had nurtured him and that he would be available for comment in pub and club on some regular basis.

Research into the relationship of the subculture to the club management has not yet been carried out but again it is possible to speculate that this relationship was a close one and that, typically, it was not threatened by different class membership or value-orientations. Certainly during the inter-war years, the prestige accorded to club directors and managers was high. Moreover, the contrast with the ambivalent attitudes of the subculture towards directors and clubs in contemporary football and the poor esteem accorded to most contemporary football managers is suggestive.[18] Hopcraft has written about the attitudes of directors and the petit-bourgeois origins of most of them, though he does not examine at any length their relationships with the supporters.[19] There is a mass of anecdotal evidence, however, to suggest that in the inter-war years, the managers and directors of football clubs, informally, and formally (through Supporters' Clubs), were involved in what was regarded by the subculture as a participatory democracy.

These relationships were formed within the working class itself. They were associated with a set of autonomously working-class values, values born of struggles and isolation, victories and defeats. From the set of values familiar in this history—and in the sociologies of Brian Jackson, Richard Hoggart and others[20]—the ones most relevant to the football subcultures within the working class were those of *masculinity, active participation,* and *victory.* Associated with these primary values, we shall suggest later, were beliefs in *fate* and *magic.*

There is no need to examine here at any length the derivations of masculinity as a focal concern. It has been dealt with exhaustively in sociological studies of the working-class family and community. Control as a focal concern, and its dimensions of participation and domination, forms part of the central thesis of this paper. However, a few words about the focal concern with victory will be in order.

There is no doubt that in the "real" world (i.e. in the empirical experience of the football supporter) victory *is* a focal concern. It is a commonplace that most supporters (whether of subcultural connections or not) place a higher value on victory in the weekly game than they do on the manner of its achievement. (This is not to deny that certain styles of playing—and of achieving victory— are more attractive and more likely to draw large crowds than others.) However, the fact that victory appears empirically to be the central focal concern should not be taken for granted or assumed. It requires sociological explanation. The emphasis on victory in soccer contrasts markedly with the concerns of other, usually middle class sports like Rugby Union and hockey where, even in competitive leagues, victory rarely assumes the status of a *central* focal concern. An explanation of the centrality of victory as a focal concern may best be located in the value-orientations of the work-situation and in the social class positions and experiences connected with it.

Even in the sociologies which emphasise the permeation of subcultures by dominant social values and the inter-penetration of subcultural values themselves,[21] there is the recognition of situational solidarity and "autonomy". In terms of subcultural theorisation, for example on delinquency, it is accepted that while it is unhelpful to conceive of an autonomous delinquent subculture possessing a set of quite distinct and ideal-typical values, it is nevertheless important to understand that, during a "drift" into delinquency, a set of values and orientations can solidify which are reminiscent of the subcultural idea. We would want to suggest that this process might be highly important in a culture like that of Britain, where a distinctive class structure has deposited a folk-tradition of working-class lore and custom, transmitted through subcultures like that of football.

Part of the burden of this paper is to argue that there exists a subcultural "rump" which is the carrier of these folk-traditions and that it is around this rump that the "solidifying"—the assertion of these values—occurs. The solidifying of the supporters around the rump can result in emphasising victory as a central focal concern, precisely because the distinguishing characteristic of the rump is its isolation from, and antagonistic relationship towards most of the institutions of the wider society—(e.g. work in industry, the school system, the law, etc.). Given that victory over these social institutions is normally impossible (except perhaps in terms of periodic strategic successes—a successful strike or theft in industry, mental breakdown brought about in teachers, discharge from court, etc.), the value finds expression in alternative arenas of which football is one important example.[22]

This highly schematic explanation will be no more satisfactory to sociologists than was Miller's explanation of autonomy in the American working-class adolescent.[23] One of the features of the working-class adolescent's world as depicted by Miller, however, was the deference exhibited by the adolescent to dominant social groups and a reluctance on his part to enter any confrontations with them. We would want to explain this in terms of the social control exercised within formal social institutions and thus to emphasise that where social control is not so highly institutionalised, as on the football terraces, the assertion of the value of victory over dominant social groups (the "bourgeoisie" of the football culture) is a possible response.

While, to a degree, the game may have functioned for the vast thousands of amateurs as relaxation and escape from the alienation of work, or in the schools as a means of character training, it was transformed at the professional level unambiguously into local struggles. In the very early days, before aristocrats and gentlemen finally opted for rugger, these struggles were veritable class struggles, for example, the games between Blackburn Rovers and Old Etonians. Later, however, the games came to reflect local rivalries nurtured particularly in the working-class communities of the north, rivalries which can still be observed where the working class is organised by district, for example, in the Miners' Lodges of the Durham Coalfield. In these games, it mattered a great deal who won, but not too much how the game was played. The horizons of these communities were such as to define an extremely catholic view of method:[24] methods which were legitimate in the struggle with the employer or the local constabulary were certainly legitimate in showing the way home to the team from down the road.

The players were the public representatives of this working-class subculture. They were expected to behave in a certain way when away from home. This is still the case to a certain extent though, strangely enough, the best example probably comes from cricket, namely the glee taken by the working-class cricket lover from South Yorkshire in Freddie Trueman's continual "disagreements" with the M.C.C. They were not expected to behave like "pansies" on the field and there was a value defining the seriousness of injuries sufficient to merit attention. In some cases, a broken ankle only just qualified. Most important of all, however, was that the player should see himself as responsible to the subculture or at least that he should participate in perpetuating the illusion of sub-cultural responsibility. Like the M.P. with his fortnightly "surgery", the football player had to appear at the latest pigeon race or darts match prizegiving for fear of attracting suspicion or scandal.

All this may appear a highly impressionistic representation of the value-orientations of working-class communities but it cannot do great violence to more systematic analyses to specify more closely the notion of control as a general value-orientation. The control was of the kind most highly valued in the working-class community: that which had grown up in the industrial work-group, the trade union, and the neighbourhood community and which had been given strength by the presence of outsiders in the shape of "boss" and "cop". The successful public representative—the footballer—when being "controlled" by the subculture, was being informed of his historical obligation to be at least an affiliate member of this working-class democracy.

The term "control" is used in two senses in the text of this paper. Each of them refers to the social context of football, i.e. to its status as a focal concern of a working-class subculture and to the goals of that subculture, particularly the goal of victory. Control is produced by the subculture's social situation and assertive of its values.

Initially, control is taken to refer to the expectation that the club (players, directors and manager) will participate in subcultural discussions and activities. Later it refers to the attempt by the subculture (or what we call the "rump" of the subculture) to exert control over—to dominate—the club, thus obstructing its "bourgeoisification". These two meanings—the first of which, for brevity's sake, might be understood as *participatory* control, the second as a *reactive* demand for *dominatory* (hegemonic) control—seem to this author to be dimensions of the same value, that is, the value placed by the subculture on the control over its external environment and focal concerns. The respective concrete expressions reflect the different contexts in which control is seen as an objective possibility by the subculture. That is, the expressions of participation or domination can be explained in terms of the differential distribution of power within the football club and the extent to which this distribution is visible. In the inter-war years, the illusion persisted that power—over the future of the club and particularly over the possibility of victory—was distributed between management, directors, players and the subculture, all of whom were seen as standing in some kind of unambiguous relationship to the working class of the area as a whole. In this context of power that was diffuse and thus relatively invisible, an assertion of participation—in the choice of team and the evaluation of performance—was characteristic. In the professionalised and bourgeoisified football of the 1960's, however, power has been alienated from the subculture and—it shall be argued—is exercised in terms of the values of the "genuine" supporter. A reaction-formation in which a dominatory power is demanded is now characteristic, there being no longer any illusion of partial control or participation. In sum, there is every justification for retaining the notion of control in this speculative paper, provided that the distinct dimensions of control in distinct social contexts are recognised.

Professionalisation and, later, internationalisation were responsible for destroying, slowly at first, more traumatically later, the illusion of participatory control. In the inter-war period, the changing structure of the game came to demand that the football player sever his links with the subculture. Certain technical developments in the game—the introduction by Arsenal of the "stopper" centre half, the abolition of the rule tying the goalkeeper to his line—came to distinguish the professional from the amateur game and to demand from the professional a dedication to full-time training and a disciplined use of leisure.

It would not be especially productive to attempt to date precisely these stages in the game's development or in the changing relationship between players and subculture. But it is clear that the *traumatic* changes were associated with the period of social reconstruction after the second war. The need for distraction in this period, particularly in the bombed out cities of Northern England, was partly answered by the provision of League football games on a vast scale. Importantly, this need for distraction was felt across the class structure: the lack of leisure facilities in post-war Britain was important for the middle as well as for the working class. It was widely observed that the clientele of the football ground in the late forties and early fifties was much more socially representative than it had been in the pre-war days. The support given to local football teams now came from the working-class football sub-culture *and* from the men awaiting their place in a reconstructed society.

Even before the abolition of the maximum wage, the illusion of control came under threat. Most immediately, the definition of control associated with the "ideal-typical local boy made good" was strained as clubs bought their way to success in the transfer market in the hope of ensuring financial stability in an industry which was clearly going to decline. There were periodic attempts to assert this definition of control by the subculture. As late as 1958, meetings were held in Sheffield to protest at the impending transfer from Sheffield Wednesday to Manchester United,[25] of Albert Quixall, known locally as "the Golden Boy".

Attempts to assert these definitions were, however, doomed to failure, since there was always a certain ambivalence in the sub-culture's response to transfers. Teams which sold also bought, thus strengthening the team "belonging" to the subculture. There were no protests in Sheffield in 1951 when the Wednesday bought Jackie Sewell from Notts. County at the then record fee of £34,000. The subculture was at one with the management in recognising the "centre-forward" problem that had arisen from the accident to local wonder boy Derek Dooley in that year. There were no protests, but there was a period of ambivalence, a testing-period in which the new arrival was scrutinised both on and off the field of play.

But in terms of our analysis, professionalisation does not consist simply of entry to the transfer market and the beginnings of large transfer fees. It is also the process whereby clubs began to accommodate themselves to their changing role in a declining entertainments industry. Developmental processes in the wider society were increasing the leisure opportunities of an increasingly differentiated working class. Football was competing for customers over and above the football subculture. In one sense, this was a technical question involving the provision of covered accommodation, increasing the number of seats, and most obviously, the fitting of floodlights to enable evening matches to be played. In another

sense, however, the process involved a transformation of the stereotype of the football supporter. Where once the stereotypical supporter was a working-class man, living for Saturday and
inextricably involved—in his own perception—with the fortunes of
the club, now he was of undefined class membership, enjoying an
escape from responsibilities, the provision of a spectacle from time
to time, and expecting fulfilment of these needs from a team of
professional entertainers. Not only did this compare very closely
with the changes made almost simultaneously in the cinema industry, and with the changes made in the stereotype of the
cinemagoer—the move from the local "flicks" to the local ABC
and from Ronald Regan Westerns to sophisticated sex spectaculars
—but it also "bourgeoisified" the game in a similar way. From the
participatory and masculine values of the working-class supporter,
and from an exclusive concern with victory, football turned its
attention to the provision of spectacle, skill and efficient performance—values understood to be important to the stereotypical
"genuine", i.e. middle-class, supporter.

Cinema and football alike can be understood as culturally-
available opportunities of escape from work in the negative sense
or, more positively, in the psychoanalytical sense for escape into
fantasy. The functions of leisure have been explored in this way
by others[26] and here it may suffice to recite the commonly heard
terrace statement, "I could have blown that one in", with its
implicit fantasy components of the type associated with certain
films—"Just me and Sophia Loren alone on this desert island".
Certainly, to approach the "bourgeoisification" of football in this
way, as a process whereby attendance at a previously working-class
occasion was legitimised for the middle class, seems useful. Clearly
to attend the Saturday game is no longer simply an activity of the
Andy Caps: the Brian Glanvilles and the Professor Ayers of this
world are also unashamedly interested. Similarly, it is no longer
necessary to go to the cinema in disguise to fulfil one's fantasies:
James Bond is "good family entertainment" and everyone will
want to see "Barbarella".

This identification of post-war professionalisation as a process of
"bourgeoisification" should not lead the thesis presented here to
be confused with that of "embourgeoisement" now receiving such
a searching examination at the hands of Goldthorpe and Lockwood.[27] The process described *here* is one which legitimises previously working-class activities for the middle class or, more
accurately, activities which previously were *seen as legitimate only
for the working class*, such as watching doubtful films and con-
gregating on the Kop. But this process *has* involved an overall

bourgeoisification of the culture of the cinema and of football, most particularly of football. There was never, after all, an autonomously working-class cinema: only a set of films thought appropriate for members of that class. Throughout this paper, however, we have been arguing that professional football did involve a set of autonomously working-class institutions: subcultures with their own traditions, folk heroes and social realities, preserved informally in memory and anecdote. In that sense, the process of bourgeoisification (professionalisation) has been particularly traumatic for the football subculture within the working class. It has been experienced most immediately in the changes of the environment of the subculture on match days. Bourgeoisification has involved the provision of amenities in certain parts of football grounds to the exclusion of others. Modern toilets, restaurants and bars have been concentrated in the stands. Seats have been built where once there was accommodation for the standing spectator. There has, in short, been intervention in the social structure of the ground. There have been changes, too, in the cultural ethos of the match day. The local works band has given way to popular records played over the public address system. The "strips" worn by the players and which are associated with salient matches in the subculture's collective memories have been altered—a change which has no obvious function other than to symbolise the *overall* cultural changes.[28]

Earlier, we stated that the response of the subculture to transfers was ambivalent. Now we can specify that the response to the changes in supporter provision and cultural ethos have been equally ambivalent. On the one hand, there is clearly a sense in which internationalisation was welcomed. The entry into and success of teams in international competition was experienced as subcultural success, as a vindication of traditional values and a continuation of an historical struggle in an extended arena. On the other hand, some of the associated cultural innovations are experienced as offensive to the traditions of the subculture encapsulated in memory and preserved by anecdote. The tradition is then reasserted. So, for example, the attempts of Vic Buckingham, Manager of Sheffield Wednesday, to introduce to the Sheffield crowd the more spectacular features of continental football—releasing team balloons before kick-off, players saluting the crowd before and after the game—met with derision and scorn, especially from the Kop end. The reassertion of traditional subcultural values can be seen in the local football press and heard at work, in pubs and at the ground itself when a team is not faring well. This reassertion would benefit from simple content analysis but again it may suffice here to recite one or two statements commonly heard on big League grounds. The statement, "What's the point of having an f . . . . g palace for a ground when we haven't got a team?" may stand as evidence for the bourgeoisification thesis and, perhaps most significant of all for the subculture thesis, the statement that was exceedingly common in the period immediately following the abolition of the maximum wage: "Hundred pounds a week! I wouldn't pay him in buttons!" On the one hand, the provisions made for the seven-and-sixer in the stand are resented: on the other, the sports-car driving, "jet-setting" inside forward is resented as a rather ambiguous public representative of the subculture.

It is important to note that what is being said here is that he is resented by the *subculture*. This is not to say that he is resented by the *crowd*. The social composition of the football crowd is undergoing processes of change and these reflect ongoing changes in the wider society. It is certainly not appropriate here to examine these changes in any depth and it is certainly not helpful, despite the trend in our argument, to characterise these changes simply as part of a process of bourgeoisification in society at large. It is, however, accurate to note that a process of structural and cultural differentiation is occurring in the working class. In structural terms, a distinction is developing between the employed worker, the unemployed worker and the unemployable worker. Within the ranks of the employed workers, cultural differentiations in the use of leisure (time not spent at work) can be observed: differential use of television, cinema, bowling alleys and night clubs; differential use of kinship and peer-group activities. One of the consequences of this differentiation is a drop in the affiliate "membership" of the *working-class* football subculture or alternatively, the adoption of temporary or irregular membership. Discrimination about attendance at games replaces compulsive identification and "ever-present" attendance.

But there is a rump, consisting of those left to carry locally the traditions of the subculture, which refuses to be seduced by worldly alternatives to the old type of ground and by the middle-class values which are being offered in place of the traditional working-class ones. We can hypothesise that this rump will include the unemployed and the unemployable, the downwardly mobile and the totally immobile, e.g. those from broken families who cling to neighbourhood ties in the absence of kin-involvements. These representatives of the subcultural rump have inherited an educational function in the subculture, a function of cultural transmission which is given considerable urgency by the catholic and critical values of the mass of the supporters.

The stand-dwellers are the target of much abuse from members of the subcultural rump in the local football press, abuse which characteristically is directed at the critical, "unfaithful" and rationalistic letters they—the stand-dwellers—produce for the very same column.[29] The stand-dweller is seen as seduced by the worldly values of spectacle and entertainment, values which are secondary to subcultural concerns. Where the stand-dweller has read Glanville on Ramsey, the Kop-ite can recite his team's forward line in 1935 and can compare the current representatives with those of that period, man for man. In the research report prepared for the Ministry of Sport, Harrington comments in a rather bewildered way that:

> We have been impressed by the amount of knowledge and memory for detail possessed by fans of limited intelligence and intellectual background.[30]

But the excellence of football education within the subculture is in danger: and mainly through teacher shortage. Where it was once true that people were socialised into constructing their social identities within that subculture and were accorded a status within it in accordance with criteria, such as attendance at away matches, and intensity of knowledge about crucial incidents in the team's history and progress, now, for the bulk of the supporters, such "Leslie Welch-like" qualities take subordinate place to qualities which contemporarily are more highly valued. It is only in certain pronouncedly traditional working-class areas that the name of Dixie Dean excites more response than that of Mick Jagger.

If we are correct in identifying the unemployed, unemployable, downwardly mobile and totally immobile as the adult reference group and educators of a subcultural rump, then we have identified precisely those groups in British society most directly affected by absolute or relative material deprivation. This is not coincidental. The better-organised worker is precisely the ideal-typical worker we specified earlier, as having diversified interests, provided for him in clubs and halls in ways to which he is accustomed and at prices he can, at least periodically, afford. He is Lockwood and Goldthorpe's "Affluent Worker". For the subcultural rump, however—the officially defined "lower-paid worker", the "lumpenproletariat" of the sixties—these opportunities and pursuits are not available and not desired. The rump has the historic task of perpetuating the traditional values of the fast-disappearing football subculture and in conditions of severe restraint. For them, *la lutte continue*, at a greater intensity and a much higher cost in terms of arrests and pillory: the subculture is involved in asserting its values in the face of bourgeoisified crowds, managements, players and press supported, in ways very familiar to the rump,[31] by local police and the courts.

In this most general struggle, the rump is constrained to employ distinctive techniques as symbolic of its values such as its distinctive degree of identification with the club and, at the most general level, its *autonomy*.[32] The Kop End on any major League ground will be concerned to assert participatory and masculine values and its desire for victory in match and League.

This *desperate assertion* can be understood in two ways. First, in a structural sense, it will result in certain restrictions on the social composition of the Kop. The female supporter and the primarily middle class football "connoisseur" will not be found on the Kop, although they are to be found, according to all available evidence, in increasing numbers in the ground at large. These two types of supporter, products of the legitimations described earlier, will be alienated from the rump by the values it displays and the techniques it uses in displaying them. Characteristically, these techniques will include the attempts at intervention described earlier as well as obscene chanting and the use of distinctively proletarian cheer-leaders.[33]

But secondly, in terms of culture and process, there is likely to be a characteristically proletarian, and in one sense irrational, belief in *fate* and *magic* exhibited in the desperate assertion of traditional values on the Kop. This is not simply to say that a set of apparently motiveless or irrational patterns of behaviour is displayed, though there is no question that this does appear to be one element in the situation. But it is to assert that while the Kop End—the subcultural rump—understands as well, if not better, than anyone else that matches are not won or lost on the terraces, and certainly not by interventions on the pitch, it is precisely this pattern of behaviour which is occurring and is, as we have suggested, the genesis of a social problem.

Malinowski[34] has propounded what can be described as a "theory of a gap" to account for the ways in which beliefs in magic arise in response to frustrating experiences and tensions in man. Using as examples, the hunter who fails to catch his quarry and the sailor who misses propitious winds, he hypothesises that:

(Man's) anxiety, his fears and hopes, induce tension in his organism which drives him to some sort of activity ... His nervous system and his whole organism drive him to substitute activity ... His organism reproduces the acts suggested by the anticipation of hope.[35]

Henslin[36] has applied Malinowski's theory to some effect to play-phenomena in his study of the "craps" (dice) game and the magical beliefs associated with it in American culture. He concludes that dice-players believe in and practise magic in as much as magic may be defined as:

... the belief and/or practice in the control over objects or events by verbal or non-verbal gestures (words or actions) where there is no empirical (natural or logical) connection between the gesture as cause and the object or event as effect.[37]

The subcultural rump on the football ground is similarly failing to catch its quarry. It is engaged in a losing struggle to assert traditional values and relationships. It is frustrated—in the sense that its assertion of faith comes to be defined as "hooliganism" while the faithless are defined as "genuine supporters". It may be that the responses of the subculture to events it knows it cannot control and processes it cannot halt are in this sense magical. The assertion of control over football players and managements who are not responsive to that control becomes not simply symbolic but magical. Particular goal-kicks can become crucial symbols. To induce a goalkeeper by distraction to kick into touch is to win a symbolic victory which may affect the result and one's side's League position. Whereas to invade the pitch when a goal is disallowed may be felt *magically* as a way of reversing the referee's decision.[38] And in the most final sense of all, to be arrested while fighting opposing supporters may be felt as a means of conveying to the management by means of some psychic process the nature of the "really genuine supporter", and the character of his identification.

Fighting—violence in the most general sense—and "hooliganism" are seen here, then, as the final assertion of traditional values —as the democratic response by the rump of a soccer subculture to the bourgeoisification of their game. The violence is neither arbitrary nor motiveless. It is explicable in terms of a subcultural theory: and it is observable in its empirical forms in reality. It is certainly not coincidental that the rump does not define property violence at home games as legitimate. The damage caused by football "hooligans" is concentrated, in the main, at away grounds, on public property, especially that of British Rail, and in the City, away from the home ground as such. In the "shrines" of the subculture, in games at home, the rump offers sacrifice rather than defiance.

One of the implications of this paper is that the "configurational" sociology offered by Elias and Dunning[39] in explanation of conflicts in the development and structure of the game itself (i.e.

of the game *on the field*) underestimates the importance of the reaction of spectators to events on the field. In the configuration that is a football ground, the interdependence of these two elements is as important as the interdependence of the two teams. It is, of course, equally important that the perspective adopted in this paper be supplemented by some examination of the importance of events on the field of play to the subcultural rump. We have already stated that, in pre-war football, the illusion persisted that the player—and the club itself—as public representative of the subculture, was under the control of the subculture, that, in other words, what the subculture said to the player at the club during the week actually influenced his play and that the advice given by the subculture to the club on tactics to adopt, junior players to watch, etc., was actually heeded. We can, perhaps, derive from this the hypothesis that the assertion of subcultural values on the terraces is linked—by the continuing strength of the values of masculinity and participation within the rump—to events on the field of play. That is, not only are events on the field important to the player as defining progress towards victory or defeat, but they are also inextricable from the processes by which the rump defines its contemporary history. Events on the field, or "incidents" as they are more commonly called, come to define esteem, identity and meaning in the life of subcultural members. These incidents are focal concerns for the player and the subculture. For the player, they can be *enabling* or *destructive*. They can enable a team or an individual player to work out agreed strategies and conform to a playing "style", or they can obstruct these strategies and style. This is particularly marked in contemporary football since the majority of successful teams play according to stringently applied collective strategies. To upset these strategies by incidents can result in total collapse and defeat. Incidents can be seen as highly dramatic confrontations in the ongoing football play, as encounters in which players and spectators alike are fearful of upset, loss of style and inevitable defeat. They are afraid, in the folk language of the terraces, that "a team will be put out of its stride" or that "it will be unable to click".

The abolition of the maximum wage for players and the increasingly remunerative occupations available in the League, heighten the drama in these situations. Players and management alike are aware that incidents of the kind described can involve the loss of considerable sums of money. A goal lost in a promotion game or in one at the top of the First Division, can mean a considerable loss of takings in the higher Division or in European competition. Players are no longer in the game for fame alone or as representatives of the subculture: they are in it for fame *and fortune*. Fame can be instrumental in "landing" advertising contracts, syndicated newspaper columns and public appearances. So, for example, Johnny Haynes, one of the "gentlemen" of British soccer has said:

> We professionals are in it for a living and it's the money that matters. Don't let anyone kid you otherwise.[40]

The incidents in the football game are dramatic confrontations in which the values and meanings associated with the social world of the player and the subculture *converge*. Victory is both a *sine qua non* of successful professionalism and a central value of the subculture. And it is in the search for victory that we might locate a "polarity" of central importance—the polarity between skill and spectacle on the one hand and victory on the other. Ideally, in the estimation of the stand-dweller and the management, the victories and successes of football teams as entertainers are achieved by skill and with spectacle. But skill is at a premium and, unlike wrestling or bullfighting, spectacle cannot be guaranteed. The unremitting search for success can define less worthy strategies as legitimate. Such strategies are identified by Arlott as responsible for violence on the field:

> Two, if not three, First Division teams of the moment can be suspected of using violence as part of policy.[41]

Of course, the search for success and affluence is most concentrated in the higher reaches of the League. The figures given below indicate that, in general, incidents, too, are concentrated in the higher divisions:

TABLE 1

Offences by League Players Resulting in Cautions,
Censures or Suspensions[42]

	1963-4	1964-5	1965-6	1966-7	1967-8
Division I	264	258	375	361	473
Division II	215	193	244	294	347
Division III	262	218	257	261	340
Division IV	295	210	297	262	268

In other words, the convergence of subcultural values with the values of players on the field is occurring and is concentrated in the incident—a confrontation between the worlds of two teams and two subcultures. This convergence can occur despite the divergence in the cultural contexts of the subculture and the club.

Whether or not one can describe a structural convergence of violence as associated with this cultural convergence, is a difficult question. It has been argued by journalists that violence on the field is imitated by violence on the terraces and that the terrace incidents in that sense structurally resemble the incidents on the field. But many incidents on the terrace appear to occur without precipitation from structural incidents observable in the game. It *may* be that incidents on the field, like "rumbles" in gang warfare, solidify the subculture, unify it behind a significant leader—a cheer-leader—and in that sense precipitate initiative or supportive violence. It may be that the comparison between the gang as *near-group*[43] and the subculture as near-group is a useful one. But whether this speculation has any validity must await a systematic analysis of the *processual* nature of "hooliganism" on the terraces of the kind Wade has undertaken for juvenile vandalism.[44] Certainly this paper is not adequate to explain the actual processes involved in crossing the threshold to violence as such. We have been concerned, rather, to characterise the cultural context in which football "hooliganism" is possible, to explain why this is socially problematic (because it is working-class action), and to relate our explanation to cultural and structural changes in the game itself. We have characterised football "hooliganism" as a sociologically explicable, "democratic" response to the loss of control exercised by a football subculture over its public representatives.

NOTES

I should like to thank the following for helpful comments on this essay: Andrew McPherson, Dept. of Education, Edinburgh University; Paul Rock, Dept. of Sociology, London School of Economics; Bridget Fowler, Dept. of Politics and Sociology, Glasgow University; and Stan Cohen, Dept. of Social Theory and Institutions, Durham University. They will not take it amiss when I say that the greatest debt is owed to my librarian parents for bibliographical help and an incomparable education in the subcultural values of the Sheffield Wednesday Football Club.

1 Becker points out in the introduction to his *Social Problems: A Modern Approach*, 1966, p. 2, that "... the objective condition is necessary but not in itself sufficient to constitute a social problem ... social problems are what people think they are". The work of the Becker school in the area of social deviance is in part a theoretical and empirical demonstration of this insight.

2 See, e.g. Eric Dunning, "The Concept of Development: Two Illustrative Case Studies" in P. I. Rose, *The Study of Society*, Englewood Cliffs,

New Jersey, 1967 and R. W. Pickford, "The Psychology of the History and Organization of Association Football", *B. J. Psych.*, XXXI, I, 80–93 and II, 129–44, 1940.

4 Becker derives this terminology, though not all the elements involved in it, from R. C. Fuller and R. R. Myers, "The Natural History of a Social Problem", *ASR*, 6, June, 1941. A series of stages are understood to be involved in the development of a social problem: perception by an individual or group of an objective condition as problematic, the sharing of this definition by others, the embodiment of the definition in the activities of an organisation and finally, the dependence of this organisation on the existence of the "problem". Something of this type of analysis could be applied here as a help in attempting to identify the stages in the development of football "hooliganism" from a troublesome matter dealt with by the police alone (up until *ca.* 1960), through a series of stages involving individual clubs, the Football League and the Football Association—in that order—in which the press came to play a crucial role, culminating finally in acceptance by the Government of their responsibility in 1967 when a research team of psychologists was appointed by the Ministry of Sport to investigate the "problem". By this stage a definition of the problem as more serious and implicitly pathological was current.

4 For a full exposition of this process, see Becker, *op. cit.*, pp. 11–14.

5 See, Stanley Cohen, "Mods, Rockers and the Rest", *Howard Journal*, 1967.

6 Here the word "practice" is important: there may be examples of other invasions before this date. Arlott's observation is here taken to imply that invasions of the pitch were not "common practice" before 1960–1. For reasons which are not obvious (and which would require explication in a comparative analysis of football in two or more cultures) invasions have apparently been "common practice" in Scotland for many years and certainly occurred frequently long before 1960. There is some suggestion that, during the period of "participatory" control which we describe later in the paper, one of the cultural axioms was that of the "sacred turf" (i.e. that the pitch was the central arena of the subculture, and thus to be preserved by all). This suggestion, if it contains any truth, further emphasises the extent to which the rump has been forced into dropping some cultural concerns in order to pursue the central concerns of masculinity, victory and control.

7 *The Guardian*, 25 October, 1968.

8 Elias and Dunning's plea for a "configurational" sociology as a synthesis of theories of group tension and theories of group harmony is centred largely on the inadequate explanatory powers of these approaches when taken apart. The plea made here for "subcultural" sociology can be seen as complementary to this. See Norbert Elias and Eric Dunning, "Dynamics of Sport Groups with Special Reference to Football", *British Journal of Sociology*, 17, 1966, pp. 388–402. See also pp. 66–80 of this volume.

9 Quoted in *The Sunday Times*, 28 June, 1968.

10 This observation might seem at first sight to imply that there *has* been an objective increase in violence around football since the inter-war years, since there are *now* apparently widespread doubts as to whether it is safe and sensible to send young children to football matches. This is not the only possible implication. Later in the paper, it is argued that the social composition of the football crowd changed markedly

during the period of "social reconstruction" after World War II. If this argument is correct, then we can advance two explanations of why it was "safe and sensible" to send one's offspring to football—in terms of the definitions of the situation in the mind of the working-class parent.

(a) As in other working-class activities (e.g. in street-games, Youth Clubs, local bars), the possibility of a brawl, or "fisticuffs" (or inter-personal conflict generally) was a general life-expectation. It was in this sense, no less dangerous, and no more dangerous, to send one's child to the football than it was to send him to the corner shop. It is not meant that football was not a violent focal concern: it only implies that it was not significantly "tougher" than others.

(b) Again, since football was a central working-class concern, not so widely patronised by other social groups in the inter-war years, violence around it was not a central "problem" for the dominant culture. It could, as it were, be "hived off" from that culture, and agencies of social control could allow that violence to be expressed within the sub-culture, without any threat to dominant or influential interests. Our argument involves the observation that football violence only comes to be defined as "socially-problematic" working-class action with the participation of other social groups in the football culture—that is, when activation of problem-definition is possible by influential social groups. When these definitions are activated (in the mass media, by agencies of social control, etc.), they are accepted by the working-class as arising from legitimate (dominant) authority. The working-class parent, as much as the middle-class parent, comes to believe that it is no longer "safe and sensible" to send his offspring to football matches. Their definition of the situation—which can perhaps be seen as an example of what has been called "moral panic"—is widely shared, and rejected only by the subcultural rump itself.

Both these explanations leave open the possibility that there has been no objective or real increase in football violence, yet recognises that there may, in quantifiable terms, be a subjective social problem and an increasing number of football "hooligans".

11 Article entitled "How long Can This Game Survive?", *The Sunday Times*, 14 July, 1968.

12 It is not entirely facetious to suggest that the introduction of the sub-stitute rule—in reality an attempt to bring Britain into line with the other football-playing nations—was interpreted by the Press as a neces-sary solution to the problem of cramp recurring on that most British of occasions, the Wembley Cup Final.

13 The spectacle and colour of professional soccer is seen as a "mimetic" activity by Elias and Dunning and functioning as a relief from the re-straint and control of "civilisation". See their, "The Quest for Excitement in Unexciting Societies", paper read to the Annual Conference of the British Sociological Association, London, April, 1967.

14 It has been suggested that the presence of Kenneth Wolstenholme or of any other well-known football commentator at a match serves as en-couragement for a display of subcultural values. Personal experience confirms that the presence of such commentators at matches is passed very rapidly round a ground by word of mouth.

15 See Elias and Dunning, *op. cit.*, 1966 and Dunning, *op. cit.*, 1967.

16 It is interesting to note that although the city of Sheffield contained the earliest organised football club in the world, Sheffield F.C., there was no

contact between the "little mester's" club and "The Club" until much later. See, e.g. R. C. Churchill, *60 Seasons of League Football*, London, 1958 and Percy F. Young, *Football in Sheffield*, London, 1965.

17 The articles by Michael Parkinson in the *Sunday Times*, a highly nostalgic treatment of his relationship with the Barnsley Club, are the best known examples of this journalistic "genre". *From Scenes Like These* by Gordon Williams, London, 1968, is a novel which exploits public definitions of football spectators in the modern day.

18 This ambivalence is similar to that exhibited towards a club's entry into the transfer market. The reactions of the subculture to the alien, wealthy industrialist who buys a majority shareholding in a declining club (to "save" it) are a subject worthy of study (cf. the recent case of Oldham Athletic). We can speculate that in times of success the industrialist will only grudgingly be acknowledged—the success will be widely understood as a subcultural initiative or vindication—and that in times of failure he will be pilloried thanklessly.

19 Arthur Hopcraft, *The Football Man: People and Passions in Soccer*, London, 1968, Ch. 2.

20. See particularly Brian Jackson, *Working Class Community*, London, 1968, and Richard Hoggart, *The Uses of Literacy*, London, 1957.

21 David Matza, *Delinquency & Drift*, New York, 1964.

22 Sexual relationships may be another example.

23 Walter B. Miller, "Lower Class Culture as a Generating Milieu of Gang Delinquency", *J. Soc. Issues*, 14, 1958, pp. 5–19.

24 The catholic view of method derives, of course, from the earlier history of the game as well. The violence and personal dangers associated with the game before it was "civilised", primarily in the public schools, have been described by Dunning, *op. cit.*, 1967 and by Pickford, *op. cit.*, 1940.

25 Only Sir Stanley Matthews could tell us whether the meeting of 3,000 Stoke supporters in 1938 to protest at the granting of his transfer request was in any way instrumental in delaying his departure until 1946.

26 In this respect, the work of Joffre Dumazedier and Roger Caillois is important.

27 Parts I and II of their *Affluent Worker* monograph series were published during 1968. Part III, the summing up of their whole research was published in 1970 under the title, *The Affluent Worker in the Class Structure*.

28 It is difficult to understand the statements made by the Arsenal and Sheffield Wednesday managements that the changes in their customary strip were made to give the teams a more "modern" appearance. Wednesday changed from a distinctive blue and white stripe to a blue shirt with white sleeves, Arsenal from red with white sleeves to all-red shirts. In 1968, Arsenal reverted to their former strip but the Wednesday have persisted with their new colours.

29 A recent example of this "paper war" is found in a series of letters in the "Green-Un", Sheffield's soccer paper, concerning incidents occurring after a goal was disallowed in a match between Wednesday and Liverpool. Cushions were thrown *from the stands* in great numbers and the referee walked off the field. On this occasion, the terraces were relatively quiet. The resentment of the terrace supporters at this lack of faith from the stands was summed up in the following letter, one of a dozen published within two weeks: "Well all I can say is that why should the younger fans be blamed for all the trouble when the biggest part of the kids can't afford

to pay for a stand or a terrace seat—and they don't supply cushions on the Kop." 30 November, 1968.

This example of "hooliganism" might lead some readers to doubt the whole of our thesis, since the "violence" cited is the violence of the stand-dweller—our "genuine supporter" of the postwar period. In fact, it tends to emphasise only the lack of density in the kind of sociological explanation offered. Clearly, in this case, *either* the rump—on the Kop—did not evaluate the situation on the field as worthy of (or suspectible to) protest and action (which would confirm our suggestion that "hooliganism" is something more than arbitrary action, and that it is contingent on certain values and processes) *or*, alternatively, the fact that the incidents occurred one minute before the end of the game may not have allowed time for collective action to develop. That is, there was no time for the necessary stages in the escalation of the incident to occur. Both these hypotheses would be illuminated by processual investigations. It needs emphasising, in any case, that the "violence" cited is a rare example of action in the stands, and one which is used mainly because of the correspondence it gave rise to in the local football press.

30 *The Harrington Report*, cyclostyled, p. 15.
31 In the sample of arrested "hooligans" discussed in the Harrington Report, 296 out of a total of 497 had previous criminal convictions. This data should not be treated as too reliable, however, since, as the report makes clear, people with previous convictions may have "a bone to pick" with the police anyway and may, on that account, be more liable to arrest than others.
32 The values we are here associating with working-class culture reflect closely the focal concerns of American working-class culture as described by Walter B. Miller: the readiness for trouble, the value of toughness, the value of smartness, a desire for excitement, a belief in fate and a concern for autonomy, i.e. for freedom from external constraint in the most general sense. See his "Lower Class Culture as a Generating Milieu of Gang Delinquency", *J. Soc. Issues*, 14, 1958, pp. 5–19.
33 The Harrington Report notes the distinctive dress and appearance of the chant-leader on the Kop and the description is very much that of a "Rocker" rather than a "Mod".
34 B. Malinowski, *Magic, Science and Religion*, London, 1948, pp. 79–81, quoted in James M. Henslin, "Craps and Magic", *A.J.S.*, 73, 3, 1967, p. 326.
35 Malinowski, *op. cit.*
36 Henslin, *op. cit.*, pp. 316–30.
37 *Ibid.*, p. 318.
38 There have been examples, however, of interventions by spectators which, though expressive or magical in this sense initially, have come to take on a distinctly instrumental character. In Scotland, one such incident is part of every supporter's range of anecdotes and is central to the folk-history of the Celtic Club. Halfway through the second half of a Scottish Cup semi-final match between Celtic and St. Mirren in March 1962—a match Celtic were expected to win easily—the Paisley club were winning 3-0. There was, apparently, no precipitating incident on the field as such but as soon as the police began the routine task of arresting someone who threw a tumbler, the crowd surged forward on to the field. This was thought, at first, to be a temporary interruption but it soon became clear to everyone that the Celtic supporters intended to stay put in the hope of cancelling the game and necessitating a replay. One report offers this

description: "The wave of brawling fans swamped the hundred-odd police on the spot. . . . Angry, threatening voices surrounded the bewildered players. Then the referee managed to herd the twenty-two players into the dressing room. Six mounted policemen galloped into the stadium. A police message went out, 'All available cars to Ibrox Park'. Before the game (could be) resumed, policemen three feet apart ringed the terracing, facing the seething, jeering, flag-waving supporters." *Scottish Sunday Mail*, 1 April, 1962. The stoppage lasted sixteen minutes and, towards the end, the Celtic supporters are reported to have behaved defiantly and triumphantly—in the belief, clearly, that they had succeeded in cancelling a game their side was obviously going to lose.

39 Elias and Dunning, *Dynamics of Sport Groups*. See pp. 66–80 of this volume.

40 Quoted in the *Football Monthly*, 207, November, 1968, p. 16.

41 In an article, "Violence as a Tactic", *The Guardian*, 1 November, 1968, p. 20.

42 *F. A. News*, September, 1968.

43 Lewis Yablonsky, "The Delinquent Gang as a Near-Group", *Soc. Problems*, Fall 1959, 7, pp. 108–17. Without accepting Yablonsky's particular choice of terminology, we may see the similarity between his "near-group"—"a mob of individuals characterised by anonymity, disturbed leadership, motivated by emotion and in some cases representing a destructive collectivity within the inclusive social system"—and the individual peer-group within the football subculture. Yablonsky describes the way in which these highly disorganised "near-groups" come together when other groups, or the police, are in the "territory" they occupy. Something of the same process can be seen to operate in the football subculture on the Kop when the police attempt to pull "hooligans" out of the crowd or when the Rail police attempt to identify those responsible for damage on football "specials".

44 Andrew L. Wade, "Social Processes in the Act of Juvenile Vandalism", in M. B. Clinard and R. Quinney (eds.), *Criminal Behaviour Systems*, New York, 1967, pp. 94–109.

Index